File

New...	⌘N
Open...	⌘O
Close	⌘W
Save	⌘S
Save As...	
Print Preview	
Page Setup...	
Print...	⌘P
1 Return on Investments	
2 Quality Control Database	
3 Rapid Transit Proposal	
4 Production Schedule	
Quit	⌘Q

Edit

Can't Undo	⌘Z
Cut	⌘X
Copy	⌘C
Paste	⌘U
Clear...	⌘B
Delete...	⌘K
Insert...	⌘I
Fill Right	⌘R
Fill Down	⌘D

Formula

Paste Name...	
Paste Function...	
Reference	⌘T
Define Name...	⌘L
Note...	
Goto...	⌘G
Find...	⌘H

Format

Number...
Alignment...
Font...
Border...
Style...
Row Height...
Column Width...

Data

Form...	
Find	⌘F
Set Database	
Set Criteria	
Sort...	

Options

Set Print Area	
Display...	
Calculation...	
Calculate Now	⌘=
Full Menus	

Macro

Run...
Record...

Window

New Window
Arrange All
✓1 Worksheet1

Worksheet Short Menus
(System 7)

Computer users are not all alike.
Neither are SYBEX books.

We know our customers have a variety of needs. They've told us so. And because we've listened, we've developed several distinct types of books to meet the needs of each of our customers. What are you looking for in computer help?

If you're looking for the basics, try the **ABC's** series. You'll find short, unintimidating tutorials and helpful illustrations. For a more visual approach, select **Teach Yourself**, featuring screen-by-screen illustrations of how to use your latest software purchase.

Mastering and **Understanding** titles offer you a step-by-step introduction, plus an in-depth examination of intermediate-level features, to use as you progress.

Our **Up & Running** series is designed for computer-literate consumers who want a no-nonsense overview of new programs. Just 20 basic lessons, and you're on your way.

We also publish two types of reference books. Our **Instant References** provide quick access to each of a program's commands and functions. SYBEX **Encyclopedias** provide a *comprehensive reference* and explanation of all of the commands, features and functions of the subject software.

Sometimes a subject requires a special treatment that our standard series doesn't provide. So you'll find we have titles like **Advanced Techniques, Handbooks, Tips & Tricks**, and others that are specifically tailored to satisfy a unique need.

We carefully select our authors for their in-depth understanding of the software they're writing about, as well as their ability to write clearly and communicate effectively. Each manuscript is thoroughly reviewed by our technical staff to ensure its complete accuracy. Our production department makes sure it's easy to use. All of this adds up to the highest quality books available, consistently appearing on best-seller charts worldwide.

You'll find SYBEX publishes a variety of books on every popular software package. Looking for computer help? Help Yourself to SYBEX.

For a complete catalog of our publications:

SYBEX Inc.
2021 Challenger Drive, Alameda, CA 94501
Tel: (415) 523-8233/(800) 227-2346 Telex: 336311
Fax: (415) 523-2373

SYBEX is committed to using natural resources wisely to preserve and improve our environment. As a leader in the computer book publishing industry, we are aware that over 40% of America's solid waste is paper. This is why we have been printing the text of books like this one on recycled paper since 1982.

This year our use of recycled paper will result in the saving of more than 15,300 trees. We will lower air pollution effluents by 54,000 pounds, save 6,300,000 gallons of water, and reduce landfill by 2,700 cubic yards.

In choosing a SYBEX book you are not only making a choice for the best in skills and information, you are also choosing to enhance the quality of life for all of us.

Mastering Excel 3 on the Macintosh

Mastering Excel 3 on the Macintosh®

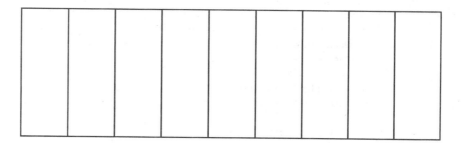

Marvin Bryan

SYBEX ®

San Francisco • Paris • Düsseldorf • Soest

Acquisitions Editor: David Clark
Editor: Judith Ziajka
Project Editor: Kathleen Lattinville
Technical Editor: Nick Dargahi
Word Processors: Ann Dunn, Susan Trybull
Book Designer: Eleanor Ramos
Layout and Art: Alissa Feinberg, Lucie Živny
Screen Graphics: Cuong Le
Typesetter: Elizabeth Newman
Proofreaders: Winnie Kelly, Dina F. Quan
Indexer: Ted Laux
Cover Designer: Ingalls + Associates
Cover Photographer: Mark Johann

Library of Congress Card Number: 91-65373
ISBN: 0-89588-800-9
Manufactured in the United States of America
10 9 8 7 6 5 4 3 2 1

To Casey Bryan—
student body president, athlete, and
Number One Son

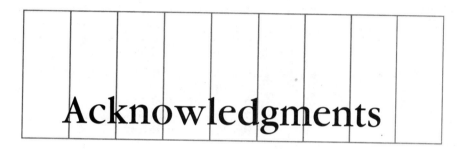

Acknowledgments

My thanks to Keri Walker, Ric Jones, and Martha Steffen of Apple and to John Dauphiny of Microsoft. They made the completion of this book a lot easier.

Contents at a Glance

Table of Contents

Part VI   **Automating Your Work**

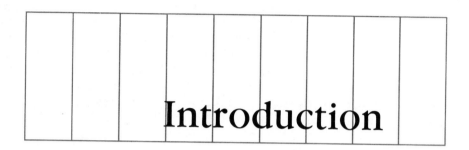

Introduction

This all-new book on Microsoft Excel covers the latest version of the best-selling spreadsheet program for the Macintosh and is intended for anyone who wants to get the most out of using it.

You may be a new user and need help in understanding the concept of an electronic spreadsheet, as well as in acquiring the knowledge that will make you productive in a hurry. You'll easily find the assistance you want here.

On the other hand, you may be an experienced user of spreadsheets and, perhaps, of other versions of Excel. You can read this book to learn about the new features and how they're affected by the Macintosh System 7 operating system (although you can run Excel under earlier versions of the operating system, starting with version 6.0.2).

Finally, you may already be using the current version of Excel for the Macintosh. However, you'd like to become a power user and to master its fine points and advanced features. This book is for you, too.

You don't have to be a math whiz to understand any of the chapters in this book. Whether a concept used is simple or complex, this book explains it in simple terms. If you are a math whiz, you can skim over background information and get on to the meat of how to apply the concept.

WHAT YOU CAN DO WITH EXCEL

In the days before computers, calculators, and adding machines, a spreadsheet was simply a large piece of paper that displayed data from various categories in columns, along with the results of manual calculations to total those columns, determine percentages, or otherwise try to obtain a meaningful analysis of the data. The purpose of the spreadsheet might have been to construct and track a monthly budget, to ascertain the costs of a contemplated project, or to forecast future sales from past performance.

Today's electronic spreadsheet is often used for the same purposes. However, it incorporates many improvements. First, you no longer have to perform calculations by hand. Instead, you enter each number into a separate box in the spreadsheet, called a *cell*; then you enter formulas into additional cells to calculate totals and percentages automatically. This automatic calculation capability also means that you can change a value in one of the cells and have the spreadsheet recalculate automatically, giving you the power to construct "what if" analyses: You can change figures as often as you like and see instantly how they affect the bottom line.

Excel has many more features. You can easily generate several kinds of graphs of your data: line, bar, pie, and combination charts; stock market performance charts; and charts that perform statistical analysis, such as linear regression plots.

You can create and maintain databases for any purpose. You can store a list of employees and their salary histories and then print a report pinpointing those who haven't had a raise in the last year. You can keep a complete file of an orchestra's repertoire and print reports showing when and where each selection has been played.

You can automate tasks you perform frequently by creating *macros*: recorded keystrokes and mouse movements that can optionally be combined with a simple macro language. With macros, you can easily build small programs that let you, by pressing a few keys, have Excel complete an entire series of actions.

NEW FEATURES OF EXCEL 3.0

In Excel 3.0, Microsoft has made major improvements that greatly increase the program's powers. However, to take advantage of these powers, the user also needs updated knowledge. Even the appearance of the Excel desktop has been changed, primarily through the addition of the Toolbar, which lets you perform many tasks without pulling down the program's menus.

Version 3.0 also offers other new features. It provides new drawing tools. Now you can create charts right on your worksheets, rather than only as separate files. You can create worksheets in an outline format and expand or collapse the outlines to view various levels of detail. Version 3.0 also offers new data consolidation abilities. In addition, you can create your own dialog boxes, solve goal-seeking problems, make three-dimensional charts and reusable templates, and enjoy hundreds of other new or enhanced features. Read this book to master them all.

ORGANIZATION OF THIS BOOK

This book is divided into seven parts, plus appendices. Part 1 discusses the fundamentals of how to use the program. Part 2 goes into detail on spreadsheet operations. Part 3 explains how to graph your data. Part 4 describes database applications. Part 5 is devoted to the fine points of printing and making reports. Part 6 is an introduction to macros and the creation of your own functions and applications. Part 7 analyzes advanced features.

The chapters include exercises you can complete to increase your knowledge through hands-on experience. Of course, if you already have a thorough understanding of a particular subject, you can simply read the section that describes that subject, looking for unfamiliar commands or special tips.

The appendices provide installation information, summaries of functions, and an orientation for those who have previously used Lotus 1-2-3.

METHODS AND CONVENTIONS USED IN THIS BOOK

Although Excel's features are explained in detail, this book invites you to learn the program through hands-on experience—by actually completing exercises that demonstrate how to accomplish specific tasks. Excel screens are reproduced frequently in each chapter, to illustrate how your worksheets and charts should appear at each stage of an exercise. The words you should type to complete an exercise are presented in **boldface**. New or unfamiliar terms or phrases are shown in *italics*.

However, if you choose not to try an exercise, or if you don't have a computer available as you read the book, you can learn the principles involved anyway by paying careful attention to the step-by-step instructions and by studying the figures that show the results you would otherwise observe on your monitor.

THE REWARDS OF USING EXCEL

Excel will reward you for the time you spend with it. You will find that it can make you more productive and give you a firmer grasp of many aspects of your business and personal planning.

Part

I

Covering
the Basics

Chapter

1

Creating and
Using a Basic
Worksheet

When you load Excel on your Macintosh, you enter a world with almost unlimited possibilities. That's because you can create formulas and macros to make the program perform almost any task you can imagine. You can also use predefined functions and a supplied macro library to handle chores such as finding the internal rate of return of a series of periodic cash flows or comparing two versions of a worksheet to see if any formulas have been changed.

In this first chapter, you'll learn the major elements of the Excel desktop. Then you'll create a simple worksheet, edit the worksheet, add a chart, and save and print your work.

If you haven't already installed Excel, read Appendix A and complete the installation before continuing with this chapter. Then double-click your Excel folder to open it and double-click the Excel icon, shown in Figure 1.1, to start the program. (If you're new to the Macintosh, you *double-click* by pressing the mouse button down twice in quick succession, after moving your mouse to position the pointer on your screen.)

TOURING THE EXCEL DESKTOP

After you start Excel, an opening screen briefly appears, followed by a blank *worksheet*. A worksheet is an individual spreadsheet file. You will soon have many worksheets stored in your Excel folder or in subsidiary folders you create. (When the pointer is on the worksheet, it assumes the shape of a large plus sign.)

The blank worksheet appears as shown in Figure 1.2. Until you save it and give it a name, the worksheet is called, by default, Worksheet1. This name appears in the title bar of the window.

The worksheet is divided into cells of equal size, arranged in rows and columns. The columns are identified by letters, and the rows are identified by numbers. A letter and number identifies each cell. For instance, the cell in the upper left corner of the worksheet is A1. This designation is known as the cell *address*.

At the top of the Excel window, you can see a *menu bar*. Here you can place the pointer on a menu title, such as File, and press the mouse button to make the menu drop down, displaying its options. The contents of the various menus are explained later in this book.

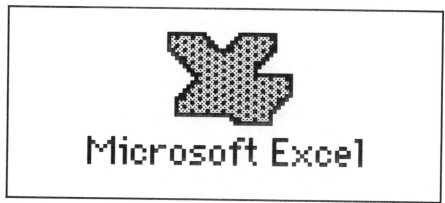

Figure 1.1: The Excel program icon

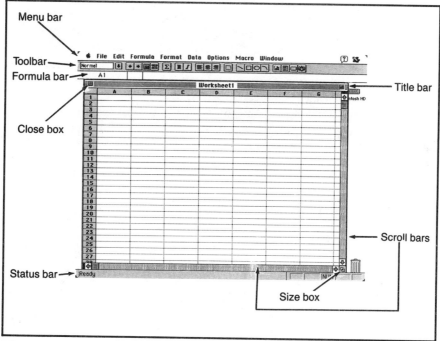

Figure 1.2: A blank Excel worksheet

CHAPTER ONE

Just below the menu bar is the *Toolbar*. You'll use some of its features in this chapter. Its other functions are explained in Chapter 2.

Below the Toolbar is the *formula bar*, which displays any formula entered into the active cell. (The cell itself displays only the formula result.) The left end of the formula bar displays the name of the active cell. In Figure 1.2, the active cell is A1. The heavy outline around cell A1 indicates that it is currently selected.

At the bottom of the screen is the *status bar,* which displays information about current Excel activity. When Excel is waiting for you to enter data or formulas, the status bar displays *Ready*. Otherwise, the message on the status bar may tell you what activity is in progress, such as copying data or recording a *macro* (saving keystrokes and mouse movements to be replayed later). The message may also inform you that Excel is in a special mode such as *edit* mode (used for editing the contents of a cell), or that it has found an error in a formula.

The worksheet is bounded on its right and bottom sides by the usual Macintosh *scroll bars* that let you shift the view in the window to display some other area of the worksheet. Incidentally, a single Excel worksheet actually contains 16,384 numbered rows and 256 columns, although you probably won't use them all. The first 26 columns are labeled A through Z. Then the labeling sequence continues with AA through AZ, BA through BZ, CA through CZ, and so on. The final column is labeled IV.

If you have a large-screen monitor, you may see more rows and columns at one time than are displayed in Figure 1.2. Conversely, if you have a small-screen monitor (such as that provided with the Macintosh Classic), you will see fewer rows and columns. You can always scroll the window to view another portion of the worksheet.

The *size box* in the lower right corner of the window lets you drag the window to resize it. To close the window, you click the *close box* in the upper left corner. Both of these features are standard in all Macintosh applications.

ENTERING TEXT, NUMBERS, AND FORMULAS

You can enter text, numbers, and formulas only into active cells. However, you can activate more than one cell at a time merely by dragging the mouse to select the cells. The following exercise demonstrates how to use text, numbers, and formulas to create a simple worksheet. Later you will revise the worksheet to see how other features work.

ENTERING HEADINGS

Your first step is to enter headings for the worksheet columns.

1. Excel selects cell A1 by *default* when you open a new worksheet. (A default selection is an action or value Excel uses unless otherwise directed.) If A1 is not highlighted, click that cell to select it.

2. Type the words **Sales Rep**. The words appear in the formula bar as you type them. Then press the → key. The words *Sales Rep* appear in cell A1, the formula bar becomes blank, and cell B1 becomes active.

3. Type the words **Gross Sales**. These words appear in the formula bar as you type them. Press the → key. The words *Gross Sales* appear in cell B1, the formula bar becomes blank, and cell **C1** becomes active.

4. Type the word **Commission** and press Return. The word *Commission* appears in cell C1, the formula bar becomes blank, and cell C2 becomes active. (The pointer moves down instead of to the right because you pressed Return this time instead of the Return key.)

FORMATTING CELL ROWS

By default, Excel aligns, or *justifies,* text at the left side of cells. Cells A1 through C1 will serve as titles for their respective columns, so you need to format them so they are centered and in boldface. Because we'll add other titles in row 1 in a later chapter, we will format the entire row now.

1. The first step is to select the entire row by clicking the heading for row 1 (the small box at the left that displays the number 1).

2. Although centering can be accomplished through options accessed through the Format menu, starting with version 3.0 Excel provides a much easier way to issue this command. Just move the pointer to the Toolbar and click the middle alignment button, which shows a group of centered lines (see Figure 1.3). Excel immediately centers the text in all cells of row 1.

3. Next, you want to make the text boldface. Again, you can make this change through options reached through the Format menu, and again, the Toolbar provides a shortcut. With row 1 still selected, just click the B button (for boldface) in the Toolbar. As Figure 1.3 shows, the boldface button is located to the left of the alignment buttons and the I button (which italicizes selected text). When you click the boldface button, the three newly centered titles also appear in boldface.

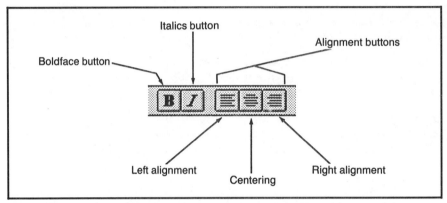

Figure 1.3: Alignment, boldface, and italics buttons on the Toolbar

ENTERING DATA

Now you can begin to enter data into the cells.

1. Drag to select cells A2, A3, and A4. These cells will contain the names of individual sales representatives. (If you're a novice at using a Macintosh, note that you *drag* by holding down the mouse button and then moving the mouse in the desired direction.)

2. Type the name **Olvera** in cell A2 and press Return.

3. Type the name **Stein** in cell A3 and press Return.

4. Type the name **Tomura** in cell A4 and press Return.

5. Now it's time to enter the gross sales figures for each sales representative. Drag to select cells B2, B3, and B4.

6. Type the number **14682** and press Return.

7. Type the number **16208** and press Return.

8. Type the number **13499** and press Return.

FORMATTING CELL COLUMNS

Now format the figures to insert a comma at the proper position. Since you'll soon need to format a cell for a total figure below these numbers, as well as cells in column C that will also contain numbers, you can save time by formatting all of the cells in columns B and C right now. Excel will apply this formatting only to numbers entered in these columns—and not to text.

1. Drag to select the column headings (the cells that display the centered letters B and C). This shortcut automatically selects the entire columns for formatting. Then pull down the Format menu and select the Number... command. The three dots following the word *Number* are called an ellipsis. They indicate that the command will not be executed instantly but, when selected, will usually bring up a dialog box, where you will be asked to make additional choices. In this case, you'll see the Format Number dialog box, shown in Figure 1.4.

2. Select the fourth number format, #,##0, and click OK. The numbers now appear formatted with a comma to indicate that the figures are in thousands. Excel also adds invisible formatting for any numbers yet to be entered in columns B and C.

ENTERING A FORMULA

You are ready to enter a formula so that Excel can calculate the sales commissions for each representative.

1. Select cell C2. Type an equal sign (=). An equal sign tells Excel you're going to enter a formula. The equal sign appears on the formula bar.

2. Click cell B2 to make it part of the formula. Excel adds the address B2 to the formula you are building.

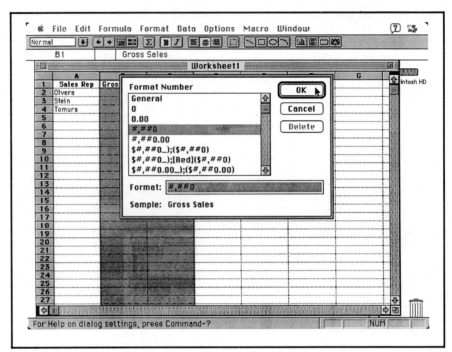

Figure 1.4: The Format Number dialog box

3. Type an asterisk (∗), the symbol for multiplication in computer formulas.

4. Type **.08** to complete the multiplication formula, which will find 8 percent (the rate of sales commission) of the value in cell B2. Your screen should now resemble Figure 1.5. Note that the message on the status bar at the bottom of the window now reads *Enter.*

5. You may have noticed that two symbol boxes appeared just to the left of the formula when you started it. One box displays a check mark and is called the *enter box.* You click the enter box to enter a formula after it's completed. Click the enter box now. (The other box displays an X. You click this box to cancel a formula.) The figure 1,175 now appears in cell C2, representing the sales commission earned by the employee named Olvera. (Note that since you previously applied number formatting to this entire column, the number in C2 has the same formatting as the numbers in column B.)

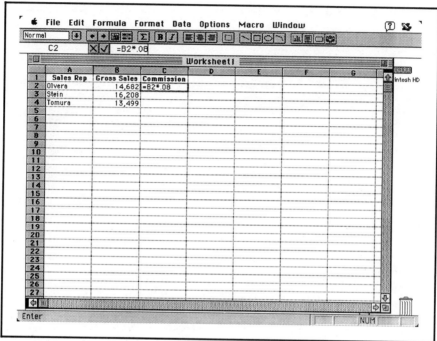

Figure 1.5: Entering a formula

COPYING A FORMULA

Now you need to copy the formula to cells C3 and C4 to find the commissions earned by Stein and Tomura.

1. First, drag to select cells C2, C3, and C4.

2. Pull down the Edit menu and select the Fill Down command. (Shortcut: Press ⌘-D.) The Fill Down command copies the formula in the first selected cell (C2) into the remaining selected cells (C3 and C4). Excel executes the copied formulas instantly. Cell C3 shows the figure 1,297, and cell C4 shows the figure 1,080. Next you'll see why these copied formulas work.

3. Click to select only cell C3. Look at the formula bar to read the formula in this cell. As you can see in Figure 1.6, the address B2 that is part of the formula in cell C2 has been adjusted automatically

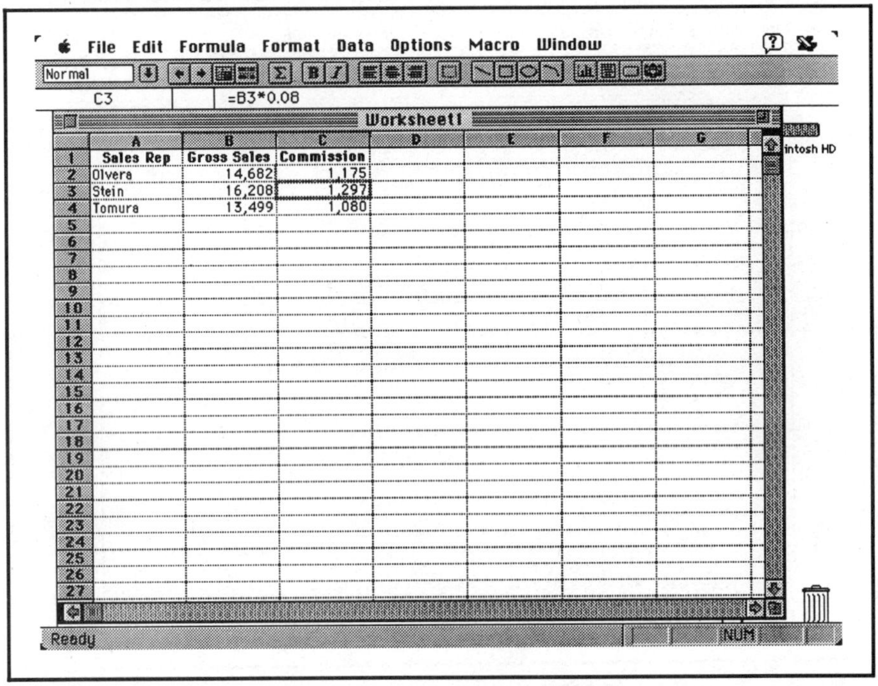

Figure 1.6: Copied formula adjusted automatically

to read B3 instead. (Observe also that Excel has added a zero before the percentage figure you typed; it now reads 0.08—which doesn't affect the functioning of the formula at all, but makes the formula conform to the way the program handles such formulas internally.)

4. Click to select only cell C4. You will see that the formula here too has been adjusted automatically and now refers to cell B4. These adjustable cell references are called *relative* cell references. Cell references in formulas can also be made *absolute,* so that some part of a formula always refers to a certain cell. For example, you could have entered the figure .08 in a cell instead of into each formula, with its cell address entered into the formulas as absolute. Then the commission percentage would have been copied into each formula from the same cell. Absolute references are explained in later chapters that discuss formulas.

DRAWING LINES ABOVE TOTALS

Let's total the number columns. First, let's draw a line in the cells above each total. Some people make such a line on a worksheet by typing a series of underlines (produced by holding down the Shift key while pressing the hyphen key). However, a line drawn in this manner—since it is an underline—will appear very close to the bottom of the cell. If you type a series of hyphens instead of underlines, they'll center vertically in the cell, but they won't be one solid line. You can also display no line above your totals, relying solely on labels to identify the totals. A fourth option is to separate columns of numbers and their totals with blank cells.

There are two better solutions to this problem. You can draw a line with the line tool located on the Toolbar (and explained in Chapter 2). You can also use *em dashes*. Em dashes are long dashes often used by printers in displaying text—like this. Using em dashes is the easiest operation to control. You'll use this method now.

1. Select cell B5. Then hold down the Shift and Option keys together, type five hyphens, and click the enter box. Instead of seeing five hyphens or underlines appear in B5, you'll see five em dashes (because you held down both the Shift and Option keys). You'll see a slight space between each em dash on your screen, but when they're printed, they'll appear as one solid line centered vertically in the cell.

2. To position the line so it appears directly underneath the column of figures above, click the right-alignment button in the Toolbar. This button is located just to the right of the center button and is represented by an icon that shows five lines that simulate right-aligned text. (Note the position of the pointer in Figure 1.7.)

3. You need a line above the total in row C too. To add the line, you can copy the contents of cell B5 to cell C5. Drag to select both B5 and C5.

4. Pull down the Edit menu and select the Fill Right command. (Shortcut: Press ⌘-R.) The formatted em dashes are copied into cell C5.

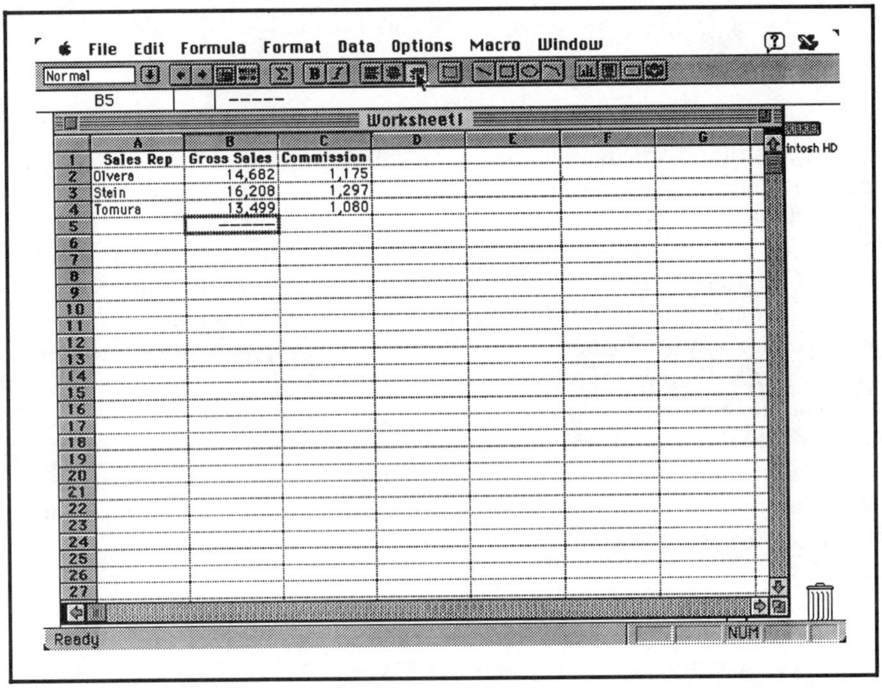

Figure 1.7: Giving a line right alignment

USING THE AUTO-SUM BUTTON

If you are using a version of Excel prior to version 3.0, you can use either of two methods to total the figures in column B and then enter the result in cell B6. You can simply click B6 to select this cell, type an equal sign (=) to start a formula, and then click, in succession, B2, B3, and B4. Excel will automatically enter this formula into the formula bar: = B2 + B3 + B4. After you click the enter box (the check mark) to complete the formula, the program will total the three cells. A second method is to pull down the Formula menu and select the Paste Function...command. You can then scroll the Paste Function dialog box and select the SUM( ) function (which automatically totals a series of referenced cells) and drag across or click the cells to be included in the formula. (Functions are explained fully in later chapters.)

If you are using version 3.0, you can still use either of these methods. However, now there's an infinitely easier way to total numbers: using the auto-sum button. You will use this method now.

1. Click cell B6 to select it and click the auto-sum button (shown with the pointer on it in Figure 1.8). This formula appears on the formula bar: = SUM(B2:B5). The colon in the formula (:) indicates that the formula includes all cells between the cells B2 and B5. Click the enter box on the formula bar to complete the formula. The result appears in B6: 44,389.

   (This automatic method of adding cells—the most common mathematical operation in spreadsheets—is accomplished by having the program look for a series of numbers above or immediately to the left of the selected cell. Note that even though the formula included cell B5, the cell did not affect the formula because it does not contain a number.)

2. In preparation for copying the formula in B6 to C6, drag to select both cells.

3. Pull down the Edit menu and select the Fill Right command. (Shortcut: Press ⌘-R.) The Gross Sales and Commission columns of the worksheet now both display correctly formatted totals.

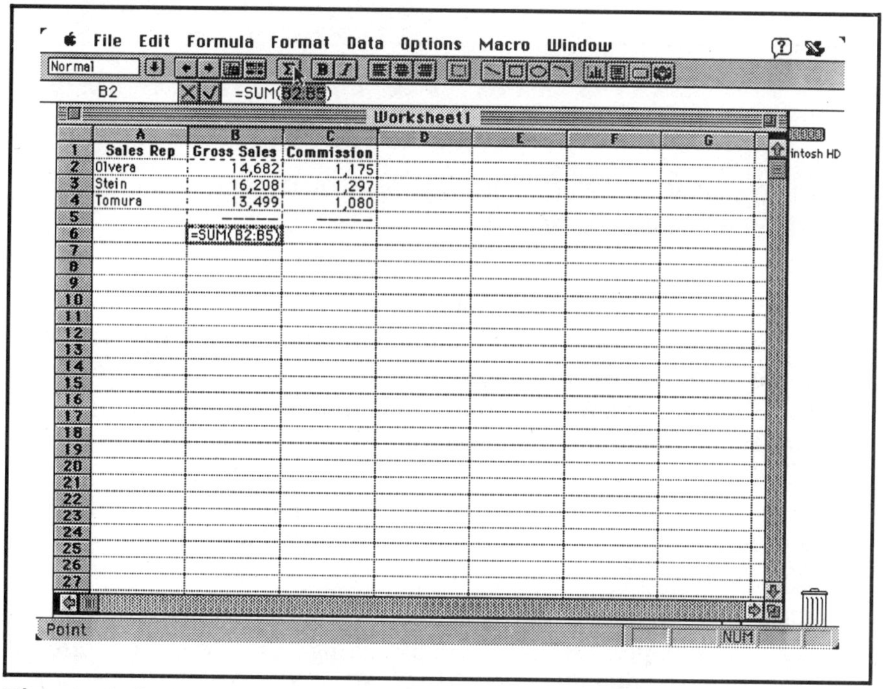

Figure 1.8: Creating a formula with the auto-sum button

SAVING THE WORKSHEET

Now save the worksheet for the first time. You'll be revising it and adding to it both in this chapter and in Chapters 2 and 3.

1. Pull down the File menu and select Save. (Shortcut: Press ⌘-S.) The Save dialog box appears.

2. Type the name **Sales Commission** in the text box and click the Save button.

Notice that the name in the worksheet title bar (Worksheet 1) has changed to Sales Commission. This title is a *file name* that can be used from now on to store and retrieve this particular worksheet. You can also add a title on the worksheet itself that will be printed as a heading for the data. You can use a large font size for the text, make the title appear in some attractive display typeface you have installed on your Macintosh, and even add a border or special background. These capabilities are discussed in Chapter 3.

EDITING THE WORKSHEET

Making changes in a worksheet is easy. Let's make some changes to the example worksheet we just created.

CHANGING A VALUE

Suppose you find out that the gross sales figure for Olvera is incorrect: This representative actually made sales of $17,682 during the period under consideration, not $14,682. Make the correction in this manner:

1. Click cell B2 to select it. Excel displays the figure 14,682 in the formula bar, as well as in the cell itself (except that no formatting, such as the comma, appears in the formula bar).

2. Click between the numbers 4 and 6 in the formula bar. A flashing vertical bar appears at that point, indicating that you can make an entry or correction there.

3. Press the Delete key once. The number 4 disappears. Type the number 7 in its place and click the enter box on the formula bar to complete the correction.

Before you made the correction, Olvera's commission was $1,175. It has been recalculated—to $1,415—to reflect the higher gross sales figure. The total for the Gross Sales column was $44,389; now it is $47,389. The total for the Commission column was $3,551; it too has changed, to $3,791. This quick modification illustrates how Excel automatically adjusts all affected parts of a worksheet to reflect the alteration of a single cell. (Of course, you won't see the dollar signs on your screen, because the number format you applied to columns B and C formats the cells only by adding commas in the proper places and rounding the numbers to display only even dollars—no cents. However, the cents are retained in memory and used in the calculations.)

INSERTING AN EMPTY ROW

Now it's time to make some cosmetic modifications to the worksheet. First, to make the worksheet easier to read, add a blank row between the column headings and the rest of the sales commission table.

1. Click the heading for row 2 (the number 2 itself at the left edge of the window). This action selects that entire row, highlighting all of its cells displayed on the screen.

2. Pull down the Edit menu and select the Insert...command. (Shortcut: Press ⌘-I.) Excel inserts an empty row just above row 2, so that row 2 becomes row 3. The entire worksheet below the column headings shifts down one row, and all formulas are automatically adjusted accordingly.

LABELING COLUMN TOTALS

Now label the two column totals.

1. Click to select cell A7. (This cell was A6 before you inserted the empty row.)

2. Type the word **TOTALS** in capital letters and press Return. The word *TOTALS* appears in the cell, and the next cell down (A8) becomes active.

RESAVING THE WORKSHEET

Press ⌘-S to resave the worksheet with the changes you've made. You'll continue to use this worksheet in Chapter 2. Your worksheet should now look like Figure 1.9.

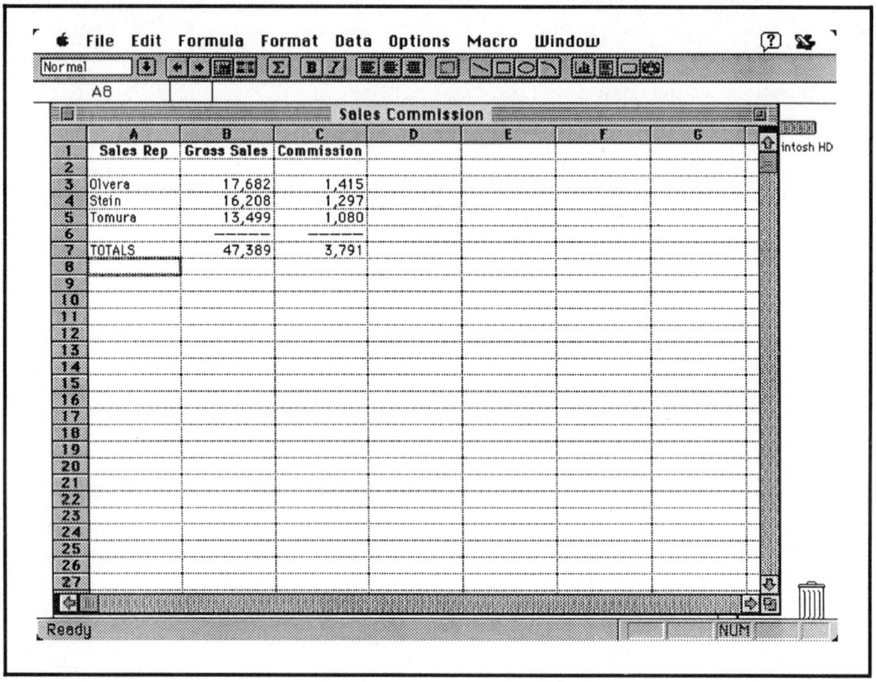

Figure 1.9: The revised Sales Commission worksheet

GRAPHING THE DATA

Why not make a graph to help those who see the worksheet understand it better? Starting with Excel 3.0, you can create any chart or graph you want right on your worksheet. (Microsoft calls such a graph an *embedded chart.*)

Follow this procedure:

1. Drag to select cells A3 through B5, as shown in Figure 1.10.

2. Click the chart tool on the Toolbar. The pointer is resting on that tool in Figure 1.10.

3. Now you must define the area where the graph is to appear. Place the pointer on cell D11 and drag down and to the right, without releasing the mouse button, to include cell G24. (If you're using a small-screen Macintosh that has not been displaying row G, the view of the worksheet will shift as you drag to the right until you can see that row.) As soon as you release the mouse button, you'll see the chart displayed in Figure 1.11. (The bars in your chart may look slightly different, depending on whether you're using a monochrome or color monitor.)

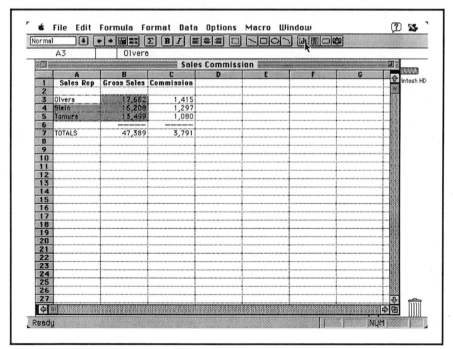

Figure 1.10: Selecting an area to graph

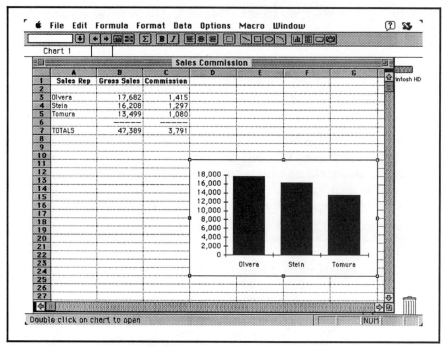

Figure 1.11: The default column chart

The chart shows the gross sales for each representative. Excel calls this particular type of chart a *column chart*—although other programs that produce graphs often call such a chart a bar chart. In Excel, a *bar chart* is one in which the bars run horizontally—frequently termed in other programs a horizontal bar chart.

CREATING A PIE CHART

The column chart is the default graph produced by Excel. However, you can select other chart types. To see a more meaningful comparison of the performance of the representatives, let's use a pie chart.

1. Double-click the displayed chart. This action activates special chart menus so you can edit the chart. (Microsoft calls the action *opening a chart window.*)

2. Pull down the Gallery menu now listed in the title bar. This menu is where you can change the kind of chart you want made from your data. Select the Pie...command, as illustrated in Figure 1.12. The Pie dialog box appears. Pick the number 6 format, which shows percentages (see Figure 1.13), and click OK. The column chart becomes a pie chart, with percentages displayed.

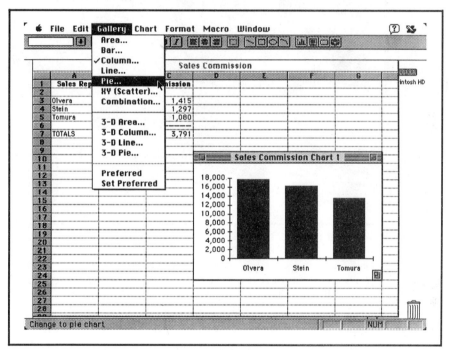

Figure 1.12: Selecting the Pie...command from the Gallery menu

ADDING A LEGEND AND TITLE

The chart still lacks a legend explaining the percentages, and it lacks a title. Add these now.

1. Pull down the Chart menu (another menu listed in the title bar when the active file is a chart). Select the Add Legend command, as shown in Figure 1.14. The result is the addition of a legend box that relates each representative to the applicable slice of the pie. The

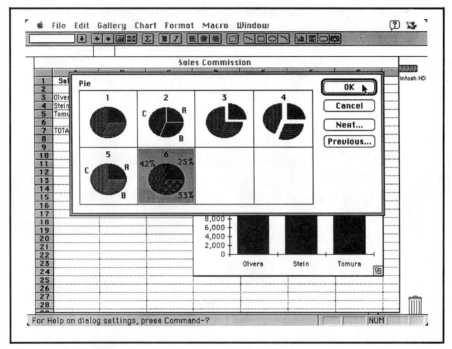

Figure 1.13: The Pie dialog box

legend box is surrounded by small black squares called *handles,* showing that the box is currently selected.

2. Click just under the title bar in the chart window to deselect the legend box.

3. Pull down the Chart menu again and select the Attach Text . . . command. The Attach Text dialog box appears. The default button already selected in this dialog box is named Chart Title. This is the button you want to use, so merely click OK. The word *Title* now appears on the chart (surrounded by small white boxes) and also on the title bar that replaces the formula bar when you're editing a chart.

4. Type this title: **Sales by Representative.** The words appear in the formula bar, as shown in Figure 1.15. Then click the enter box. The

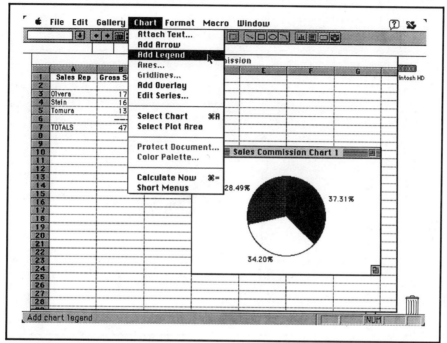

Figure 1.14: Selecting Add Legend from the Chart menu

title now appears at the top of the pie chart, in boldface. (You could pull down the Chart Format menu and select the Font...command to change the size or typeface of the title.)

COMPLETING THE WORKSHEET

Now view your revised worksheet and save it again.

1. Click twice anywhere on the worksheet outside the chart area. You return to the normal worksheet mode, the title is no longer sur-rounded by white boxes, and the chart is no longer selected. Your screen should now resemble Figure 1.16.

2. Save your work again. (Pull down the File menu and select the Save command. Shortcut: Press ⌘-S.) You'll use this worksheet again in Chapters 2 and 3.

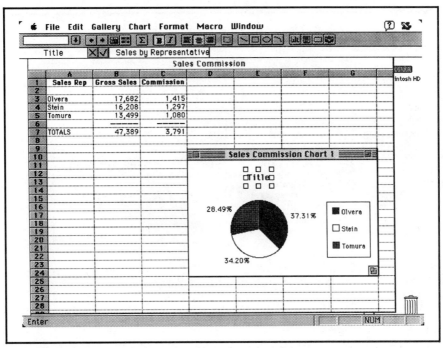

Figure 1.15: Adding a title to the pie chart

TIP

You can reposition an Excel graph on a worksheet simply by dragging the graph to a new location. Also, you can resize a graph by selecting it and then dragging one of the handles that appear on its boundaries.

PRINTING THE WORKSHEET

You can print this worksheet with its pie chart, using the usual Macintosh commands.

1. Pull down the File menu and select the Print...command. The Print dialog box appears.

2. Click OK to start printing.

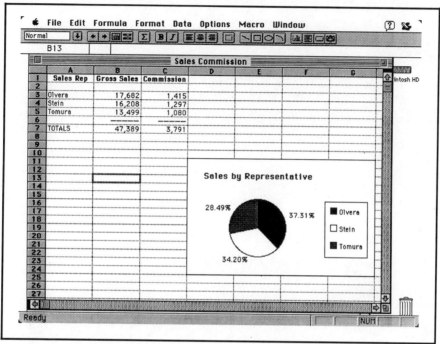

Figure 1.16: The worksheet with the completed graph

If you want to continue on to Chapter 2 without taking a break, leave this Sales Commission worksheet on the screen. Otherwise, pull down the File menu and select Close, or click the close box, to close the worksheet. Then, to leave Excel, pull down the File menu again and select Quit. (Shortcut: Press ⌘-Q.)

SUMMARY

This chapter provided a brief introduction to some of the basic features of Excel. You learned how to enter text, numbers, and formulas; edit a worksheet; make a graph from your worksheet data; and print your files.

Even if you've never used a spreadsheet program before, you should now be able to create and use simple worksheets effectively. The remainder of the book introduces you to many, many additional features that can make you a true power user.

Chapter

Sales Rep	Gross Sales	Commission
Olvera	17,682.00	1,414.56
Stein	16,208.00	1,296.64
Tomura	13,499.00	1,079.92
TOTALS	47,389.00	3,791.12

Sales by Representative

28.49%

37.31%

34.20%

Understanding Excel's New Look

If you've used previous versions of Excel, you've become accustomed to accomplishing tasks by using certain menus and commands. These familiar options are still available to you in Excel 3.0, but they have been augmented by new capabilities and—most noticeably when you load the new version—by the Toolbar.

The Toolbar provides the quickest and easiest way to perform many common tasks in Excel. You used this added feature briefly in Chapter 1. In this chapter, you learn all about it.

After introducing all of the icons on the Toolbar, this chapter provides a brief tour of the Excel worksheet menus. This section tells newcomers to the program where to find menu items they'll soon need and brings experienced users up-to-date on new and enhanced commands.

Before continuing with this chapter, be sure the Sales Commission worksheet is on your screen. If you closed it after completing Chapter 1, start Excel, pull down the File menu, and select Open.... (Shortcut: Press ⌘-O.) From the Open Document dialog box that appears, double-click the Sales Commission file to open it, or alternatively, highlight the name of the file and click the Open button.

USING THE TOOLBAR

You use the Toolbar by clicking icons that represent commands and options (see Figure 2.1), as you discovered in Chapter 1. You can access some commands and options through the menu system too. Others are major new features accessible only through the Toolbar.

STYLE BOX

The option at the left end of the Toolbar is called the *style box*. By default, it says *Normal*. Using this box, you can choose or create styles to apply to a cell or group of cells. To apply an existing style, you merely select the cells to be formatted and then click the name of the style you want applied. To create a new style, you format a cell with the attributes you want to assign to the style or select a cell that already has been formatted with those attributes; then you provide a new style name.

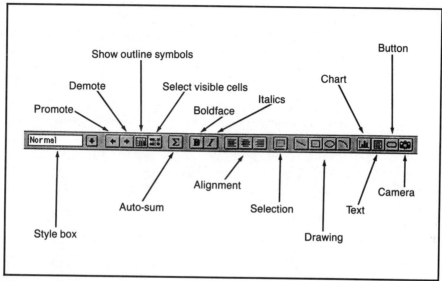

Figure 2.1: The Toolbar

The Normal style assigns the standard Excel default attributes to the selected area of the worksheet (removing other formatting from those cells, if you've added it). Excel includes three additional styles, which you can access by pressing the down-pointing arrow to the right of the word *Normal.* These predefined style options are *Comma*, *Currency*, and *Percent—* all for formatting number cells.

Try the following example to see how the style box feature works.

1. With the Sales Commission worksheet displayed on your screen, drag across the headings for columns B and C to select those columns. The entire columns will be highlighted.

2. Place the pointer on the down-pointing arrow next to the style box and click to see the options available other than Normal.

3. Highlight the Currency option and then release the mouse button. Excel reformats all of the number cells in columns B and C to show dollars and cents. The column headings and the lines in cells B6 and C6 are not changed, since their cells do not contain numbers.

Note that the currency format leaves one blank space to the right of the number in each cell. This space allows negative numbers to be enclosed in parentheses, with the decimal points of both positive and negative numbers appearing at the same position in each cell (see Figure 2.2).

Don't save this change in the worksheet—nor any of the other changes you make in this chapter. You're making these changes only to try some of Excel's new features. In Chapter 3 you'll work with the Sales Commission worksheet again—in the same condition you left it at the end of Chapter 1.

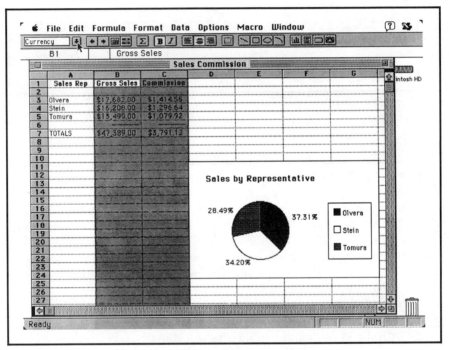

Figure 2.2: Number cells reformatted for Currency

PROMOTE AND DEMOTE BUTTONS

Just to the right of the down-pointing arrow are left- and right-pointing arrows. These are called the *promote* and *demote buttons.* These buttons let you collapse the view of a worksheet to show less detail or expand it to show more detail. You can change a worksheet into an outline format almost instantly, right from the Toolbox, using these buttons. Try it now:

1. Drag to select the headings for rows 3 through 6 (displaying the numbers 3, 4, 5, and 6). This action selects the entire rows. These particular rows contain the names of the sales representatives, individual gross sales, and the amount of commission each representative has earned, as well as the lines you inserted above the column totals.

2. Press the demote button (the right-pointing arrow). A new column appears to the left of the headings for the rows (see Figure 2.3). At the top of this column, the numbers 1 and 2 appear in small white boxes, called *row level buttons,* indicating that an outline has been created that has, at present, two levels. (An Excel outline can have up to seven sublevels of information.) The four rows you selected are bracketed by a symbol called a *row level bar.* The row level bar

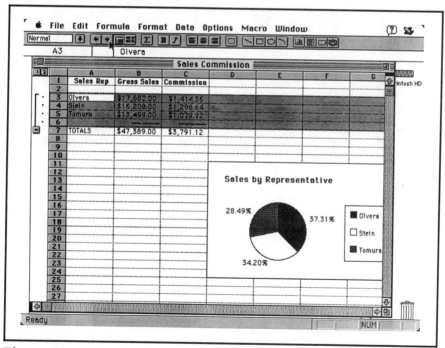

Figure 2.3: Sales detail section demoted to form an outline

displays a minus sign in a box (called a *collapse button*), which can be used to collapse (or hide) this level of the outline. (You can create outline levels in both row and column formats.)

3. Click the collapse button at the end of the row level bar. Rows 3, 4, 5, and 6 disappear. They're hidden, not erased. A plus sign (+) now appears in the outline column beside the heading for row 7 (see Figure 2.4).

4. Click the plus sign button to make the hidden rows reappear.

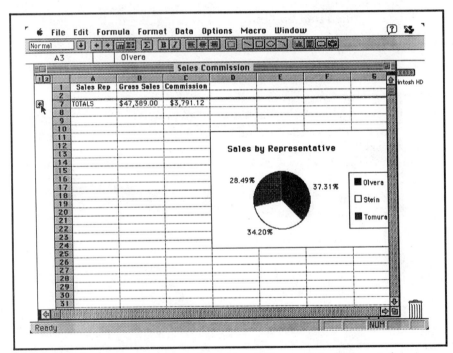

Figure 2.4: The worksheet collapsed to hide rows 3, 4, 5, and 6

What is the advantage of hiding rows 3, 4, 5, and 6? In a small worksheet like the Sales Commission sample, hiding details does emphasize the totals, but the advantage is certainly inconsequential.

However, when you create a long worksheet that covers several pages, the advantage is obvious. You could display totals on a single page, so that readers wouldn't have to read column after column and page after page of detail merely to obtain an overview of the ''bottom line'' of the worksheet.

SHOW OUTLINE SYMBOLS BUTTON

The next option on the Toolbar is the *show outline symbols button,* which you use to display or hide the outline column.

1. Click the show outline symbols button. The new outline column disappears.

2. Click outside the data area of the worksheet, to deselect rows 3 through 6. The worksheet now has no visible indication that an outline has been created. However, you can bring back the outline symbols at any time by clicking the show outline symbols button again.

SELECT VISIBLE CELLS BUTTON

The *select visible cells button* is the last of the group of buttons connected with outlining. This button allows you to select all of the cells currently visible, excluding those that are temporarily hidden because you collapsed the worksheet. This button has several uses. You may want to copy only the summary information (the part that is not collapsed) into another document or application, such as a word processor, where you are preparing a report. Or you may want to create a graph right on the worksheet from this summary information. You can also apply special formatting, such as boldface or italics, only to the key information on the worksheet and not to the temporarily hidden detail.

AUTO-SUM BUTTON

You used the *auto-sum button* in Chapter 1. This button automatically creates a formula to total numbers in the group of cells immediately above or to the left of the currently selected cell.

BOLDFACE AND ITALICS BUTTONS

The *boldface* and *italics buttons* turn boldface or italic formatting on or off in cells currently selected. You used the boldface button in Chapter 1.

ALIGNMENT BUTTONS

You met the *alignment buttons* too in Chapter 1. They center the contents of currently selected cells or align contents at the left or right edge of the cells.

SELECTION TOOL

Click the *selection tool* to change the pointer into a selection tool, so you can select objects you want to move, size, or format. You can drag with the selection tool to select a group of objects at the same time. As you drag, the objects are enclosed in an expanding rectangle formed with dashed lines. When you release the mouse button, the rectangle disappears, and all of the objects entirely within the rectangle remain selected.

DRAWING TOOLS

Use the *drawing tools* to call attention to areas of a worksheet. The tools are (from left to right), the *line*, *rectangle*, *oval*, and *arc* tools. Simply select one and drag to create the graphic object. After you've finished, you can add colors and styles with the *Patterns command* on the Format menu, or you can drag to change the object's size or location.

The operation of the drawing tools is similar to that of the text box tool, described later in this chapter. The discussion of the text box tool includes a demonstration of its features.

CHART TOOL

The *chart tool* icon resembles a miniature bar chart. You used the chart tool in Chapter 1. Using the chart tool, you can create a graph by selecting cells with data to be charted, clicking the chart tool, and then dragging to define an area on your worksheet where you want the graph to appear. That's all! As soon as you release the mouse button, the default bar chart of your data appears. You can change this chart format to any of numerous other formats, through menu options.

Part 3 discusses the charting features of Excel in detail.

TEXT BOX TOOL

The *text box tool* lets you add rectangular boxes of notes to work-sheets (or to macro sheets, described in Part 6). You can format these notes with any size font you like, using any typeface installed on your system, a variety of borders, and colored and patterned backgrounds. The completed box can be resized and dragged to any new location on your worksheet that you wish.

Test this tool now.

1. Click the text box tool (the icon that looks like several lines of text surrounded by a border; the text box tool is immediately to the right of the chart tool).

2. Position the pointer at the left edge of cell A9 and drag down and to the right until you reach the right edge of cell B14. Release the mouse button. A white rectangle, called a *text box*, forms in the area you've selected. The text box covers the gridlines that mark the cell boundaries in that region of the worksheet.

3. A flashing vertical bar inside the text box indicates that Excel is waiting for you to enter text. Type these words: **SALES FIGURES CURRENT AS OF JANUARY 31**. Click outside the text box to end the text entry.

4. Click inside the text box to select the text box itself. It will now be surrounded by eight square handles: one at each corner of the box and four more centered in each of its four boundary lines. You can drag any of the corner handles to resize the box proportionally, or you can drag one of the centered handles to stretch or compress the box in only one dimension.

5. Experiment with dragging the handles until the borders of the box are close to the text on all sides, with the words *SALES FIGURES CURRENT* on the first line and *AS OF JANUARY 31* on a second line. As you resize the boundaries, the text rearranges itself auto-matically to fit its new dimensions. However, if you make the rec-tangle too small, some of the words will be hidden.

6. Click outside the box to deselect it. Then drag the box until it overlaps the top left corner of the embedded pie chart on the worksheet.

7. The final step is to center the text. First, click inside the text box to select it once more. It will be surrounded by handles again.

8. Click the alignment button that centers text. The words *AS OF JANUARY 31* become centered on the second line.

9. Click outside the text box to deselect it.

Your worksheet should now resemble Figure 2.5.

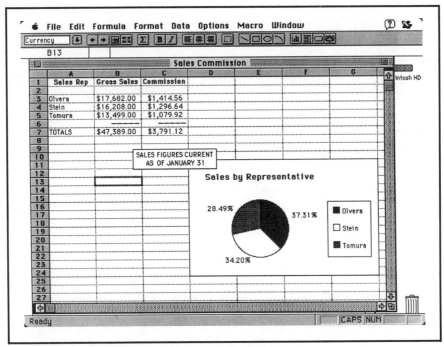

Figure 2.5: Worksheet with text box added

BUTTON TOOL

The *button tool* is an exciting new feature of Excel. With this tool (located to the right of the text box tool), you can create your own buttons on worksheets that will execute macros when they're clicked. You can name these buttons anything you like and even control their appearance. You'll use the button tool in Chapter 15.

CAMERA TOOL

With the *camera tool* (at the right of the Toolbar, represented by the icon that's shaped like a camera), you can capture a section of a worksheet or macro sheet, move it as a "picture" to the clipboard, and paste it into an Excel chart or even into another application. (If you're new to the Macintosh and unfamiliar with the functions of the clipboard, see "Edit Menu" later in this chapter.) The picture remains linked to the original data: Change the data on the worksheet, and the contents of the picture changes wherever the picture appears.

To use this feature, simply select the cells you want to copy, click the camera tool, activate the sheet on which you want to paste the picture, and click a cell. The picture will appear at that location.

LEARNING EXCEL WORKSHEET MENUS

The final section of this chapter familiarizes you with the options on the Excel worksheet menus. Some of the options are complicated and are explained later in this book, occasionally in chapters of their own. Others are simple, and you will be able to use them easily after reading the description here.

Excel lets you display either *short menus* or *full menus*. If you choose the Short Menus option, you'll see only the commonly used commands on each menu. This choice can be convenient if you use only the basic functions of the program.

However, for the purposes of learning many of the advanced Excel features explained in this book, you should choose the Full Menus option. You'll find both options at the bottom of the Options menu, though only one option appears at a time; the menu lists only the option that is *not* selected.

At this time, be sure that full menus are displayed. Just pull down the Options menu and look at its contents. If the bottom command is Short Menus, you know that no change is needed; Full Menus are the current choice. Otherwise, select the Full Menus command.

As you pull down the menus and look at the commands described, note that often the commands have shortcuts listed beside them. These shortcuts usually involve simultaneously pressing the Command key (⌘) and a letter key and can be executed without pulling down any menus. For example, pressing ⌘-Z lets you undo a command you've just executed. The alternative is to pull down the Edit menu and select the Undo command—a longer process.

FILE MENU

The purpose of most of the items on the *File menu* (see Figure 2.6) will be obvious to you if you're an experienced user of Macintosh applications, or even if you've used Windows applications on computers running under MS-DOS. However, there are variations specific to Excel.

For example, the first option on the File menu is the *New . . .* command. When you select it, you'll be asked if you want to create a new *worksheet*, *chart*, or *macro sheet*. The default selection, which is highlighted, creates a

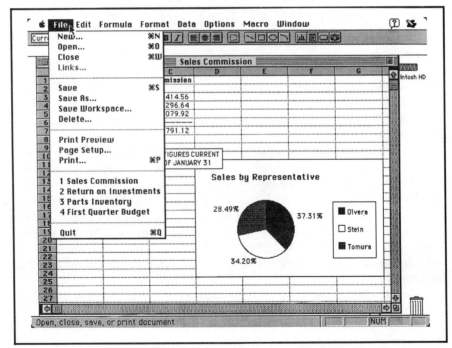

Figure 2.6: The File menu

worksheet. You make your selection by moving the highlight with the pointer, if necessary, and then clicking OK (or the Cancel button to cancel the command). If you choose to create a new worksheet, a blank worksheet will appear, containing only empty cells.

The second option on the menu is *Open....* Pick this one, and you'll see a typical Macintosh Open Document dialog box, showing the name of the current folder (initially, it will probably be Excel 3.0) and a list of the files and other folders available for access from within that folder. You can place the pointer on the name of the current folder and press your mouse button to see a list of other, higher-level folders you can access (if any), plus the desktop of the current drive itself.

The Open Document dialog box has several buttons that let you change drives, eject a floppy disk, open a highlighted file or folder, or cancel the Open... command.

Two additional options in the Open Document dialog box—Read Only and Text...—are specific to Excel. Clicking the Read Only box helps you prevent accidental changes to a highlighted file. Clicking the Text...button displays options that let you import ASCII text data from other Macintosh applications or from Microsoft Windows, DOS, or OS/2 files (see Figure 2.7). You can select either a tab or a comma as the column delimiter: the symbol you want Excel to use in separating the imported data properly into columns.

The *Close* command closes the current file. If you haven't saved changes, you'll be prompted to do so.

The *Links...* command provides a list of files linked to the current file (see Chapter 7).

Of course, the *Save* command saves the current file (without closing it). You should save your work frequently, to guard against power failures and other mishaps. A shortcut to save a file and continue working is to press ⌘-S.

The *Save As...* command gives you the options of renaming a file and saving it in other formats.

To save a file in a different format, you need to access the subsidiary Options dialog box. Click the Options button in the Save As dialog box. Then, in the Options dialog box, place the pointer on the arrow beside the File Format text box to display the list of available file formats (Figure 2.8). You can choose among many, including three Lotus 1-2-3 formats. In addition, you can save the file as a template so that you can reuse it, including all formatting you've added, for some recurring purpose, such as the preparation of weekly reports in the form of worksheets.

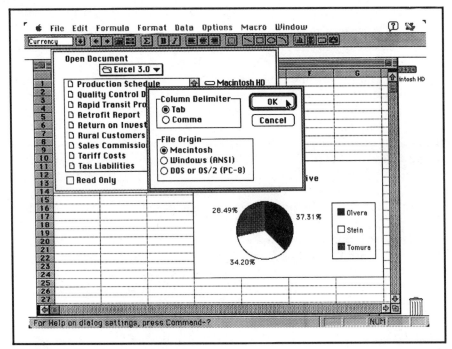

Figure 2.7: The Text dialog box

This Options dialog box also contains password security features, which are explained in Chapter 21.

Clicking the Create Backup File box creates a backup copy of the previous version of your current worksheet every time you save the file—a very good idea, unless you're critically short of disk space. Only one backup copy of the file is on disk at any time: the most recent previous version. Thus, you don't have to worry about taking up space with numerous backup versions of the same worksheet.

The first time you save a file, the Save command displays the same dialog box as the Save As... command so you can give your new file a name.

To save all of the documents you've had open at the same time in a work session (to return to the session later), select the *Save Workspace...* command. The default file name provided by Excel is Resume, but you can give this workspace file any name you like. Open the file to return to the work environment in effect when you left the previous session, with all of the same worksheets, charts, and other files open.

Use the *Delete...* command to delete a document.

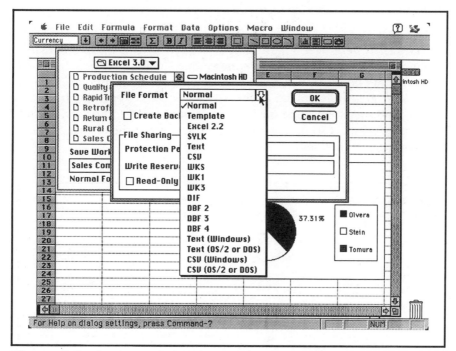

Figure 2.8: File format choices in the Save As Options dialog box

Use *Print Preview* to see how your worksheet will look when printed. This command and the Print Preview window are explained in Chapter 14, which discusses printing.

The *Page Setup...* and *Print...* commands bring up typical Macintosh dialog boxes to perform page setup and printing functions. These dialog boxes, too, are explained in Chapter 14.

At the bottom of the File menu, you'll see a handy list of the last four Excel files opened (except on some small-screen Macintoshes). This feature lets you reopen files you've used recently, so you can continue working in them without first searching through files in the Open Document dialog box. The list also includes any workspace files you may have created (provided they too are among the last four files opened in your previous Excel session).

The final option is *Quit*, which, of course, takes you out of Excel. If you issue this command and have not previously saved your current work, the program reminds you to do so before returning you to the desktop.

EDIT MENU

The *Edit menu* (see Figure 2.9) is headed by the *Undo* command (which changes to the *Can't Undo* command in situations where the Undo command can't be used), followed by the *Repeat* command (which changes to the *Can't Repeat* command in circumstances where repeating is not an option). Undo lets you wipe out the result of a command or action and return the worksheet to its state just before you made the change. Repeat lets you repeat the last command or action.

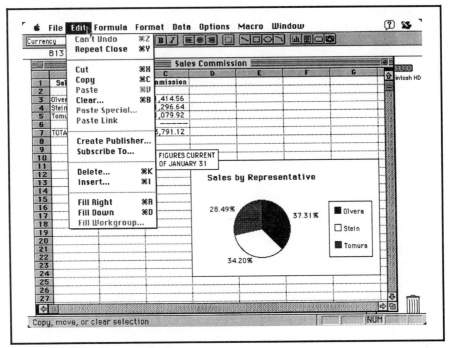

Figure 2.9: The Edit menu

You can undo a command or action only immediately after it has been completed—in other words, before you make other changes to the worksheet. If you haven't completed an applicable command or action recently, the menu displays the Can't Undo and Can't Repeat commands. However, these options are dimmed, indicating that they're not available for selection until a command has been issued or an action performed (see Figure 2.9).

Below the Undo and Repeat options, you'll see the usual Macintosh *Cut*, *Copy*, *Paste*, and *Clear* commands. The Cut and Copy commands let you either move or copy a selected area of the worksheet to the *clipboard:* that area of computer memory reserved for the temporary storage of data or objects to be placed elsewhere.

The Paste command lets you paste the contents of the clipboard into a worksheet at a location you selected before using the command.

The Clear command, which normally erases selected data or objects, is slightly different in Excel than in other Macintosh applications. It is followed on the menu by an ellipsis, indicating that a dialog box appears when the command is issued. The options in the Clear dialog box are buttons that let you clear all of the contents of the selected cell or area, formats only, formulas only, or notes only. You click OK after you make your selection.

Excel also provides three Paste options you won't find in some other applications: the *Paste Special...*, *Paste Link*, and *Insert Paste...* commands. The first two commands appear dimmed on the Edit menu when they're not available. The Insert Paste... command appears on the menu only when the clipboard actually stores something.

Paste Special... displays a dialog box that allows you to paste all of the contents of a cell or selected area, formulas only, values only, formats only, or notes only. You select the option you want by clicking the appropriately labeled button.

A separate Operations section of the Paste Special dialog box lets you perform an operation with the data as you paste. You can join a formula from the clipboard to a formula in a destination cell, using add, subtract, multiply, and divide operators. You can also use these operators to combine values from the clipboard with values in destination cells. You'll learn more about using formulas in Chapter 5.

You can also click boxes in the dialog box to skip blank cells in pasting or to transpose data (switch rows and columns).

Use the Paste Link command to paste the contents of the Clipboard into a worksheet other than the one where the data originated. Using this command automatically creates a link between the data in the original worksheet and the same data in the copy. When you update the original, the applicable cells in the second worksheet are also updated. With this command you can also link a file from another application (provided the other application supports the Paste Link feature).

The Insert Paste... command lets you insert the contents of the clipboard into an area of the worksheet that already contains data, without losing or overwriting the existing data. A small dialog box gives you the option of shifting existing cells to the right or down to make room on the work-sheet for the clipboard data.

If you're running System 7, you'll see Create Publisher... and Subscribe to... commands, which let you designate data by *publishing*. Other documents can display and update published data automatically, by *subscribing* to the data.

The *Delete*... command displays a dialog box that lets you decide what to do with the gap created by the deletion of selected cells. You can pick buttons to shift the remaining cells left or up, or you can delete entire rows or columns.

If the clipboard is empty, the normal *Insert*... command replaces the Insert Paste... command. The Insert... command offers options opposite to those for the Delete... command: You can insert data by shifting existing cells that contain information to the right or down, or you can choose between buttons that insert entire rows or columns.

The *Fill Right* and *Fill Down* commands let you copy the contents of a cell into adjacent cells. These commands are used most often for copying a formula. You simply drag across both the cell that contains the formula and the cells to which you want it copied. Then select either the Fill Right or Fill Down command, according to whether the destination cells are below or to the right of the original cell.

Use the *Fill Workgroup*... command if you have previously identified a group of worksheets as a workgroup, using the Workgroup... command (on the Window menu, which is described later in this chapter). The Fill Workgroup... command copies the contents of selected cells into the same cells in the other worksheets in the group. In other words, the command copies the contents of a range such as cells A3 through F4 to cells A3 through F4 in each additional worksheet in the group.

FORMULA MENU

The *Formula menu* (see Figure 2.10) contains commands that help you create or modify formulas. For instance, these commands let you paste in functions and name specific cells and groups of cells. Calling a range of cells in a formula Expenses, for example, makes the formula easier to understand than if the range is merely identified by a worksheet address such as E14:E29.

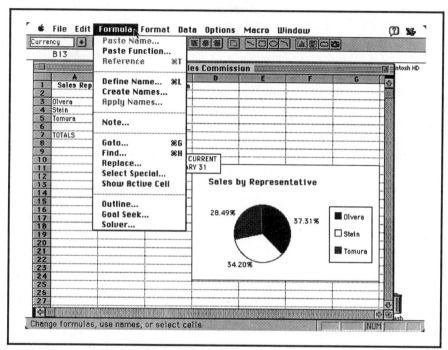

Figure 2.10: The Formula menu

You can also use the Formula menu to find and replace elements throughout the worksheet. For example, if a local sales tax rate is increased from 7 percent to 7.5 percent, you easily replace all references to 7 percent with 7.5 percent, using the *Replace...* command.

Some of the Formula commands are discussed in more detail in Chapter 5, which is devoted to formulas.

The *Select Special...* command can help you locate logical errors in your worksheets. If the total in a cell doesn't look right, you can quickly pinpoint all its precedents: those other cells that affect the total. The subject of finding and preventing errors is discussed in detail in Chapter 8.

In a large worksheet, you can use the *Show Active Cell* command to find your place.

The *Note...* command lets you attach a note to a cell or read, modify, or delete an existing note, through a Cell Note dialog box. The Note... command is especially useful for documenting a worksheet, explaining the logic of certain complicated formulas so they can be understood immediately by those unfamiliar with their structure or remembered by their creator weeks or months after their creation. These notes differ from the text boxes you can enter from the Toolbar, which are usually intended for continuous display. Cell notes don't receive fancy formatting and are usually hidden until a question arises about a formula. Their presence is denoted by a small square that appears in the upper right corner of an annotated cell. You'll use this feature in Chapter 8.

Use the *Outline…* command to turn a selected range into an outline. You simply click the Create button in the Outline dialog box. Another option lets you have Excel apply its default style formatting to the outline. Two other options (selected by default) place summary rows below, and summary columns to the right of, the detail rows and columns.

The *Goal Seek…* command is explained in Chapter 25, which is devoted to the Excel's goal-seeking feature.

The *Solver…* command, explained in Chapter 23, solves optimization problems. An example would be finding the kinds and quantities of products a manufacturer should produce to achieve maximum profits, considering constraints such as the cost or availability of components.

FORMAT MENU

The *Format menu* (see Figure 2.11) is where you set the form in which numbers appear, cell alignment, typeface, borders, patterns, styles, row height, column width, justification, and grouping and placement of objects. You'll use most of these commands in Chapter 3, "Changing and Formatting a Worksheet."

DATA MENU

Use the *Data menu* (see Figure 2.12) in connection with Excel's database features, which let you create and maintain simple databases, such as records for all employees or all customer orders.

Databases and related commands are the subjects of Chapters 12 and 13.

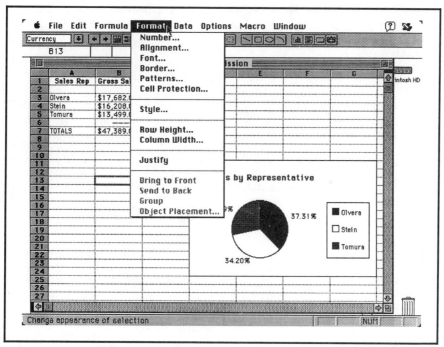

Figure 2.11: The Format menu

OPTIONS MENU

As its title suggests, the *Options menu* (see Figure 2.13) contains a mixed bag of commands not related to one specific subject. Here you will find commands related to printing: You can specify an area for printing, select text to be used as titles, and determine where page breaks occur. You can also select, through the *Display...* command, whether you want to display formulas, gridlines, row and column headings, zero values, and outline symbols; the location of automatic page breaks; and the color to be used for gridlines and headings. You can choose to display or hide the status bar, the Toolbar, the scroll bars, the formula bar, and the symbol that shows that notes are attached to certain cells.

Also from the Options menu, you can protect the cells, windows, and objects in your document with a password. You can determine how and

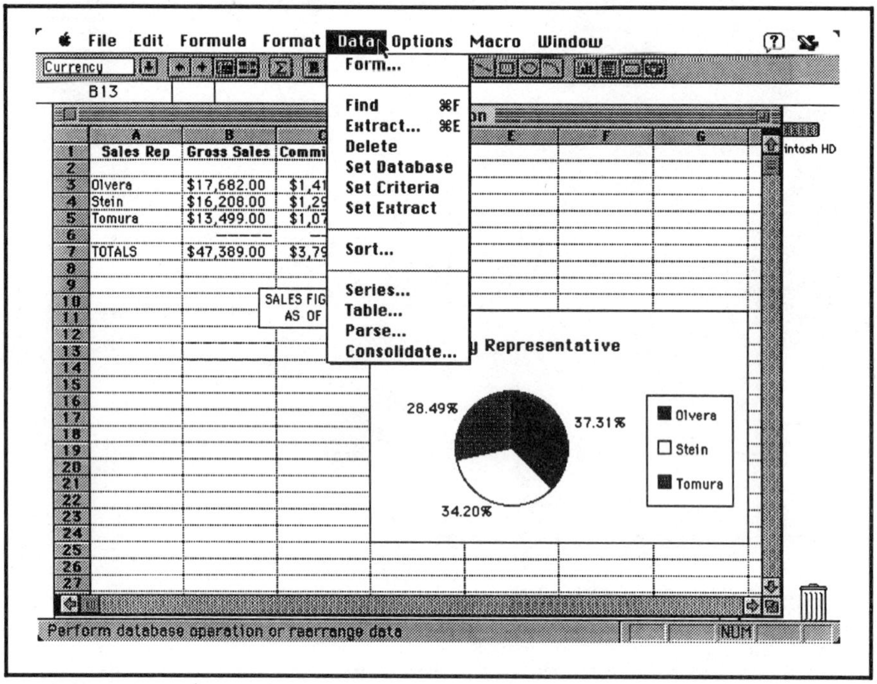

Figure 2.12: The Data menu

when the worksheet is calculated and with what degree of precision. As mentioned earlier in this chapter, you can switch between short menus and full menus.

MACRO MENU

Macros are featured in Part 6 of this book. Macros let you automate repetitive tasks to an amazing degree and even help you create custom applications. The commands on the *Macro menu* (see Figure 2.14) refer primarily to macros you can record. To create such macros, you simply perform a procedure and have Excel keep track of the keystrokes and mouse movements you use. You can then play back that macro later and have all of that recorded activity reproduced for you automatically. For example, you can create a macro to load and print a certain report that you use every week.

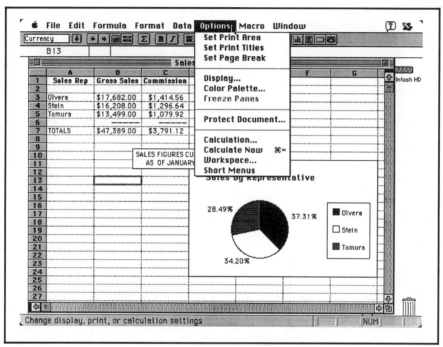

Figure 2.13: The Options menu

Through the macro menu, explained completely in Part 6, you can both record and run macros.

WINDOW MENU

The *Window menu* (see Figure 2.15) lets you display or hide program windows. If you're running your Macintosh under a version of the operating system prior to System 7.0, here is where you can call Excel's on-line Help screens, using the *Help...* command. It will be the first option on the menu. However, if you're using System 7.0 or a later version of the operating system, you call Help screens through a separate Help menu, explained in the next section. (Exception: if you're using a small-screen Macintosh running under System 7, you may still find help commands only on the Window menu.)

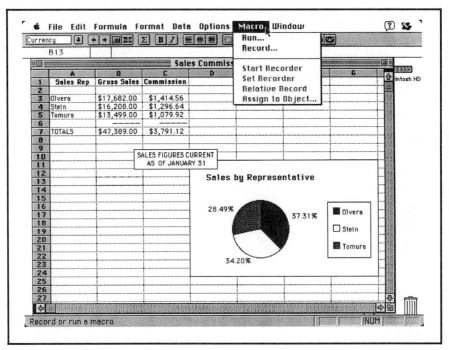

Figure 2.14: The Macro menu

From the Window menu, you can switch from one Excel file window to another (the name of the current window appears with a check mark before it). In addition, you can create a new window that provides a different view of your worksheet or display the current contents of the clipboard or all of the information relating to a current cell, including any formula or note attached. You can hide the current window temporarily, using the *Hide* command.

You can also select worksheets to be combined into a workgroup, using the *Workgroup...* command, and display all of those related worksheets simultaneously, using the *Arrange All* command. The workgroup features are especially useful when you want to work with several closely related worksheets, such as a series of sales summaries for regional offices, that use almost identical formats and formulas (see Chapter 7).

HELP MENU

Starting with System 7.0, the *Help menu* is located to the right of the Window menu (but is not displayed on some small-screen Macintoshes). It is

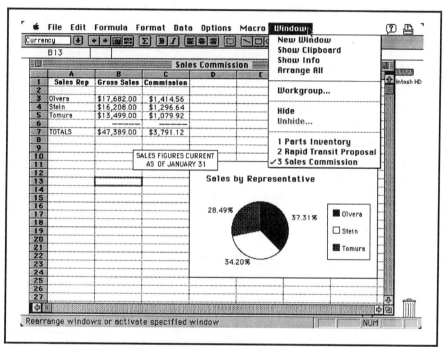

Figure 2.15: The Window menu under System 7.0

represented by a question mark enclosed in a dialog balloon similar to those used in newspaper comic strips. (See Figure 2.16.)

From the Help menu you can call up a brief screen that describes how to use the *balloon Help,* show or hide Help balloons, and access the standard Excel Help screen structure, including the Help index.

Balloon Help displays an explanation enclosed in a balloon as you place the pointer on some element of your screen. For example, if you move the pointer to the close box of a window, you'll see the message, *Close box. To close this window, click here.*

Apple provides this handy feature to help you learn how to use the elements of your desktop and windows. Fortunately, Microsoft has added to these operating system explanations, so you can also place the pointer on items specific to Excel and obtain instant help regarding their functions and uses. Figure 2.17 shows the balloon you see when you position the pointer on the selection tool icon on the Toolbar (provided you've issued the command to show the balloon Help).

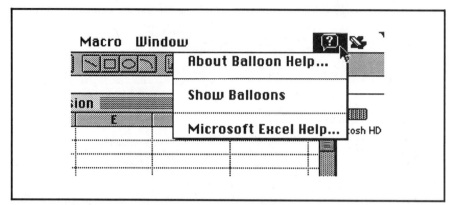

Figure 2.16: The Help menu under System 7.0

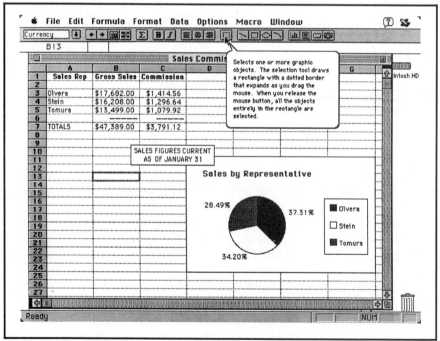

Figure 2.17: Balloon Help on the selection tool

When you're working in Excel under any version of the operating system, you can use a shortcut to access the regular Help screens: Press ⌘-/ (the Command key plus the slash key). If you've chosen a command, or if a message appeared on the screen just before you called Help, the Help window will automatically provide information about that specific command or message. This feature is called *context-sensitive* Help. Otherwise, you'll see a Help index, from which you can select the subject you want. You can also press ⌘-/ and click an Excel feature to bring up the Help screen that describes that feature.

If you have an extended keyboard (a large keyboard with 12 function keys along its top edge), you can call Help by pressing the Help key, which is labeled Ins Help. This key also operates as the Insert key when you run an MS-DOS application. The INS Help key is located immediately to the left of the Home key.

As mentioned previously, if you're using a version of the Macintosh operating system prior to System 7.0, you can also access Help from the Window menu.

APPLICATION MENU

The *Application menu* is a feature of System 7. This menu is denoted by a changing icon in the upper right corner of your Macintosh screen. The icon displayed changes to represent the application or system feature currently active. For example, when you're in Excel, you'll see a miniature version of the same Excel icon you double-click to start the program.

You use the Application menu to switch between applications without closing them. Previous versions of the operating system gave you the option of switching between applications by activating the MultiFinder. Under System 7, the switching feature is always on.

You pull down the Application menu to hide an application temporarily or make another application active, as shown in Figure 2.18. The application currently active has a check mark beside its name on the menu.

CAUTION

Remember to keep track of the applications you have currently open, since each one uses part of your available system memory. By closing an application promptly when you know you're finished with it, you help avoid the problem of having insufficient memory to use Excel features.

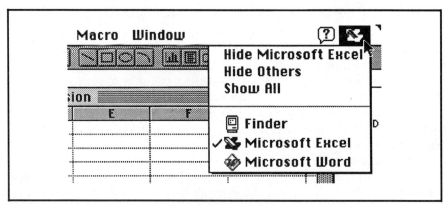

Figure 2.18: The Application menu

APPLE MENU

Every Macintosh has an *Apple menu,* marked by a small reproduction of the Apple Computer logo in the upper left corner of the screen. As Figure 2.19 shows, this menu provides access to options that let you choose a printer, select control panel features, activate the system alarm clock, and perform other actions. The content of your Apple menu depends upon the applications, accessories, and utilities you have installed in your system. For example, in Figure 2.19 the Word Finder utility is listed twice. These listings represent two different versions of this thesaurus program that are provided with two separate word processing applications.

You can select the *About Excel...* item on this menu (visible only when you're working within Excel) to display a window with the following useful information: the version of Excel you're running, the licensee of your copy of Excel, the serial number of your copy of Excel, the amount of free memory available to Excel at the moment, and whether or not your computer has a math coprocessor installed. (A math coprocessor chip speeds up certain calculations.)

CONCLUDING
THE TOUR OF EXCEL MENUS

This concludes your introduction to the Excel menus. Close the version of the Sales Commission worksheet you've used in this chapter *without*

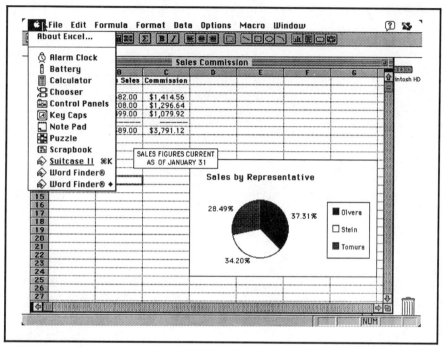

Figure 2.19: A typical Apple menu

saving it. As mentioned earlier, in Chapter 3 you'll continue using the worksheet in the form in which you saved it at the end of Chapter 1.

SUMMARY

This chapter acquainted you with the enhanced Excel desktop, including the options on the Toolbar and the revised worksheet menus. In the chapters to come, you'll acquire hands-on experience with the fine points of the subjects introduced here.

However, already you know where to find many of the commands you'll be needing in the future.

Chapter

Changing and Formatting a Worksheet

$\mathbf{T}$he commands and procedures illustrated in Chapter 1 are only a tiny fraction of those available for building and displaying a worksheet. You'll use more of Excel's capabilities in this chapter.

ADDING SALES QUOTAS

Your first task is to expand the worksheet you created in Chapter 1 by including sales quota information for each sales representative. You'll need two more columns, to be placed next to the names of the representatives.

1. Drag to select the headings for columns B and C, thereby selecting the entire columns.

2. Pull down the Edit menu and select the Insert... command. (Shortcut: Press ⌘-I.) You selected two columns, so Excel inserts two blank columns in place of columns B and C. The previous contents of columns B and C shift right and become columns D and E. Excel adjusts the formulas automatically to reflect the move, as Figure 3.1 shows.

If you had wanted to insert two blank rows, you would have selected two *rows* before issuing the Insert... command.

ENTERING THE SALES QUOTAS

Now enter the sales quota for each representative, in dollars.

1. Click to select cell B1.

2. Type **Quota** and press the Return key twice. This action enters the text and moves the pointer down two cells, to the new cell B3. The word *Quota* now appears centered and in boldface, since in Chapter 1 you formatted the entire row 1 with those attributes.

3. In cell B3, type the amount **15000** (for $15,000) and press Return, to activate the cell below. (You'll format the numbers in this column later.)

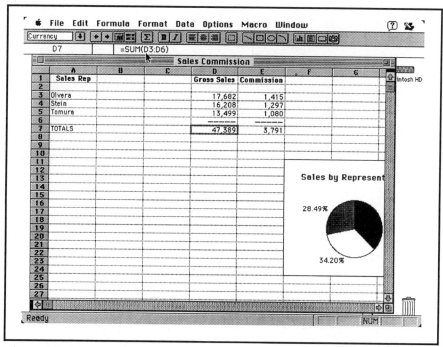

Figure 3.1: Formulas adjust when columns are inserted

4. Type **17000** in cell B4 and press Return.

5. Type **13000** in cell B5 and press Return.

6. Drag to select cells D3 through D5.

7. Pull down the Edit menu and select Copy. (Shortcut: Press ⌘-C.) A *marquee* (a moving dashed line that resembles the moving border of lights on the marquees of some movie theaters) surrounds cells D3 through D5.

8. Move the pointer to cell B3 and click.

9. Pull down the Edit menu again and select the Paste Special... command. The Paste Special dialog box appears (see Figure 3.2.)

10. Click the Formats button. Then click OK. Cells B3 through B5 acquire the formatting of cells D3 through D5.

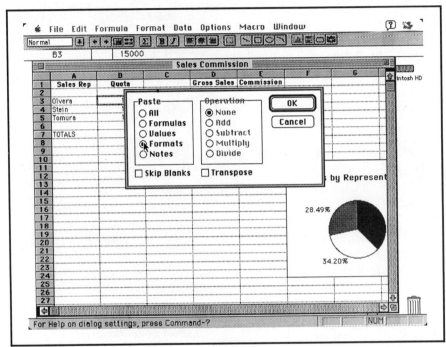

Figure 3.2: The Paste Special... dialog box

11. You still need to copy the line to indicate totals (the series of em dashes), the cell formatting from D6 to B6, and the formula and formatting from D7 to B7. You can accomplish these goals all at once. First, drag to select both D6 and D7. Press ⌘-C (the shortcut for the Copy command).

12. Click cell B6 and press ⌘-V (the shortcut for the Paste command). In B6, Excel duplicates the line and formatting from cell D6 and copies the formula into B7, causing the figure 45,000 (representing $45,000) to appear in that cell.

CALCULATING PERCENTAGES OF QUOTA

The next modification to the worksheet will be to show what percentage of their quotas the representatives have sold. To obtain this information, you must divide the actual (Gross Sales) figure by the quota figure. For this task, you use the second column you added to the worksheet: the new C column.

1. First click cell C1 and enter this heading: **% Quota Sold**. Because you previously formatted row 1 for centered text and boldface, Excel adds these attributes automatically to the words you type (although the characters fill up the cell from its left to right margins anyway, leaving no need for centering).

2. Press Return twice, to move the active cell down to C3.

3. Type an equal sign (=) to indicate that you're starting a formula. Then click D3 to enter the first cell address you'll need: where you'll find the actual gross sales amount for representative Olvera.

4. Enter a slash (/), the symbol for division.

5. Click cell B3, which contains Olvera's sales quota. Then click the enter box on the formula bar. The number 1.1788 immediately appears in cell C3.

6. Now reformat the display of the number to make it more understandable. Pull down the Format menu and select the Number... command. The Format Number dialog box appears.

7. Scroll the box until you can see this number format: 0%. Click the format to select it and then click OK. Cell C3 shows that Olvera's sales were 118 percent of quota.

8. Copy the formula you entered for Olvera to the two cells immediately under C3. Drag to highlight cells C3 through C5. Then press ⌘-D, the shortcut for the Fill Down command on the Edit menu. Now you can see, as Figure 3.3 shows, that Stein's sales were 95 percent of quota, and Tomura's were 104 percent. The complete formula in cell C3 is still visible in the formula bar.

USING A CONDITIONAL STATEMENT

Let's add another enhancement to the worksheet. Assume that a representative will receive a bonus of 1 percent if sales for a given month are more than 15 percent above quota. You can provide for this additional benefit by entering an appropriate formula.

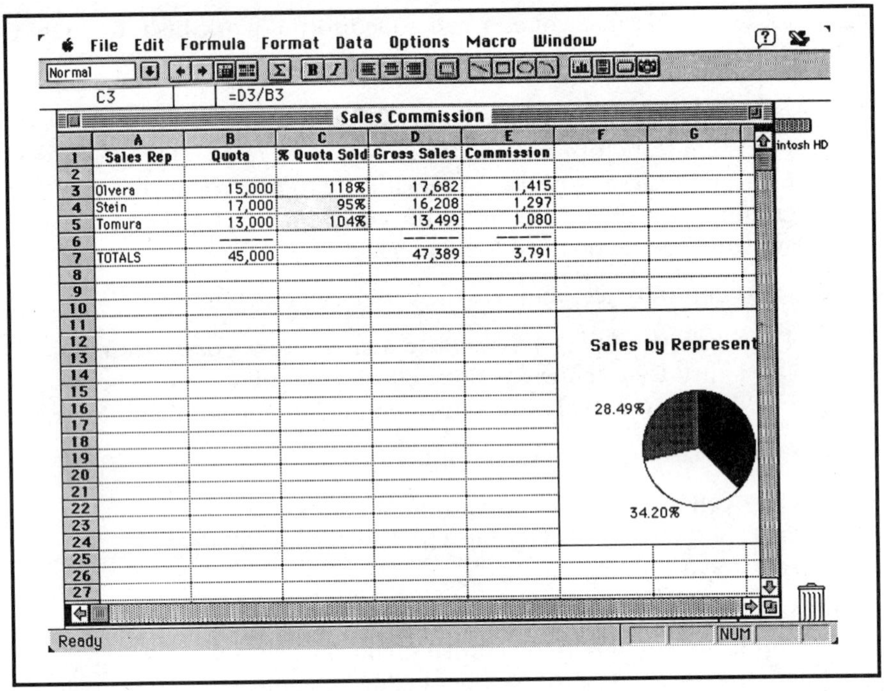

Figure 3.3: Copying the percent-of-quota formula

1. Click cell F1 and type the word **Bonus** as a heading for the column. Then click the enter box. The word *Bonus* appears in the cell, centered and in boldface.

2. Click cell A10 and type **Bonus Percent**.

3. Click cell B10 (another method of completing the entry in A10 and activating B10).

4. Enter this value in B10: **.01**. Then click the enter box. The number appears in B10 as 0.01. This cell will provide the source for the 1 percent bonus amount to be included in the formula. (You could enter the value .01 directly into the formula, as you did when you calcualted the previous percentages in this worksheet: Both methods accomplish the same goal, at least so long as the worksheet remains unchanged. Entering a cell reference instead of a specific value is especially handy if you expect the percentage for the bonus

to change frequently. It's easier to change the number in a single cell than to rewrite a series of formulas. In some cases, as we discuss later, an absolute reference is essential.)

5. Pull down the Format menu, select the Number... command, and scroll to this format: 0%. Click to select the format and then click OK. The value .01 is now displayed as 1%—a much more meaningful value to anyone who reads the worksheet.

6. Click cell F3 and type an equal sign (=) to start a formula.

7. Pull down the Formula menu and select the Paste Function... command. (A function is a sort of predefined formula. Functions require arguments to work. An argument is a value or independent variable used by the function. Functions are explained in detail in Chapter 6.)

8. Scroll the Paste Function dialog box until you see this function: IF( ). Click to select it.

9. At the bottom of the Paste Function dialog box is a small box titled Paste Arguments. By default, this box has an X in it, to show that it has been selected. Click the box to deselect it and remove the X. Then click OK. The IF( ) function now appears both in the formula bar and in cell F3.

    If you select the Paste Arguments option, the IF( ) function appears in a subsequent dialog box with a list of arguments it can use. The arguments are presented in the form of placeholders: text explanations that you must replace with actual values in order to use the function. This Paste Arguments feature is helpful in some situations, but would only clutter our example here.

10. Click cell C3 to add it to the formula. This cell address now appears in the formula between the parentheses.

11. Type a greater-than symbol (>), then the number **1.15**, and then a comma (,).

12. Click cell B10 to add the percentage amount in cell B10 to the formula. Then press ⌘-T to convert the characters *B10* in the formula to B10, making this cell reference an *absolute reference*. (Because the reference is absolute, the formula will always refer to cell B10, even if the formula itself is copied to other cells. The dollar signs before each part of the cell address are what make the cell reference absolute.)

13. Type an asterisk (∗—the computer symbol for multiplication) and click cell D3. The formula now says, "If C3 is greater than 1.15 (115 percent of quota), multiply B10 (the 1 percent bonus figure) by D3 (the gross sales for the first representative on the list, Olvera)"—in other words, issue a bonus payment of 1 percent of Olvera's gross sales.

14. To complete the formula, you must stipulate what happens if a representative's sales are not 15 percent above quota. (The IF function is really an IF/ELSE logical test: If the outcome of the test is evaluated as true, the program follows one course of action; if the outcome is evaluated as false, the program follows another course of action.) So to complete the formula, type another comma (,) and then a zero (**0**).

15. Click the enter box to enter the formula. You've now stipulated that, if the representative does not attain gross sales 15 percent above quota, the bonus is zero. The complete formula in the formula bar now reads = IF(C3 > 1.15,B10∗D3,0). Cell F3 displays 177—the result of the formula instead of the formula itself.

16. Now you need to copy the formula into cells F4 and F5 to determine the bonuses for the other two sales representatives. Drag to select F3 through F5. Then press ⌘-D (the shortcut for the Fill Down command on the Edit menu). Zeros appear in cells F4 and F5, since the other two representatives did not attain sales 15 percent above quota.

17. To enter a line in cell F6 and a formula in F7 to total column F, drag to select both E6 and E7. Press ⌘-C (the shortcut for the Edit Copy command), click F6 to select that cell as the top destination cell, and press ⌘-V (the shortcut for the Edit Paste command). A line appears in F6, and the formula in E7 is copied to F7, resulting in the figure 177 appearing in that cell. Your worksheet should now resemble Figure 3.4.

18. Press ⌘-S to save your work.

    You learn much more about using formulas in Chapter 5.

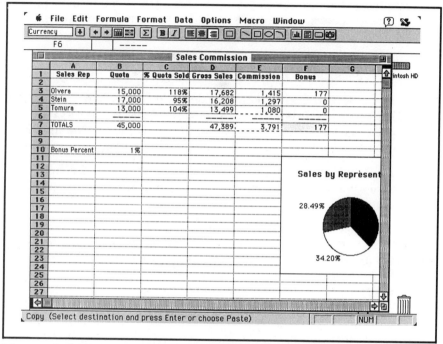

Figure 3.4: The Sales Commission worksheet with Bonus added

TITLING THE WORKSHEET

If your worksheet is to be printed and distributed to corporate executives, it should have a title. This title will consist of two lines of text. Although you could use the text box tool to create a title, you'll type this title into worksheet cells so you can learn how to add special formatting to the cells, and so you can see how Excel adjusts the cells to meet your needs.

Your first step is to add empty rows at the top of the worksheet, to make room for the title.

1. Drag to select the headings for rows 1, 2, and 3. This action selects the entire rows.

2. Press ⌘-I (the shortcut for the Insert... command on the Edit menu). Since you selected three rows, this command inserts three

empty rows above rows 1, 2, and 3, thereby moving the headings orginally in those rows to 4, 5, and 6. In fact, the number designations for all rows now increases by three.

3. Click to select cell C1. Pull down the Format menu and select the Font... command. The Font dialog box appears.

4. Select an appropriate display typeface for the worksheet title from those installed on your system. Figure 3.5 shows Helvetica as the typeface selected. Select 18 from the Size list, or type **18** in the size box, to indicate that you want the font size to be 18 points.

5. Click Bold in the Style box to make the title boldface. (A sample of the font you've selected appears in the Sample text box—a very useful Excel feature.)

6. Click OK. When the dialog box closes, you'll see that the height of all cells in the new blank row 1 has increased automatically to accommodate the large font point size. (Incidentally, typefaces are

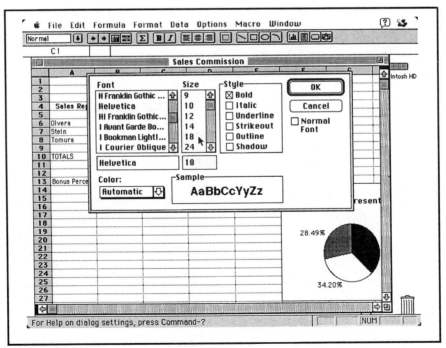

Figure 3.5: The Font dialog box

usually measured in points. A point is approximately 1/72 of an inch. Technically, a font is a specific typeface in a specific size and style. For example, 18-point Helvetica bold is a different font from 18-point Helvetica italic.)

7. Type two spaces and then the title **January Sales**. (The spaces make the text center better over the remainder of the worksheet. Since the text will be too wide to fit into cell C1 alone, the normal Center command won't help.) Press Return to enter the text and activate cell C2. The title appears in cell C1. Because the title is too wide to fit into cell C1 alone, and because the cells to the right are empty, Excel automatically lets the title overlap into D1. (If D1 already contained text or data, Excel would truncate the title and display as much text as would fit in C1.)

8. Now type a second line for the title, in C2. Pull down the Format menu and select the Font… command again. Change the font to a smaller size—for instance, 12 points—and click OK. The height of row 2 increases to accept the font.

9. Type two spaces (again, for centering purposes) and then the sub-heading **By Representative ($)**. Press Return. This text appears in C2 and overlaps into D2, below the words *January Sales*. The dollar sign in parentheses (**$**) indicates that the figures on the worksheet are shown in dollars and eliminates the necessity of cluttering up individual columns with dollar signs.

Your worksheet should now look like Figure 3.6.

ADDING FORMATTING

To try other formatting commands, why not place a shaded border around the worksheet title area?

1. Drag to select cells C1 through D2, thereby selecting both cells C1 and C2 that actually contain the text, plus the cells to the right of these cells into which the text overlaps.

2. Pull down the Format menu and select the Border… command. The Border dialog box appears.

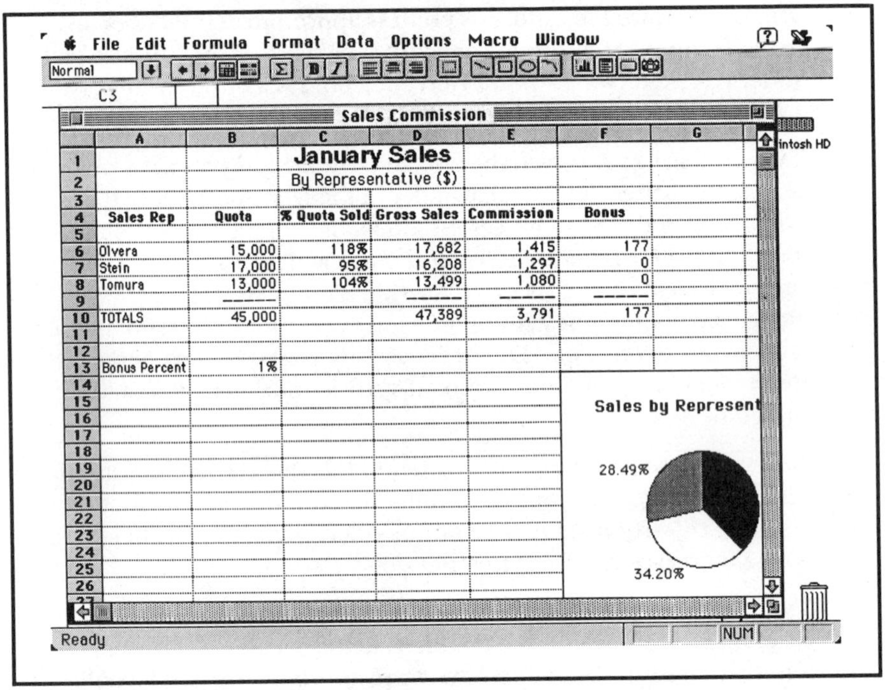

Figure 3.6: The worksheet with a two-line title added

3. In the Border section of the dialog box, click Outline box to outline
    the entire selected area. (Instead of this choice, you could also place
    a border only to the left, right, top, or bottom of the area.)

4. In the Style section of the dialog box, click the box at the far right
    of the top row that contains a wide black line.

5. Also click the small box titled Shade to place a default background
    shading inside the border. The dialog box should now look like
    Figure 3.7.

6. Click OK to close the dialog box and put the changes into effect.
    The heading lines now appear in a shaded box.

7. If you want to print this worksheet on one vertically oriented page
    (using tall, or portrait, mode), you'll find that the pie chart does not
    fit on the same page as the data. Correct this problem by dragging
    the pie chart until its upper left corner touches the upper left corner
    of cell B15.

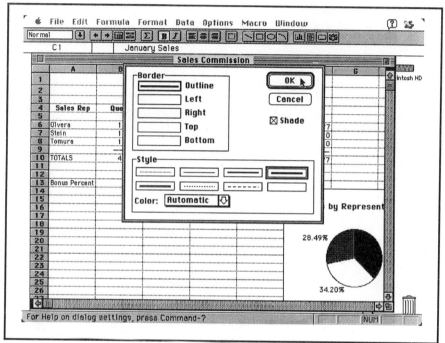

Figure 3.7: The Border dialog box

8. Press ⌘-S to save your work.

Your worksheet is done. However, you may worry that the worksheet now calculates incorrect amounts for the bonuses. Remember that you created a formula with an absolute reference to cell B10, which stored the percentage rate of 1 percent. This cell became B13 when you added the extra rows for the title, moving all rows down.

If you had used a relative reference, you know that the formula for calculating the bonus for representative Olvera would still be correct: When you added the title, the formula would have changed automatically to refer to B13. However, the copied bonus formulas for the other representatives would have been incorrect: Both before and after the three rows were added, these formulas would have referred to blank cells.

The absolute reference to B10 was necessary. Do you have to adjust it now so it will refer to B13?

The answer is no. When you add entire rows, Excel adjusts even absolute reference to accommodate changes in cell addresses entered in formulas.

PRINTING THE WORKSHEET

If you have a printer connected to your Macintosh and you'd like to print the worksheet and pie chart at this time, press ⌘-P (the shortcut to display the Print dialog box) and click the Print button. (Note: For versions of the operating system prior to System 7.0, the button is labeled OK.) The resulting output should look like Figure 3.8.

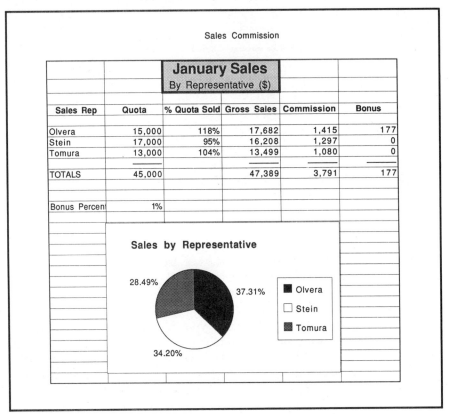

Figure 3.8: A printout of the Sales Commission worksheet

SUMMARY

In this chapter you learned how to expand a worksheet by adding rows or columns of additional elements. You created new formulas, including one that employs a conditional statement. You saw an example of how important an absolute reference can be. You created a two-line title for the worksheet and watched Excel increase the height of rows automatically to accommodate larger fonts. You moved a graph to a new location. Finally, you saw how cosmetic formatting can be applied to cells.

In the next five chapters you'll investigate many other aspects of worksheets, beginning with how to plan to achieve the most effective worksheet organization.

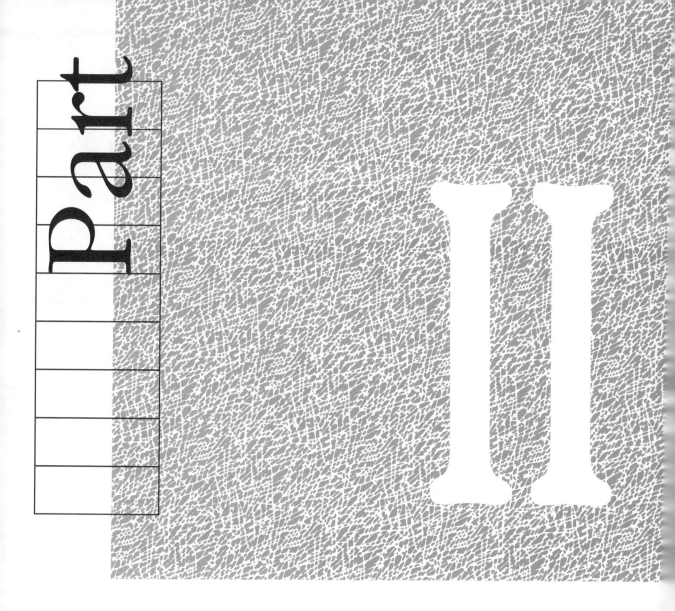

Part II

Making Great
Worksheets

Chapter

4

Planning and Organizing for Results

The manner in which a worksheet is organized can have a strong effect on how easy the worksheet is to use and keep free from error. The organization can even determine whether or not the worksheet actually performs the functions for which it is intended. If you engage in a little planning before you start to construct your Excel worksheets, you can prevent many headaches later on.

For example, if you cluster formulas in an area separate from where you enter data, you can more easily protect the formulas from being accidentally changed or overwritten. Also, if you give names to cells and ranges of cells that perform specific functions, you may make fewer mistakes in writing formulas (see Chapter 5). A formula that subtracts *EXPENSES* from *INCOME* is easier for many people to understand than one that subtracts cell *C4* from cell *C3*.

However, many worksheets fail in even more basic ways: The logic is wrong, or the information is incomplete. In most cases, the shortcomings are not caused by the incorrect use of advanced mathematical concepts, but by hasty decisions and foggy thinking.

For instance, accounting operations may seem mystifying to those unfamiliar with the accounting field. Nevertheless, the formulas involved are usually simple, consisting of little more than addition and subtraction. The example that follows—a budgeting problem—does not use higher math. It does demonstrate how you can construct a worksheet that seems to do its job, but does not.

MANAGING
A PRODUCTION BUDGET

The worksheet in Figure 4.1 presents a manufacturing production budget that appears at first glance to be adequate. Cell A4 states the volume to be produced: 10,000 units. (This text can overlap into B4 because B4 is blank.) Each cost is clearly allocated to its source. Only one formula is needed: to total the anticipated costs.

How well did the company do in handling the budget? The report shown in Figure 4.2 seems to provide an encouraging answer. Compare budgeted figures to actual costs, and you can see that, as the large type in the large text box proclaims, "Production costs were $3,541 under budget for this period." The

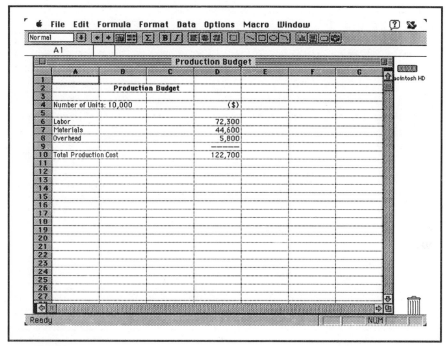

Figure 4.1: A basic production budget

figure was obtained by subtracting the total of the Over (budget) column from the total of the Under (budget) column, and the math is correct. Should the production manager be in line for a raise or promotion?

Well, not on the basis of this report, if you examine it more closely.

Compare the report with the original budget worksheet. The actual costs have been compared against the budgeted costs, and the only runover seems to have been overhead—by a mere $66. However, look at the number of units produced. The plant made only 8,000 units of the product, instead of the planned 10,000. Doesn't that fact affect the accuracy of the budget report?

It certainly does. The trouble with the original worksheet is that it shows a fixed budget. It provides the basis for an accurate report only if the company manufactures exactly 10,000 units.

The company should have used a worksheet based on a flexible budget. Figure 4.3—more appropriately titled "Performance Report"— shows the real result of the cost-containment effort. In fact, the production

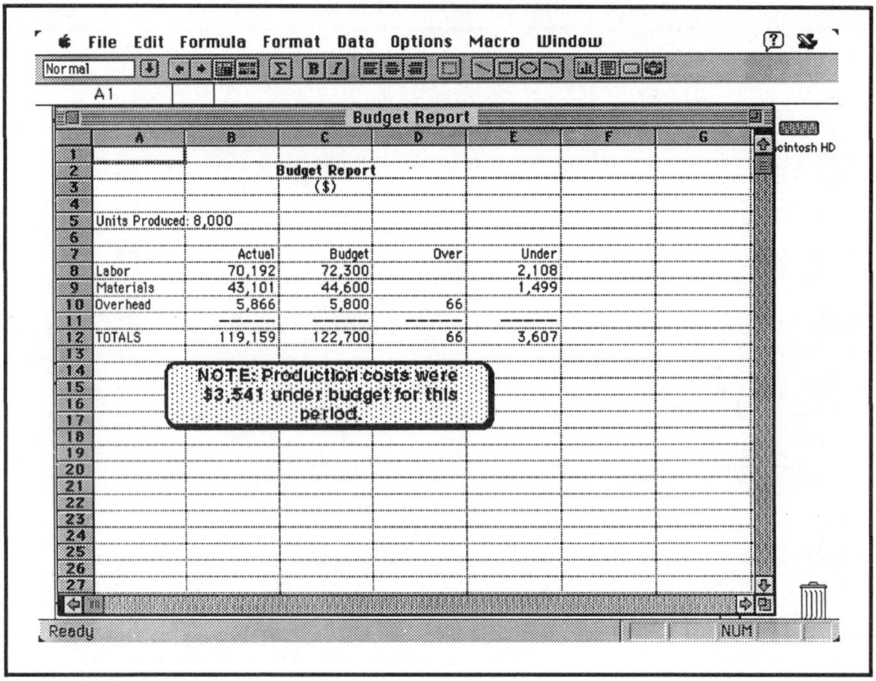

Figure 4.2: A report based on the budget

manager didn't stay within the budget in a single category, and the total costs exceeded the budget by a total of $20,999!

The worksheet in Figure 4.3 applies a flexible budgeting technique to the production costs that provides for variations in the number of units produced. Simple division reveals that the projected labor cost per unit on the worksheet in Figure 4.1 was $7.23 ($72,300 divided by the 10,000 units to be produced). The same math applied to materials and overhead results in per-unit costs of $4.46 and 58 cents, respectively. When you multiply these per-unit costs by the number of units actually produced, you obtain the correct budget figures for a production run of 8,000. When you subtract the actual cost from the correct budgeted cost, the overruns become glaringly apparent.

BUILDING A MEANINGFUL REPORT

Let's recreate the performance report in Figure 4.3 and make it as foolproof as possible. Before you begin, start a new worksheet and be sure

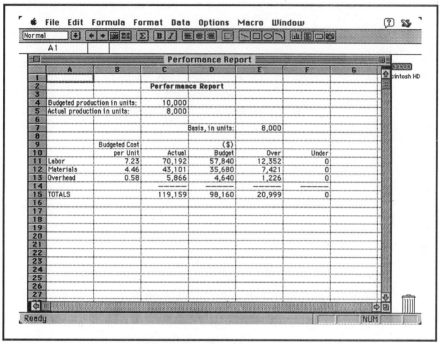

Figure 4.3: A revealing performance report

you're using the Full Menus option (the option needed for many of the examples and exercises in this book).

1. First, enter the heading for the report. Click cell D2 to select it and type these words: **Performance Report**. Add four spaces after the word *Report* and then click the enter box on the formula bar. (We placed the title in row 2 instead of row 1 simply to make it stand out by surrounding it with blank cells. We added the four spaces to help center the title horizontally. If we click the Center icon on the Toolbar to center text in a cell, text too long to fit in the cell will overlap equally into blank cells on the left and right. However, since our worksheet has an even number of columns, centering text in a cell will not center it over the worksheet as a whole.)

2. With D2 still selected, click the boldface icon on the Toolbar to make the heading appear in boldface.

3. Click the right alignment icon on the Toolbar to move the heading to the left so that it extends into the blank cell C2 and is approximately centered over the six columns of information you'll be entering.

4. Click cell A4 to select it. Then type the following text: **Budgeted production in units:**. The text overlaps into the blank cell B4 to the right. Press Return to enter the text and move the pointer to the cell below.

5. In A5, type **Actual production in units:**. This text too overlaps into the cell to the right.

6. Click cell C4 to select it and type **10000**. (You'll format numbers later to add a comma where appropriate.) Press Return to enter the number and move the pointer to C5.

7. In cell C5, type **8000**.

8. Click cell D7 and type **Basis, in units:**.

9. Click cell B9 and type the first line of the column heading: **Budgeted Cost**. Then click the enter box on the formula bar to enter the text. Click the right alignment icon on the Toolbar to right-justify the text over the numbers that you will add underneath.

10. Click B10 and complete the column heading by typing **per Unit**. Press Return and drag to select cells B10 through F10. Click the right alignment icon to right-justify the text just entered in B10 and also to format the remainder of the cells to the right in that row, to prepare them for the right-justified text you're about to enter.

11. Click cell C10 to select it and type **Actual**. Excel right-justifies your entry automatically. Press the Tab key to move the pointer to D10.

12. In D10, type **Budget**. Press Tab.

13. In E10, type **Over**. Press Tab.

14. In F10, type **Under**.

15. Click A11 and type **Labor**. (You will use the default left-justification for the remainder of the text you enter in this worksheet.) Press Return to enter the text and move the pointer to the cell below.

16. In A12, type **Materials**. Press Return.

17. In A13, type **Overhead**. Press Return twice to skip one row and move the pointer to cell A15.

18. In A15, type **TOTALS**, using all capital letters.

19. Click cell B11 to select it and type **7.23**, the per-unit cost of labor obtained by dividing the budget total for labor in the Budget Report by 10,000, the number of units to be manufactured. Press Return.

20. In cell B12, type **4.46**, the per-unit cost for materials. Press Return.

21. In cell B13, type **.58**, the per-unit cost of overhead. The program automatically adds a zero before the decimal point.

22. Click cell C11 to select it and type **70192**, the actual labor cost for the units produced. (You'll format this group of total costs shortly.) Press Return to enter the number and move the pointer to cell C12.

23. In cell C12, type **43101**, the actual cost of materials. Press Return.

24. In cell C13, type **5866**, the actual cost of overhead. Press Return.

25. In cell C14, hold down the Shift and Option keys simultaneously and press the Hyphen key five times to enter five em dashes in the cell. This operation draws a line above a total that you'll soon add.

26. Click the enter box on the formula bar. Then click the right alignment icon on the Toolbar to right-justify the line you created with the em dashes.

27. Drag to select C14 through F14. Then press ⌘-R (the shortcut for the Fill Right command on the Edit menu) to copy the line in C14 into the three cells immediately to the right.

28. Now add some formatting: Drag to select cells C4 through F15. Pull down the Format menu, select the Number... command, and select the fourth option: #,##0. Click OK. Numbers entered in the selected area are now formatted with commas, and the formatting is in place in those cells that don't contain figures yet.

ADDING FORMULAS

It's time to start adding formulas. The purpose of the formulas is to automate every aspect of the worksheet that relates to the actual number of units produced, so that changing the quantity from 8,000 to some other amount will instantly result in a new valid comparison of budgeted costs and actual costs.

1. Start with the easiest formula. Click cell E7 to select it, type an equal sign (=) to begin a formula, click C5 to include that cell in the formula, and click the enter box on the formula bar. That's it! The completed formula is = C5. This formula takes whatever number you enter into C5 as the amount of units actually produced and copies the number into cell E7, after the text in D7 that reads *Basis, in units.*

2. Now you need to calculate the correct budgeted cost for the three items in cells A11 through A13 based on the quantity of the product actually manufactured. Thus, for labor you need to multiply the number in B11 (the per-unit budgeted cost) by C5 (or by E7, since the value in this cell is the same as that in C5). Click D11 to select it. (D11 shows the total budgeted labor costs for the units actually produced.)

3. Type an equal sign (=) to start the formula, click cell B11 to add it to the formula, type an asterisk (∗) to indicate multiplication, and click cell C5 to add it to the formula. Press ⌘-T (the shortcut alternative to pulling down the Formula menu and selecting the Reference command). This operation makes C5 an absolute reference (so the formula will still refer to this cell when you copy the formula into other cells).

4. Click the enter box on the formula bar to complete the formula. The formula now is = B11 ∗ C5. The result—57,840—appears in D11.

5. Drag to select cells D11 through D13. Press ⌘-D (the shortcut for the Fill Down command). Excel copies the formula in D11 to D12 and D13, producing the results 35,680 and 4,640.

Your worksheet should now resemble Figure 4.4.

USING THE IF( ) FUNCTION

To perform the calculations for rows E and F, you need to make a slightly more complicated use of the IF( ) function, introduced in Chapter 3.

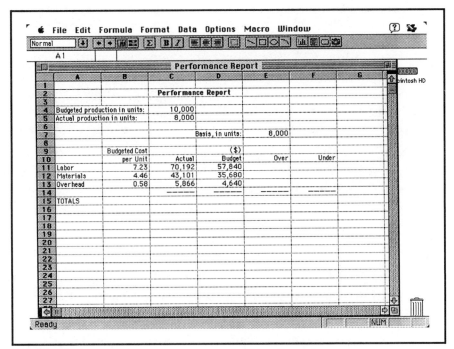

Figure 4.4: The report after adding budget forumlas

1. Click E11 to select that cell.

2. Pull down the Formula menu and select the Paste Function... command. Scroll the list of functions and select the IF( ) function. Click the Paste Arguments box to deselect the box. Click OK. The function now appears both in cell E11 and on the formula bar. (Excel automatically adds an equal sign to start a formula.)

3. Click C11 to include that cell in the formula. Then type a greater-than symbol (>).

4. Click D11 to add this cell to the formula. So far, the formula says, "If the actual amount in C11 is greater than the budgeted amount in D11...."

5. Type a comma (,) to separate the parts of the formula. Then click C11 again.

6. Type a minus sign (−). Then click D11 again.

7. Type another comma (,) and then a zero (**0**). Click the enter box on the formula bar. The completed formula now says, "If the actual amount in C11 is greater than the budgeted amount in D11, subtract D11 from C11. Otherwise, enter a zero." The actual formula is = IF(C11>D11,C11-D11,0).

8. Drag E11 through E13 and press ⌘-D to copy the formula in E11 into E12 and E13. No absolute references are needed here; you want the copied cell references to remain relative.

9. Now you need a slightly different version of the same formula in cells F11 through F13. Click cell F11 to select it.

10. Pull down the Formula menu, select Paste Function..., and select the IF( ) function again. (The Paste Arguments box should still be deselected.) Click OK.

11. Click cell C11 to add it to the formula. Type a less-than symbol (<).

12. Click cell D11 to add it to the formula. Type a comma (,).

13. Click cell D11 to add it to the formula a second time. Type a minus sign (−).

14. Click C11 again, type a comma (,) and a zero (**0**), and click the enter box on the formula bar. This new formula says, "If the actual cost in C11 is less than the budgeted cost in D11, subtract C11 from D11. Otherwise, enter a zero." The actual formula is = IF(C11<D11,D11-C11,0).

15. Drag to select F11 through F13 and press ⌘-D to copy the formula in F11 into cells F12 and F13.

16. Now the only formulas you still have to enter are those to total columns C through F. Click C15 to select it and click the auto-sum icon on the Toolbar. Click the enter box. Excel automatically creates and enters the following formula into C15: = SUM(C11:C14).

17. Drag to select cells C15 through F15 and press ⌘-R to copy the formula in cell C15 into cells D15 through F15.

You've finished entering the formulas, and you've accomplished your goal. You've duplicated the worksheet shown in Figure 4.3.

PROTECTING
THE WORKSHEET STRUCTURE

The Performance Report worksheet can now be used by others to enter new actual production figures for analysis. To ensure that users do not alter formulas and other data in certain cells accidentally, thus producing incorrect results, you should protect the cells that you don't want users to change.

The easiest way to handle cell protection in this worksheet is to protect the entire worksheet first and then remove from protection the few cells in which you want the user to be able to change or enter data.

1. Drag to select cells A2 through F15. This area includes all cells that contain any information.

2. Pull down the Format menu and select the Cell Protection... command. You'll see the Cell Protection dialog box shown in Figure 4.5.

3. The dialog box contains two selection boxes. The top one is labeled Locked and is selected by default. The bottom one is labeled Hidden; selecting this option hides selected cells from view. Leave the Locked box selected and click OK. Now all of the cells in the worksheet are set up for protection—but, as you'll see, protection is not in effect yet.

4. Click to select cell C5. Pull down the Format menu and select the Cell Protection... command. Then click the Locked box to deselect it and click OK.

5. Drag to select cells C11 through C13. Pull down the Format menu again and select the Cell Protection... command. Click the Locked box to deselect it and click OK. In steps 4 and 5 you removed C5 and C11 through C13 from the planned cell protection. These are the only cells a user needs to change to determine whether a production run is over or under budget.

6. Next, to place cell protection in effect, pull down the Options menu and select the Protect Document... command. You'll see the

dialog box in Figure 4.6. This dialog box gives you the option of protecting cells, windows, or objects. The Cells and Objects options are selected by default. Leave them selected. For now, ignore the Password option and click OK to put protection in effect. You could also enter a password, without which no one could later remove the protection from the selected cells. Note that this option does not keep people who don't know the password from looking at your worksheet; it only stops them from changing protected cells. If you want to restrict access entirely, you can use an option in the Save As dialog box, activated through the File menu. See Chapter 21 for details.

7. Press ⌘-S to save your work. In the Save dialog box that appears, name the worksheet **Performance Report** and click Save.

Now test the protection. Click cell B11—the budgeted labor cost per unit—and try to change the number. If you've followed the preceding

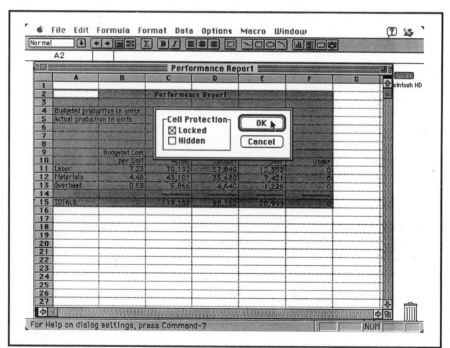

Figure 4.5: The Cell Protection dialog box

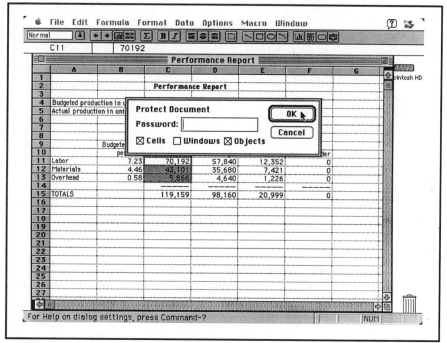

Figure 4.6: The Protect Document dialog box

directions carefully, you won't be able to alter the cell. Instead, you'll see a warning box that states, "Locked cells cannot be changed."

Next test the ability of this worksheet to analyze new production numbers. Click cell C11 (which you *can* change) and type a new amount for the actual cost of labor: **50000**. Click the enter box. Immediately, figures in columns E and F change as well. Labor is now $7,840 under budget!

These tests show that you can change the numbers displayed in protected cells, provided the numbers are created by protected formulas resident in those cells. However, you cannot enter new data directly into protected cells.

If you need to make a direct change to the contents of a protected cell, you can easily pull down the Options menu and select the Unprotect Document... command. All protection will immediately be removed. The Unprotect command replaces the Protect Document... command on the menu whenever cell protection is in force.

If you enter a password when you activate cell protection, you have to enter that password again when you select the Unprotect Document...

command. A small dialog box appears that requires you to type the password to remove the protection.

After you make the changes you need, you can immediately select Protect Document... again to reactivate cell protection.

Don't save the changes you've just made in the Performance Report worksheet. You saved the worksheet in the proper form in step 7. Don't drag this worksheet into the trash, either. You'll need the worksheet again in Chapter 8.

SUMMARY

This chapter illustrated the importance of creating versatile worksheets that fully accomplish your goals. For instance, when worksheets relate to budgets, you've seen that flexible budgeting makes results valid under many more circumstances than fixed budgeting.

You added to your basic knowledge of formulas, particularly in connection with the use of the IF( ) function. (Formulas are discussed in depth in Chapter 5, and formulas and functions are discussed in Chapter 6. You can even create your own functions, as you'll discover in Chapter 18.) In addition, you learned the fundamentals of cell protection. (Security matters are discussed in detail in Chapter 21.)

Chapter

5

Building Effective Formulas

Formulas in Excel can perform many tasks. You can even use text in formulas.

In this chapter you'll create several example formulas, all of which can be entered on a single worksheet.

FORMULA PRINCIPLES

As is the case with all computer spreadsheet programs, most formulas in Excel are based on simple algebraic principles that you probably learned in high school, if not earlier. However, the ability of the computer to manipulate numbers and perform other spreadsheet operations makes using Excel far more efficient than struggling over formulas with pencil and paper. This chapter demonstrates a few of the chores that formulas can accomplish in Excel and how you can execute them.

WRITING A TEXT FORMULA

First, let's enter a *text formula*.

Why would you want to include text in a formula? There are many reasons. For example, suppose you use the IF( ) function demonstrated in Chapters 3 and 4 in preparing a worksheet to calculate and report net profit for a series of retail stores. The formula can insert the words *DATA TO COME* in a cell whenever the formula encounters a blank cell instead of a sales figure.

Some spreadsheet programs refer to text formulas as *string formulas*. Let's see how text formulas work.

1. Open a new worksheet.

2. In cell A1, type **WORK**.

3. Press Tab to enter the word and move to cell B1.

4. In B1, type the formula **=A1&"SHEET"** and click the enter box on the formula bar. Instantly, the word *WORKSHEET* appears in B1, as Figure 5.1 shows.

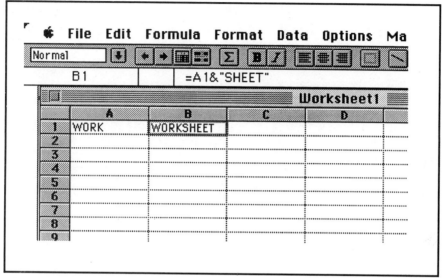

Figure 5.1: A simple text formula

Here's an explanation of what you've just done.

You've written a formula that combines the contents of cell A1 (which happens to be text only: the word WORK) with additional text within the formula itself and then displays the result in the cell that contains the formula: cell B1.

The ampersand symbol (**&**) is an *operator* that joins text. An operator is a mathematical symbol you use in a formula to represent a relationship between two values. Some other operators are + – * / (which indicate, respectively, addition, subtraction, multiplication, and division).

When you include text in a formula, you must enclose it in double quotation marks. Otherwise, Excel interprets the text as a name that has been assigned to a cell or range of cells, as the name of a function, or as a number.

If you want to insert a space between words to be displayed by a formula, simply include the space between double quotation marks. In many instances, you may want to place a space immediately before or after a word in a formula.

ORDER OF EVALUATION

Excel evaluates operators in a specific order. For example, Excel calculates multiplication or division in a formula before it calculates addition or subtraction, unless an addition or subtraction operation is enclosed in parentheses. Table 5.1 shows the order in which Excel evaluates operators.

Try this:

1. Click cell A3 to select it.

2. Type the formula $= 8 + 64/2$. Press Tab to enter the formula and move the pointer right, to cell B3. The result of the formula—40—appears in cell A3.

Table 5.1: Order of Evaluation of Operations

OPERATOR	FUNCTION
%	Percent
^	Exponentiation
* and /	Multiplication and division
+ and –	Addition and subtraction
&	Text joining
= < > <= >= <>	Comparison
Operators with equal priority are evaluated from left to right. Operators enclosed in parentheses are evaluated first.	

Excel divided 64 by 2 first (since division has a higher priority than addition). Excel then added the division result—32—to 8 and entered the final result, 40, in A3.

If you want Excel first to add 8 and 64 and then to divide the total by 2, you can change the order of evaluation by enclosing the first two figures in parentheses. Excel always evaluates numbers in parentheses first.

Now try this:

1. In B3, type the formula $= (8 + 64)/2$.

2. Press Return. The addition is completed first, and the result in cell B3 is now 36 instead of 40.

HANDLING NUMBERS TOO LARGE FOR DISPLAY

What happens if a formula produces a number too large to be displayed in a cell? Although row height increases automatically when you use a font that is too tall for a cell, Excel provides no such automatic adjustment of cell sizes when the results of formulas produce numbers that are too long to fit. Instead, if a cell has the default General formatting, Excel displays a number that is too wide to fit in scientific notation. If the number is still too long, or if the cell has some formatting other than General, Excel fills the cell with a series of number signs (######).

When numbers in a column are too long to fit, you can, of course, adjust the width of the column to correct this problem. However, you can't change the width of one individual cell.

See how these features work for yourself:

1. Click cell A5 to select it. Type the formula =2^60 and click the enter box to complete the entry. The formula raises the number 2 to the 60th power; the caret (^) in Excel is the exponentiation operator. Cell A5 now displays the result of the formula in scientific notation: 1.1529E + 18.

2. With A5 still selected, place the pointer on the down-pointing arrow next to the style box (at the left end of the Toolbar) and press the mouse button. From the drop-down menu that appears, select the Comma format. Cell A5 now displays a series of number symbols (#) instead of the number in scientific notation.

3. Position the pointer on the border line between the headings for columns A and B. The pointer changes from the normal plus-sign shape it assumes on the cells of a worksheet to a vertical line with arrows pointing toward the left and right.

4. Hold down the mouse button and drag the pointer to the right, just beyond the position normally occupied by the heading for column C. Column A expands to about three times its normal width (see Figure 5.2). Now the column has enough room for the result of the formula to appear in normal Arabic numerals. Cell A5 displays 1,152,921,504,606,850,000.00.

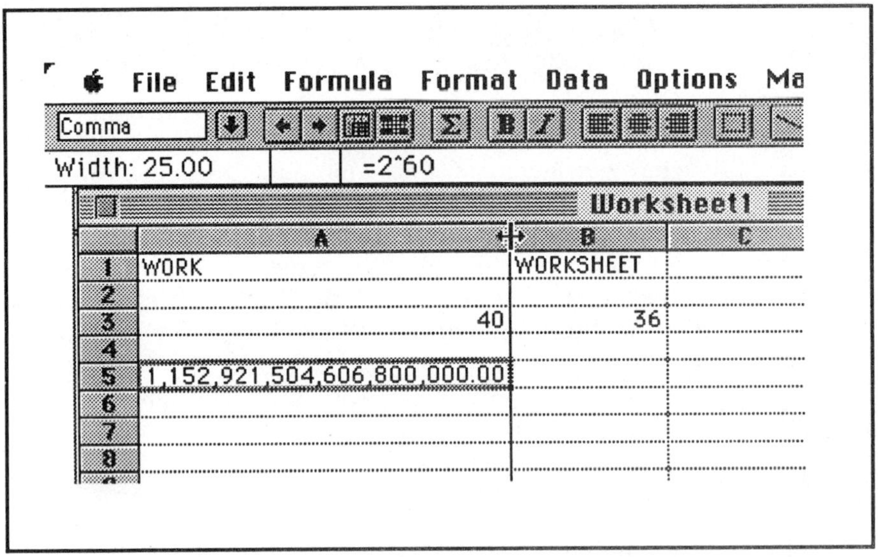

Figure 5.2: Widening a column to display a large number

(You can also change the height of a row manually by dragging the border between two rows. An alternative method of changing row and column sizes is to pull down the Format menu and select either the Row Height... or Column Width... commands; a dialog box appears, giving you the option of specifying the row height in points or the column width in characters. In addition, you can choose to hide selected rows or columns or return the height or width to the default size, called Standard.

The Column Width dialog box provides one more option: a Best Fit box you can click to adjust the size of the column automatically to accommodate the largest entry in any of the cells in the column (see Figure 5.3).

A shortcut for activating the Best Fit option is to position the pointer on the border between column headings and double-click (click the mouse button twice in rapid succession). Try this now.

1. Position the pointer again on the border between the headings for columns A and B until the pointer assumes the shape of a vertical line with left- and right-facing arrows.

2. Double-click. Column A shrinks until it's just wide enough to display the largest number in the column, in cell A5.

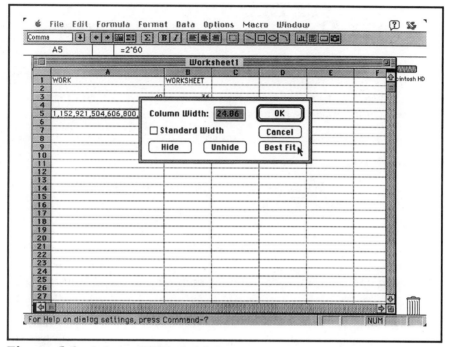

Figure 5.3: Column Width dialog box

You can select more than one row or column for size changes, by dragging across the headings or holding down the Shift key as you click the headings. However, you can select only a contiguous group: rows or columns next to each other. For example, if you hold down the Shift key and click the heading of column A and then click the heading of column D, columns B and C will be selected too because they lie between columns A and D.

NAMING CELLS AND RANGES

As mentioned in Chapter 4, naming cells and ranges can help you create formulas with fewer errors. Instead of having to include a mysterious cell reference such as D18 in a formula, you can name that cell something meaningful, such as Taxable Income.

Let's try this technique now.

SUBTRACTING ONE CELL ADDRESS FROM ANOTHER

First, let's create a simple formula in the usual way.

1. Click cell B7 to select it and type **Revenue**. Press Return to enter the word and move the pointer down to B8.

2. In B8, type **Expenses**. Press Return.

3. In B9, type **Net Income**.

4. Click C7, and in that cell type **10640**. Press Return.

5. In C8, type **8293**. Press Return.

6. In C9, type an equal sign (=). Click C7 to include this cell in the formula, type a minus sign (–), click C8 to include this cell in the formula, and click the enter box on the formula bar. Your formula now read = C7 – C8, and the number 2347 appears in cell C9.

7. Now format the number cells you're using. Drag to select cells C7 through C9.

8. On the Toolbar, press the down-pointing arrow next to the style box to see the drop-down list of options. Highlight Currency to select it. The cells that contain numbers now appear in a dollars-and-cents format.

SUBTRACTING ONE CELL NAME FROM ANOTHER

You can convert the cell addresses in the formula into names almost instantly.

1. Drag to select cells B7 through C9.

2. Pull down the Formula menu and select the Create Names... command. You'll see the small Create Names dialog box shown in Figure 5.4. Note that a box labeled Left Column already has an X in it. If you accept this default setting, Excel uses the column to the left of the numbers to find names to apply to the number cells. You can

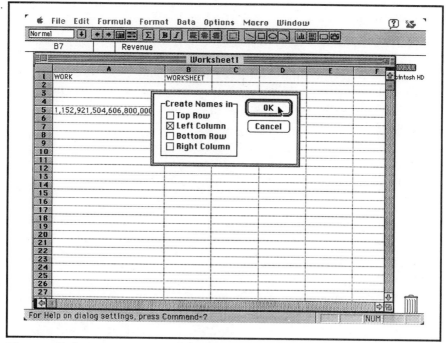

Figure 5.4: The Create Names dialog box

also instruct Excel to choose names from the top row, bottom row, or right column of a selected area.

3. Click OK to accept the default setting. This action creates the names for the number cells. All six cells remain selected, and no change is visible on your worksheet.

4. Now you have to apply the names you've created. Pull down the Formula menu again and select the Apply Names... command. The Apply Names dialog box appears. This dialog box lists the new cell names alphabetically. All cell names are selected (highlighted). Note that the name Net Income has become Net_Income. The program has replaced the space between the two words with an underline because you can't use spaces in a cell name. (When Excel applies cell names to existing formulas, by default it assigns both the row and column names of a cell as the cell's name in a formula if the cell doesn't have a name of its own. This feature is described later in this chapter in the section, "Using the Apply Names Options." Excel

separates the row and column names with a space, called the *intersection operator*.)

5. You could just click OK to apply the new names to any formulas in the selected area, since the default settings in the Apply Names dialog box will work fine for this particular example. However, before you do this, click the Options button in the dialog box, just to learn what these options are. The dialog box now appears as shown in Figure 5.5.

6. Note that each option has an X in the box preceding it to show that it's selected by default. (The first two options were displayed even before you clicked the Options button.) The next section, ''Using the Apply Names Options,'' explains each option. Now click OK to apply the cell names.

7. Click cell C9 to select it. Look at the formula bar. The formula that previously read = C7 – C8 now reads = Revenue – Expenses; it uses cell names instead of cell addresses.

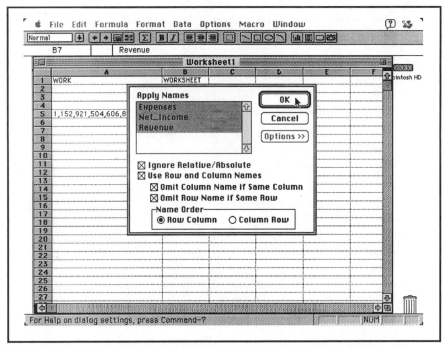

Figure 5.5: The Apply Names dialog box, showing all options

Even though you've named the cells, you can continue to use the cell addresses to reference to them in other formulas on the worksheet. However, you can also use the names, as you'll soon see.

Before we discuss this feature, though, let's take a brief look at the options in the Apply Names dialog box.

USING THE APPLY NAMES OPTIONS

The Apply Names... command causes the program to examine the formulas in all cells of the area you've selected. Whenever a formula mentions a cell for which a name has been defined, Excel changes the cell reference to the name. The ApplyNames options add fine-tuning to this process.

Here are the ApplyNames options:

- **Ignore Relative/Absolute**. This check box is selected by default. When it's selected, Excel replaces cell references with names without considering whether the cells contain an absolute reference. You'll usually want the command to work this way. Sometimes, you may want to retain the relative/absolute characteristics of a cell in a formula, if you plan to copy the formula to another location. However, most cell names are absolute references. Since Excel will replace references only when it can do so with a name that has the same attribute—absolute, relative, or mixed (where only the column or the row reference is absolute)—if you click this box to turn off this option, you'll find very few names added.

- **Use Row and Column Names**. This box is also selected by default. When it's selected, Excel substitutes row and column names from the range that contains the cell when no name has been assigned to a particular cell. When the box is not selected, Excel does not make this substitution. Usually, the substitution adds to the understandability of the formula and offers no disadvantage. However, if you want to use only exact names for specific cells, deselect this option. Then any references to cells that have not been specifically named will remain as cell addresses.

The following options appear in the Apply Names dialog box after you click its Options button:

- **Omit Column Name If Same Column**. This option, selected by default, causes Excel to replace a cell without a specific name of its own with just the row name if the cell is in the same column as the formula. If you want the cell to be named with a combination of the row and column names, deselect this option.

- **Omit Row Name If Same Row**. This option, selected by default, causes a cell without a specific name of its own to be replaced with just the column name if the cell is in the same row as the formula. If you want the cell to be named with a combination of the row and column names, deselect this option.

- **Name Order**. This option, displayed in a small box at the bottom of the dialog box, shows a Row Column button selected by default. You can alternately click a Column Row button. (These buttons are what are known in Macintosh parlance as *radio buttons,* because they work like the buttons on a push-button radio. Clicking a button automatically deactivates the previously selected button, and you can't select more than one of the buttons at the same time.) When you select the Row Column button, Excel lists the row name first, using names that the program applies to cells without names of their own. When you select the Column Row button, Excel lists the column name first.

DEFINING NAMES FOR CELLS, VALUES, AND FORMULAS

So far, you've learned how Excel can create names for cells automatically from existing labels and then apply those names to existing formulas. However, there may be no nearby labels that can be used, or you may prefer to use some name not used for a label, or you may want to label ranges of noncontiguous cells (cells that aren't located next to each other). In these cases, you can use another command on the Formula menu: the Define Name... command.

You can also use the Define Name... command to name a formula or to make a name refer to a value rather than a cell. In each instance, you handle these operations through the Define Name dialog box.

Try this example:

1. Click cell B11 to select it. Type **720**. Press Return to enter the number and move the pointer to B12.

2. In B12, type **106**. Press Return.

3. Press ⌘-L (the shortcut for pulling down the Formula Menu and selecting the Define Name... command). The Define Name dialog box appears.

4. In this dialog box, you need to select cell addresses by clicking to select the cells in which you've just entered numbers. However, the Define Name dialog box is positioned over those cells so they can't be seen. Simply drag the title bar of the dialog box to move the box to the bottom of the screen so you can again see the cells that contain the numbers.

5. In the Name text box of the dialog box, type **Rent**. Do not press Return, since that action would cause the program to enter the cell address it has proposed as the cell to be named. This address is B13, an absolute reference to B13, the cell that Excel activated automatically when you pressed Return after entering a number in B12 (step 2 above). Instead, press Tab. The Refers To box in the dialog box is highlighted (see Figure 5.6).

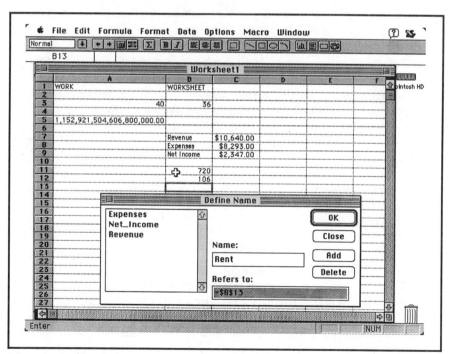

Figure 5.6: The Define Name dialog box

6. Click cell B11 to enter it into the Refers To box. Excel proposes this cell as an absolute reference too, which is what you want. (To make the cell reference relative, you would edit the Refers To box.)

7. At this point, you could click OK to enter the name and close the dialog box. However, you need to make more entries, so click the Add button instead. Excel adds the name Rent to the list box at the left, which contains a list of defined names.

8. The Name text box in the dialog box is highlighted again. Type the word **Maintenance** and press Tab. The Refers To box is highlighted again.

9. Click cell B12 to select it as the cell to receive the name Maintenance. Then click Add once more. The Name box is highlighted.

10. In the Name box, type **Utilities** and press Tab.

11. In the Refers To box, now highlighted, type the number **43**. Click OK.

What have you done so far? You've named cell B11 Rent, and you've named cell B12 Maintenance. These steps are easy to understand.

However, what happened next? You entered the name Utilities and—instead of making the name refer to a cell—you made it refer to a number, 43, which represents the cost of utilities. This action illustrates a different way in which you can use the Define Name... command. When you make a name refer to a number in this fashion, you can change the number, and all formulas using that name will be updated instantly.

Now we'll create a formula that uses all of these names, plus the formula itself will have a name. Follow this procedure:

1. In cell B13, which should still be selected, press ⌘-L again to bring back the Define Name dialog box. Drag the dialog box to the bottom of the screen again.

2. In the Name box, type the name **Housing** and press Tab.

3. In the Refers To box, now highlighted, you'll enter a formula. First, type an equal sign (=) to start the formula. Then click B11 to include this cell in the formula, type a plus sign (+), click B12 to add this cell to the formula, type another plus sign (+), and type the word **Utilities**. Since Excel, by default, creates absolute references for the cells selected, the formula now reads = \$B\$11 + \$B\$12 + Utilities. Click OK to complete the formula.

You may expect cell B13 to display the result of the formula you just defined. However, it doesn't. You only gave that formula a name; you didn't apply it. That's what you'll do next.

For the final step in this demonstration of the Define Name dialog box, you enter a formula directly into cell B13 that utilizes the formula you've named. You find the Housing expense for a 12-month period (assuming that the Housing formula determined this expense for only one month) by multiplying the Housing formula by 12.

1. Type an equal sign (=) to start the formula, type the number **12**, and type an asterisk (∗) (the computer symbol for multiplication).

2. Complete the formula by pulling down the Formula menu and selecting the Paste Name... command. Highlight the word *Housing* in the list box of the Paste Name dialog box and click OK. (You could have used this method of entering the word *Utilities* in the Housing formula; it's an alternative to typing the name in the formula and eliminates the possibility of making a typing error when entering a defined name.)

3. The formula now reads = 12∗Housing. Click the enter box on the formula bar to enter the formula.

The number 10428 appears in cell B13. This number is a 12-month total for Housing, which is the sum of cells named Rent and Maintenance, plus the value 43, which represents the name Utilities, a category not directly entered into any cell.

Remember, that the named formula Housing isn't actually stored in any specific cell either. The advantage of this approach is that you can use the Housing formula again and again in the worksheet by merely pasting in its name, without taking up storage space on the worksheet with the formula itself.

You can even use the formula in other worksheets without storing it there—a tremendous advantage if the formula is long and complicated. To enter the formula into another worksheet, merely type the name of the worksheet on which you named the formula, type an exclamation point (!), and type the name of the formula. For example, if you create the Housing formula in a worksheet called Expenses, you can use the formula in another worksheet by typing **Expenses!Housing** in that worksheet.

Of course, you could type labels into adjoining cells to identify the numbers displayed in the example you just completed.

Incidentally, you'll probably want to keep defined names short for the sake of convenience. However, names can contain up to 255 characters. The first character must be a letter. The other characters must be letters, numbers, periods, or underlines and cannot resemble a cell reference (like A1, for example). You can use either capital or lowercase letters; Excel treats both the same.

WORKING WITH ARRAYS

Excel uses two kinds of *arrays*. An *array range* is a rectangular group of cells that shares a single formula (called an *array formula*). An *array constant* is a group of constants arranged in a special fashion and used as an argument in a formula. When you need to perform the same operation on a group of cells, arrays can often save you time in writing formulas. Arrays also require less memory and disk storage space than writing formulas separately.

USING ARRAY FORMULAS

Suppose you want to multiply a series of numbers in column B of a worksheet by another series of numbers in column C and place the products of these factors in column D. Try this:

1. Click cell B15 to select it, type the word **Quantity**, and press Tab. The word is entered, and C15 is selected.

2. In C15, type the word **Price** and press Tab. D15 becomes the active cell.

3. In D15, type the word **Cost** and press Return.

4. Drag to select B15 through D15 and click the right-alignment icon on the Toolbar. This operation aligns the titles in the selected cells over the numbers that you'll soon enter.

5. Click to select B16 and type the number **25**. Press Return.

6. In B17, type the number **50**. Press Return.

7. In B18, type the number **100**. Press Return.

8. Click to select C16 and type the number **.62**. Press Return. (By default, Excel adds a zero when displaying numbers that start with a decimal point.)

9. In C17, type the number **.49**. Press Return.

10. In C18, type the number **.35**. Press Return.

11. Drag to select the range D16 through D18, select the Currency format from the style box on the Toolbar to format these cells to show dollars and cents, and type an equal sign (=) to start a formula.

12. Drag to select cells B16 through B18 and include them in the formula. Then type an asterisk (*) to indicate multiplication and drag to select C16 through C18 to include these cells in the formula.

13. Now, instead of just pressing Return to complete the formula, hold down the ⌘ key while you press Return. This action enters the formula as an array formula.

14. Click D16 so the formula bar displays the formula for that cell.

Your worksheet should now look like Figure 5.7. Cells D16 through D18 now contain the same formula: { = B16:B18*C16:C18}. Excel has enclosed the formula in braces ({ }) to show that it is an array formula. This single formula has multiplied B16 by C16 to obtain the product $15.50, multiplied B17 by C17 to obtain the product $24.50, and multiplied B18 by C18 to obtain the product $35.00—all automatically!

You cannot edit an array formula for an individual cell in the array; you must edit the formula as a whole. And you cannot merely type an array formula and add your own braces; if you do so, Excel will treat the formula as text. You must use the key combination ⌘-Return (or ⌘-Enter, using the Enter key on the number keypad) to enter the formula and tell Excel that you want the formula created as an array. Excel will then add the braces. (As you'll see in the next section, you do, however, enter braces yourself within a formula to create an array constant.)

To test whether you need to edit an array formula as a whole, try this experiment:

1. Click to select cell D16 only. Then click within the formula bar to create an insertion point just after the asterisk (the multiplication operator).

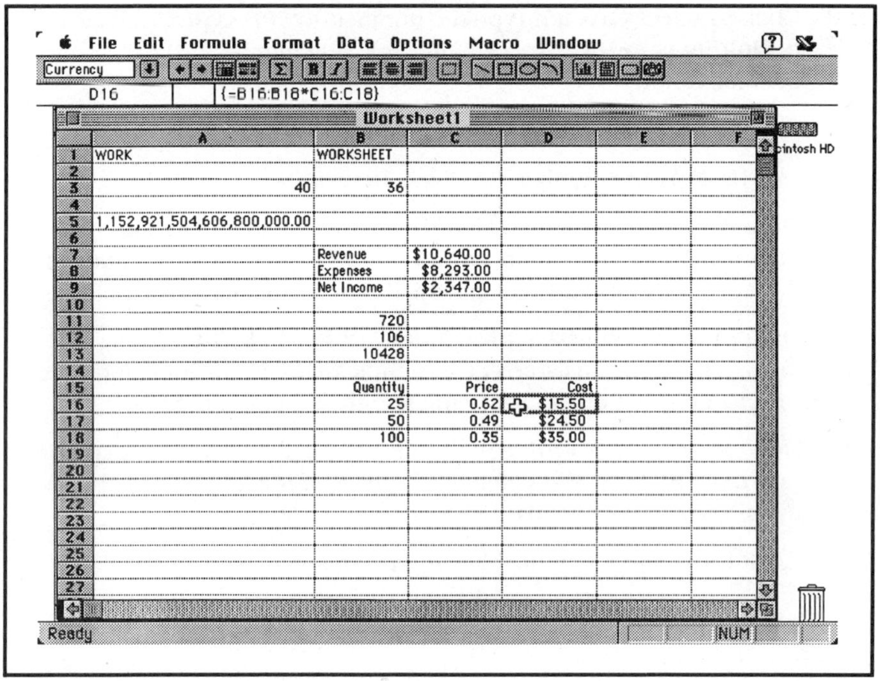

Figure 5.7: A completed array formula

2. Press the Delete key to backspace and erase the asterisk. Type a minus sign (–) to replace the asterisk.

3. Click the enter box in the formula bar to save your changed formula. As soon as you do this, you'll see the following warning message: *Cannot change part of an array.*

4. Click OK to acknowledge the message. Then click the cancel box in the formula bar to abort the attempted change to the formula.

USING ARRAY CONSTANTS

You can use the same example formula to see how to use an array constant. You'll eliminate the reference to the range C16:C18 and replace it with an array constant that contains the multipliers previously picked up from column C.

1. Drag to select cells D16 through D18 (all of the cells that contain the array formula).

2. In the formula bar, click to establish an insertion point at the end of the formula (after the closing brace). Then press Delete until you erase the reference to C:16:C18 (that part of the formula to the right of the asterisk). Note that the braces surrounding the formula disappear.

3. When you create an array constant, it must be enclosed in braces, just like an array formula. For an array constant, however, you enter the braces; the program won't do it for you. Type this new completion to the formula (starting to the right of the asterisk): {.62;.49;.35}.

4. Enter the revised formula by holding down the ⌘ key while you press Return. Excel encloses the revised formula in braces again, so it now contains two nested sets of braces: the set you entered to identify the array constant, and the set entered automatically by the program.

Note that the revised array formula produces exactly the same results as the previous version. However, using the array constant has eliminated the need for column C entirely.

RULES FOR ARRAY CONSTANTS

Bear several rules in mind in creating array constants:

- Type semicolons (;) between numbers to use the numbers with successive *rows* of a worksheet. (You did this in the example, because you needed to multiply the prices in the array constant by the quantities shown in the range B16:18.)

- Type commas (,) between numbers to use the numbers with successive *columns* of a worksheet.

- You can use an array constant for a rectangular range. Just use the appropriate combination of semicolons and commas to specify the rows and columns.

- An array constant must use constant values, not formulas. In other words, although an array constant can be contained within a formula, the constant cannot contain a format such as {1 + 2;3 + 5}.

- An array constant can contain numbers, text, logical values, or error values, but it cannot contain punctuation such as dollar signs or percent symbols. Text must be enclosed in double quotation marks.

- Cell references must be in the form C16:C18. You cannot list cells individually or use defined names. As an alternative to listing cells, you can use their values directly as constants (as you did in the example).

You can use arrays and array constants with functions, a subject you'll explore in Chapter 6.

At this point, discard the practice worksheet used in this chapter if you like. You won't need it again for the exercises in later chapters. However, you may want to save it so you can refresh your mind later regarding some of the principles that it demonstrates.

SUMMARY

You've covered a lot of territory in this chapter: some of the fine points of creating formulas, using text, changing the sizes of rows and columns, creating and using cell and formula names, and working with arrays.

Formulas are still in the spotlight in the next three chapters, so you'll have plenty of opportunity to sharpen your newly acquired skills.

Chapter

6

Letting Functions
Do the Work

A *function* is a special kind of formula that has been prepared in advance to perform a variety of chores. Every function performs some operation on a value or group of values in order to produce another value or set of values.

Functions always have the same general format. For example, if you start a formula with a function, you begin with the usual equal sign, followed by the name of the function, and then *arguments* that are enclosed in parentheses. Arguments are the values you must provide so a function can do its job.

You've already used the SUM( ) and IF( ) functions in earlier chapters. Excel provides many other useful functions: database, date and time, financial, information, logical, lookup, mathematical, matrix, statistical, text, and trigonometric. For instance, SUM( ) is a mathematical function, and IF( ) is a logical function.

In this chapter you explore some of Excel's built-in functions. In Chapter 18 you learn how to create your own functions.

Excel provides two general types of functions: *worksheet functions* and *macro functions.* You can use worksheet functions either on a worksheet or on the separate *macro sheets* that are used to store macros. However, you can use macro functions only on macro sheets. Macro sheets are separate files that store both recorded macros (consisting of keystrokes and mouse movements that have been captured for replay, to automate spreadsheet chores) and macros written in Excel's macro language to perform specific operations or serve as functions. Chapters 15 through 20 explain the many uses of macros and custom macro functions.

This chapter discusses only worksheet functions. The examples in this chapter—using the AVERAGE( ), SQRT( ), COS( ), RATE( ), and VLOOKUP( ) functions—show you how Excel worksheet functions work.

In preparation for trying the examples in this chapter, open a new worksheet.

AVERAGING NUMBERS

Basic statistical functions are useful to almost everybody. Let's try the AVERAGE( ) function, which finds the average (or mean) of a series of numbers.

To set up headings for the numbers to be averaged, you'll use Excel's Series... command, located on the Data menu.

1. Click to select cell A1, if it's not already selected.

2. Type **Jan-92**, click the enter box in the formula bar, and click the boldface icon on the Toolbar to apply boldface to the text.

3. Drag to select cells A1 through C1.

4. Pull down the Data menu and select the Series... command.

5. In the Series dialog box (shown in Figure 6.1), you see that Excel has already recognized your entry as a date format to be entered in a row rather than a column. However, in the Date Unit section, it has proposed the increment to be used for the series as Day. Click the Month button to have the series increase in increments of months instead of days.

6. In the Step Value box, Excel displays the number 1, the default step value. (If you wanted to show quarterly data, you would change the 1 to a 3.) In this example, 1 is what you want, so click OK to accept your entries and close the dialog box.

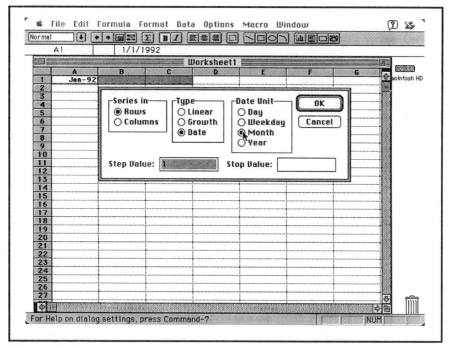

Figure 6.1: The Series dialog box

You'll now see a series of column headings, starting with Jan-92 and ending with Mar-92. Since you added the boldface attribute when you typed the information for the first cell in the series, the entries in B1 and C1 also appear in boldface.

Next you will add a fourth heading, identify the cell that displays the average, and enter the numbers to be averaged and the function that accomplishes this task.

1. Select cell D1, type the word **Average**, click the enter box in the formula bar to complete the entry, and click the boldface icon on the Toolbar to make the text appear in boldface.

2. Click the right alignment icon on the Toolbar to right-align the text so that it matches the headings of the other columns. (Excel right-aligned the other headings automatically because it interpreted them as headings for columns of numbers.)

3. Drag to select cells A2 through C2. (You'll be using an alternative method of entering data. If you preselect a series of cells, you can press Return or Enter after typing a number in a cell, and Excel will automatically select the next cell in the series for you—in this case, as if you'd pressed Tab after each entry.

4. In cell A2, type **38** and press Return.

5. In cell B2, type **42** and press Return.

6. In cell C2, type **43** and press Return.

7. Click to select cell D2, pull down the Formula menu, and select the Paste Function… command.

8. In the Paste Function dialog box, click the Paste Arguments box to deselect it.

9. Scroll until you see AVERAGE( ), highlight that function to select it, and click OK. The function appears in the formula bar, with the pointer—which appears as a vertical line between the parentheses after the function name—positioned for entry.

10. Drag to select cells A2 through C2 (the cells that contain the numbers to be averaged). The formula in the formula bar now reads = AVERAGE(A2:C2).

11. Click the enter box in the formula bar to complete the formula.

Your screen should now look like Figure 6.2. The result of the formula appears in D2. You see that the average of the three numbers is 41.

The numbers in cells A2 through C2 could represent sales for three consecutive months (in thousands of dollars), average temperatures for three consecutive months, or the number of patients admitted to a particular hospital for major surgery. The procedures for using the function are the same.

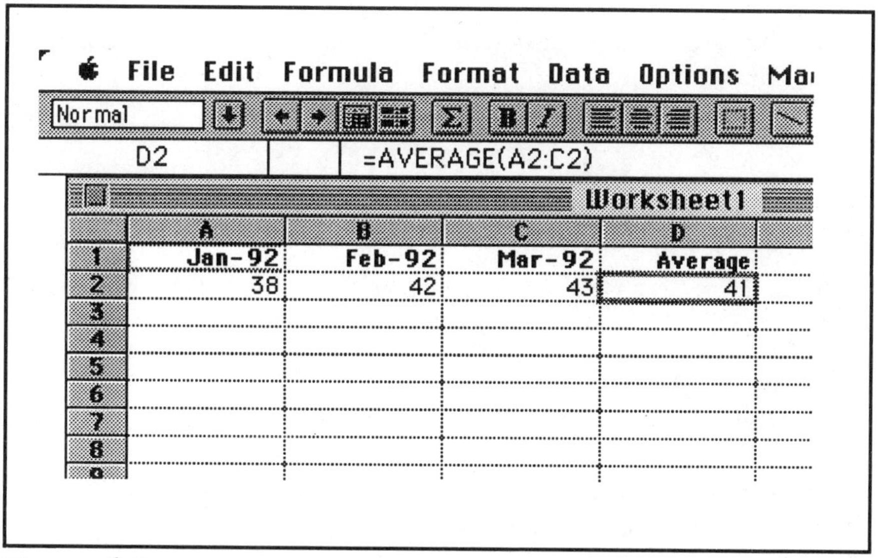

Figure 6.2: Using the AVERAGE( ) function

FINDING A SQUARE ROOT

You can quickly find the square root of a number with the SQRT( ) function.

Try this:

1. Select cell A4 and type the number **400**. Press Tab to enter the figure and move to the next cell to the right.

2. With cell B4 selected, pull down the Formula menu and select the Paste Function... command.

3. Scroll to find the SQRT( ) function. Highlight the function to select it and click OK.

4. Click cell A4 to insert it into the formula. The formula now reads = SQRT(A4).

5. Click the enter box in the formula bar to complete the formula.

Cell B4 now displays the number 20, which is the square root of 400, the value in cell A4.

GETTING HELP WITH TRIG: COSINES

Excel provides a variety of trigonometric functions. Let's look at the COS( ) function, which returns the cosine of a given angle.

1. Select cell A6 and enter the value **.435821**, which we'll assume to be the measurement of an angle in radians. Press Tab to move to cell B6.

2. Pull down the Formula menu. Select the Paste Function... command and then the COS( ) function.

3. Click A6 to include it in the formula and click the enter box in the formula bar.

Cell B6 displays the result of the formula: .90652376.

TIP

If the measurement of an angle is in degrees, you must convert this value to radians so the function can use it. You accomplish this conversion by using another function, PI( ), which returns the mathematical constant pi (3.14159265358979—accurate to 15 digits). Although PI( ) does not require or use an argument, you must include the parentheses so Excel will recognize it as a function. To convert a value from degrees to radians, multiply the value by PI( ) and divide the result by 180. In other words, the formula takes this form: = value*PI( )/180.

DETERMINING AN INTEREST RATE

Let's look now at one of Excel's many financial functions: RATE( ). The RATE( ) function finds the interest rate per period for an annuity. (In financial terms, an annuity is a series of continuous cash payments made on a regular basis, such as a mortgage or a car loan or the proceeds from an insurance policy or pension fund.)

The RATE( ) function requires several arguments. First, you enter the total number of payment periods and the amount of the fixed payment required for each period (usually, principal and interest, but no taxes or other charges). Then you enter the present value (how much a series of future payments is worth now) and the future value (or cash balance) you have as a goal after the last payment is made. (If you omit this argument, future value is assumed to be zero.) Next, you enter the type. (You enter a zero if payments are due at the end of each period or a 1 if payments are due at the beginning of the period. If you omit this argument, the type is assumed to be zero.) Finally, you enter a guess. (The guess is your own estimate of what the rate will be. If you don't provide a figure here, Excel assumes a rate of 10 percent. The program determines the actual rate through an iterative process; in other words, Excel recalculates the formula repeatedly, with each iteration hopefully coming closer to the correct answer. The program uses the guess argument as the starting point in the rate calculation.)

You can add these arguments individually to the function, separating them with commas, or you can designate cell addresses where the information resides. Worksheets are frequently designed using the latter method, to achieve some measure of automation. Some of the arguments require the use of other functions to obtain the input needed; for example, you use the PV( ) function to determine present value.

Let's use the RATE( ) function now. Assume that the amount of a loan is $16,000, to be repaid in 60 monthly payments of $342 each. In this case, the amount of the loan is considered the present value. We will use Excel's default values for the last three arguments, so we can complete this formula using only the data in this paragraph.

1. Select C8 and type **Amount of Loan**. Press Tab.

2. In D8, type **16000** and click the enter box in the formula bar. Press the down-pointing arrow next to the style box on the Toolbar and select the Currency format. The number appears as $16,000.00.

3. Select C9 and type **No. of Payments**. Press Tab.

4. In D9, type **60**.

5. Select C10 and type **Monthly Payment**. Press Tab.

6. The text you typed in C9 and C10 won't quite fit into those cells. Place the pointer on the border between the headings of columns C and D and drag slightly to the right to widen column C until all of the characters you entered in C10 are displayed entirely within that cell.

7. In D10, type **342** and click the enter box in the formula bar. From the style box on the Toolbar, select the Currency format. The cell now displays the number as $342.00.

8. Select C11 and type **Annual Int. Rate**. Press Tab.

9. In D11, pull down the Formula menu and use the Paste Function... command to paste the RATE( ) function into the cell.

10. Click D9 to add the contents of this cell (the number of monthly payments) to the formula.

11. Type a comma (,), type a minus sign (–), and click D10 to add the amount of the monthly payment to the formula. You must precede the monthly figure payment with a minus sign since you're reducing the indebtedness by that amount. If you were a financial institution figuring the loan from its point of view (determining the rate of return), you would precede the present value figure, not the monthly payment, with a minus sign. In either case, the result of this particular formula would be the same.

12. Type another comma (,) and click D8 to add the amount of the loan to the formula.

13. The formula is now complete—provided you want the result to show the *monthly* interest rate. Usually, however, the *annual* interest rate is what is wanted. So click the formula bar to the right of the closing parenthesis after the function name and type ∗**12** (an asterisk followed by the number 12, to convert the monthly interest rate to an annual interest rate).

14. The formula now reads = RATE(D9, – D10,D8)∗12.

15. Click the enter box in the formula bar to enter the formula and start the iterative process.

16. The answer, in cell D11, is 0.10259592. This number may not seem to make much sense; it represents the annual interest rate, but it needs formatting for clarity.

17. To obtain a two-decimal-place precision in the display, *don't* pick the Percent option from the style box. Instead, pull down the Format menu, select the Number... option, and select the format that looks like this: 0.00%. As soon as you click OK, the annual interest rate appears as 10.26%. (The choice from the style box would have displayed the rate simply as 10%—with less precision than most financial analysts would prefer.)

Your screen should now look like Figure 6.3.

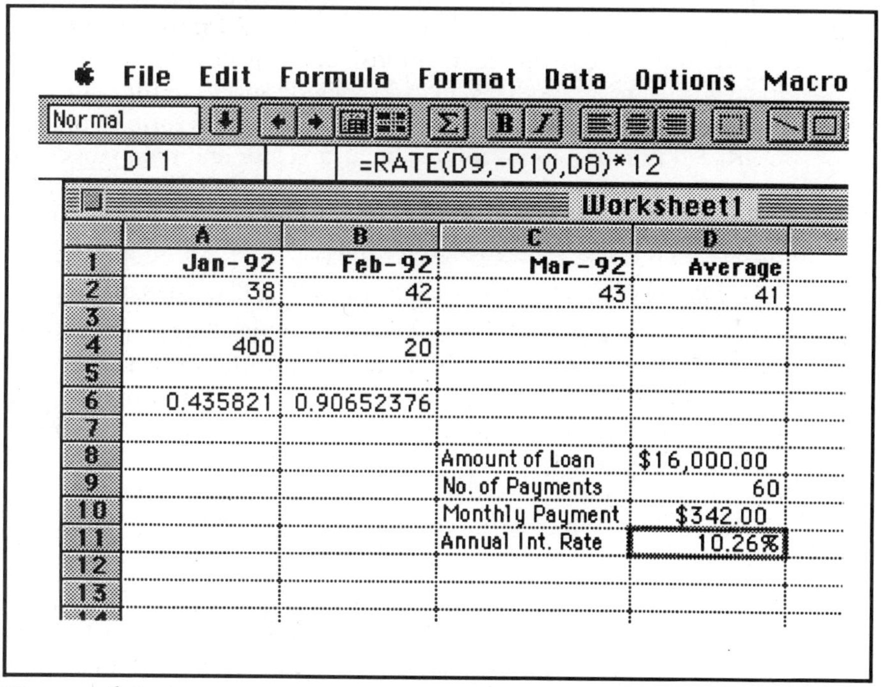

Figure 6.3: Determining annual interest rate

You use Excel's other financial functions by following a similar series of steps.

USING LOOKUP FUNCTIONS

Excel provides three lookup functions that return a value from a reference or array: LOOKUP( ), HLOOKUP( ), and VLOOKUP( ). The LOOKUP( ) function has two forms.

- **LOOKUP( )—vector form**. LOOKUP( ) function operation depends on the arguments used. The *vector* form of this function uses these arguments: (*lookup_value,lookup_vector,result_vector*).

- A vector is an array consisting of only one row or column. To use the LOOKUP( ) function for vectors, you simply replace the argument placeholders with an actual value (entered manually or determined from a cell reference) and range addresses for the vectors. (An underline used in an argument instead of spaces between individual words indicates that you can't include spaces in the actual value you substitute for the placeholder.) The vector form of the LOOKUP( ) function looks for a value in a vector and then moves to the same position in the second vector and returns the value found in the first vector. In this form of the function, you can specify the range in which you want to match values.

- **LOOKUP( )—array form**. The array form of the LOOKUP( ) function uses only two arguments: (*lookup_value,array*). This form looks only in the first row or column of the array for the value and then moves down or across to the last cell of the array to return the value. If you want to operate on an array other than a vector, you're better off using HLOOKUP( ) or VLOOKUP( ), described next, because they're more versatile. Excel includes this form of the LOOKUP( ) function only for compatibility with other spreadsheet programs.

- **HLOOKUP( )**. This function gives you more control than the array form of the LOOKUP( ) function. It includes more arguments: (*lookup_value,table_array,row_index_num*). HLOOKUP( ) looks in the top row of a specified array for a value and returns that value to a specified cell.

- **VLOOKUP( )**. This function is the companion to VLOOKUP( ). Use VLOOKUP( ) when you want the program to search for a value in a column instead of a row. VLOOKUP uses these arguments: (*lookup-_value,table_array,col_index_num*).

To see how a lookup function works, let's use VLOOKUP( ) now. We will have VLOOKUP( ) look in the left column of a specified array for the row that contains a value that is less than or equal to the lookup value, find a second value in another column of that same row, and return that value to the cell that contains the formula.

Assume that you're working for a steel mill that charges distant customers a percentage of the amount of each invoice as a shipping charge, based on the mileage involved. Customers 100 miles or less from the mill do not pay a shipping charge. However, customers between 101 miles and 200 miles away pay 6 percent, customers between 201 miles and 300 miles away pay 9 percent, and customers more than 300 miles away pay 11 percent. You can include the VLOOKUP( ) function in a daily sales worksheet to look up the correct percentage charge for each customer, using a separate table located elsewhere in the worksheet.

1. First enter the headings for the columns. Drag to select cells A13 through F13. Click the right-alignment and boldface icons on the Toolbar to format the cells for the text you'll enter.

2. Type the word **Distance**. Excel enters it in A13. Press Return.

3. Type the word **Rate**. Excel enters it in B13. Press Return twice to leave a blank column between the area that will contain the lookup table and the cells with the customer information. D13 becomes the active cell.

4. Type the word **Customer** in D13 and press Return.

5. Type the word **Mileage**. Excel enters it in E13. Press Return.

6. Type the word **Charge** and press Return. This entry completes the column headings.

7. Now enter the table array, starting with the numbers representing the distances over 100, 200, and 300 miles away. Click to select A14 and type the number **100**. Press Return.

8. In A15, type **200**. Press Return.

9. In A16, type **300**. Press Return.

10. Drag to select B14 through B16. You'll use this range to enter the percentages customers are billed for shipping charges.

11. Type **.06**. This percentage appears in B14. Press Return.

12. In B15, type **.09** and press Return.

13. In B16, type **.11** and press Return.

14. The range B14:B16 remains selected. Press the down-pointing arrow to the right of the style box on the Toolbar to display the list of styles and select Percent. Cell B14 now displays 6%. Excel formats the other two cells in the range in the same way.

15. Click D14. Type the name of a customer: **Johnston Steel**. Press Tab.

16. In E14, enter a number for the mileage involved in shipping the Johnston Steel order: **286**. Press Tab.

17. In F14, you'll enter the formula that determines the percentage charged to the customer. Pull down the Formula menu, select the Paste Function... command, and highlight the VLOOKUP( ) function. Click OK.

18. Click E14 to enter the first argument, which is the cell reference for the value to be looked up: 286 miles. Type a comma (,) to separate this argument from the next one.

19. Drag to select the range A14:B16 to enter the data in columns A and B as the table array argument. Type another comma (,).

20. You must provide a *column index number*: the number of the column in the array that contains the percentage shipping charge displayed in F14. You listed the percentages in column B, the second column of the array A14:B16, so type the number **2**.

21. The formula now reads = VLOOKUP(E14,A14:B16,2). Click the enter box in the formula bar to complete the formula.

22. Cell F14 displays .09. Select the Percent format again from the style box on the Toolbar. The display changes to 9%. Your screen should now look like Figure 6.4.

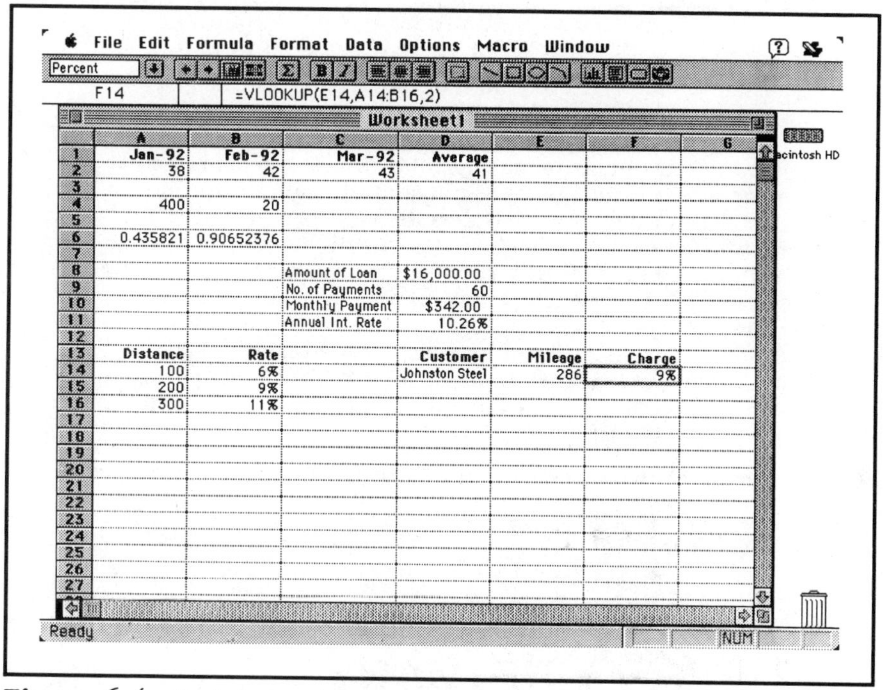

Figure 6.4: Worksheet with VLOOKUP( ) function added

Excel determined the answer as follows. Excel started with the lookup value, the number 286, which it found in E14. The program then searched for the lookup value in the first column of the table array, which is where this function always searches for a lookup value. It couldn't find that exact number in the first column, so it settled on 200, the value in the table that is less than or equal to the lookup value. Since we specified the second column of the table array as the column index number (2), Excel stayed in the row containing 200 (row 15) and looked in the second column of that row for the value to be returned in F14. The second column of the row is cell B15, which contains 9%. Therefore, Excel returned the value 9% in F14.

This is the final example of the chapter. At this point you can abandon the worksheet if you like, since you won't need it in later chapters. However, you may want to save it for future reference. If so, you may want to name the worksheet **Functions** (or give it a similar name that indicates its contents).

TIP

When you use the VLOOKUP( ) function, the values in the first column of the table array must be arranged in ascending order. Otherwise, you may not get the correct answer. If you have a long column that is not in this order, or if you're not sure exactly what the order should be (for example, negative numbers must come before positive numbers), you can use Excel's Sort command (on the Data menu) to place the values in the proper sequence.

Three error values may appear in cells when you use the VLOOKUP( ) function. If you enter a column index number less than 1 (perhaps by adding a decimal point or minus sign due to a typing mistake), Excel displays the error value *#VALUE!* If you enter a column index number greater than the number of columns in the table array, Excel displays *#REF!* If your lookup value is smaller than the smallest value in the first column of the table array, Excel displays *#N/A.*

SUMMARY

In this chapter, you sampled some of Excel's useful worksheet functions. You averaged a series of numbers, found a square root, calculated the cosine of an angle, determined an interest rate, and used a lookup function. Appendix B contains a list of Excel's functions.

Chapter 13 discusses database functions, Chapter 17 explains macro functions, and Chapter 18 tells you how to create your own functions.

Chapter

7

Linking and
Consolidating
Data

Excel lets you easily include the same data in a series of worksheets; link part of a worksheet to another worksheet or even another application for automatic updating; and consolidate input from multiple sources for comprehensive summaries, analyses, and reports.

CREATING AND USING WORKGROUPS

Organizations often want their various departments all to use the same format for calculating overhead or sales or presenting other information. Excel's *workgroup* feature is ideal for creating a series of similar worksheets. For example, you can enter individual department names or other unique elements on worksheets one at a time and then group those worksheets and add headings and formulas that you want to be common to all. Once the worksheets are in a group, data that you enter in one worksheet will automatically appear in the same cells of all other worksheets in the group.

Excel does not limit the number of worksheets you can place in a workgroup. You are restricted only by the amount of memory you have available.

Experiment with the workgroup feature now.

GROUPING WORKSHEETS

1. Close any Excel worksheets you currently have open.

2. Open a new worksheet.

3. Click cell B1 and enter the title **Chicago Office**. Click the boldface icon on the Toolbar to make the text boldface.

4. Open a second new worksheet. It will appear on top of Worksheet1 and will bear the temporary name Worksheet2. (If you have previously opened worksheets in your current Excel session, your worksheet names may carry higher numbers.)

5. Click cell B1 in Worksheet2 and enter the title **New York Office**. Click the boldface icon to make the text boldface.

6. Pull down the Window menu and select the Workgroup... command.

7. The Select Workgroup dialog box that appears shows both Worksheet1 and Worksheet2 in the list box and highlights these two files by default (see Figure 7.1). Click OK to form a workgroup with those two files. (The selection list displays only currently open files.)

8. Pull down the Window menu again and select the Arrange Workgroup command. The two worksheets now appear side by side on your screen, with the first few columns of each visible. The word *Workgroup* in brackets appears after each of the worksheet names. Your screen should resemble Figure 7.2.

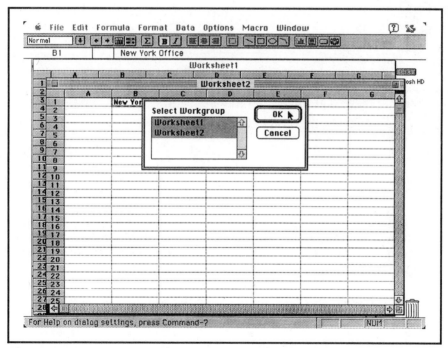

Figure 7.1: The Select Workgroup dialog box

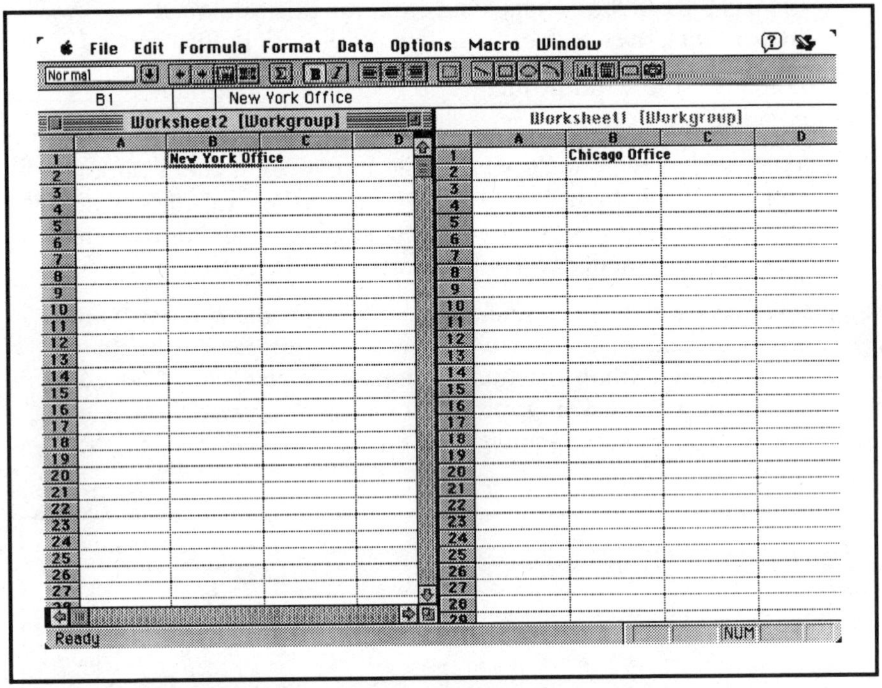

Figure 7.2: A Workgroup displayed with the Arrange Workgroup
command

ENTERING SHARED
DATA IN A WORKGROUP

The active worksheet (since you opened it and worked with it last) is
Worksheet2. You can easily determine the active worksheet by glancing at
the screen: Only the active file is framed by scroll bars. With Worksheet2
still active, you'll now make some entries.

1. Drag to select the range A3:A5. Type the words **Orders Processed**.
   Press Return. Excel enters the words in A3 and highlights A4.

2. In A4, type the words **Orders Shipped** and press Return.

3. In A5, type the words **Back Orders** and press Return.

4. Move the pointer to the border between the headings for column A and column B and drag to the right until column A is wide enough to display all of the text in A3 (the widest label).

5. Click B5 to select it and type an equal sign (=) to start a formula. Then click B3 to add the cell to the formula, type a minus sign (–), and click B4 to add this cell too. The formula now reads = B3 – B4.

6. Click the enter box in the formula bar to complete the formula.

Excel duplicates all of your work in Worksheet2 in Worksheet1: the labels, the widening of column A, and the formula in B5. B5 in both worksheets displays a zero, since no numbers have been entered into B3 and B4 of either worksheet to complete the subtraction operation called for in the formula.

ENTERING INDEPENDENT DATA IN A WORKGROUP

When you enter a value in B3 of Worksheet2 to represent the number of orders processed by the New York office, you don't want that figure echoed to Worksheet1 for the Chicago office. So before you enter data, you need to dissolve the workgroup so the worksheets retain what has been entered into them so far but become independent again. All you have to do is click anywhere on a worksheet that is not active—in this instance, on Worksheet1.

1. Click cell B3 in Worksheet1.

2. Type the number **322**, the number of orders processed by the Chicago office. Press Return.

3. In cell B4, type the number **318** and press Return. Your screen should resemble Figure 7.3. Notice that your new entries in Worksheet1 were not duplicated in the same cells of Worksheet2, because you dissolved the workgroup.

4. Now enter order information for the New York office. Click anywhere on Worksheet2 to activate it. Then click B3. Enter **587** as the number of orders processed and press Return.

5. In B4, enter **581** as the number of orders shipped. Press Return. The formula already present in B5 subtracts B4 from B3 and displays the result—6—in B5 as the number of back orders.

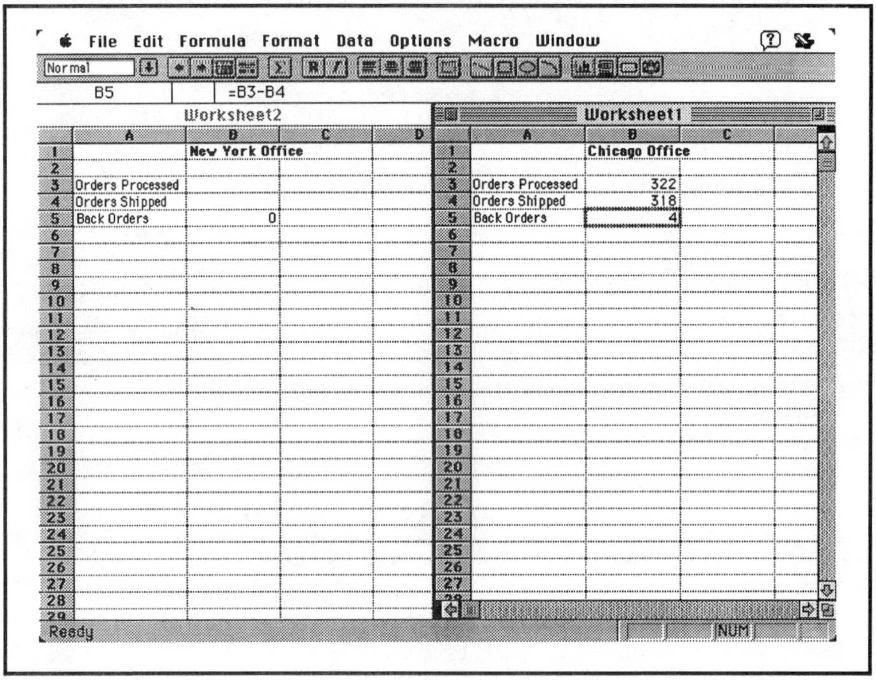

Figure 7.3: Data entry after dissolving the workgroup

COPYING DATA WITH
THE FILL WORKGROUP... COMMAND

What if you enter something on one worksheet and then want to transfer it to other, currently independent worksheets later? For instance, suppose you decide to add a proposed shipping date for the back orders to each worksheet. Even if you have many worksheets in this series, for branch offices throughout the country, you can form them into a workgroup and update them all with one command. Try this:

1. Select cell A6 in Worksheet2 and type **BO Ship Date**. Click the enter box in the formula bar.

2. To group the worksheets again, pull down the Window menu and select the Workgroup... command.

3. The Select Workgroup dialog box should show only Worksheet1 and Worksheet2, since these are the only Excel files open. By default, both worksheets are highlighted, so merely click OK to group them again. (If you had many worksheets open, you would manually highlight those you wished to group.)

4. Since Worksheet2 was the active worksheet before you issued the Workgroup... command, it is still selected. In fact, cell A6 is still selected too. Now you must use a special command to copy selected areas of a grouped worksheet to the other worksheets in the group. Pull down the Edit menu and select the Fill Workgroup... command.

5. The Fill Workgroup dialog box contains three buttons for specifying the elements to be copied. You can choose among All, Formulas, and Formats (see Figure 7.4). By default, All should already be selected, so click OK.

The text *BO Ship Date* now appears in cell A6 of Worksheet1 as well.

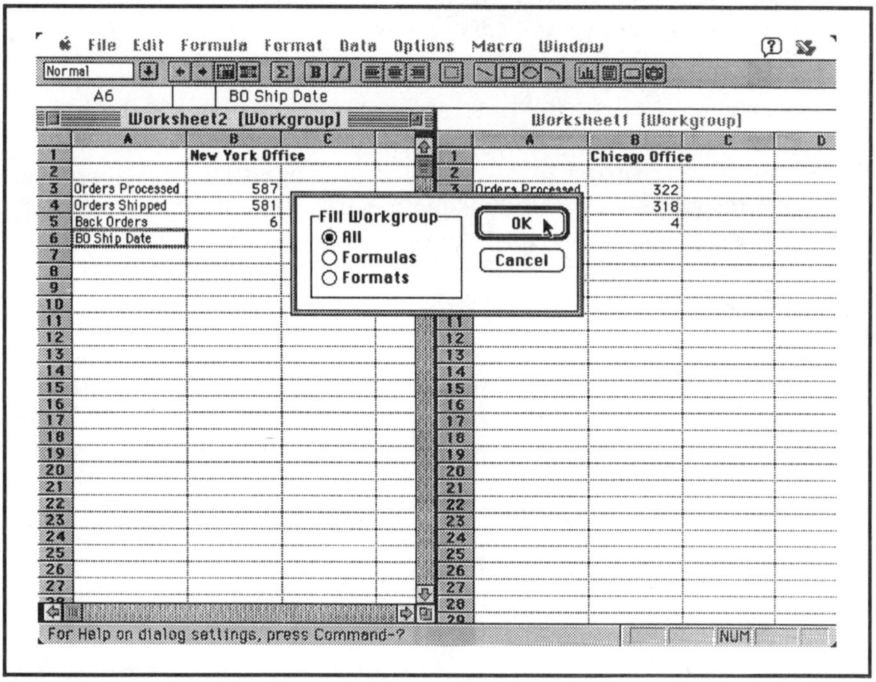

Figure 7.4: The Fill Workgroup dialog box

SAVING THE WORKGROUP

Save these worksheets because you'll use them again later in this chapter. To accomplish this, you have a choice of two commands. If you pull down the File menu and select Save (shortcut: press ⌘-S), Excel saves all of the sheets in the workgroup, one at a time. If you pull down the File menu and select the Save Workspace... command, Excel saves all of the sheets in the workgroup as a workspace file. This second choice allows you to open the files again later in the same configuration. (Any time you use the Save Workspace... command, you can select the workspace file by name to reopen all files that were open when you issued the command; the files will be just as you left them. However, if you want the files grouped after they're reopened, you'll have to reissue the Workgroup... command. The default name for workspace files is Resume, but you can select any name you like.)

Use the Save Workspace... command, since you'll need both worksheets open at the same time later in this chapter.

1. Pull down the File menu and select the Save Workspace... command. You'll see the Save Workspace dialog box, which is almost identical to the Save As... dialog box.

2. Rather than accepting the default workspace name Resume, type the name **WORKGROUP EXERCISE**, so you can apply the default Resume name on another occasion without overwriting the specifications for this particular workspace. (A handy trick to use in saving a workspace is to use all capital letters for the filename. This stratagem lets you later, when you look at the list of files in the Open Document dialog box, easily differentiate between normal worksheet files and workspace files.)

3. As soon as you give the workspace a name, you'll see dialog boxes asking if you want to save the changes in each worksheet, one by one. In each case, answer Yes. Excel then asks you to name the worksheets. Name Worksheet1 **Chicago** and Worksheet2 **New York** (without using all capital letters, since these are individual files you're saving at this point, not the workspace). The file names now indicate the file contents and also match references to the worksheets you'll encounter further on in the chapter.

Don't confuse the Workgroup... and Save Workspace... commands. The first command groups files temporarily; the second saves your current working environment, consisting of any open Excel file, so you can later resume working where you left off.

LINKING FILES

You can link two or more Excel files together. The link can be between worksheets, or between worksheets and macro sheets or charts. In addition, you can create a link between an Excel worksheet or chart and a document in another application. First, let's explore links between Excel files.

CREATING LINKS BETWEEN EXCEL FILES

You link one worksheet to a second worksheet by referring to the second worksheet in a formula. This type of reference is called an *external reference*. The formula lists the name of the second worksheet, then an exclamation point (!), then a cell or range reference. (You can use named cells or ranges too.)

Try this now:

1. Close the open worksheet files (which you just saved) and open a new worksheet. Since you've created two other worksheets in this session, the new worksheet bears the default name Worksheet3.

2. In cell A1, type this heading: **Sales Expense**. Click the enter box in the formula bar. Then click the boldface icon on the Toolbar to make the text boldface.

3. Select A3 and type **Salaries**. Press Return.

4. In A4, type **Commissions**. Press Return.

5. In A5, type **Office Expense**. Press Return.

6. In A6, type **Advertising**. Press Return.

7. In A7, type **TOTAL**. Press Return.

8. Select B3 and type **56034**. Press Return.

9. In B4, type **10093**. Press Return.

10. In B5, type **32016**. Press Return twice (to skip B6).

11. With B7 selected, click the auto-sum icon on the Toolbar. This action enters the formula = SUM(B3:B6) in B7. Click the enter box in the formula bar to complete the formula. The total 98143 appears in B7.

12. Drag to select the range B3:B7. From the style box on the Toolbar, select the Currency format for these cells. Excel now displays the numbers in column B as dollars and cents.

13. Click a blank cell such as A8 to deselect the range and press ⌘-S to save the file. In the Save dialog box, name the worksheet **Sales Expense** and click the Save button.

Your worksheet should now look like Figure 7.5.

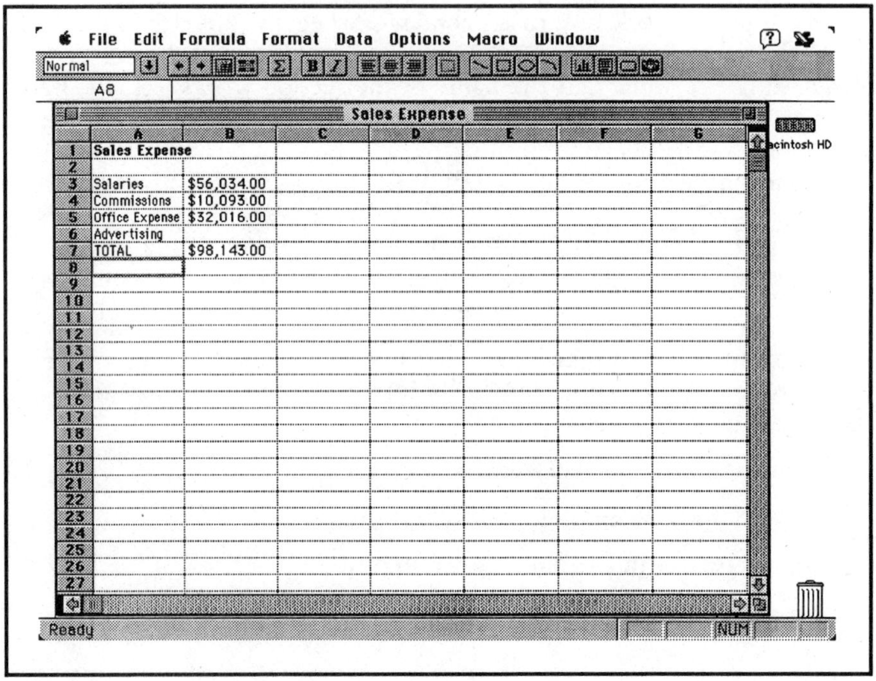

Figure 7.5: The Sales Expense worksheet

Later you'll enter a formula in B6 to insert a value for advertising expense from a total on a second worksheet. Right now you'll reduce the size of the Sales Expense worksheet so you can see both worksheets simultaneously. Then you'll create that second worksheet.

1. Place the pointer over the size box (located at the intersection of the vertical and horizontal scroll bars, at the lower right corner of the window) in the Sales Expense worksheet.

2. Drag to reduce the width of the worksheet until only columns A through C are visible.

3. Press ⌘-N to start a new worksheet. Initially, this worksheet fills most of your screen and covers the Sales Expense worksheet. Drag the size box of this second worksheet until it is approximately the same size as the Sales Expense worksheet.

4. Drag the title bar of the second worksheet to move the worksheet to the right until the first and second worksheets appear side by side.

5. In cell A1 of the second worksheet, type the heading **Advertising**. Click the enter box in the formula bar to complete the entry and click the boldface icon on the Toolbar to make the heading boldface.

6. Select A3 and type **Production**. Press Return.

7. In A4, type **Magazine**. Press Return.

8. In A5, type **Newspaper**. Press Return.

9. In A6, type **Radio**. Press Return.

10. In A7, type **Television**. Press Return.

11. In A8, type **TOTAL**. Press Return.

12. Select B3 and type **8989**. Press Return.

13. In B4, type **12117**. Press Return.

14. In B5, type **5667**. Press Return.

15. In B6, type **16321**. Press Return.

16. In B7, type **28082**. Press Return.

17. With B8 selected, click the auto-sum icon on the Toolbar and the enter box in the formula bar. The number 71116 appears in cell B8.

18. Drag to select the range B3:B8 and then select the Currency format from the style box on the Toolbar. Excel displays the numbers in column B as dollars and cents.

19. Click a blank cell such as A9 to deselect the range. Then press ⌘-S to save the worksheet. In the Save dialog box, type the name **Advertising** and click the Save button.

The Advertising worksheet is now complete. The final chore is to enter the formula in the Sales Expense worksheet to link the two worksheets.

1. Click anywhere in the Sales Expense worksheet to activate it.

2. Click cell B6 and enter this formula: **=Advertising!B8**. The word *Advertising* is, of course, the name of the other worksheet. The exclamation point indicates that you want to link the Advertising and Sales Expense worksheets, and that B8—the location of the total for advertising expenses—is the specific cell you want linked.

3. As soon as you click the enter box in the formula bar, the amount $71,176.00 appears in cell B6 of the Sales Expense worksheet. Cell B6 has picked up the value shown as the total of advertising expenses in the other worksheet.

4. Notice that B7, the cell in the Sales Expense worksheet that is supposed to present the total of all sales expenses, instead displays a series of number signs (###). This occurs because column B is now slightly too narrow to display the value for the total. To correct this problem, select B7. Then pull down the Format menu and select the Column Width... command. In the Column Width dialog box, click the Best Fit button. Excel now properly displays the total as $169,319.00. (Alternatively, you could place the pointer on the border between the headings for columns B and C and drag slightly to the right until the total is displayed correctly—or you could double-click the border between the column headings as a faster way to execute the Best Fit command.)

Your screen should now resemble Figure 7.6 (except that the figure shows cell B6 reselected to emphasize the formula that links the two worksheets).

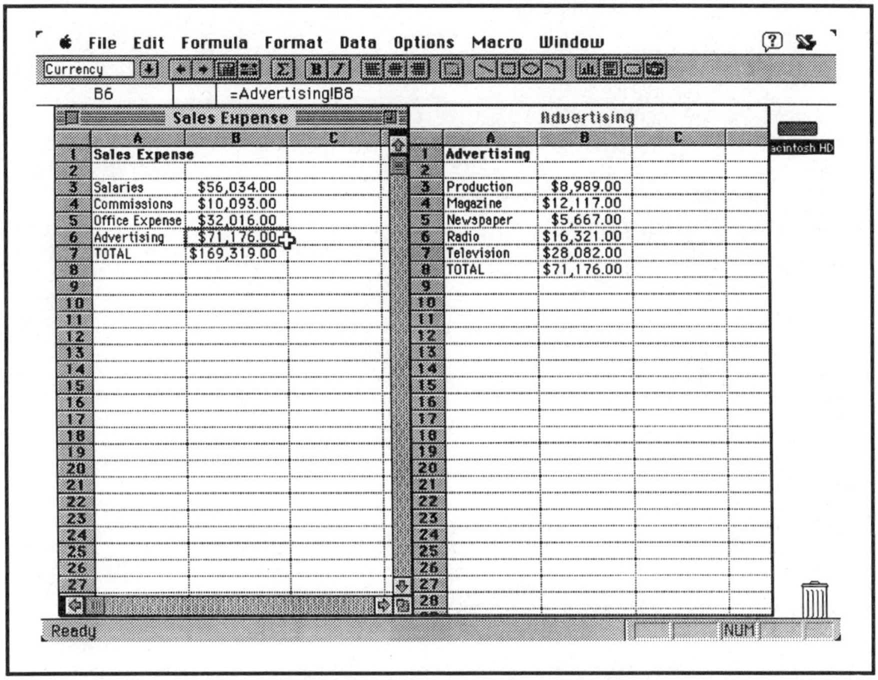

Figure 7.6: Two worksheets linked through the formula in cell B6

Once you've created links, you can open supporting documents for an active worksheet by using the Links . . . command on the File menu. The File Links dialog box, shown in Figure 7.7, lists all documents that have been linked to the active worksheet.

If you want to preserve the linked files in this example in their final form, press ⌘-S to save the latest changes in the Sales Expense worksheet. Then click the close box. Advertising now becomes the active worksheet. Press ⌘-S to save the changes in this worksheet too. Then click its close box.

When you reopen a worksheet, such as Sales Expense, that contains a file-linking formula, you'll immediately see an alert box (identified by a graphic symbol consisting of an exclamation point inside a triangle) asking you if you want to update references to unopened documents. You respond by clicking either a Yes button or a No button. If you click the Yes button, any changes you made that affect the total in the linked Advertising worksheet will automatically be reflected in the linked cell in the Sales Expense worksheet—without your actually opening the Advertising worksheet.

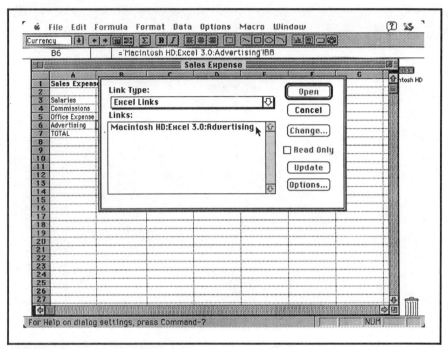

Figure 7.7: The File Links dialog box

This updating capability is one reason that some creators of complicated worksheets employ linking frequently. They use a series of linked
worksheets instead of making one giant worksheet. In this way, they can
build complex spreadsheet applications without using much computer
memory, since supporting worksheets need not be open.

CREATING LINKS
WITH OTHER APPLICATIONS

To create a link between Excel and another application, you can create
a formula similar to those used to link two Excel worksheets. Another
option is to use special commands to paste a selected cell or range from
Excel into the other application.

Using the Formula Method

First, we'll discuss the formula method. Suppose you want to transfer information from a cell in an Excel worksheet to a field in a database. This is the format to use in the formula you enter in that cell:

    = 'ApplicationName' | 'DocumentName'!SpecificArea

The first element in this format (after the standard equal sign to indicate the beginning of a formula) is the name of the application, enclosed in single quotation marks. For example, you could enter **'FileMaker'**.

Next, a pipe character (|) is used as a divider. This character is located on the same key as the backslash, but in the shifted position.

The name of the document, enclosed in single quotation marks, follows the pipe character. For example, you can specify a database file named **'Employees'**.

The fourth element is another divider: an exclamation point (!) in this case, not the pipe character.

After the exclamation point, you list the cell, range, or database field where you want the Excel information to appear. This element of the formula is not enclosed in quotation marks. For instance, you could specify a field named **HireDate**.

Here's a completed formula using the example names:

    = 'FileMaker' | 'Employees'!HireDate

This formula would pick up the date an employee was hired from the Excel worksheet and copy the date through the link to a FileMaker database field.

Using the Paste Method

To use the paste method to create a link between Excel and another application, both applications must currently be loaded into memory. As explained in Chapter 2, you can handle this requirement easily through the Macintosh operating system, starting with System 7.0. You simply load each application and switch between applications through the Applications menu at the upper right corner of your screen.

If you're using a previous version of the operating system, you must switch from the normal Finder mode to MultiFinder mode in order to have more than one application loaded at a time. Here's how:

1. From the Macintosh desktop (without being in any application), pull down the Special menu and select the Set Startup... command. You'll see a dialog box where you click buttons to choose between Finder and MultiFinder. You can also click buttons to have Excel reopen selected items or open applications and desk accessories automatically at startup. The default setting activates only MultiFinder at startup.

2. If you change your mind about switching to MultiFinder, you can click the Cancel button in the dialog box. Otherwise, click OK to record your selections and close the dialog box.

3. Now your desktop looks just as it did before you pulled down the Special menu. To activate MultiFinder, you must restart the computer (using what some computer users call a warm boot). Pull down the Special menu again and select Restart. Your Macintosh restarts, and a MultiFinder icon appears in the upper right corner of your screen, indicating that this feature is available for use.

4. Once you have applications loaded into memory, click the MultiFinder icon in the upper right corner of your screen to cycle through the applications until the one you want to use is displayed and active.

Whether you use the System 7 Application menu or MultiFinder, here's how to paste a portion of an Excel worksheet into another application, with linking:

1. Open Excel and the worksheet from which you want to copy information—for instance, the Sales Expense worksheet.

2. Use the Application menu or click the MultiFinder icon to return to the Macintosh desktop without closing Excel.

3. Open the other application and the document into which you want to paste Excel data. For instance, you might open a new file in Microsoft Word.

4. Activate your Excel worksheet again.

5. Select the cell or range you want to duplicate and link to another application. For example, you might want to drag to select the data area of the Sales Expense worksheet.

6. Pull down the Excel Edit menu and select Copy. (Shortcut: Press ⌘-C.)

7. Make the other application (such as the new document in Microsoft Word) active again.

8. Pull down the Edit menu in the other application and select the Paste Link command. Assuming Microsoft Word as the example again, Excel now displays the entire contents of the Sales Expense worksheet in the Word document (see Figure 7.8). Above this information, a header describes the disk, folder(s), and Excel file name involved. Do not remove this header because it defines the link. In Word, the header is automatically formatted as *hidden*. This format means that when you print the worksheet as part of your Word document, all you have to do to keep the header from printing is to make certain that the Print Hidden Text box is *not* selected in the Print dialog box (see Figure 7.9). (By default, hidden text is not printed.)

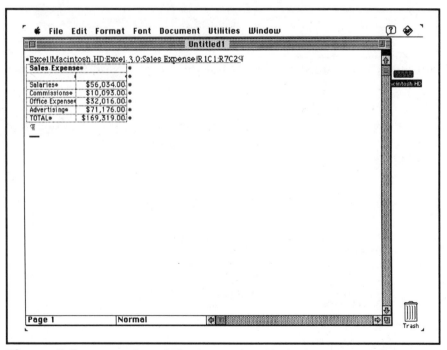

Figure 7.8: An Excel worksheet pasted and linked to a Microsoft Word document

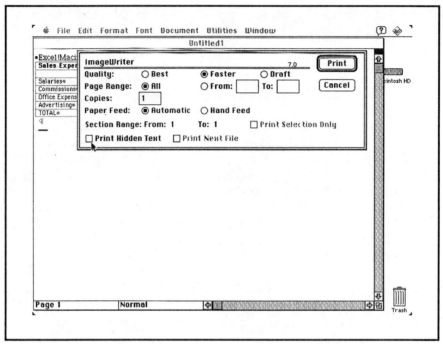

Figure 7.9: The Word Print dialog box showing the Print Hidden
Text box

If you want to print the Microsoft Word document in the example at
some later time, you can ensure that the Excel worksheet in the document
contains the latest data: You simply pull down the Word Edit menu and
select the Update Link command.

CAUTION

If the Edit menu of the application to receive the data from Excel
does not offer a Paste Link command, you cannot use this method
of linking. You could, of course, use the ordinary Paste command.
This command would copy the information from Excel into the
other application, but it would provide no link for updating. You
would have to perform any updating manually.

CONSOLIDATING WORKSHEETS

You can use the Consolidate... command from the Data menu to consolidate information from individual worksheets. We'll explore this very versatile command in this final section of the chapter.

These are the basic features of the Consolidate... command:

- You can consolidate information from the same cell address on a series of worksheets. Thus, if you work for a company with branch offices that all use identical worksheet templates to report their sales, you can combine the totals in cell A24 of all of the worksheets in cell A24 of a master worksheet serving as a corporate report. This operation is called *consolidating by the position of the data*.

- You can consolidate by category. For example, you can have Excel total cells labeled Sales, no matter where those cells are located on their respective worksheets. This versatile feature lets you import data from worksheets designed entirely differently from one another to meet local requirements and preferences.

- You can specify up to 255 sources for consolidation, and the worksheets don't have to be open during the consolidation process (however, they must have been saved).

- You're not restricted to using the SUM( ) function to add the values from the various worksheets. You can also use 10 other functions: AVERAGE, COUNT, COUNTA, MAX, MIN, PRODUCT, STDEV, STDEVP, VAR, and VARP. (These functions are explained in Appendix B.)

- You can create links between the worksheet that contains the results of the consolidation and the worksheets that contain the source data. When you create such links, Excel automatically updates the consolidated worksheet whenever changes are made in source data. Excel also creates an outline of the consolidated worksheet, with the supporting data stored on a second level that can be either displayed or hidden at will. In other words, you can see the individual values that were used in obtaining the consolidated figure merely by expanding the outline to show its second level.

USING CONSOLIDATION

Try the powerful consolidation feature now:

1. Load the Chicago and New York worksheets you created earlier in this chapter into memory: Select the Open… command from the File menu (shortcut: press ⌘-O) and then select the workspace name you applied to the workgroup that contains those two files (the book used the name WORKGROUP EXERCISE).

2. Click the Open button in the dialog box, and the New York and Chicago worksheets appear side by side, just as they were when you experimented with the Workgroup… command. However, now they are not grouped.

3. Press ⌘-N to open a new file. Click OK to use the worksheet file type. The new worksheet appears on top of the other worksheets, concealing most of them.

4. Drag the new worksheet down by its title bar until you can see the contents of the Chicago and New York worksheets at the same time. Your screen should now resemble Figure 7.10.

5. Now copy some titles to the new worksheet. Click the New York worksheet to activate it and drag to select the range A3:A5. (Do *not* include A6 in this range.)

6. Press ⌘-C (the shortcut to copy the selected cells to the clipboard).

7. Click the new, unnamed worksheet to select it. Then click to select cell A4.

8. Press ⌘-V (the shortcut for the Paste command). The first three titles in column A of the New York worksheet appear in the new worksheet, starting one cell lower (in the range A4:A6). You're not using exactly the same range the titles occupy in the New York worksheet because you need an extra row to accommodate a two-line title you'll create now.

9. Click cell B1 in the new worksheet and type **Order Summary**. Press Return.

10. In B2, type **(All Offices)**. Press Return.

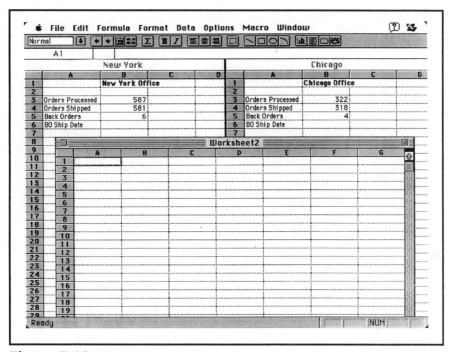

Figure 7.10: Three open worksheets

11. Drag to select both B1 and B2 and click the boldface icon on the Toolbar to make the two-line title boldface.

12. Place the pointer on the border between the headings for columns A and B and drag to the right slightly to widen column A so the words *Orders Processed* fit into A4 without overlapping into B4. (The column widths now match those in the New York and Chicago worksheets.)

13. Next you'll consolidate the New York and Chicago worksheet values on the new worksheet. However, before you proceed, save the new worksheet, using the name **Order Summary**.

14. On the newly saved Order Summary worksheet, drag to select the range A4:B6. This action provides a destination area for the data to be consolidated, even telling Excel where the titles for the data cells are located.

15. Pull down the Data menu and select the Consolidate... command. You'll see the Consolidate dialog box. Drag this dialog box by its title bar to move it any time it obscures or hides an area on a worksheet that you need to select.

16. Drag the Consolidate dialog box now to reposition it so you can see the data areas of all three worksheets. Your screen should resemble Figure 7.11.

17. Note that a Function area appears at the left of the dialog box, with SUM already selected in the list box. You'll use SUM in this exercise, so don't change the selection. To the right of the function area is a smaller area, By Categories. Since the destination range on the Order Summary worksheet is slightly different than the source range on the other two worksheets, you'll want to consolidate by categories rather than position of data. Therefore, in this instance, click the Left Column box. This action causes Excel to look for cell titles in the column to the left of the value cells (obviously, you'd

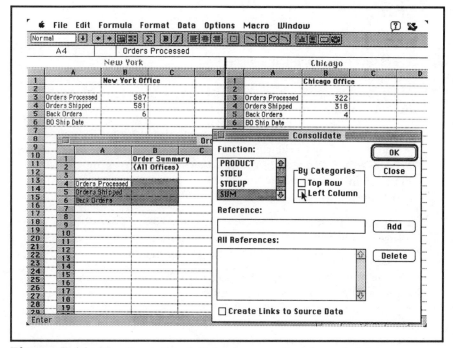

Figure 7.11: The Consolidate dialog box used with worksheets

use the other choice—Top Row—if your cell titles were located above the data).

18. Click the New York worksheet to activate it and drag to select the range A3 through B5. This move causes an entry to appear in the Reference box of the Consolidate dialog box. This entry lists the name of the New York worksheet enclosed in single quotation marks, an exclamation point, and the range just selected shown as an absolute reference (with $ signs).

19. The entry in the Reference box is what you want, so click the Add button in the dialog box.

20. Repeat the preceding process for the Chicago worksheet: Select the worksheet, select the range A3:B5, and click Add in the dialog box. Both worksheet references now appear in the bottom list box of the dialog box, titled All References. Your screen should resemble Figure 7.12.

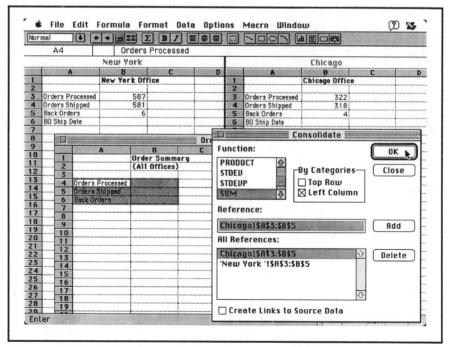

Figure 7.12: References added to the Consolidate dialog box

21. Click OK to enter the references and close the dialog box.

As shown in Figure 7.13, the Order Summary dialog box displays consolidated data from the New York and Chicago worksheets. The SUM( ) function totaled the categories Orders Processed, Orders Shipped, and Back Orders on both source worksheets.

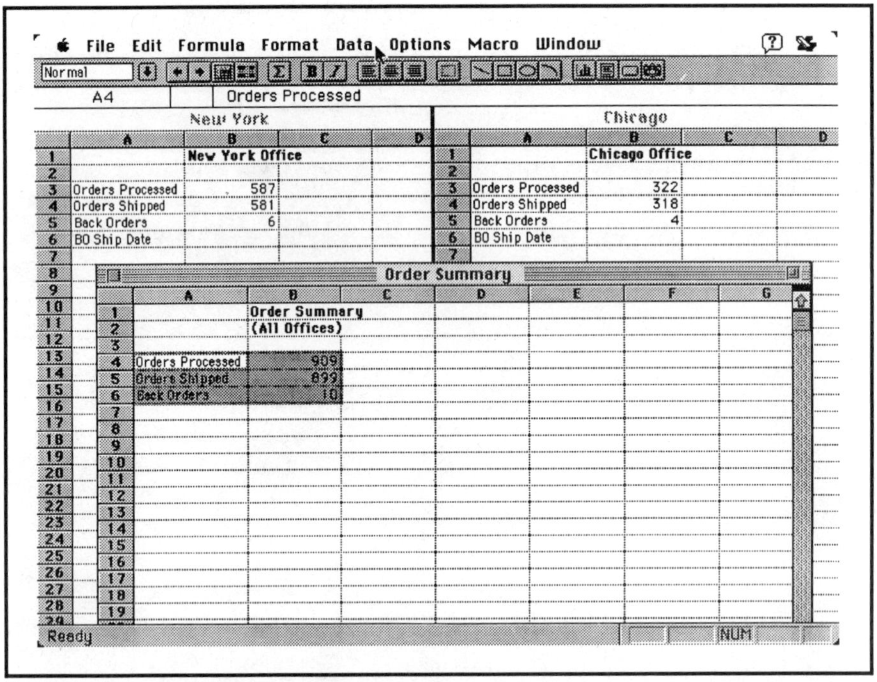

Figure 7.13: Data consolidated on the Order Summary worksheet

USING THE CONSOLIDATED OUTLINE

To see how the outlining feature of the Consolidate... command works, try this:

1. With the range A4:B6 still selected on the Order Summary worksheet, pull down the Data menu again and reselect the Consolidate... command.

2. In the Consolidate dialog box, click the selection box at the bottom labeled Create Links to Source Data. Then click OK.

Now the source worksheets are linked to the Order Summary worksheet, and outlining has been completed. You can see a vertical outline bar at the left of the window. Click the number 2 at the top of this bar to display the second level of the worksheet. A labeled display includes the individual source data. Your screen should look like Figure 7.14. Note that the cell locations of the data have been adjusted to accommodate the outline format.

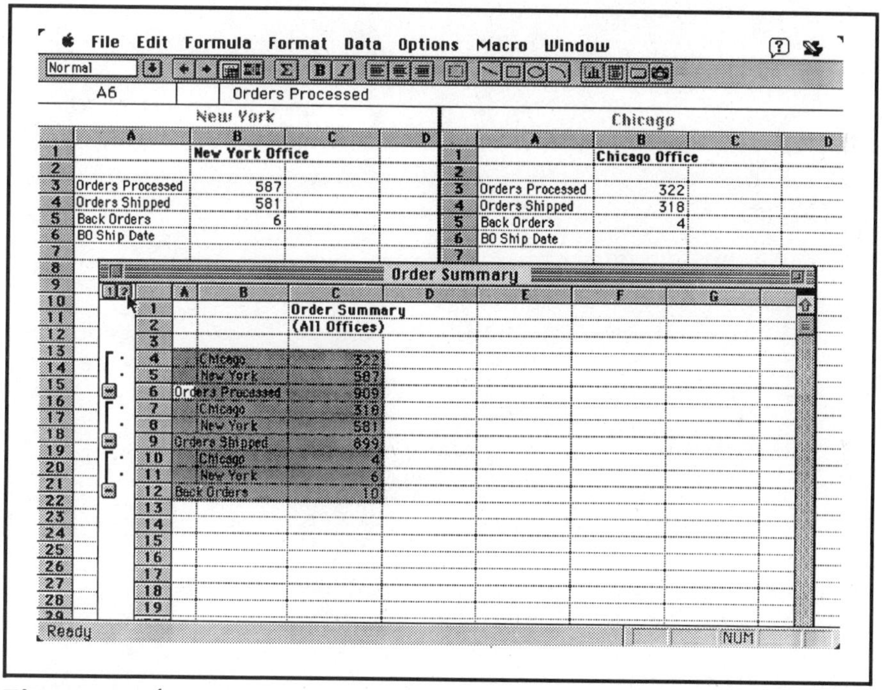

Figure 7.14: The Order Summary worksheet with outlining added

Chapter 2 discusses further how Excel handles outlines.

Save the three worksheets as **WORKSPACE**. You'll use them again in Chapter 15.

SUMMARY

In this chapter you learned how to use workgroups, link data between files and even between applications, paste and link files, and take advantage of Excel's powerful consolidation capabilities.

Chapter

Preventing
Errors

Once you learn the basics, Excel is an extremely easy program to use. You can build complex worksheets very quickly.

However, the program's very accessibility means that you can also quickly and easily introduce errors into your worksheets. Moreover, if cells are not protected (see Chapter 4), other users of your worksheets can also introduce errors. You can create a formula with a *circular reference*, in which the formula obtains data by referring to itself rather than other cells, creating an endless circle. Or you can create a formula that refers to other cells, but they're the wrong cells. Or someone can accidentally update a worksheet by replacing the formula in a cell with a value; thereafter, in subsequent updates, that cell and all cells that refer to it will contain incorrect values.

All of these possibilities mean that you need the capability of auditing worksheets both before and after you create them. This chapter discusses several Excel features that can help you create and maintain accurate worksheets.

Before you proceed further, open the Performance Report worksheet you created in Chapter 4. Use the Save As... command from the File menu to make a copy. Name the copy **Error Checking**. You'll use this copy to explore some of Excel's error-checking features.

USING THE FIND... COMMAND

Many Excel users develop giant worksheets that cover several pages. You don't have to be a power user to find yourself in this situation. For example, you might create a worksheet that projects the revenue from each of a line of products in all of the markets where they're distributed. If you have, say, 14 products sold in 65 cities throughout the United States and 23 expense categories affecting the profit picture in each market, and you want a worksheet that projects sales for the entire company, you could end up with a real extravaganza. The formulas could consist of nothing more elaborate than addition, subtraction, and multiplication (the multiplication would be used to determine costs per unit)—yet the opportunity for errors would be substantial. In fact, just locating a particular section of the worksheet for examination or updating could take many minutes of scrolling and selecting cells to examine formulas.

Fortunately, Excel provides an easier way of finding information in a worksheet: the Find... command.

FINDING CHARACTERS

With the new Error Checking worksheet open (the copy you just made of the Performance Report worksheet), you can easily locate specific characters or character combinations with the Find... command.

1. Pull down the Formula menu and select the Find... command. You'll see the Find dialog box shown in Figure 8.1. In this dialog box, you enter the characters you want to find. You type the characters in the Find What box. Note that you can search for particular cell contents in formulas, values, or notes; you can search for characters as whole items or as parts of items (such as strings contained

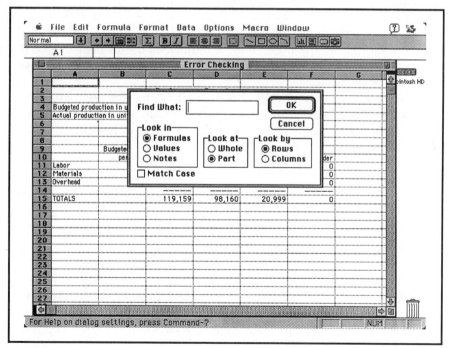

Figure 8.1: The Find dialog box

in formulas); and you can search by rows or by columns. If the Match Case box is checked, Excel searches only for perfect capitalization matches for any text you type. For example, if you type TOTAL, the program ignores any cells containing Total.

2. You will search for instances of the IF( ) function. In the Find What box, type **if**.

3. Don't change the default settings: You want to search for parts of formulas by rows. Do not click the Match Case box. Click OK to begin the search. Excel immediately highlights cell E11, the first instance in the worksheet of the IF( ) function.

4. Press ⌘-H to continue the search. Excel stops at the next occurrence of IF in the same row (the program is searching by rows, remember)—cell F11.

5. Press ⌘-H once more. Since there are no more IF( ) functions in formulas in row 11, the program moves down to the next row and highlights E12, the next occurrence of IF.

Once the Find... command has located all instances of the specified characters, pressing ⌘-H causes Excel to cycle through all of the highlighted cells again. To search for other characters, you have to select the command again from the Formula menu.

If you want to search for the same character combination in a series of worksheets, all you have to do is load a worksheet and press ⌘-H. The search specifications you've set up continue to be in effect until you either change them in the dialog box or exit Excel.

If your keyboard contains a row of function keys at the top (an *extended keyboard*), you can press F7 instead of ⌘-H to continue a search. You can also press Shift-F7 to find the preceding occurrence of the specified characters (or Shift-⌘-H).

Using Wildcards

Excel lets you use two *wildcard* characters—∗ and ?—to search for nonspecific strings. You can use the wildcard character ∗ (an asterisk) in the Find What box to locate a character or group of characters followed by anything whatsoever. For example, you can type **TOTA**∗ to find both *TOTAL* and

TOTALS. Or you can type **sum(∗)** to find the SUM function used with any arguments whatsoever; however, this search would not find a title containing the word *Summary* because the characters *Sum* in this instance are not followed by parentheses.

You can use the wildcard character **?** (a question mark) to find any one character in a certain position. For instance, you can type **MI?(** to locate occurrences of both the MID( ) and MIN( ) functions. (These functions are explained in Appendix B.)

Note that if you want to find a cell containing the multiplication operator (∗), you must type a tilde (˜) before the asterisk: ˜∗. This action tells Excel that you want to find the ∗ operator. If the tilde is not present, the program interprets the symbol as a wildcard character. On the other hand, if you want to find a question mark, you simply type **?**.

FINDING PROBLEM CELLS

Now let's test the Find... command's ability to locate problems. Imagine that the Error Checking worksheet is enormous, consisting of many screens of data-filled cells. You want to find any cells containing the error value #VALUE! (This error code appears in a cell when you use the wrong kind of argument or operand.)

First, though, you have to create an error for Excel to find.

1. Select cell D13, where this formula appears: = B13∗C5. The last part of this formula is an absolute reference to cell C5, which displays the actual production in units: 8,000. Change the first part of the formula, B13, which references the budgeted cost per unit for overhead (to be multiplied by 8,000).

2. Click the formula bar just after the letter B. Backspace to delete the B and type an A in its place. The formula now refers to cell A13, which is only a text label.

3. Click the enter box in the formula bar to enter the revised formula.

Immediately, the error value #VALUE! appears in six cells: D13, the one in which the error was introduced, and five additional cells that contain formulas that depend on the data in D13. Your screen should now resemble Figure 8.2.

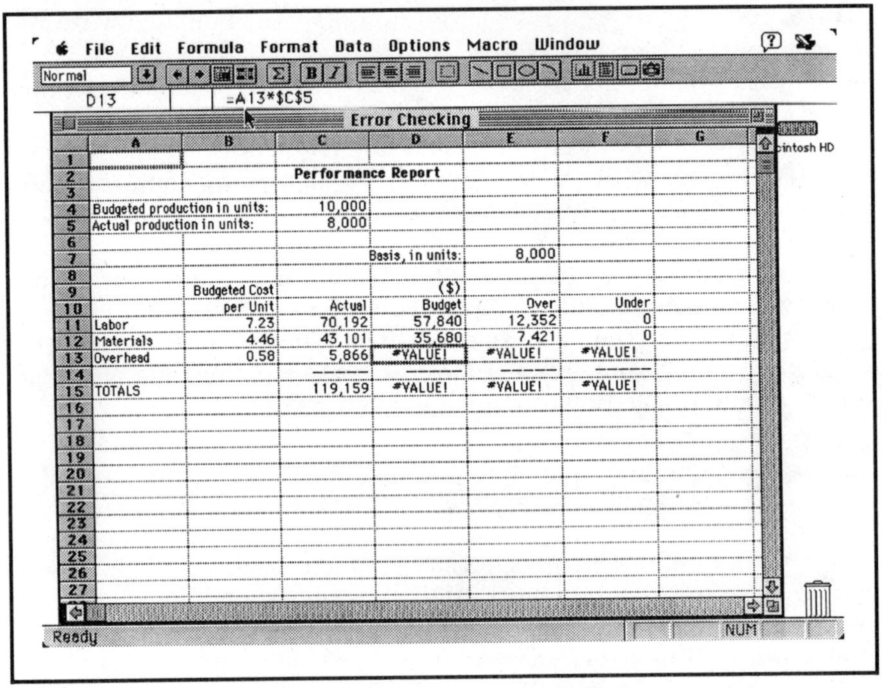

Figure 8.2: The Error Checking worksheet with error values

Now use the Find... command to locate all the erroneous values in your worksheet. If this were a large worksheet, the Find... command could be a real lifesaver in finding all the problem cells.

1. Click A1 to select a cell not involved with the error.

2. Pull down the Formula menu and select the Find... command.

3. In the Find dialog box, type #VALUE! in the Find What box.

4. Since your search in this case will be for a value and not a formula (#VALUE! is considered an error *value*), click the Values button in the dialog box. Then click OK.

Excel highlights the first occurrence of the error value.

To find each additional cell that contains the error value, you could press ⌘-H or F7, as previously discussed. However, you can also use another command—the Select Special... command—to highlight all of the cells simultaneously.

USING THE
SELECT SPECIAL... COMMAND

The Select Special... command can conduct several kinds of specialized searches for you. We'll use it now to find the error values.

1. Pull down the Formula menu and pick the Select Special... command. You'll see the Select dialog box shown in Figure 8.3. Here you can search for notes attached to cells (the default setting), constants, formulas, blank cells, cells that differ from one another, the last cell in the worksheet, objects such as graphic images, cells upon which the selected cell is dependent (called *precedent cells*), or cells that are dependent upon the selected cell (our goal in this instance).

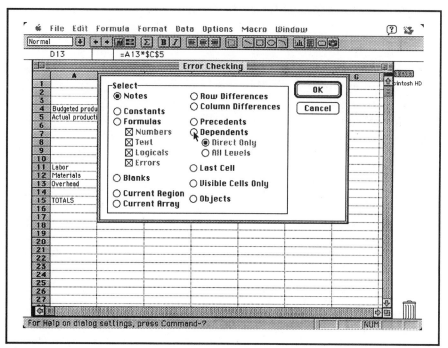

Figure 8.3: The Select dialog box

2. Click the Dependents button to select it. The Notes button is automatically deselected.

3. You now have a choice of two buttons under Dependents. The Direct Only option finds only the cells directly dependent upon the selected cell. The All Levels option finds cells at any level that are dependent upon that cell. Let's try both options to see the difference. First, leave the Direct Only button selected (the default setting) and click OK. Cells E13, F13, and D15 are now highlighted.

4. Click D13 to reselect it. (After the previous search, E13 became the selected cell.)

5. Pull down the Formula menu and pick the Select Special... command again. This time, click the Dependents button and then the All Levels button.

6. Click OK.

Now all five cells that depend in any way upon D13 are highlighted.

USING THE SHOW INFO COMMAND

You can obtain a list of the cells dependent upon a cell (and much additional information about the cell) by selecting the Show Info command.

1. Click D13 to reselect the cell.

2. Pull down the Window menu and select the Show Info command. The menu bar at the top of your screen changes, and an Info window opens.

3. Pull down the Info menu now displayed on the menu bar. This menu lists information about the selected cell that you can display in the Info window: the cell address, any formula, any value, the cell formatting (including the font in use), whether or not the cell is protected, any name for the cell, whether or not a note is attached to the cell, and specific lists of precedent and dependent cells.

4. To see all of the information available, click each of the options on the Info menu (if the item is not already selected, as indicated by a check mark). You'll have to pull down the menu repeatedly to accomplish this. The Precedents... and Dependents... options each display an additional dialog box, where you can select Direct Only or All Levels. Select All Levels, to display the maximum amount of information.

The contents of the Info window should resemble Figure 8.4.

TIP

You can display the Info window continuously while you work. This feature can be handy when you're having trouble locating a worksheet error. With your worksheet already open, pull down the Window menu and select the Show Info command to display the Info window. Then pull down the Window menu again and select Arrange All. Excel will display the Info window and the worksheet window side by side. You can switch between the windows either by clicking the inactive window or by pressing ⌘-F6. If some of the data you want is not visible, you can use the scroll bars, drag the size box at the lower right corner of each window to resize the window, or drag either window by its title bar to move it to a new position.

After you've read all of the displayed information, click the close box on the Info window to close that window and return to the regular Excel menus.

FINDING COLUMN DIFFERENCES

Earlier in this chapter, we discussed how someone could replace a formula in a cell with a value and thus produce incorrect results when the worksheet is updated. Let's now look at how to quickly find many errors of this kind: using the Column Differences button in the Select Special dialog box.

1. Select D13 again and change the first cell reference from A13 back to B13.

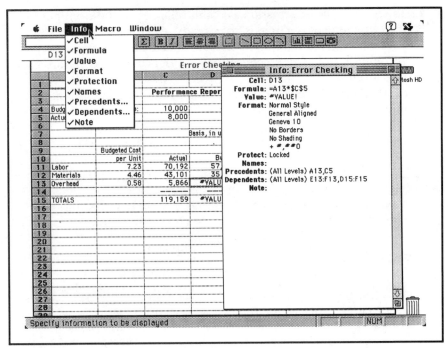

Figure 8.4: The Info menu and window

2. Click the enter box in the formula bar. The error values in the worksheet disappear, and cell D13 displays the value 4,640, just as it did before the previous change you made.

3. With D13 still selected, replace the formula with the value it produces. Type **4640** in the formula bar and click the enter box.

4. Click cell D11 to select it. Now that D13 is no longer selected (you can no longer see the cell's true contents in the formula bar), you cannot tell by looking at your screen that a problem exists in the worksheet. However, you can check for such problems.

5. Drag to select the range D11 to D13.

6. Pull down the Formula menu and pick the Select Special... command once more.

7. This time click the Column Differences button. Excel now searches for differences between the cells in the selected portion of the column.

8. Click OK. Immediately, D13 is highlighted because the other cells in the range contain formulas, and this cell does not (since you converted the formula to the value it represented to test this feature).

You can use the Column Differences command to search multiple selected columns in the same way. You can also search for differences between the contents of cells in selected rows rather than columns, by selecting rows and clicking the Row Differences button instead.

USING THE REPLACE... COMMAND

You can use the Replace... command to locate specified characters and then replace them with other characters. The Replace dialog box resembles the Find dialog box. However, the Replace dialog box contains an additional box where you can type replacement characters. It also provides three buttons: Replace All (to replace all occurrences of the search characters with one command), Find Next (to search for occurrences one at a time), and Replace (to replace a single occurrence that has been highlighted).

You can use wildcards in the Replace dialog box in the same manner as in the Find dialog box.

Figure 8.5 shows the Replace dialog box.

ADDING NOTES TO CELLS

You've already seen references to notes. Attaching a note to a cell is a good way of documenting a formula, both for the enlightenment of others who may use your worksheet and to remind yourself of the purpose and result of a particular formula.

Add a note to your worksheet now.

1. Select E11. This cell contains a formula that uses the IF( ) function. The formula could be confusing to someone not aware of what it does.

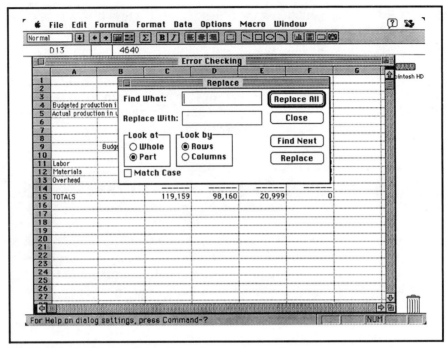

Figure 8.5: The Replace dialog box

2. Pull down the Formula menu and select the Note... command. The Cell Note dialog box appears. This dialog box lists all of the notes currently in the worksheet. You can select any of these from the Notes in Sheet box to delete or edit them. Because you have not created any notes yet for this particular worksheet, the box is empty. The large Note text box is where you add a note to the selected cell.

3. A vertical line flashes in the Note box, indicating that Excel is waiting for your entry. Type this: **If the value in C11 is greater than the value in D11, subtracts D11 from C11. Otherwise, enters a zero.**

4. Click Add to add the note to the cell. Your screen should now resemble Figure 8.6.

5. Click OK to close the dialog box.

A small square appears in the upper right corner of the cell to indicate that a note is attached. On a color monitor, this square is red.

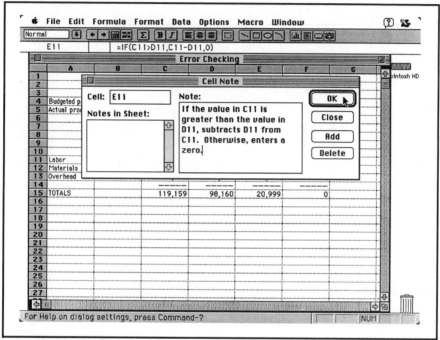

Figure 8.6: The Cell Note dialog box

To view the note, you simply select the cell again, pull down the Formula menu, and select the Note... command. (Shortcut: Double-click the cell that contains the note.)

Resave the Error Checking Worksheet. You'll use it again in its present form when you reach Chapter 16.

SUMMARY

In this chapter, you learned how to use the Find..., Show Info..., and Select Special... commands to locate data and find and prevent errors.

You also learned how to add notes to cells—a good way to document the logic of your worksheets. Remember that naming cells and ranges can be helpful too, especially in large worksheets.

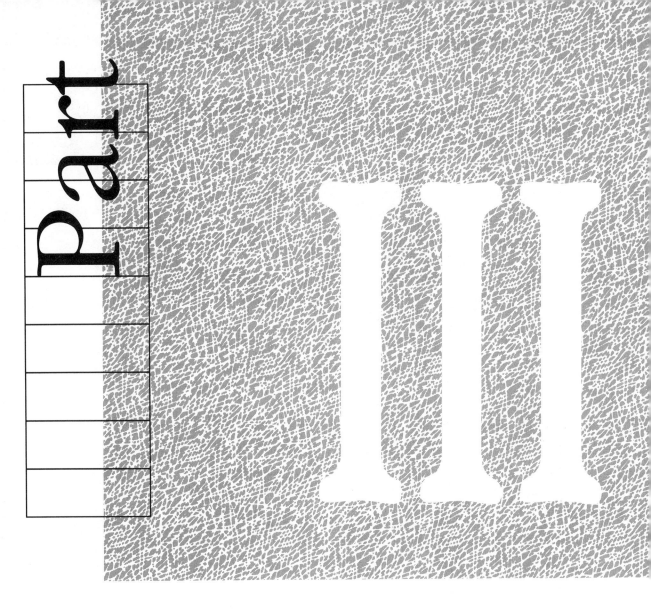

Part III

Turning Numbers
into Charts

Chapter

9

Selecting the
Right Chart
Type

In Chapter 1 you created a simple pie chart as part of a basic worksheet. Now it's time to get into the subject of creating charts more seriously. This chapter explains how Excel searches for and allocates the data it uses to generate charts. Then you learn more about the kinds of charts that are available and how each is best used.

SETTING COLOR MONITORS
TO GRAY-SCALE DISPLAY

If you have a color monitor, you should be aware of a potential color reproduction problem before you start making charts.

You'd probably prefer to run most programs in color. Color gives a cheerful, vibrant appearance to files and often helps you differentiate among items on your screen. However, if you won't be printing Excel charts in color, it's a good idea to set your monitor to gray-scale, rather than color, display before having Excel create those charts.

The reason for using gray-scale display is that when Excel senses you're using a monitor set for color, it assigns colors to your data series that will print well in color—but not necessarily in black and white. For example, in creating a default column chart with three data series, Excel assigns red bars to represent the first series, green bars to represent the second series, and blue bars to represent the third series. However, when the chart is printed on other than a color printer, all three sets of bars appear as solid black, so that no one can distinguish among the three data series.

On the other hand, if you set your color monitor to gray-scale display, Excel automatically creates that same column chart using black for the first data series, white for the second data series, and gray for the third data series—a combination that will be very easy to read on a black-and-white printout. The program assigns black, white, and shades of gray in identifiable sequences for data series in all other kinds of charts as well.

You use the Monitors dialog box to alternate between showing colors and grays. Figure 9.1 shows the System 7 version of this dialog box.

Here's how to change your color monitor to a gray-scale display:

1. Pull down the Apple menu and select Control Panels (called Control Panel in versions of the operating system preceding System 7).

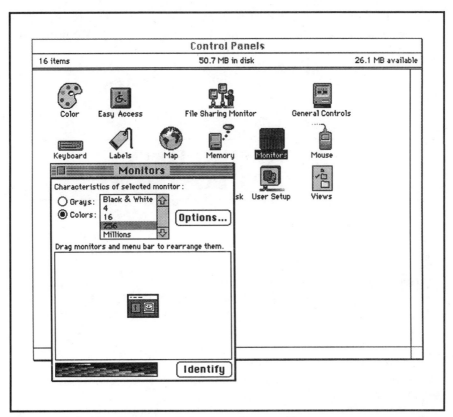

Figure 9.1: The Monitors dialog box (System 7)

2. Double-click the Monitors icon. (With older versions of the operating system, you may have to scroll the list box to see this particular icon.) The screen displays the Monitors dialog box, where you can click a button to switch between gray-scale (Grays) and color (Colors) displays. Pick Grays. (You can also select the number of grays you want displayed—Black & White, 4, 16, 256, or Millions— depending on the capabilities of the video card installed in your Macintosh. For example, if you select 16, your monitor will display 16 shades, or gradations, of gray.)

3. After setting your monitor to Grays, click the close box in the Monitor dialog box and then the close box in the Control Panels dialog box to return to the desktop or your current application. Your color

monitor now displays only black and white, plus shades of gray. (If you're using a version of the operating system released prior to System 7, you have to click only the close box on the Monitors dialog box to return to the desktop.)

To switch back to color display, follow steps 1 and 2 again, except click the Colors button.

ASSIGNING DATA TO CHART POSITIONS

You may remember that in Chapter 1 Excel seemed to know exactly where to find and place text and data. Simple rules govern these default procedures.

Excel always assumes that you will use fewer *data series* than *categories* or *data points*. For example, a typical chart might show Sales and Expenses (two separate data series) for three regional offices (categories) over a period of a year (12 or 52 or even 365 data points). Therefore, when you drag to select a range to be plotted that includes data and labels, the program assumes that the long dimension of the range represents the data points or categories. If the range is square, Excel selects the horizontal dimension for categories or data points.

Occasionally, Excel isn't certain which dimension to use for categories or data points: for example, if Excel finds no text in the first column of the range, as in Figure 9.2. In that case, the program displays the First Row Contains dialog box, which asks you if the first row contains the first data series, category (X axis) labels, or X values for an XY chart. You click the appropriate button so Excel can allocate the data properly and then click OK to create the default chart (a column chart).

Figure 9.3 shows the results of charting the data in Figure 9.2 with each of the three First Row Contains buttons selected. Note that since the third option calls for X values on an XY chart, Excel automatically creates a scatterplot in this instance instead of the default column chart.

For each of these charts, you would need to add appropriate labels so that viewers could understand the meaning of the data, since the worksheet contains no text for that purpose.

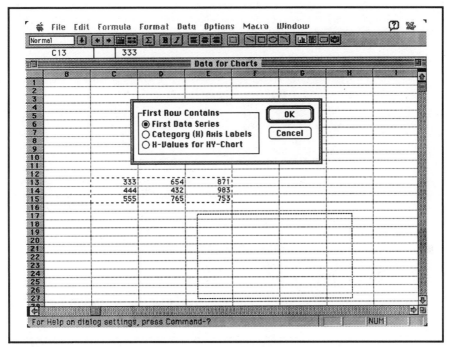

Figure 9.2: The First Row Contains dialog box

Of course, you can change the default plotting sequence Excel uses. For instance, you can simply rearrange your worksheet so Excel picks up the data in a different order. Other approaches are discussed in Chapter 10.

MATCHING THE CHART TYPE TO THE DATA

In Chapter 1 you changed the default column chart to a pie chart. You can create 11 kinds of charts in Excel—column, horizontal bar, area, line, pie, XY(scatter), combination, 3-D area, 3-D line, 3-D column, and 3-D pie charts—with many variations. Several of these may adequately display the data in one of your worksheets; others may not be appropriate at all. Usually, only one type of chart presents your data with maximum effectiveness.

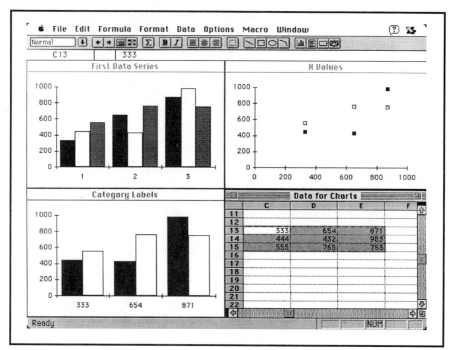

Figure 9.3: Results of First Row Contains options

Let's quickly create a worksheet and plot its contents to verify these statements.

CHARTING
TEMPERATURE COMPARISONS

You'll create a list of cities and their high temperatures for five consecutive days. This simple worksheet requires no formulas at all. Then you'll chart this data in different ways and evaluate the results.

1. Open a new worksheet and select cell D1.

2. Type this heading: **High Temperatures**. Press Return.

3. In D2, type this subheading: **(Fahrenheit)**. Press Return.

4. Drag to select both D1 and D2. Then click the boldface and center icons on the Toolbar to make the heading and subheading appear centered and in boldface.

5. You need to enter headings representing days of the week. (You can't use Excel's Data Series... command—demonstrated in Chapter 6—for this, because these headings will not represent complete dates, which must include the year. The Data Series... command manipulates dates based on serial numbers—stored values representing the number of days since January 1, 1904.) Select B4 and type **Sat**. Press Tab to move to C4.

6. In C4, type **Sun**. Press Tab.

7. In D4, type **Mon**. Press Tab.

8. In E4, type **Tue**. Press Tab.

9. In F4, type **Wed**. Press Tab.

10. Drag to select the range B4:F4 and click the boldface and right-alignment icons on the Toolbar to display the days of the week in boldface and right-aligned so they'll be above the temperature readings to be entered in the rows below.

11. Look at Figure 9.4 and complete the worksheet by entering the city labels shown in column A (the series labels) and the temperature readings shown in columns B through F (the data points).

12. Save the worksheet, using the name **High Temperatures**.

TRYING THE DEFAULT COLUMN CHART

To chart the temperatures in your worksheet, first try creating the default chart Excel produces automatically. This is a vertical bar chart, called a column chart in Excel.

1. Drag to select the range A4:F7 in the High Temperatures worksheet.

2. Click the chart tool icon on the Toolbar and drag to select the range B9:F25 on the worksheet. The column chart shown in Figure 9.5 appears. What's wrong with it? Well, it does present the worksheet data; however, it has defects—the most glaring being that the chart does not identify what the individual bars represent.

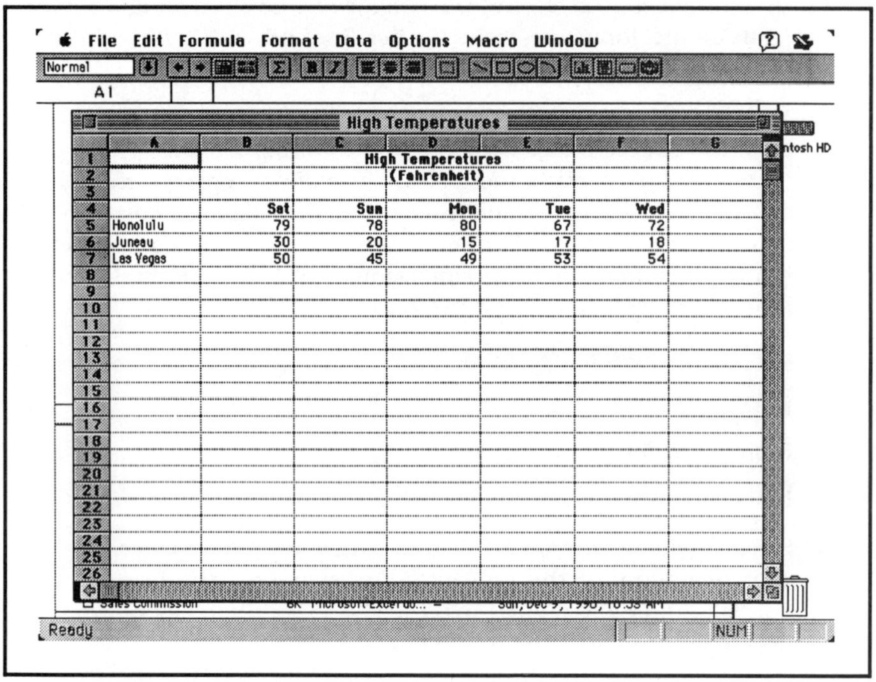

Figure 9.4: The High Temperatures worksheet

3. Correct this shortcoming by double-clicking the chart to open the chart window so you can edit it using the separate chart menus.

4. Pull down the Chart menu that appears in the chart window (introduced in Chapter 1) and select the Add Legend command. Instantly, Excel adds a small legend box that indicates that the bars represent the cities of Honolulu, Juneau, and Las Vegas (see Figure 9.6). The legend box is selected, as the eight black handles that line its boundaries show; thus, you can now move the box or change its default formatting. (Excel picked up the text for the legend box automatically because the data range you selected included the series labels in column A.)

5. Click the chart window just under the title bar to deselect the legend box without selecting the chart area as a whole.

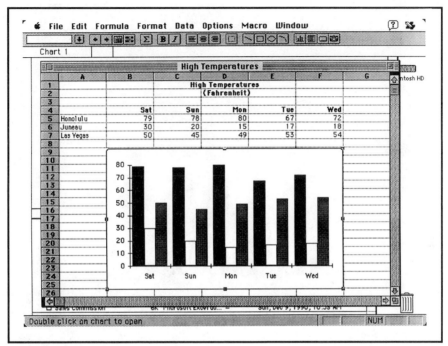

Figure 9.5: The default column chart

In a moment, we'll discuss the other failings of this chart type in representing this particular data.

Incidentally, if you have a color monitor (unless you're using it in a black-and-white or gray-scale configuration), the first data series (Honolulu) in the chart you now see will be represented by red bars. The Juneau bars will be green, and the Las Vegas bars will be blue. If you have a monochrome monitor (or a color monitor set for a black-and-white or gray-scale display), the Honolulu bars will be black, the Juneau bars white, and the Las Vegas bars gray.

As you'll learn in Chapter 10, you can change the default appearance of either color or black-and-white bars, using different colors or patterns. You can also move and reformat the legend box. In fact, you can add headings, comments, backgrounds, borders, and otherwise customize the look of the chart to suit both your individual taste and the message you're trying to get across.

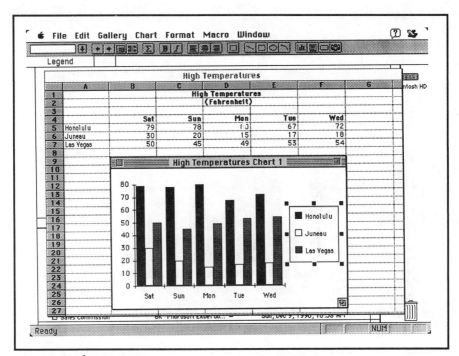

Figure 9.6: The column chart with a legend added

However, your first task is to select the chart type that best represents the data.

Why is the default column chart less than ideal? It now has a legend box to identify the cities symbolized by each series of bars. By analyzing the chart, you can see which cities have the highest or lowest temperatures and how one day of the week compares with another. However, this chart provides no real sense of flow, of change over time. A column chart can be a good choice when your goal is to compare individual values—but that is not our goal here.

TRYING A HORIZONTAL BAR CHART

Once you've selected a format option for a chart type (or have accepted the default format), you'll find the most similar format highlighted when you select a different chart type. For instance, try displaying your High Temperatures worksheet data using a horizontal bar chart, identified on the chart window Gallery menu simply as Bar.... This option displays horizontal bars, while a column chart displays vertical bars.

1. Pull down the Gallery menu. This menu is where you change chart types, as discussed in Chapter 1. Select Bar... to display the Bar dialog box shown in Figure 9.7. The Bar dialog box offers seven different horizontal bar configuration options. The first option is highlighted.

2. The most appropriate bar chart format available is option 7, which displays value labels for each temperature reading. Highlight this option to select it and click OK. Figure 9.8 shows the result.

Remember that you previously specified a legend box. Excel retains this box in the display when you change the chart type.

This format is the best we can do with the bar chart type, but it still gives little sense of temperature continuity for the three cities. A horizontal bar chart is an excellent choice if you want to deemphasize the time aspect of the data series.

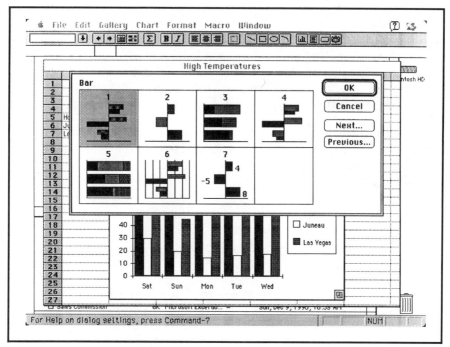

Figure 9.7: The Bar dialog box

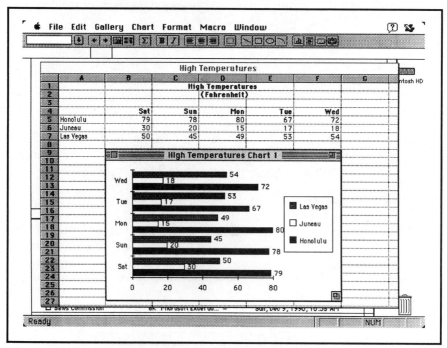

Figure 9.8: A bar chart with value labels and a legend box

Bar and Column Chart Formats

Bar and column charts have similar format options. In addition to the seven options offered for bar charts, column charts offer an eighth option, which eliminates space between column groups. Here is a summary of the bar and column chart formats shown in Figure 9.7:

- **Option 1** is the default format. This option produces the simplest form of a bar or column chart.

- **Option 2** produces a bar or column chart for one data series with varied patterns.

- **Option 3**, the stacked option, displays all data series in the form of one bar or column for each category label (a category in the High Temperature example being one day of the week).

- **Option 4**, the overlapped option, causes parallel bars or columns to overlap, requiring less space for each category.

- **Option 5**, the 100 percent stacked option, displays one bar or column for each category label (like format 4), except that the bars or columns are all the same length or height, and each data series is shown as a percentage of the column. (This kind of display is completely unsuited for the display of temperatures.)

- **Option 6** is like option 1, except that Excel adds gridlines to help readers determine the approximate values represented by bar or column lengths.

- **Option 7** adds value labels for each data point. (If you use this option for the example, there will be no question as to the exact temperature represented, because the value is displayed at the end of the bar or column.)

- **Option 8** shows no spaces between the categories (the column groups). This option is available for column charts only, not for bar charts.

TRYING AN AREA CHART

An area chart is similar to a pie chart in that it shows the relative importance of one data series in relation to the whole. It has an advantage for our temperature chart in that it can emphasize flow: the change in temperatures over time. A disadvantage, however, is that the labels on the default Y axis (the vertical axis of the chart) display cumulative values for all series; in other words, you'll find that, on the warmest day, the sum of the temperatures in the three cities was 160 degrees. The total, of course, is meaningless for this kind of data.

Display an area chart to see how it fits our purposes.

1. Pull down the Gallery menu again and select the Area... command.

2. In the Area... dialog box (see Figure 9.9), merely click OK to accept the first option, which is highlighted. The default area chart appears, as in Figure 9.10. As mentioned, this format displays cumulative values, which are meaningless here.

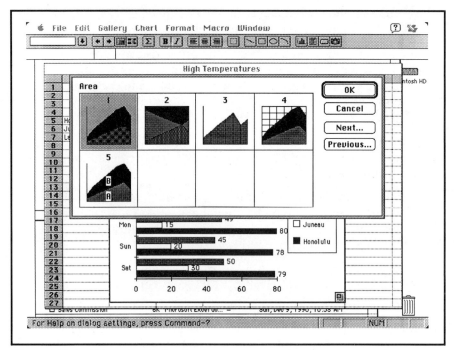

Figure 9.9: The Area dialog box

Option 5 is a more promising area chart for our purpose, since you can also remove the misleading Y-axis labels. Try this variation now.

1. Pull down the Gallery menu and select Area... again.

2. Click option 5 in the Area dialog box and click OK. The area chart appears with value labels. Now you don't need the legend box (since the values displayed in this particular chart are the city names), so it has vanished automatically.

3. To remove the Y-axis labels, pull down the Chart menu and select the Axes... command. You'll see the Axes dialog box shown in Figure 9.11.

4. Click to deselect the box labeled Value (Y) Axis. Then click OK.

Now you have the result shown in Figure 9.12. You have no confusing cumulative temperature values, and you do have each data series clearly

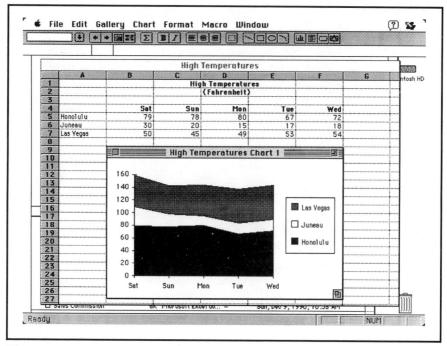

Figure 9.10: The default area chart

labeled, right in the middle of the series itself. You can see the category labels (the days of the week involved) along the horizontal (X) axis. However, you don't have a clue as to the temperatures recorded!

No, none of the area charts is suitable for our purpose. Nevertheless, remember that area charts really shine when your goal is to display cumulative values.

Area Chart Formats

Here is a summary of the area chart format options shown in Figure 9.9:

- **Option 1**, the default format, is a simple area chart (as in Figure 9.10).

- **Option 2**, the 100 percent area chart, shows each data series as a percentage of the whole.

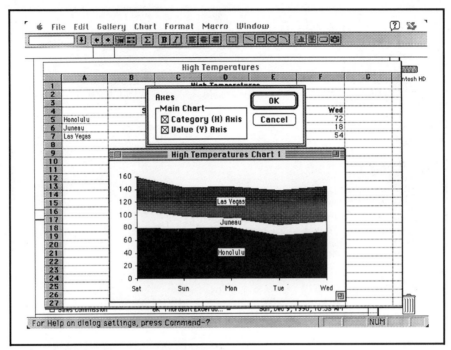

Figure 9.11: The Axes dialog box

- **Option 3** is similar to option 1, except that Excel adds drop lines to separate the categories. (In our example, the categories are the individual days of the week.)

- **Option 4** adds gridlines behind the displayed data series. (Gridlines are not very useful unless some of the categories contain very small values, since you may hardly able to see the lines; the grid is visible only in those areas that do not display values. However, you can pull down the Format menu, select Main Chart..., select the Drop Lines box, and click OK to add drop lines to this option.)

- **Option 5** is like option 1, except that Excel adds value labels within each data series.

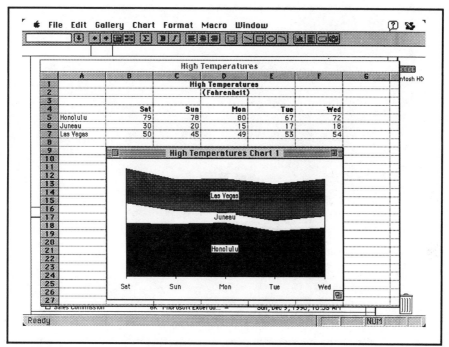

Figure 9.12: An area chart with value labels and no Y values

TRYING A LINE CHART

A line chart is an excellent tool for showing change over time—or a trend. A line chart can also depict differences between data series in a manner that's easy to comprehend.

1. Pull down the Gallery menu and select Line.... The Line dialog box appears (see Figure 9.13).

2. In the Line dialog box, click OK to accept the first formatting option (the default format).

3. You need a legend box again. Pull down the Chart menu and select the Add Legend command.

4. Click just under the title bar for the chart window to deselect the legend box. Now your screen should resemble Figure 9.14.

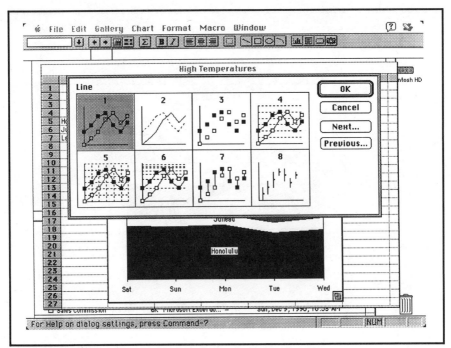

Figure 9.13: The Line dialog box

The default chart looks pretty good. However, option 5 (with the legend box added) is probably the best line chart choice for our high temperatures chart, because it adds a grid that helps readers associate the data points with the days of the week and to determine the approximate temperatures represented. Try this format:

1. Pull down the Gallery menu again and select Line....

2. In the Line dialog box, select option 5 and click OK. The result should look like Figure 9.15.

Line Chart Formats

Here's an explanation of the line chart formatting options shown in Figure 9.13:

*   **Option 1**, the default format, displays lines with markers at each data point.

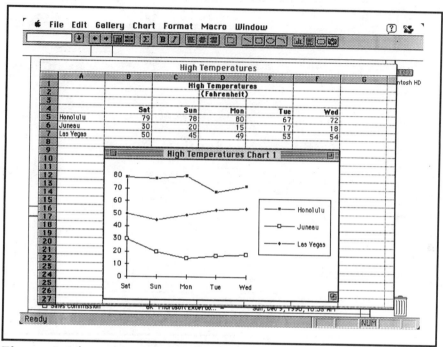

Figure 9.14: The default line chart with a legend box added

- **Option 2** displays lines only.

- **Option 3** displays markers only.

- **Option 4** is the same as option 1, except that Excel adds horizontal gridlines.

- **Option 5** is the same as option 4, except that Excel adds both vertical and horizontal gridlines.

- **Option 6** displays lines and markers with gridlines and a logarithmic scale.

- **Option 7**, the hi-lo chart, shows markers and hi-lo lines. (Hi-lo lines extend from the highest to the lowest values in each category.)

- **Option 8**, the hi-lo-close chart, used for stock quotations, adds points representing the final value within the hi-lo range.

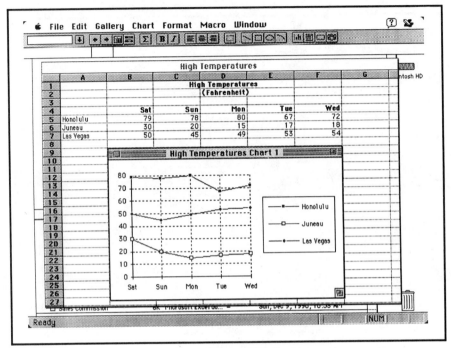

Figure 9.15: Line chart with gridlines added

TRYING A PIE CHART

Like an area chart, a pie chart shows the relationship of parts of the data to the whole (a feature inappropriate for our temperature data). A pie chart is usually easier to read than an area chart, since you can see at a glance the size of each slice of the pie. You can even show specific percentages for each slice, as you discovered in Chapter 1.

However, a pie chart is even less suited for our data than an area chart. At least the area chart provides a depiction of change over time. A pie chart does not. Nevertheless, apply the pie chart type to the data to observe the result.

1. Pull down the Gallery menu and select Pie.... The Pie dialog box appears.

2. Click OK to accept the default format, number 1. You'll see the chart in Figure 9.16.

  Note that Excel ignored two of the data series entirely and constructed the slices of the pie using only the daily temperatures for Honolulu! The legend box now identifies days of the week. (Excel chooses the first data series displayed—in this case, the values for Honolulu.)
  Let's see what happens when we change to a different pie format.

1. Pull down the Gallery menu and select Pie... again.

2. In the Pie dialog box, select option 5, which labels the slices. Figure 9.17 shows this new version.

  As you will observe, we're no better off. Now the slices are labeled with the days of the week, making the legend box unnecessary, but the chart

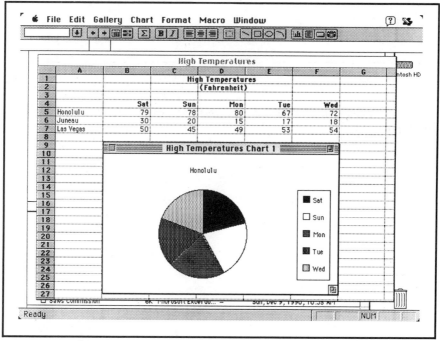

Figure 9.16: The default pie chart

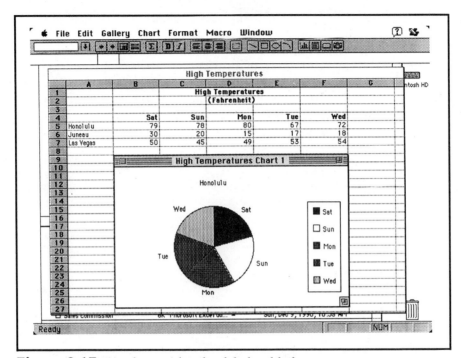

Figure 9.17: Pie chart with value labels added

is still meaningless for comparing the temperatures in three cities over a period of five days.

Pie Chart Formats

Here are the pie chart formatting options (shown in the Pie dialog box, reproduced in Figure 1.13 in Chapter 1):

- **Option 1**, the default format, is an unadorned pie, with each slice a different color.

- **Option 2** shows all slices the same color, but labeled with categories.

- **Option 3** is the same as option 1, but with the first slice exploded (moved out from the pie).

- **Option 4** is the same as option 1, but with all slices exploded.

- **Option 5** is the same as option 1, but with category labels added.

- **Option 6** is the same as option 1, but with value labels expressed as percentages.

Although a pie chart is not suited to our task, it's the best chart type for displaying percentages.

TRYING AN XY (SCATTER) CHART

XY (scatter) charts are often used for scientific or statistical analysis. The X axis must be numerical, and Excel calculates the labels on this axis, just as it does for the Y axis. The program plots data points as XY coordinates. XY charts (also called scatterplots) are very good for displaying the relationship between variables.

Now see how choosing this chart type affects our temperature data.

1. Pull down the Gallery menu and select the XY (Scatter)... command. You'll see the XY (Scatter) dialog box shown in Figure 9.18.

2. The first option in this dialog box assigns a format that indicates data points with markers only; it does not use connecting lines. We know this format won't be appropriate for our purpose. Actually, Excel proposes another option anyway, number 2, which is exactly the same chart but with lines connecting the data points. Click OK to accept this selection. Figure 9.19 shows the result. The chart displays a legend box too, because you activated it for previous chart types.

This XY (scatter) chart resembles the line chart you created earlier. However, at the *tick marks* on the X axis (the evenly spaced marks, which indicate points on a scale), you see numbers representing, in this case, the five temperature readings, not the names of the days of the week when the temperatures were recorded.

XY (Scatter) Chart Formats

Here's an explanation of the options for the XY (scatter) dialog box:

- **Option 1**, the default format, shows markers only.

- **Option 2** adds lines connecting the markers in each series.

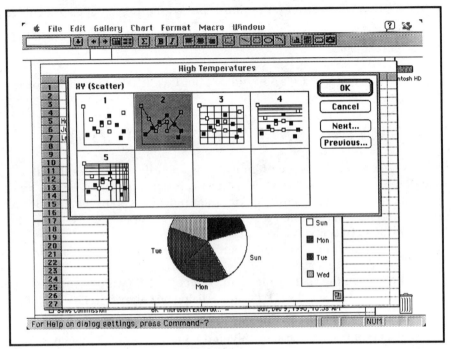

Figure 9.18: The XY (Scatter) dialog box

- **Option 3** displays markers with both horizontal and vertical gridlines.

- **Option 4** displays markers with semilogarithmic gridlines.

- **Option 5** displays markers with log-log gridlines.

TRYING A COMBINATION CHART

Combination charts let you compare data using different graphic methods, choosing from among the chart types you've already encountered, and even show data on different scales simultaneously, using up to four axes.

The default combination chart produces surprising results from our High Temperatures worksheet.

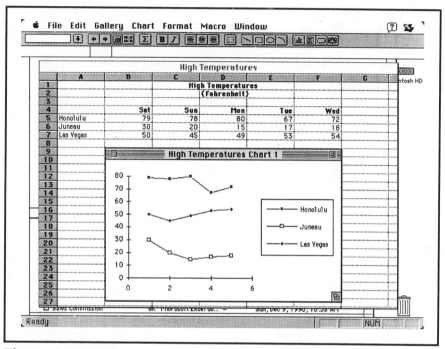

Figure 9.19: XY (Scatter) chart with format option 2 and a legend box added

1. Pull down the Gallery menu and select the Combination... command. The Combination dialog box appears, as shown in Figure 9.20.

2. Click OK to accept the default option 1 formatting. You'll see the chart displayed in Figure 9.21.

The default combination chart formatting offers an effective comparison of the temperatures in Las Vegas for the five-day period with those recorded for the other cities. The Las Vegas data series is shown as it would be on a line chart: by markers, with lines connecting the five values. The temperatures for the other two cities are represented by columns (vertical bars). The result makes Las Vegas the standard against which the other cities are compared. If that particular comparison was your goal, this chart type, with option 1 formatting, would be an excellent choice.

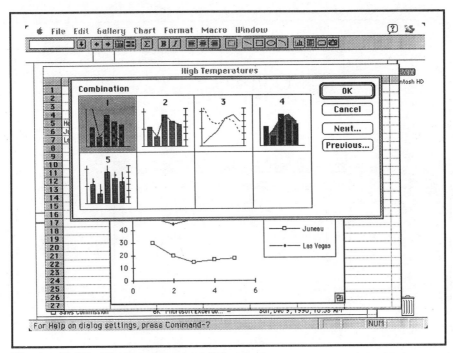

Figure 9.20: The Combination dialog box

Combination Chart Formats

Here is the list of options for the combination chart as shown in Figure 9.20:

- **Option 1**, the default format, is a column chart with a line chart overlaid.

- **Option 2** is the same as option 1, but with an independent Y-axis scale added.

- **Option 3** is the same as option 2, except that both charts are line charts.

- **Option 4** is an area chart with a column chart overlaid.

- **Option 5** is a column chart overlaid with a line chart that contains three data series. This chart is intended for showing high, low, and closing stock prices.

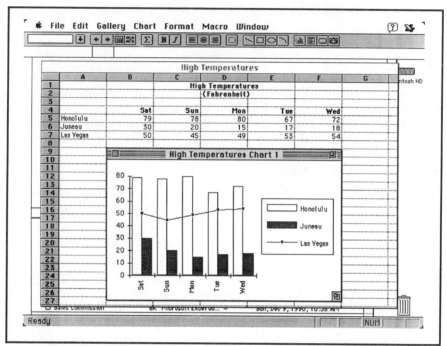

Figure 9.21: Combination chart with default formatting and a legend box

Notes on Using Combination Charts

Be aware that if you convert an existing chart into a combination chart with the Combination... command after you've added custom formatting (such as changing fonts or inserting background patterns), all of your custom formatting will be lost. To retain this formatting, instead create the combination chart with the Add Overlay command (located on the Chart menu). When you add an overlay chart to an existing chart, you're actually creating a combination chart, since you produce combination charts by superimposing one chart over another. (The Add Overlay command is explained in Chapter 11, along with more tips on creating combination charts.)

Note that you cannot turn a three-dimensional chart (discussed in the next sections) into a combination or overlay chart. Furthermore, if you've created a combination chart and then issue the Gallery menu command to turn the main chart into a 3-D chart, Excel automatically deletes the overlay in the chart and replots all data on the main chart alone.

TRYING A 3-D AREA CHART

Excel provides three-dimensional versions of four chart types you've already tried. These often do far more than, say, give a 3-D effect to the bars of a chart. They can add a different, related data series or category to the values displayed. What's more, as you'll learn in Chapter 11, you can rotate 3-D charts to obtain a variety of views of the data.

The first chart of this kind you'll try is the 3-D area chart.

1. Pull down the Gallery menu and select the 3-D Area... command. The 3-D Area dialog box shown in Figure 9.22 appears.

2. As the dialog box clearly shows, option 1 would display the three data series on top of one another. In fact, although you can't tell from the dialog box, option 1 would display the same cumulative temperature values on the Y axis that made a two-dimensional area

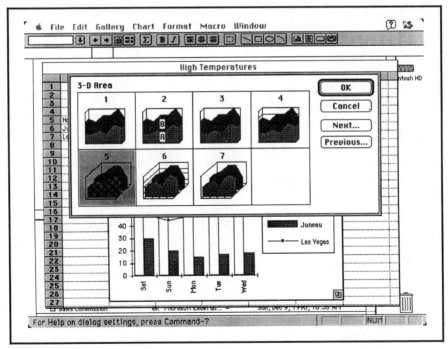

Figure 9.22: The 3-D Area dialog box

chart a poor choice for our data. Because of your previous selections, Excel proposes option 5, which displays the series individually. However, option 6 is even better; it adds gridlines that help identify the exact temperatures better. So click option 6.

3. Click OK. You'll see a 3-D area chart with a legend box that is not needed, since this three-dimensional format identifies the three data series at the right of the chart itself. (See Figure 9.23)

4. Pull down the Chart menu and select the Delete Legend command. The legend disappears.

As you can see, this choice might be appropriate, except that the Honolulu data series, with by far the highest temperatures, is displayed in front of the other series. The Honolulu values thus cover up almost all of the Juneau and Las Vegas data series, making the chart useless. However, if the Honolulu data were shown behind the others, the chart might be a good bet.

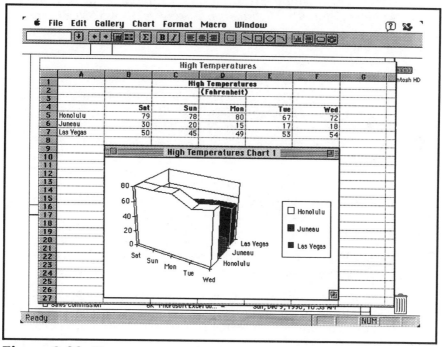

Figure 9.23: The temperature data as a 3-D area chart

Although you'll learn other ways to accomplish this kind of change in Chapter 10, you can easily try out the effect of moving the Honolulu data now. You'll move the Honolulu data series so it becomes the bottom, or last, row of data, instead of the first.

1. Click the worksheet outside of the chart area to close the chart window and make the chart an embedded part of the worksheet again. Then press ⌘-S, the shortcut to save the worksheet and chart in their present form. (You'll be using this version of the worksheet again in Chapter 10.)

2. Now make a new version of the worksheet in which to experiment with another sequence for the three data series. Pull down the File menu and select the Save As... command.

3. In the Save As dialog box, type a new name: **High Temperatures Rev** (for *Revised*).

4. Click the Save button. The name on the title bar of the worksheet window changes to *High Temperatures Rev*. Now you can experiment with another version of the worksheet without altering the original.

5. Drag to select the range A5:F5 (the Honolulu data series).

6. Pull down the Edit menu and select the Cut command. (Shortcut: Press ⌘-X.) The Honolulu data series will be surrounded by a marquee, if you're running under System 7; if you're using an earlier version of the operating system, the data series will disappear temporarily.

7. Click cell A8 to select it. Then pull down the Edit menu again and select the Paste command. (Shortcut: Press ⌘-V.) The Honolulu data series appears below the Las Vegas series. However, this change leaves row 5 blank.

8. Click any cell in row 5, pull down the Edit menu, and select the Delete... command to delete the row. (Shortcut: Press ⌘-K.)

9. You'll now see the Delete dialog box shown in Figure 9.24. You can select buttons to shift cells left or up after deleting selected cells or to delete an entire row or column. Be sure that the button selected

is Entire Row. Click OK. The extra row disappears. (This sequence helps accustom you to the uses of this Delete dialog box. However, a faster way of deleting the row is to select the row heading: the number 5 itself. Then, when you issue the Delete... command, you won't even see the dialog box; the row will simply disappear. If you make a mistake, you can bring back the row by selecting Undo Delete from the Edit menu.)

10. Click the embedded chart to select it. Then press ⌘-B, the shortcut to delete the chart. The chart disappears.

11. Drag to select the range A4:F7 (all of the data on the worksheet, with row and column titles) and click the chart icon to create a new embedded chart from the rearranged data.

12. Drag the range B9:F25 to define the area where you want the chart to appear. You'll now see the default column chart.

13. Press ⌘-S to save the worksheet with the new embedded chart.

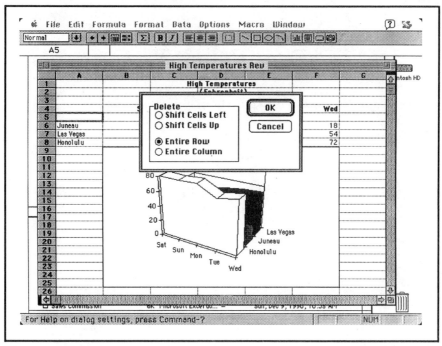

Figure 9.24: The Delete dialog box

14. Double-click the new chart to open a chart window. Then select the Gallery menu from the chart menus.

15. Select the 3-D Area... command.

16. From the 3-D Area dialog box, click option 6 to select it. Then click OK. The revised 3-D area chart appears.

17. Click outside the chart window to close it and embed the chart in the worksheet again. Press ⌘-S to save the worksheet and chart in their new configurations.

Your screen should now resemble Figure 9.25.

Now you can see all of each data series perfectly, since the series with larger values are behind those with smaller values. This kind of arrangement is usually good when you're working with 3-D charts. Of course, in some instances changing the order of the various series is not possible because the data series must appear in alphabetical order on the worksheet, or must

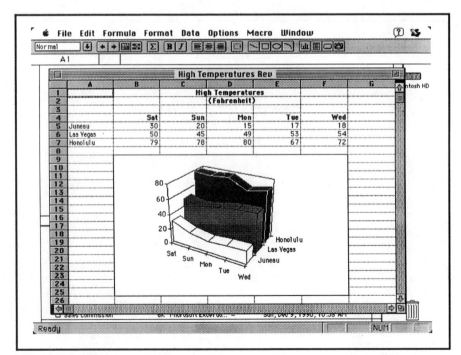

Figure 9.25: Revised 3-D area chart

be shown in groups, or must meet some other organizational criteria. However, even in these situations you can change the plotting order of the series, as you'll discover in Chapter 10. You may also be able to rotate the 3-D chart to obtain an unobstructed view of a hidden series, as discussed in Chapter 11.

Note that the 3-D chart option in our example identifies the cities, the temperatures, and the days of the week without using a legend box.

3-D Area Chart Formats

Here is an explanation of the options for a 3-D area chart, shown in Figure 9.22:

- **Option 1**, the default format, shows all data series as part of one area, with 3-D markers. The top of the Y-axis scale displays a value greater than or equal to the total of the largest values in all series.

- **Option 2** is like option 1, except that Excel labels the areas of individual data series.

- **Option 3** is like option 1, except that Excel extends drop lines to the markers on the X axis.

- **Option 4** is like option 1, except that Excel shows gridlines behind the data series in blank areas.

- **Option 5** plots each series individually.

- **Option 6** is the same as option 5, except that Excel adds gridlines.

- **Option 7** is the same as option 5, except that Excel connects gridlines with axes only.

TRYING A 3-D LINE CHART

Like a 3-D area chart, the 3-D line chart can display categories as well as data series without using a legend box (in our temperature examples, remember that the categories are the days of the week that accompany each data series). The data series themselves, shown as lines on the normal two-dimensional line chart, appear as three-dimensional ribbons. This kind of display is particularly helpful when the individual lines that represent data series cross because they contain similar values. The 3-D display makes it easier for the eye to differentiate between the series.

Turn the 3-D area chart into a 3-D line chart now.

1. Double-click the chart to open the chart window again, pull down the Gallery menu, and select the 3-D Line... command. You'll see the 3-D Line dialog box shown in Figure 9.26. The second option should already be highlighted, since it matches most closely the attributes of the previous chart you created with the temperature data.

2. Click OK. The result is the 3-D line chart displayed in Figure 9.27.

This chart is easy to understand and represents the data well. Of course, the addition of explanatory text such as a heading and a title for the Y axis would add to its readability.

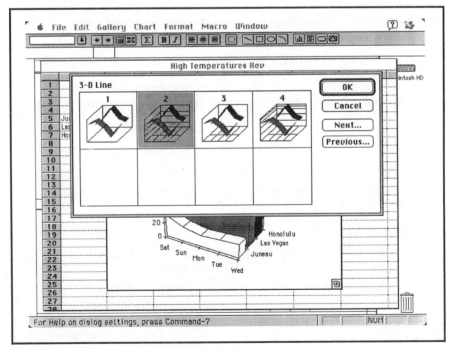

Figure 9.26: The 3-D Line dialog box

3-D Line Chart Formats

These are the 3-D line chart options shown in Figure 9.26:

- **Option 1**, the default format, is a basic 3-D line plot.

- **Option 2** is the same as option 1, with gridlines added.

- **Option 3** is the same as option 1, except it includes X-axis and Y-axis gridlines only.

- **Option 4** is the same as option 1, with logarithmic gridlines added.

TRYING A 3-D COLUMN CHART

A 3-D column chart is good for comparing individual data points, which this format emphasizes more than it does the flow of the data. Its

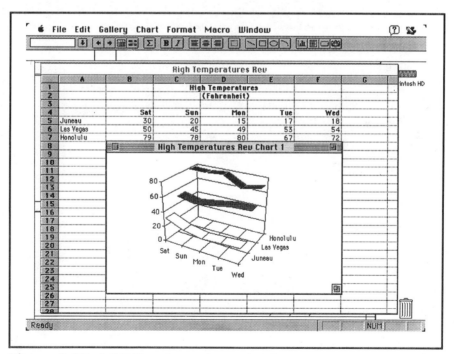

Figure 9.27: A 3-D line chart using option 2

advantages over a two-dimensional column chart (which it shares with other 3-D area charts and with line charts) are that it shows categories without the need for a legend box, and it can be rotated to change the viewing angle (discussed in Chapter 11).

Take a quick look at this chart type:

1. Pull down the Gallery menu and select the 3-D Column... command. You'll see the 3-D Column dialog box shown in Figure 9.28. Option 6 should already be highlighted, since it most closely matches the format used previously for the 3-D line chart.

2. Click OK. You'll see the chart shown in Figure 9.29.

This chart does not display temperature trends nearly as well as the 3-D area and line charts you created. Instead, it emphasizes the daily readings.

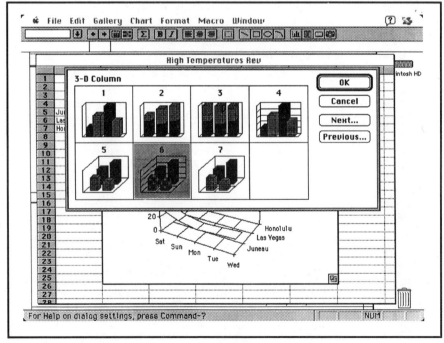

Figure 9.28: The 3-D Column dialog box

3-D Column Chart Formats

Here are the 3-D column chart options shown in Figure 9.28:

- **Option 1**, the default format, is a simple chart with three-dimensional columns but no category labels.

- **Option 2**, the stacked format, stacks the columns on top of one another, with a Y axis scaled to accommodate the total of the largest individual values shown in the various data series. This format does not include category labels (unless you add a legend box).

- **Option 3**, the 100 percent stacked format, adjusts the sizes of stacked columns so that each column equals 100 percent of a category, and the data series divisions indicate the percentage of the whole contributed by each series. This format does not include category labels (unless you add a legend box).

- **Option 4** is the same as option 1, with gridlines added.

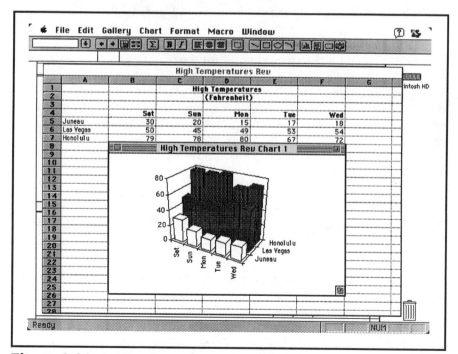

Figure 9.29: A 3-D column chart using option 6

- **Option 5** shows individual 3-D columns for each data point, with category labels added.

- **Option 6** is the same as option 5, with gridlines added.

- **Option 7** is the same as option 5, except it includes X-axis and Y-axis gridlines only.

TRYING A 3-D PIE CHART

A 3-D pie chart has the same advantages and disadvantages as a two-dimensional pie chart, except that the 3-D appearance of the pie places additional emphasis on the front slices. The formatting options are exactly the same as for a two-dimensional pie chart.

Look at this final chart type now:

1. Pull down the Gallery menu and select the 3-D Pie... command.

2. Click to select option 5 to add labels.

3. Click OK. You'll see the chart shown in Figure 9.30.

This chart shows how much temperature each day contributed to the temperature total for the city of Juneau for the five days for which data was collected (a completely meaningless chart for temperature data). If you were still using the original High Temperatures worksheet—which displays the Honolulu data series in the first data row—this chart would have been exactly like the two-dimensional pie chart you created in Figure 9.17, except for the three-dimensional appearance of the slices. Since Juneau is the first data series in the High Temperatures Rev worksheet, that series is depicted here instead.

CREATING AN UNEMBEDDED CHART

If you want to create a chart that is not embedded in a worksheet, you have two choices:

- You can pull down the File menu, select the New... command, highlight the word Chart to select it, and click OK. Excel then

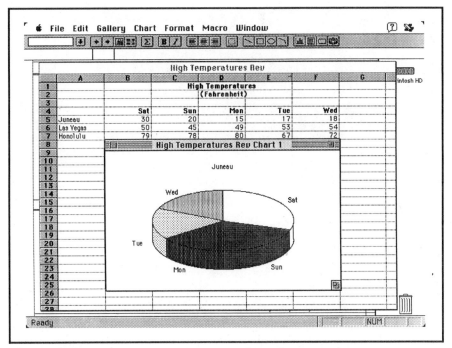

Figure 9.30: A 3-D pie chart using option 5 formatting

creates a separate chart, not embedded in the worksheet, using the data from the worksheet.

- You can convert an embedded chart into a separate chart by double-clicking the chart to open a chart window, pulling down the File menu, selecting either the Save or Save As... command, giving the chart a name in the resulting dialog box, and clicking OK to save the new version.

A chart you create in either of these ways will still be linked to the data in the worksheet.

Be sure to retain the original High Temperatures worksheet. You'll use it again in Chapters 10 and 11.

SUMMARY

You learned how Excel makes automatic selections in plotting data. Then you tried out all of the chart types available, with some variations in automatic formatting options, and discovered the purposes for which each type is suited.

In the next chapter you learn how to edit charts and add custom formatting.

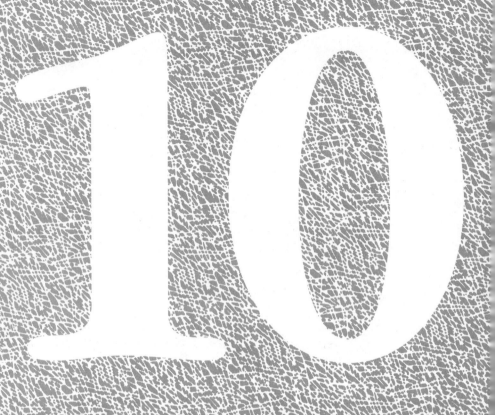

Chapter

10

Editing and
Formatting
Charts

You can perform almost any kind of editing or formatting operation on an Excel chart. You can add a border or a colored background, change typefaces, switch the order in which data series are plotted, and even assign drawings to represent the subject matter of the data. For example, a chart showing real estate sales could display a series of small houses for each data series instead of a bar or column.

This chapter explores some of the editing and formatting possibilities for charts.

EDITING DATA SERIES

In Chapter 9 you created two versions of the High Temperatures worksheet. You created the second version primarily to change the order in which the series were plotted: to place the large values of the Honolulu series behind the other series on 3-D charts. Your first task in this chapter is to investigate data-series editing—an often easier alternative to changing or rearranging worksheet data to accomplish your goals.

1. If you have any Excel files loaded, close them, so that only the program itself is in memory.

2. Open the original High Temperatures worksheet. If you saved it as requested in Chapter 9, you'll see it displayed with an embedded 3-D area chart. The Honolulu data series will be in the foreground, hiding most of the other two series.

3. Double-click within the chart to open it as a chart window. It now acquires its own title bar.

4. Pull down the Chart menu and select the Edit Series... command. This action opens the Edit Series dialog box shown in Figure 10.1.

USING THE EDIT SERIES... COMMAND

The Edit Series dialog box contains several elements. First, you'll notice a list box on the left. Here the three data series in the chart are listed

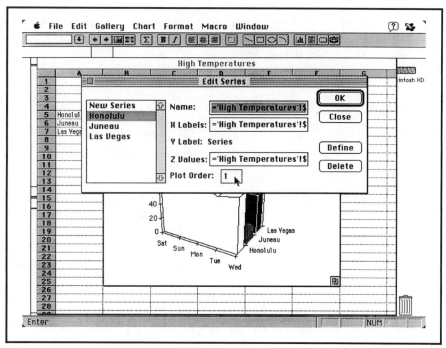

Figure 10.1: The Edit Series dialog box

by name. The heading above these names is New Series. You select this option to add another existing series to the chart. In the center of the dialog box, you identify the new series and specify the locations of its X-axis labels and, if appropriate, its Z-axis values, either by clicking cells in the worksheet to add them to the series formula or by typing the name of the series wanted. (The Z-axis is the third axis present in 3-D charts.)

The OK, Close, and Delete buttons on the right serve their usual functions. You click one of these to accept your changes or entries and close the dialog box, close the dialog box without making any changes, or delete a highlighted data series. You click the Define button, also in this area, to enter a series definition or your changes. After you click Define, you remain in the dialog box so you can make additional changes.

The Edit Series dialog box contains one more item: *Plot Order*. Here is where you can quickly rearrange the order in which Excel plots the data series on the chart.

1. Highlight the Honolulu series in the list box.

2. Click the Plot Order box just after the number 1, which the box now displays. A flashing vertical line appears, indicating that the box is waiting for data entry.

3. Press the Delete key to backspace and delete the number 1.

4. Type the number 3 in its place.

5. Click OK.

6. Click outside the chart window to close the window so the new plot order can take effect.

The dialog box closes, and Excel displays the Honolulu series behind the other series—an effect that took you 16 steps to achieve in Chapter 9 by making a new version of the worksheet and changing the order of the data series on the worksheet itself. This change made in the Edit Series dialog box appears only on the chart and in no way affects the content or arrangement of the worksheet itself.

USING THE PATTERNS... COMMAND

If you have a color monitor, you may discern another problem with the 3-D area chart displayed. The chart deals with temperatures, yet the default color assignments display the data series with the highest temperatures in blue and the series with the lowest temperatures in red.

To make the colors fit our usual conventions for hot and cold, let's change them. (If you have a monochrome monitor, you still can do this exercise. Instead of seeing the actual colors in the dialog box described, you'll see the names of the colors, provided you selected color in the control panel. You can select the colors by name only and still have them printed correctly on a color printer.)

1. Double-click the chart to open a chart window again.

2. Click the Honolulu data series. It becomes surrounded by white handles. If the handles were black, they would indicate that the series is an object that you can change directly. White handles indicate that the series is selected, but you can change it only indirectly, usually through menus.

3. Pull down the Format menu and select the Patterns... command. You'll see the Patterns dialog box, which we'll discuss in more detail in a moment. Press the down arrow to the right of the Foreground box in the Area section of the dialog box. A display of colors drops down.

4. Change the current foreground color displayed, which is blue, to red, as illustrated in Figure 10.2.

5. Click OK. The Honolulu data series appears in red instead of blue.

6. Now the chart has two red series, since Juneau is red too. Repeat steps 2 through 5 with the Juneau data series selected. This time, change the Foreground color from red to blue.

7. Click outside the chart area to close the chart window. Then press ⌘-S to save the revised High Temperatures worksheet, preserving the new plotting order for the three data series and the new color assignments.

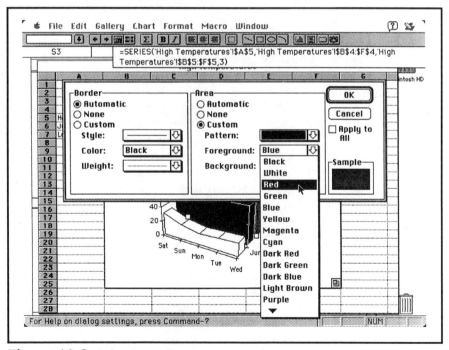

Figure 10.2: Selecting colors on a monochrome monitor

PATTERNS DIALOG BOX OPTIONS

The options the Patterns dialog box displays depend on the object or objects selected. Let's look at the options available in each section.

Patterns Area Options

You use the patterns area buttons to control the type and placement of patterns used in your chart. Excel provides these options:

- **Automatic button**. Press this button to assign contrasting colors (or patterns, on a monochrome display) to selected objects.

- **None button**. Select this button to remove all patterns and colors from selected objects.

- **Custom button**. This button must be selected before you can use the remaining three Area options. However, choosing any of these options (Pattern, Foreground, or Background) selects the Custom button automatically.

- **Pattern box**. Press the down arrow to the right of this box to display a long list of available patterns to apply to selected objects. If you choose a foreground or background color (other than white) from the Foreground or Background box below, the patterns appear in that color. If you choose both foreground and background colors, the pattern appears in a combination of those two colors. (For example, if the foreground choice is red and the background choice is yellow, a pattern of stripes appears in the Pattern box as red and yellow stripes. If the foreground and background colors are red and yellow but you select a dot pattern that would otherwise appear as a gray, the Pattern box displays orange, mixing the two colors equally. This mixing capability means that you can create almost any color you want by combining Pattern, Foreground, and Background options.)

- **Foreground and Background boxes**. Pressing the down arrow next to one of these boxes displays colors you can choose for the foreground or background of selected objects. As noted in the preceding discussion of the Pattern box, you can combine a pattern and foreground and background colors to create an almost unlimited variety of colors and effects. (If you're using a monochrome display, as mentioned earlier, you'll see the names of the colors in the Foreground and Background boxes instead of the colors themselves. However, they will be printed correctly if you use a color printer.)

Patterns Border Options

The Border section of the Patterns dialog box allows you to place a border around selected objects. (For example, in the 3-D area chart currently displayed, you could place a border around any data series or around the chart itself.) The Border section contains Automatic, None, and Custom buttons with the same functions as the buttons with these names in the Area section. Here's an explanation of the other options:

- **Style box**. Press the arrow to the right of the box to pull down a display of styles you can choose for a border. The styles include a solid line and various dashed, broken, and patterned lines.

- **Color box**. Assign a color to a border using the same procedures as for the other boxes.

- **Weight box**. Assign a weight or thickness to a selected border using the same procedures as for the other boxes.

Other Patterns Dialog Box Features

The right side of the Patterns dialog box contains the familiar OK and Cancel buttons. This area of the dialog box also includes two other features:

- **Apply to All box**. Excel displays this box only if a selected object is a data point, data series, or related text. If you click to activate the box, Excel applies color, pattern, and border choices you've made for the selected object to all data points in the series.

- **Sample box**. Excel displays the result of your choices in this box before you click OK to apply them to a selected object.

Figure 10.3 shows custom selections made in the Patterns dialog box and how they look when applied to the Juneau data series.

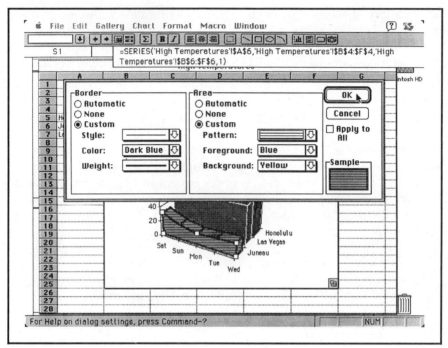

Figure 10.3: Custom Patterns selections for data series

DIRECTLY EDITING
DATA SERIES FORMULAS

Look again at Figure 10.3. The formula bar displays a formula using the SERIES() function. Excel uses this function only in charts. The program uses a separate formula with the SERIES() function to plot each data series. The formula is created automatically when you start a new chart and is modified automatically when you use menu options to change the plotting of the data series through menu options.

For example, look at the last argument of the formula, just inside the closing parenthesis: the number 1. A number in this position in a data series formula indicates the plotting order of that particular data series. Recall that you used a menu option to change the Honolulu series from the first to be plotted to the last (so its large values would appear behind the others on the chart). This action made Juneau number 1 in the plotting order. You could also have changed the plotting order of these data series by manually editing each data series formula.

Figure 10.4 identifies the elements of the series formula for the Juneau data series.

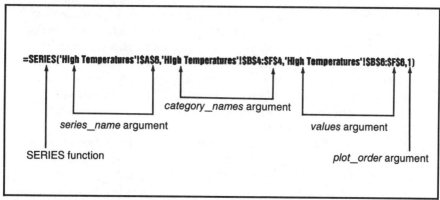

Figure 10.4: Formula for Juneau data series with SERIES() function arguments labeled

You edit a data series formula directly (rather than through menus) in this manner:

1. Double-click the chart to display it in a chart window (unless, of course, the chart window is already open).

2. Click the data series displayed on the chart to select it. It becomes surrounded by white handles (indicating that it is selected but cannot be edited directly). At the same time, Excel displays the series formula for that data series in the formula bar.

3. Click within the formula in the formula bar to select the point where you want to make a change. A flashing vertical line appears at that point in the formula, and the formula enter and cancel boxes appear in their usual positions.

4. Make the changes you want and click the enter box to enter your changes.

5. Click the chart outside the data series itself to deselect the series. The white handles surrounding the data series disappear.

SERIES( ) Function Arguments

Here is an explanation of the arguments used with the SERIES( ) function.

- **The *series_name* argument**. This argument tells Excel where to find the name of the data series. In the case of the Juneau data series, the argument consists of (after the opening parenthesis that indicates the beginning of the argument sequence) the name of the High Temperatures worksheet enclosed in single quotation marks and followed by an exclamation point, then an absolute reference to the cell where the name *Juneau* appears, and then a comma to complete the argument and separate it from the one that follows. If you're creating a formula yourself (rather than using an Excel default formula), you can eliminate this argument if you don't want the data series labeled. You can also type the name of a different worksheet before the exclamation point or apply a name to the data series that doesn't appear on any worksheet by entering the new name; both worksheet and data series names must be enclosed in quotation marks. This argument is where Excel obtains the information for a chart legend box.

- **The *category_names* argument**. This argument lists the name of the worksheet that contains the category names. The worksheet name appears enclosed in quotation marks and followed by an exclamation point. An absolute reference to the worksheet range that contains the category names, followed by another comma, completes the argument.

- **The *values* argument**. This argument is constructed exactly like the category names argument, except that the worksheet range refers to the location of the values (or numbers) to be plotted for the data series.

- **The *plot_order* argument**. This number, which follows the last comma in the formula, determines the order in which Excel plots the various data series. As mentioned earlier, the Juneau data series is currently number 1 (plotted in front of the other series in the 3-D area chart), so a 1 appears as the argument in this particular formula.

Of course, the formula must end with a closing parenthesis after the last argument.

Excel treats absolute references in chart formulas differently from those in worksheet formulas. If you add or delete a row or column in a worksheet referenced in a chart formula, Excel updates absolute references to ranges automatically to reflect their new locations.

TIP

You can manually edit chart formulas that use the SERIES() function to quickly insert linked data from two or more worksheets into a chart. Simply add the appropriate arguments, providing the location of category names and values.

FORMATTING YOUR CHARTS

Excel provides many ways for you to make your charts more attractive, more distinctive, or more indicative of the subject matter they represent. You learn about some of these options in this section of the chapter.

MAKING A PICTOGRAM

Beginning with version 3.0 of Excel, you can easily create *pictograms*. (Excel manuals refer to pictograms as *picture charts*.) Pictograms are charts that represent data series with graphic images that reflect the nature of the series. For example, instead of using ordinary vertical bars in a column chart that reports sales revenues, a pictogram might display stacked bags of money.

Very few graphics or spreadsheet programs give you the capability of creating this type of chart. In Excel you can make a pictogram from any two-dimensional, bar, or line chart. (In a line chart, you do this by replacing the data markers with graphic images, rather than by altering the lines themselves.)

Where do you obtain these graphic images? You can create them within Excel by using the drawing tools on the Toolbar, you can create them in another application, or you can use commercial clip art—you can use any graphic on which you can perform a cut-and-paste operation through the clipboard.

TIP

Many people unsuccessfully try to copy artwork to the clipboard
that is in EPS (encapsulated PostScript) format. However, copying
EPS files is not difficult to do. EPS files are composed of two elements: QuickDraw code to make the image appear on the screen
of your Macintosh properly and PostScript code to print the
image. To copy these ''two-headed'' files to the clipboard, just
hold down the Option key as you select the Copy command from
the Edit menu.

Try making a pictogram based on the High Temperatures worksheet.
You'll save an independent copy of the chart currently embedded in the
worksheet, convert it to column chart format, create a simple graphic image
with Excel's drawing tools, and import your image into the chart.

Creating an Unembedded Column Chart

The first step in creating your pictogram is to create an unembedded
column chart.

1. With the High Temperatures worksheet open, double-click the chart
   to open a chart window.

2. Pull down the File menu and select the Save As... command (or
   press ⌘-S). The Save As dialog box appears.

3. Name the chart **Pictogram** and click the Save button.

4. Your screen is unchanged. To see the new Pictogram chart, you
   must now load it. Pull down the File menu and select the Open...
   command.

5. Scroll the list box in the Open Document dialog box until you see the
   name Pictogram. Double-click the name to open the chart. The chart
   appears directly in front of the chart embedded in the worksheet.

6. Pull down the Gallery menu and select the Column... command.

7. In the column dialog box, select the first option, a simple standard
   column chart, and click OK. Excel converts the 3-D area chart to a
   two-dimensional column chart.

8. Pull down the Chart menu and select the Add Legend command. A legend box appears, surrounded by black selection handles.

9. Click just under the Pictogram title bar to deselect the legend box. Your screen should resemble Figure 10.5.

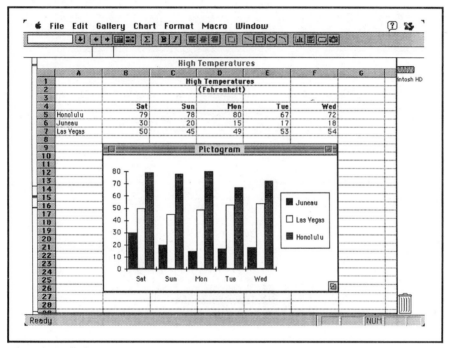

Figure 10.5: Pictogram chart in column format

Drawing an Image of the Sun

Now you need to activate the worksheet again so you can draw the graphic images to be used. You'll be creating a *pictograph* of the sun. (What symbol could be more appropriate for a temperature chart?)

1. Click the worksheet to activate it. The Pictogram chart disappears from view, behind the worksheet.

2. Find a blank area on the worksheet (scroll down if necessary) and click the oval tool on the Toolbar to activate the tool.

3. Hold down the Shift key and drag to draw a small oval. Holding down the Shift key constrains the oval tool, causing it to draw a perfect circle, which you can use to represent the sun.

4. With the drawing of the sun complete, click the line tool and drag to create a diagonal line representing a ray. Repeat this operation until your little sun is surrounded by rays and looks something like Figure 10.6.

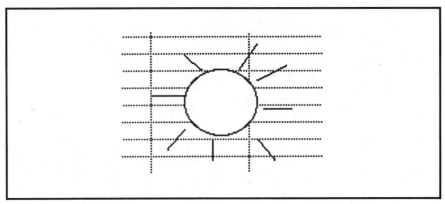

Figure 10.6: A drawing of the sun

Sizing and
Duplicating the Sun Pictograph

With the sun graphic complete, your next task is to make it the proper size. Then you need to make two slightly different copies to distinguish each data series in the Pictogram chart with a recognizably different symbol.

1. To group the circle and the lines that make up the sun and its rays so they become one symbol, click the selection tool to activate it and drag to create a rectangle around the sun and its rays, thereby selecting all of these objects.

2. Pull down the Format menu and select the Group command. The sun and its rays now are bordered by one group of six handles, indicating that you can consider them as one object.

3. Drag the sun object by one of its corner angles to reduce it in size until it's approximately the width of one of the vertical bars on the Pictogram column chart. (You can also move a drawn object anywhere you like by dragging it; it's not attached to a cell.)

4. Pull down the Edit menu and select the Copy command. (Shortcut: Press ⌘-C.) Excel copies the grouped sun image to the clipboard.

5. Click a nearby blank cell on the worksheet to select it. Then pull down the Edit menu again and select the Paste command. (Shortcut: Press ⌘-V.) A copy of the sun symbol with its rays appears at this location in the same reduced size.

6. Repeat step 5 so you have a total of three sun symbols.

7. With the last symbol still selected, pull down the Format menu and select the Patterns... command.

8. In the Patterns dialog box, select a gray pattern and click OK. The dialog box closes, and Excel displays the selected sun image in gray.

9. Click to select another sun symbol on the worksheet and repeat steps 7 and 8, except this time select black as the pattern. Your worksheet should now have a white sun, a black sun, and a gray sun, as in Figure 10.7.

10. Press ⌘-S to save the changes to the worksheet.

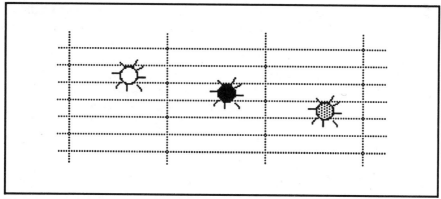

Figure 10.7: Worksheet with three sun symbols

Applying Symbols to Data Series

All that remains for you to do is apply each of the three symbols to one of the data series in the Pictogram chart.

1. Click the black sun to select it. Then press ⌘-C to copy the black sun to the clipboard.

2. Pull down the Window menu and select the Pictogram chart to display and activate the chart again.

3. Click any of the vertical bars representing Juneau in the column chart. This action activates the entire Juneau data series and places white boxes in three of the bars in the series.

4. Press ⌘-V to paste the sun into the Juneau data series as its data point symbol. Excel replaces each bar in the series with an elongated sun the same height as the bar that was formerly in its place.

5. This elongated single symbol would be appropriate for some graphic images. For example, if the image was a drawing of a man, each man would vary in height according to the value he represented. However, in this example, another option will work better. Pull down the Format menu for the chart and select the Patterns... command. You'll see a dialog box quite different from those you've used with this command before (see Figure 10.8). This Picture Format dialog box allows you to stretch the single image (using Stretch, the default option, which is already in use), to stack the image (displaying a series of images stacked on top of one another to achieve the height represented by each value), or to stack and scale the image (defining the unit represented by each symbol stacked on a bar; for example, each symbol could represent 1,000 workers or $10 million dollars). If you want to apply the same symbol to all data series in your chart, you click the Apply to All box at the right side of the dialog box.

6. Select Stack and click OK.

7. Click to activate the worksheet again and repeat steps 1, 2, 3, and 4, except this time apply the gray sun symbol to the Las Vegas data series. (Excel selects the Stack option automatically for all data series now, since you selected it for the first one.)

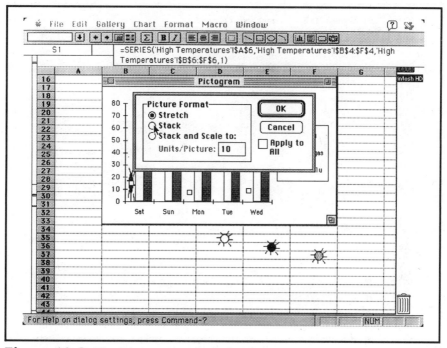

Figure 10.8: The Picture Format dialog box

8. Activate the worksheet once more and repeat steps 1, 2, 3, and 4 a final time, this time applying the white sun to the Honolulu data series.

9. Click under the Pictogram title bar to deselect the data series. This action completes the pictogram (except for adding titles and other enhancements). The chart should now resemble Figure 10.9.

As you can see, the city with the lowest temperatures (Juneau, Alaska) is represented by a series of black, or very much occluded, suns. Las Vegas, with higher temperatures, is represented by gray suns (possibly hiding behind thin cloud cover?). Honolulu, with the highest temperatures, is represented by clear, white suns symbolizing a sunny, hot day.

Press ⌘-S to save the changes in the Pictogram chart. Then get ready to explore additional formatting options for this chart.

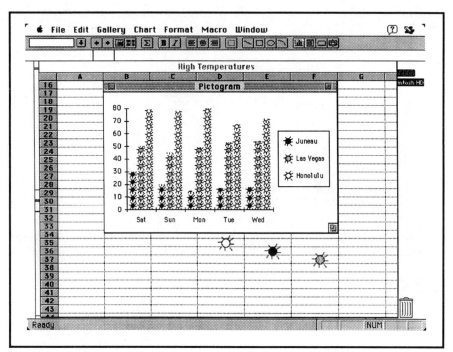

Figure 10.9: The completed pictogram

ENHANCING THE PICTOGRAM

You already know that a chart window displays some menus and options that differ from those in a worksheet window, and you've used a few of these options that change the appearance of a chart—most notably the chart type options on the Gallery menu. Certainly, switching from a column chart to a pie chart results in a different look for your data. However, Excel lets you change less obvious features too.

Making Changes through the Chart Menu

Pull down the Chart menu (see Figure 10.10) and look at the options. Using these options and their additional commands, you can customize your charts in numerous ways to enhance their readability and their capacity for conveying precise and varied information.

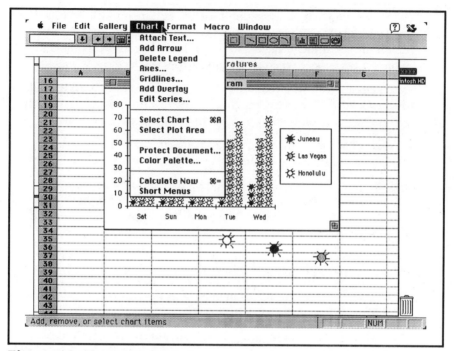

Figure 10.10: The Chart menu

Here is a brief summary of the Chart menu options:

- **Attach Text...** This command displays the Attach Text dialog box. Here you can click the Chart Title button to place a title on your chart. You can also add a label to the value (Y) axis, the category (X) axis, or a data series (even a data point, in line charts). For example, you could label the Y axis of the Pictogram chart with a heading indicating that the values (from 0 to 80) on this axis are temperature readings in degrees Fahrenheit. (Actually, the meaning of these particular Y-axis values should be obvious if the chart is properly titled.) You can also attach text to overlay axes, as discussed in Chapter 11.

- **Add Arrow**. This command displays an arrow on the chart, with a black handle at each end. You drag either of these handles to rotate the arrow or change its length. You drag the arrow shaft to move the arrow to a new location. An arrow is normally used in combination with a note to highlight some aspect of a chart. You must select an arrow to remove it, but you don't use the Edit menu's Clear command or the Delete key to complete this procedure; instead, you must pull down the Chart menu again and select the Delete Arrow command, which appears only when an existing arrow is selected.

- **Add Legend**. You've already used this command to make a legend box appear on a chart. When an existing legend box is selected, the Delete Legend command replaces the Add Legend command.

- **Axes...** This command brings up a small dialog box where you can click boxes to specify whether or not an X axis or a Y axis is displayed.

- **Gridlines...** This command displays a dialog box with boxes to click to display major and minor gridlines on either or both axes. (*Minor gridlines* are additional gridlines that appear between the major data points.)

- **Add Overlay**. Choose this command to add an overlay to a chart. Overlays are discussed in Chapter 11.

- **Edit Series...** This command manipulates the data series on a chart, as explained in detail earlier in this chapter.

- **Select Chart**. This command provides an alternative method of selecting the entire chart area. You can also select the entire chart area by clicking the chart just outside the plot area.

- **Select Plot Area**. This command provides an alternative method of selecting the entire plot area of the chart. You can also accomplish this goal by clicking anywhere inside the plot area of the chart so long as the pointer is not resting on a specific feature of the chart.

- **Protect Document...** Use this command to apply a password to the chart or its related windows, so that a user must enter the password to change the chart.

- **Color Palette...** This command lets you apply colors to objects and to mix new colors. For details, see Chapter 24.

- **Calculate Now**. Use this command to recalculate worksheet data and replot displayed values accordingly. Use this command only if you have previously switched Excel from automatic recalculation to manual recalculation by using the Calculation... command on the worksheet Options menu. Calculate Now is useful when you change values on the chart that affect other values (see the next section, "Changing Data Values").

- **Short Menus**. This command changes the display of chart menus to short menus with only basic options (to help avoid confusion for users who do not need advanced options). When short menus are displayed, the item in this position on the Chart menu is Full Menus. Select Full Menus to toggle the display to full menus, the type used throughout this book.

Changing Data Values

In addition to changes you can make to charts for the sake of aesthetics or clarity, you can actually alter the values depicted on two-dimensional line, bar, and column charts by dragging data points on the charts themselves. If a supporting worksheet includes formulas for the calculation of results from several series of values, this dragging capability provides an easy way to play "what-if" because it lets you try out different values and observe the results right on the chart.

Follow this procedure:

1. Make sure the worksheet that contains the data displayed on the chart is open. If the worksheet is not open, when you try to resize a data point, you'll see the warning message shown in Figure 10.11.

2. Open the chart you want to alter (if it's not already open).

3. Hold down the ⌘ key as you click to select the bar or line data point you want to change: for instance, the Sunday temperature for Las Vegas. In a bar or column chart, the individual bar will be framed by four white handles, with a single black handle displayed between the two handles at the end of the bar (see Figure 10.12). In a line chart, the line will be marked by a white handle at a data point other than the one you clicked, and the data point you clicked will change into a black handle.

4. Release the ⌘ key and drag the black handle to increase or decrease the value of the data point you selected. The worksheet changes automatically to reflect the new value. (If you're playing "what-if" and don't want to retain changes of this sort permanently, just close the files when you're finished without saving them. Don't save the changes you made in this example.)

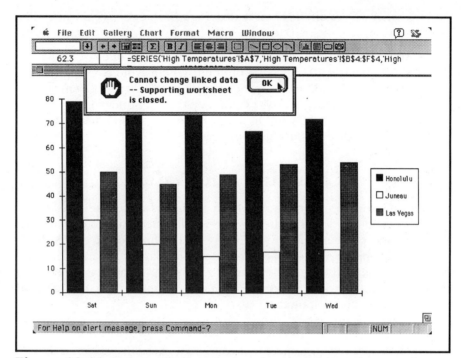

Figure 10.11: Message displayed when the user tries to change a chart value with the supporting worksheet closed

Note that you cannot drag a data point so that it represents a value larger than the highest value displayed on the Y axis.

Also, dragging a data point that has itself been calculated by a formula automatically activates the supporting open worksheet and displays the Goal Seek dialog box accessed from the worksheet Formula menu. Excel assumes that you now want to perform a goal-seeking operation and adjust formula variables to reach a target value. Goal seeking is the subject of Chapter 25.

If your worksheet is set for manual recalculation (see the previous section) and you change a value that affects other values, don't forget to issue the Calculate Now command on the Chart menu.

Making Changes through the Format Menu

The options available on the Format menu (those options not displayed in dimmed text) change according to what you select before you pull

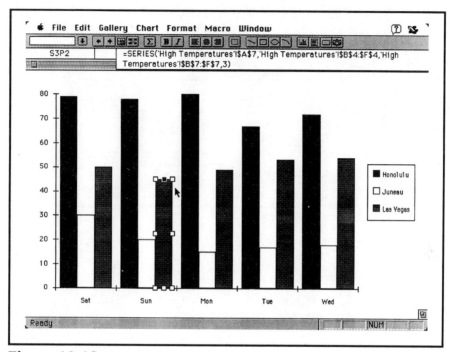

Figure 10.12: Data point selected for change of value

down the menu. For example, if you select a group of bars that represents a data series, the Font... command is dimmed because, obviously, you can't assign a typeface to a chart element that contains no text. The contents of the dialog boxes accessed through this menu vary too, again according to the object you select before you issue a command.

One option on the Format menu is the Patterns... command. You've already worked with different Patterns dialog boxes. You'll work with yet another Patterns dialog box right now, as you begin to reformat the Pictogram chart using a variety of options on this menu.

1. With the Pictogram chart still on the screen, click the Y axis (the vertical axis that displays the scale of temperatures) to select it. A white box appears at each end of the axis to indicate that it is selected.

2. Pull down the Format menu and select the first option, the Patterns... command. You'll see the dialog box shown in Figure 10.13.

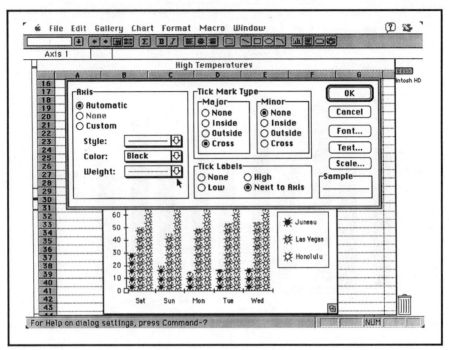

Figure 10.13: The Patterns dialog box for the Y axis

Note that this box contains some options that you haven't seen previously. You can specify the kind and style of the tick marks that denote points on the axis, as well as the location of their related labels. You can click one of the buttons at the right—under the usual OK and Cancel buttons—to move directly from this dialog box to the Font, Text, or Scale dialog boxes.

3. While the Patterns dialog box is still open, move the pointer into the Axis area of the box and click the arrow beside the Weight option. A display of line widths drops down for your selection.

4. Select the next-to-widest line (the one next to the bottom of this display) to make the Y axis more prominent. You'll be selecting this line width (a heavier line) for other elements of the chart too.

5. Click the Font... box at the right of the dialog box to display the Font dialog box shown in Figure 10.14. Here you can select any typeface installed on your system; change the size, style, and color

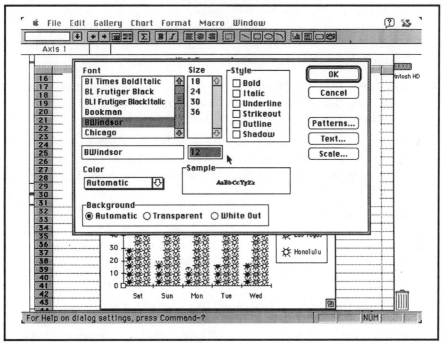

Figure 10.14: The Font dialog box

of any font; and select a font background format from among three
options: Transparent (which lets other chart elements show
through), White Out (which masks out other chart elements, such
as the Y axis itself, in the immediate vicinity of a font character),
and Automatic (which lets Excel choose between Transparent and
White Out so that all chart elements are displayed as well as possible). This dialog box also has OK and Cancel buttons, plus buttons
to switch to Patterns, Text, and Scale dialog boxes. In addition, the
Font dialog box provides a handy Sample box, which displays a
previous sample of any font selected.

6. Scroll the Font list box in the Font dialog box and choose a typeface
   that is easy to read and relatively bold: for instance, our example
   uses Windsor Bold.

7. In the Size box, select or type **12**, for 12-point type. This type size
   makes the text slightly larger than the default 10-point size. (A point
   in the printing industry is a measurement signifying approximately

$1/72$ of an inch.) Use the default settings for the other options (unless you need to click Bold in the style box to make your typeface appear in boldface; Windsor Bold is one of many typefaces in which the bold attribute is included in the design and need not be applied separately).

8. Click OK. The dialog box closes. The axis line becomes darker and wider, and the numbers on the Y axis change to the bold typeface you chose.

9. Repeat steps 1 through 8 to reformat the X axis. Click to select the X axis. Then use the Patterns and Font dialog boxes to make the axis line heavier and to change the font to the same one you used for the Y axis.

10. Reformat the legend box in the same manner. Click to select the legend box. In its Patterns dialog box, make the border line heavier and select the Shadow box to add a drop-shadow to the legend box (see Figure 10.15). In the Font dialog box, change to the bolder font you've been using, again choosing the 12-point size.

11. Let's add gridlines, so readers can more easily see the temperature readings in the data series. Click under the Pictogram title bar to deselect the legend box. Then pull down the Chart menu and select the Gridlines... command. You'll see the Gridlines dialog box shown in Figure 10.16.

12. Click the Value (Y) Axis Major Gridlines box to select it. (Leave the other boxes unselected because they would add unnecessary clutter to the chart. Selecting X-axis major gridlines would add lines extending up from the days of the week, and selecting minor gridlines would add more lines between major gridlines.) Click OK. Gridlines now extend horizontally across the chart from the numbers on the Y axis.

13. Now you need to make the gridlines heavier by using the same line width you used in the rest of your formatting. The default light gridlines are difficult to separate visually from the stacked sun symbols. Click to select any of the gridlines below the top line of the chart. Then (as usual, through the Format menu) increase the weight of the line in the Patterns dialog box and click OK.

14. Finally, add a title to the chart. Click just under the Pictogram title bar to deselect the gridline. Then pull down the Chart menu and

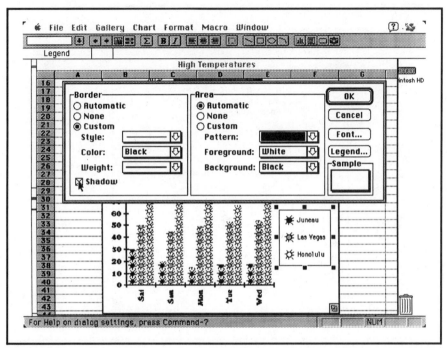

Figure 10.15: Adding a drop-shadow using the Legend Patterns dialog box

select the Attach Text... command. The Attach Text To dialog box appears, as shown in Figure 10.17. Note that in addition to adding a chart title with the Chart Title option (which you used in Chapter 1), you can add text to the X or Y axis, to a data series, or to a data point. (This dialog box also offers overlay options, discussed in Chapter 11.)

15. Click OK to accept the default selection, Chart Title. The dialog box closes, and as you discovered in Chapter 1, the word *title* appears in the formula bar and at the top of the chart surrounded by white boxes.

16. Type these words: **Temperatures Compared**. Click the enter box in the formula bar. The title appears at the top of the chart in the default typeface.

17. With the title still selected, pull down the Format menu and select the Font... command.

18. In the Font dialog box, select the same bold typeface you've been using throughout this example, this time in 36-point size.

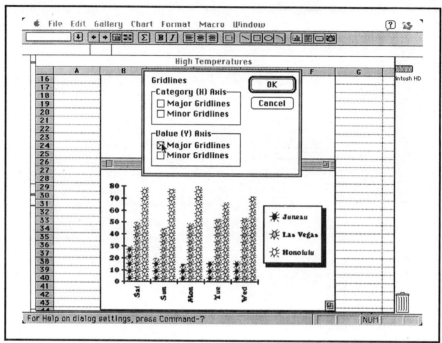

Figure 10.16: The Gridlines dialog box

19. Click OK. Click outside the chart area to deselect the title and press ⌘-S to save your new version of the chart. Your screen should now resemble the printout in Figure 10.18 (except that your typeface will probably be different from the Windsor Bold shown).

CAUTION

Bear in mind that you have specified 12- and 36-point fonts from a particular type family. Excel will maintain those sizes, even in a small window, automatically rearranging the data on the chart and abbreviating some text as necessary so that the type will fit (as Figure 10.19 demonstrates). However, the disk file will not have changed. All you have to do is click the zoom box to restore the chart to full screen, and everything will be arranged again just the way it was before.

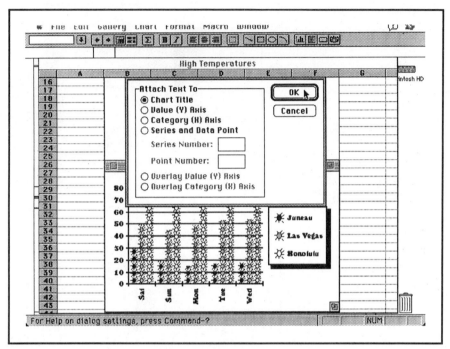

Figure 10.17: The Attach Text dialog box

From the Format menu, you can also add text to label the axes (using the Text... command to position the text either upright or sideways), add a background to the chart and the legend box (which in our example would make them harder to read), and rescale an axis (using the Scale... command).

Take a look at the Scale... command now.

Rescaling an Axis

To rescale an axis,

1. Click to select the Y axis.

2. Pull down the Format menu and select the Scale... command. The Scale dialog box appears, as in Figure 10.20.

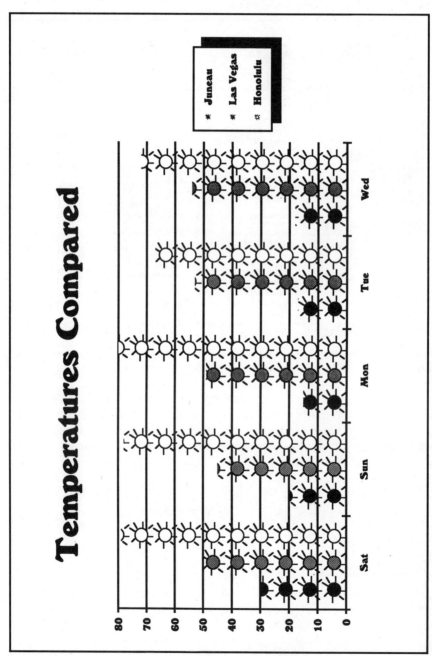

Figure 10.18: The reformatted temperature chart

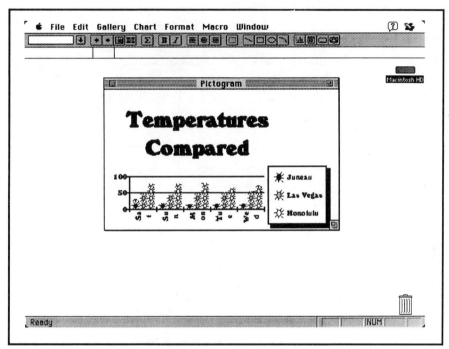

Figure 10.19: Temperature chart in a smaller window

Note that you can set the maximum and minimum values and major and minor divisions of the scale. You can also provide for negative values, using the Category (X) Axis Crosses At box, and you can specify a logarithmic scale and display values in reverse order.

Formatting Using the Main Chart Command

You can customize additional aspects of a chart by pulling down the Format menu and selecting the Main Chart command. Several of the options in the Main Chart dialog box relate to the display of data markers. However, you can also change even the depth of a 3-D chart in relation to its width. Figure 10.21 shows the Main Chart dialog box.

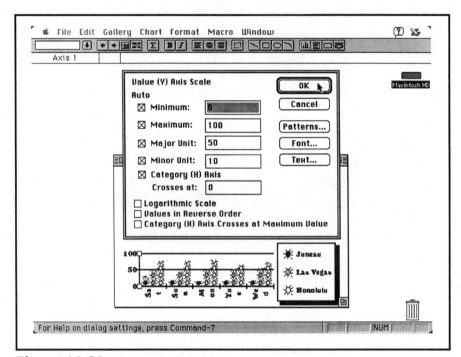

Figure 10.20: The Scale dialog box

These are the options in the Main Chart dialog box:

- You can change the chart type. (This feature can also be accessed through the Gallery menu. It is included in both places for convenience.)

- You can select the arrangement you want for data markers (called the *data view* in the dialog box).

- You can specify the amount of overlap in bar and column marker clusters as a percentage of the marker width.

- You can set the distance between bar and column marker clusters as a percentage of the marker width (called the *gap width*).

- You can display each marker in a different color pattern, by selecting the Vary by Category box. This option applies only when a chart shows just a single data series.

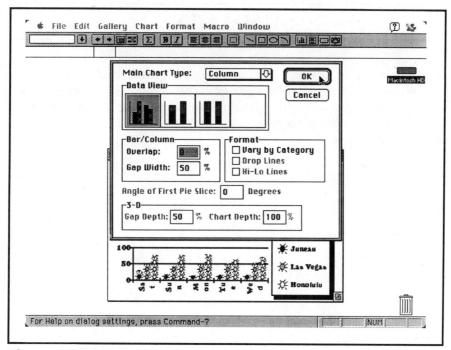

Figure 10.21: The Main Chart dialog box

- Add drop lines extending from the highest value in each category down to the X axis. This feature applies only to line and area charts.

- Add hi-lo lines extending from the highest value to the lowest in each category. This feature applies only to line and area charts used to show stock performance.

- In a pie chart, you can indicate where you want the first slice by specifying an angle, starting clockwise from the top of the pie.

- In 3-D charts, you can specify the distance between data series as a percentage of the marker width.

- In 3-D charts, you can specify the depth of the chart as a percentage of the chart width.

    Close the chart now. Additional Excel formatting options are explored in Chapter 11.

SUMMARY

You've learned how to edit a data series and how to perform many formatting operations, including how to replace bars, columns, and line markers with graphic images. Use these powerful features judiciously. Remember that not all formatting options are appropriate for every chart, as the exercise you just completed proved.

Chapter

11

Using Overlays
and 3-D Angles

Sometimes you may want to make changes in the way your charts are displayed that go beyond choosing a different chart type or font or adding a drop shadow to your legend box. For example, you may want to combine two sets of information with an overlay, possibly even displaying two X or Y axes with individual scales, or you may want to change the effect of a 3-D chart completely by rotating it on its axes. These advanced formatting options are the subject of this chapter.

ADDING AN OVERLAY

In Chapter 9, one of the chart types you used was a combination chart. This kind of chart is actually a main chart with an overlay added. You created this chart by using the Combination... command on the Gallery menu. As mentioned in Chapter 9, when you add an overlay in this way, any custom formatting you added to the main chart is erased. Instead, Excel uses the default settings. To retain custom formatting, you must use the Add Overlay command on the Chart menu. Try this command now.

DISPLAYING TWO SETS OF DATA

When you add an overlay to a chart, both the chart and the overlay obtain their data from the same worksheet. For this overlay demonstration, you'll use the High Temperatures worksheet you created in Chapter 9. You'll need additional information on the worksheet, so you will add a new data series. You will also delete two data series you won't be using.

Assume that you work for an ice cream store in Honolulu. You're interested in showing how sales are affected by temperatures from day to day.

Creating a Default Column Chart

First create a default column chart of the worksheet data.

1. Close any Excel files you have open. Then load the High Temperatures worksheet. The worksheet appears, showing an embedded

3-D area chart of the data (the chart you were using when you last saved the worksheet in Chapter 9). Delete this chart and create a new one.

2. Click the chart to select it. Then press the Delete key to erase the chart from the worksheet. (Pressing the Delete key removes a selected object just as if you had issued the Clear... command from the Edit menu. A third way to remove a selected object is to press ⌘-B.)

3. Now delete two of the data series: the Juneau and Las Vegas data series. Drag to select the range A6:F7. Since this range is not an object, you must use the Delete command (or the shortcut, pressing ⌘-K) to remove these rows. Click OK in the Delete dialog box to confirm the deletion.

4. Click cell A6 to select it and type this heading: **Sales ($)**. Press Tab to move to cell B6.

5. Add sales data. In B6, type **346**. This number represents $346 in sales for Saturday, the first day listed on the worksheet. Press Tab.

6. Type **388**. Press Tab.

7. Type **291**. Press Tab.

8. Type **302**. Press Tab.

9. Type **298**. Press Tab.

10. You need to select a range of data to include in a new chart. Drag to select the range A4 through F6.

11. Click the chart tool on the Toolbar. Then drag to select the range B8:F24, the area where the chart will appear. A default column chart appears (see Figure 11.1).

Note that since Excel can't at this point tell the difference between the temperature readings and the dollar sales amounts, the program combines both data series on one chart, using one set of bars for temperatures and another set of bars for sales and a default Y axis that displays a maximum value of 400. The result is completely meaningless, but you'll soon alter the chart to correct its problems.

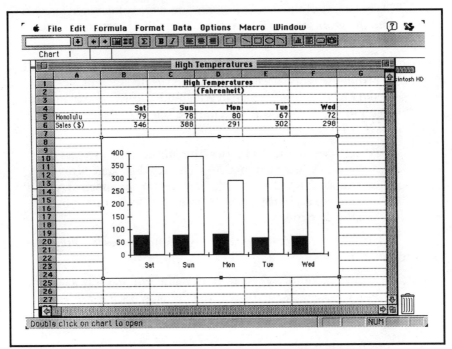

Figure 11.1: Default column chart showing the added data series

Adding the Overlay

To separate the two types of data on your chart, add an overlay.

1. Double-click the chart to open a chart window. Then pull down the Chart menu and select the Add Overlay command. The resulting combination chart is no better. As Figure 11.2 reveals, the chart now displays the bottom series on the worksheet—the daily sales accomplished—as a line chart overlay instead of as a series of bars like those still used to represent Honolulu temperatures. However, the chart continues to use the same scale for both temperatures and dollars. To correct this problem, add a second Y axis to the main chart to represent the sales data alone.

2. Pull down the Chart menu and select the Axes... command. You'll see the Axes dialog box. In the Overlay section, click the Value (Y) Axis box (see Figure 11.3) and click OK. A second Y axis appears at

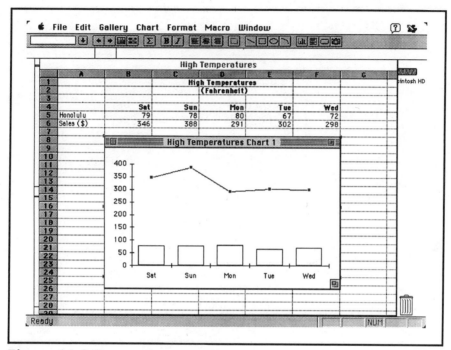

Figure 11.2: Bottom data series plotted on an overlay

the right side of the chart showing the values for the data series that reports sales in dollars.

The left Y axis now peaks at 80, the highest temperature recorded. The chart begins to make more sense (see Figure 11.4). But how could someone receiving this chart determine which Y axis is connected to the line and which is connected to the bars?

Adding Symbols and Labels

To clarify the chart, let's start by using the stacked sun symbols again on the bars to connect the bars in a viewer's mind with temperatures rather than money.

1. The sun symbols you created should still be at the bottom of your worksheet. Click outside the chart area to close the chart window. Then scroll the worksheet down until you see the drawings.

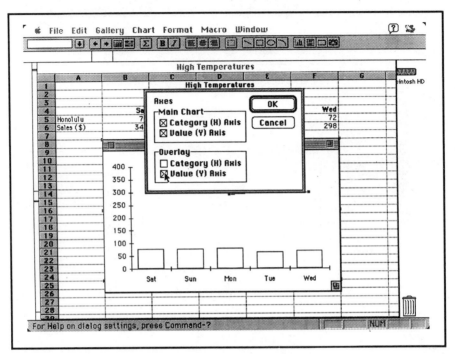

Figure 11.3: The Axes dialog box

2. Select the white sun and press ⌘-C to copy this object to the clipboard.

3. Scroll the worksheet back up to the top. Then double-click the chart again to open the chart window.

4. Click a bar of the Honolulu data series to select the series.

5. Press ⌘-V to paste the sun symbol into the data series. The bars of the series now each show one elongated sun, the length depending upon the size of the value for each data point.

6. To convert the stretched sun symbols into columns of stacked sun, pull down the Format menu, select the Patterns... command, click the Stack button, and click OK.

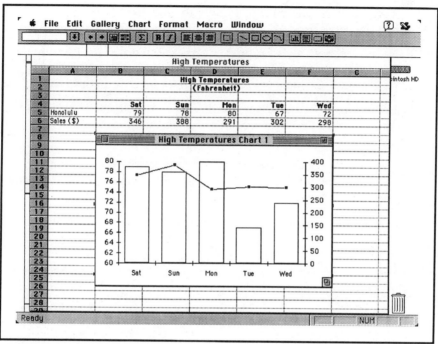

Figure 11.4: The combination chart with two axes

7. Next, add a legend box. Pull down the Chart menu and select the Add Legend command. A legend box appears to the right of the bars, identifying the Honolulu series with the sun symbol and the daily sales with a line that contains a centered data point.

8. The line that represents sales would stand out better if it were heavier. Also, it doesn't need to display the data points; the points where it crosses each bar of sun symbols are obvious. To begin making these additional changes, click the line for the data series on the chart to select it.

9. Pull down the Format menu and select the Patterns... command.

10. In the Patterns dialog box, change the weight of the line to the heaviest available.

11. In the Marker section of the dialog box, click the None button. Then click OK and click just under the title bar of the chart to deselect the data series. Your screen should now resemble Figure 11.5.

12. Next, label both axes for further clarity. Pull down the Chart menu and select the Attach Text... command. (You could also use this command to add labels to one or all data points on your chart.)

13. In the Attach Text dialog box, click the button labeled Value (Y) Axis and click OK. The letter Y surrounded by white squares appears to the left of the main chart Y axis.

14. Type **Degrees Fahrenheit** and click the enter box on the formula bar. This label now appears beside the left Y axis, printed vertically and reading from the bottom up.

15. Again, pull down the Chart menu and select the Attach Text... command.

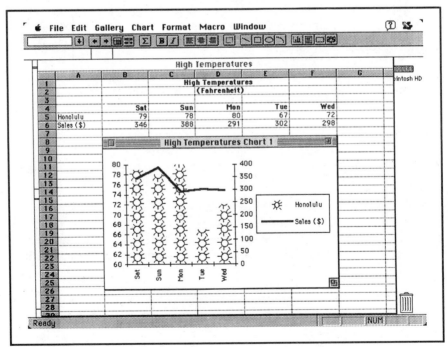

Figure 11.5: Chart with sun symbols and legend box added

16. In the Attach Text dialog box, click the button labeled Overlay Value (Y) Axis (as shown in Figure 11.6) and click OK.

17. Type **Sales ($)** and click the enter box on the formula bar. This label appears beside the Y axis for the overlay: the right Y axis. Both axes now have labels, as Figure 11.7 shows.

18. The label for the overlay (right) Y axis doesn't look quite right. It seems to face away from the main part of the chart. It would look better if it were flip-flopped 180 degrees (so it reads from the top down). To make this change, pull down the Format menu and select the Text... command.

19. In the Text dialog box, in the Orientation section, click the vertical text box on the right (as shown in Figure 11.8). Then click OK. The labels for both axes now face toward the chart. Click under the chart title bar to deselect the axis.

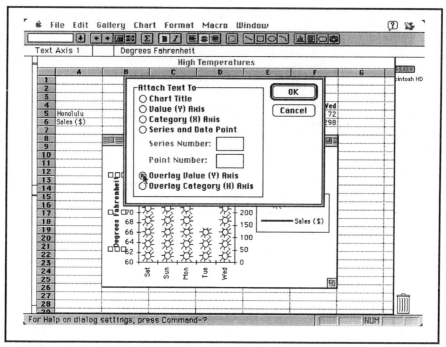

Figure 11.6: Labeling the overlay Y axis

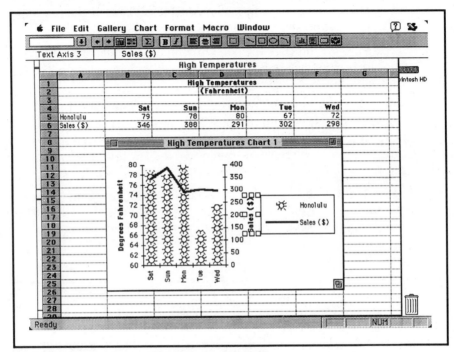

Figure 11.7: Chart with both axes labeled

Completing the Chart

Your chart is almost complete.

1. To complete the chart, add a title. Pull down the Chart menu again and select the Attach Text... command.

2. In the Attach Text dialog box, accept the default button selection, Chart Title, and click OK.

3. Type the words **Temperatures vs. Ice Cream Sales** and click the enter box on the formula bar. Your screen should now resemble Figure 11.9.

4. Click outside the chart area to embed the chart in the worksheet again.

5. Use the Save As... command to save this version of the worksheet under the name **Temps vs. Sales**.

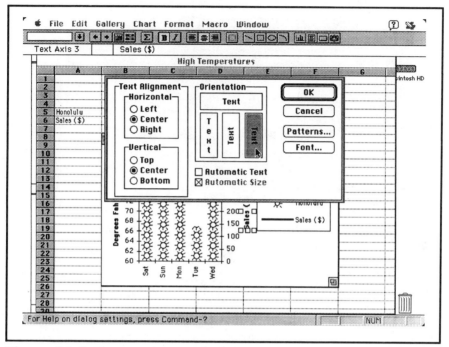

Figure 11.8: Rotating the overlay Y-axis label

The new chart lets you easily see that, apparently, changes in temperature had little effect on ice cream sales. For example, Tuesday was the coldest of the five days recorded; yet sales didn't dip accordingly. Furthermore, Monday was the hottest day, yet sales went down. In fact, analyzing the chart more closely, you can see that the highest sales were realized on Saturday and Sunday, when more people are home and have the time and inclination to buy ice cream.

Thus, you can see how an overlay can help you contrast and analyze two different kinds of data effectively.

REASSIGNING
DATA SERIES TO OVERLAYS

When a worksheet has only two data series, Excel automatically moves the second series to the overlay when you issue the Add Overlay command.

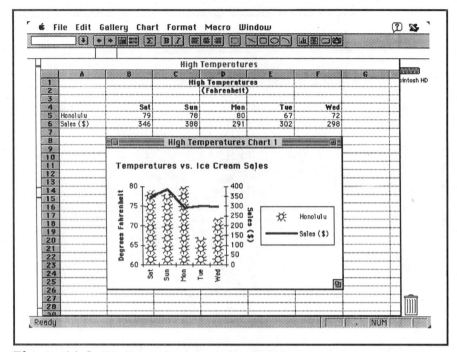

Figure 11.9: Worksheet with completed chart

These are the rules the program follows when it has more series to consider:

Excel always tries to divide data series into two equal groups, assigning the first half to the main chart and the remainder to the overlay. It always assigns the series with the highest plot numbers to the overlay. (As you will see, you can change these default plot numbers.) If your worksheet contains an uneven number of data series, Excel assigns the extra one to the group on the main chart. For example, if you have either four or five data series, in both instances Excel plots only the last two series on the overlay.

On many occasions this default division won't be what you want. For instance, if you want to compare sales for three individual ice cream stores (three data series) against the five-day temperature readings for Honolulu (one data series), you will want all but one data series (the temperatures themselves) shown in line-chart format on the overlay. Or, forgetting temperatures for a moment, you may want bars on a column chart to represent sales for three individual stores during this time period and an overlay line chart to display a line representing the company sales quota (assuming that each store has the same quota). You can then easily see whether a particular

store met the quota for any day in the series by observing whether or not the
bar for that particular sales value extends to or above the line.

You do not have to use Excel's default format if it does not suit your
needs. You can easily specify which data series appear on the overlay, and
you have a choice of methods.

Choosing the First Series for an Overlay

Try using the First Overlay Series button to specify the series displayed
on the overlay.

1. Double-click the chart on the Temps vs. Sales worksheet to open
   the chart window again.

2. Pull down the Format menu and select the Overlay... command.
   You'll see the Overlay dialog box shown in Figure 11.10.

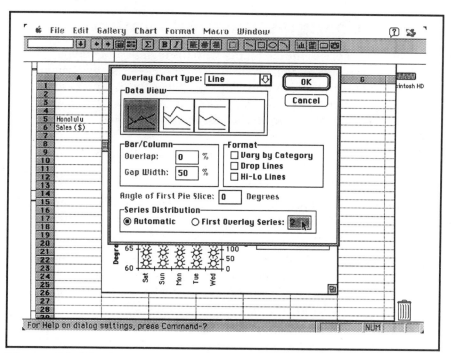

Figure 11.10: The Overlay dialog box on the Format menu

This dialog box closely resembles the Main Chart dialog box on the same menu. However, it has a Series Distribution section at the bottom, with Automatic and First Overlay Series buttons. Excel selects the Automatic button by default and then proceeds in the manner just explained. In the entry box to the right of the First Overlay Series button, you can see the number 2, indicating that the second data series (sales) has been selected for plotting on the overlay—in this case, because the supporting worksheet contains only two data series.

If the worksheet contained more data series, all you would have to do to reassign the data series to be shown on the overlay would be to type a new number in the First Overlay Series box. Then Excel would plot the data series with that number, plus any data series with higher plot numbers, on the overlay.

You can use this method if the data series you want to appear on the overlay are grouped together and have higher plot numbers than the data series you want plotted on the main chart.

Changing the Plot Number

Since Excel places the data series with the highest plot numbers on the overlay, you can control what is displayed on the overlay by changing the plot number of one or more series. You can change the plot order in the Edit Series dialog box or in the worksheet formula.

To change the plot order in the Edit Series dialog box,

1. Click the Cancel button to close the Overlay dialog box.

2. Click the line representing the sales data series to select that series.

3. Pull down the Chart menu and select the Edit Series... command. You'll see the Edit Series dialog box, which you encountered previously in Chapter 10.

4. To change the plotting order of the selected series, you simply type a new number in the Plot Order box. With this particular chart, you could type **1**. Then the sales figures would appear on the main chart, and the temperatures would appear on the overlay.

To change the plot order in the worksheet formula, you edit the formula bar.

1. With the line still selected (now it represents temperatures), look at the formula bar. As explained in Chapter 10, you can edit the formula itself to change the plotting order.

2. Click the formula just before the closing parenthesis and then change the last argument from 2 (currently displayed) to another number. Of course, the only other number available for this worksheet is 1.

Bear in mind that in some charts you may have to both change the plot order of individual series and specify a new starting series for an overlay to obtain the results you want.

Close the chart window and the Temps vs. Sales worksheet without saving your most recent changes.

CHANGING 3-D ANGLES

You also don't have to be satisfied with the default view of any of Excel's 3-D charts. You can rotate 3-D charts in any of the three dimensions and make other adjustments as well, through the 3-D View... command on the Format menu. You can use these capabilities to obtain a less obstructed view of a particular data series (which may be hidden behind others) or to emphasize a particular feature of the chart. For example, lowering the elevation from which a pie chart is seen tends to make the slices in front seem more important

Here are your options:

- **Elevation**. You can change the apparent height from which the reader views the chart. You measure the change in degrees, from – 90 to 90 degrees, except on pie charts, where the range is 10 to 80 degrees.

- **Perspective**. You can make the markers in back seem further away than the ones in front. You specify perspective as a ratio of the front of the chart to the back. The possible range is 0 (no perspective) to 100.

- **Rotation**. You can rotate the plot area around its vertical axis. The range is 0 to 360 degrees. Specifying 180 degrees creates the effect of looking at the back side of the area.

- **Right Angle Axes**. When the Right Angle Axes option is on, the X and Y axes appear at right angles to one another, so you can't specify changes in perspective. You click a box to turn the feature on and off.

- **Height**. You can control the height of the Z axis (the vertical axis) in relation to the width of the X axis or the base of the chart. Height is measured as a percentage of X-axis length. For example, a height setting of 200 percent would make the height of the Z axis twice the length of the X axis.

Let's try the 3-D View . . . command:

1. Close any Excel files you have open.

2. Load the High Temperatures worksheet. It should still display an embedded chart in a 3-D area chart format.

3. Double-click the chart to open the chart window.

4. Pull down the Format menu and select the 3-D View . . . command. You'll see the 3-D View dialog box shown in Figure 11.11. You don't have to type percentage figures to use this dialog box. You can click any of the boxes containing arrows to make the sample chart in the box rotate so you can evaluate the effect of various settings.

5. Experiment with clicking the various arrows and observing the result on the sample chart. If you find you've rotated the chart until it's unrecognizable, just click the Default button to return its appearance to the way you found it.

6. When you achieve a combination you'd like to try on the High Temperatures 3-D area chart, click the Apply button. Then click OK and

observe the result. Repeat steps 4 through 6 as many times as you like to experiment with different effects.

7. Pull down the Gallery menu and select the 3-D Pie... command.

8. In the 3-D Pie dialog box, select format option 5 and click OK.

9. Experiment again with the 3-D View... command to see how rotation affects a 3-D pie chart.

10. When you feel comfortable using the 3-D View... command with the various 3-D chart types, click outside the chart to return it to its embedded state on the worksheet. Then close the worksheet without saving your changes.

Figure 11.12 shows the effect achieved by using an 80 percent perspective on the High Temperatures chart with the 3-D column type selected.

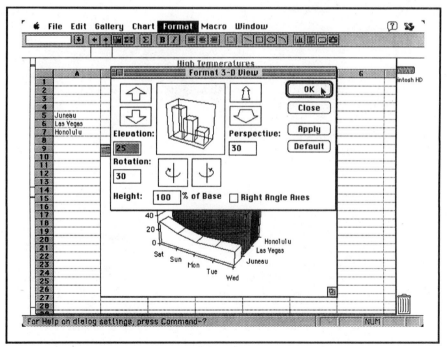

Figure 11.11: The 3-D View dialog box

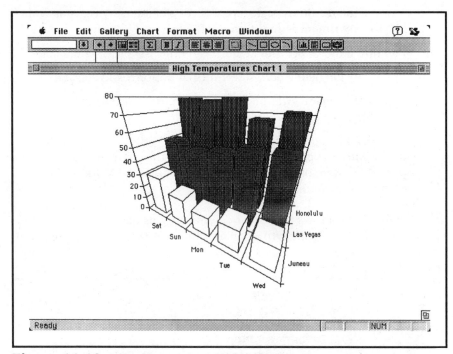

Figure 11.12: 3-D column chart with heightened perspective

SUMMARY

You've seen how useful 3-D angles and overlays (combination charts) can be in exhibiting your data.

Remember that all of the data series used in a combination chart must be available on the same worksheet, and that this kind of chart has two main advantages: You can combine different chart types to highlight one or more data series, and you can show two X or Y axes to display a separate scale for overlay data points.

Part

IV

Constructing
Databases
on Worksheets

Chapter 12

Learning
Database
Basics

Although Excel is a spreadsheet program, it can serve as a database program too. You can create and manage a database right on a worksheet.

You can use a database to store and retrieve records for almost any purpose. You can also perform statistical calculations on an Excel database. For example, you might set up a database containing employee records and then use database functions and formulas to determine how long the average employee has been with the company or which department turns in the most overtime.

In this chapter you'll create a new database and then use it to familiarize yourself with Excel's database features.

DATABASE COMPONENTS

Excel databases use three different kinds of special ranges:

- The **database range** is an area you set up on a worksheet to store the records that comprise the database.

- The **criteria range** is a smaller area where you specify the information you want to retrieve from the database.

- The **extract range** is the area you set up to store the retrieved information that matches your criteria.

Database ranges contain these components:

- **Records**. A record in an Excel database is one row in the database that contains the same categories (or fields; see the next item) of information as all the other records. For example, in an employee database, the data pertaining to a single employee would be stored in one row. Since an Excel worksheet can contain over 16,000 rows, an Excel database can contain that many records. (However, see the Caution note that follows.)

- **Fields**. A field is one category within a record. In an employee database, an employee's last name might be one field, the employee's first name might be another, and the date the employee was hired might be a third. Each column in an Excel database range is a different field. A field name can contain as many as 255 characters; however, short names are easier to read and much easier to use in formulas. The name of a field appears at the top of its column. The first row of a database range always contains the field names, which must be text constants. If a field name contains numbers, you must enclose the name in quotation marks so Excel will know it's a name. You can't use logical values (TRUE or FALSE), error values, or formulas as field names.

- **Computed fields**. A field that contains formulas or functions is called a computed field. You don't enter data directly into this type of field; Excel calculates the data using values in other fields and then displays the result in the cell of the computed field.

A note of caution here: Although an Excel worksheet can contain 16,384 rows and 256 columns, your Macintosh may not be able to hold in memory simultaneously all of the data that a database worksheet that big would contain. Since having access to all of the data at the same time is essential for the correct operation of a database, you may have to construct smaller databases. The exact size depends on the amount of *RAM* (random-access memory) installed in your computer and the complexity of the database (including the kind and number of formulas used).

If you need to use a larger database than your Macintosh can handle, you can solve your memory problem in any of three ways:

- *Add more memory*, if your Macintosh has room for it and you can afford the expense. You can install as much as 32 megabytes of RAM on some Macintoshes. If you don't know how to do this yourself, ask your Macintosh dealer.

- *Store records externally*. If you are an advanced user and have access to an external database capability (including a company mainframe computer), you can store most of your data externally and use Apple's CL/1 Data Access Language to import subsets of the data as needed. See Chapter 26 for more information.

- *Use virtual memory*. If you're using a recent version of the Macintosh operating system—System 7.0 or higher—you may be able to use virtual memory. This means that when your Macintosh runs out of memory, it can automatically store some data on disk temporarily and then reaccess it as needed. However, to take advantage of the System 7.0 virtual memory feature, you must be using a Macintosh with an 68030 (or higher) central processing unit. If you don't know whether your computer has this capability, ask your dealer.

SETTING UP AN EMPLOYEE DATABASE

The best way to learn how an Excel database functions is to use one. Let's enter information pertaining to employee records into a new worksheet. Let's then create a new database using this range of cells and both locate and extract specific data with criteria and extract ranges. Figure 12.1 shows the data we'll use.

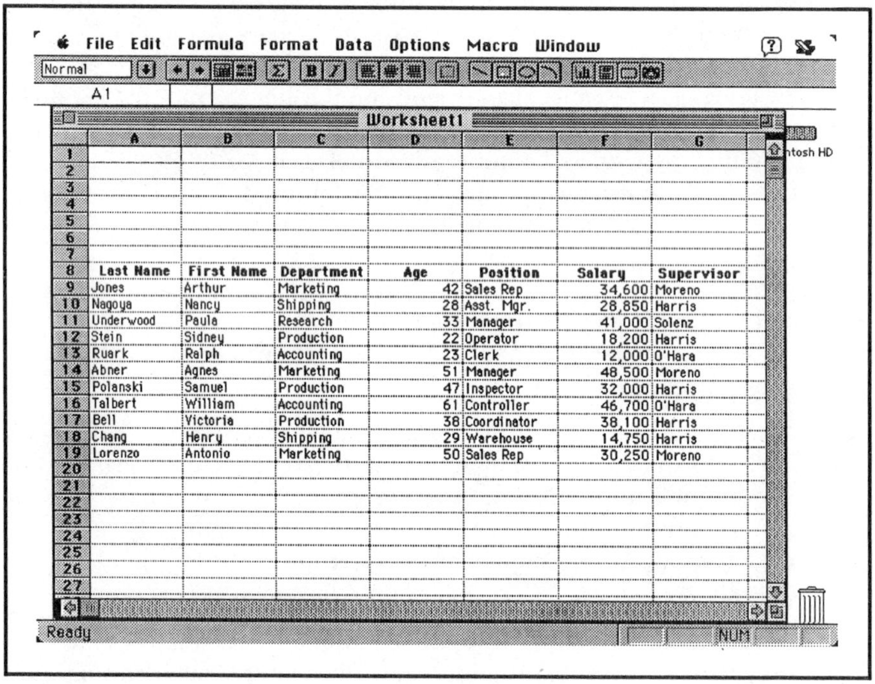

	A	B	C	D	E	F	G
8	Last Name	First Name	Department	Age	Position	Salary	Supervisor
9	Jones	Arthur	Marketing	42	Sales Rep	34,600	Moreno
10	Nagoya	Nancy	Shipping	28	Asst. Mgr.	28,850	Harris
11	Underwood	Paula	Research	33	Manager	41,000	Solenz
12	Stein	Sidney	Production	22	Operator	18,200	Harris
13	Ruark	Ralph	Accounting	23	Clerk	12,000	O'Hara
14	Abner	Agnes	Marketing	51	Manager	48,500	Moreno
15	Polanski	Samuel	Production	47	Inspector	32,000	Harris
16	Talbert	William	Accounting	61	Controller	46,700	O'Hara
17	Bell	Victoria	Production	38	Coordinator	38,100	Harris
18	Chang	Henry	Shipping	29	Warehouse	14,750	Harris
19	Lorenzo	Antonio	Marketing	50	Sales Rep	30,250	Moreno

Figure 12.1: Records for the employee database

1. Close any Excel files you may have open and select the New... command from the File menu to start a new worksheet.

2. Duplicate the worksheet displayed in Figure 12.1 on your new worksheet. To accomplish this, create the field names first. Start by selecting cell A8 and entering the words **Last Name**. Press Tab to move the pointer to the next cell to the right: B8.

3. Continue to enter the field names shown in Figure 12.1 until you've entered them all.

4. Drag to select all of the cells that contain field names: the range A8:G8.

5. Click the boldface and center-alignment icons on the Toolbar to format the field names to appear in boldface and centered in their cells.

6. Select cell A9 and—cell by cell—enter the information for the individual employees that is shown in Figure 12.1. Be careful that you type the abbreviated words in the Position field as shown; note that Sales Rep is not followed by a period, whereas both abbreviations in Asst. Mgr. do have periods. Be especially cautious when you enter the supervisor names, since some of them appear more than once. If one of these cells contains a typing error, some data retrieval operations won't work correctly; the result will be as if a certain department had two supervisors with slightly different names.

7. When you've completed typing the information, the only additional formatting you'll need is for the numbers in the Salary field. Drag to select the range F9:F20. (This range includes a blank row below the data, so you can easily expand the database later.) Pull down the Format menu, select the Number... command, and select the fourth option in the Format Number dialog box—the format that looks like this: #,##0.

8. Click OK. The dialog box closes, and Excel displays the numbers in the Salary field formatted with a comma.

9. Finally, turn the rows of information into a database. Drag to select the range A8:G20. (As in the formatting in step 7, you include the blank row 20 in the range to facilitate future expansion.) Pull down the Data menu and select the Set Database command. That's all that's required! Excel automatically names the range Database, and you can use it as such.

10. You've done considerable typing, so press ⌘-S to save the work-sheet (to guard against possible power failure). Name the worksheet **Employee**.

TIP

Including a blank row at the bottom of a range you define for a database allows you to add more records later without redefining the database. To add another record, you simply select the blank row, pull down the Edit menu, and select the Insert command. This procedure inserts a new row above the blank row, where you can enter the data for your additional record. Since the new row is above the last row, the range expands automatically to include the new record.

Without a blank row at the bottom of the range, you have to redefine the database every time you add a record.

SORTING DATA

It's usually a good idea to store information such as employee records in alphabetical order. Excel can sort data by rows or columns on up to three *keys* at a time. (A key is a field you specify by which to sort a database.) For example, you could sort your employee records initially keyed by last name. Since you might have two or more employees with the same last name, you would probably also want to sort with a first-name key. Large companies may even have two employees with both the same first and last names, so a third key—such as the department in which the individual works—might be desirable too.

Let's sort the employee records database.

1. Drag to select the range A9:G19. This range excludes the field names (you certainly don't want to sort them along with the employee names!) and the blank record (row) at the end of the database.

2. Pull down the Data menu and select the Sort... command. You'll see the Sort dialog box shown in Figure 12.2.

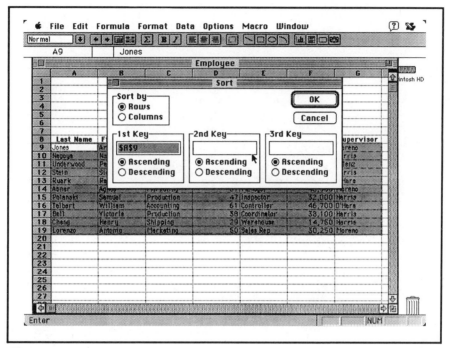

Figure 12.2: The Sort dialog box

3. You can sort by rows or by columns. Here you want to sort by rows (the default selection), so be sure the Rows button is selected. As you select fields to include in the sort, leave the Ascending button selected (the default choice) to perform the sort in ascending rather than descending order.

4. The default 1st Key for sorting is the first cell in the first column of the range. This is what you want, so move on to specify the second key. Click the entry box for 2nd Key. Then click any cell in the second column to select that column (the First Name field) as the second key for sorting.

5. Click the entry box for 3rd Key. Then click any cell in the third column to make Department the third key for sorting.

6. Click OK to execute the sort. The database should now look like Figure 12.3.

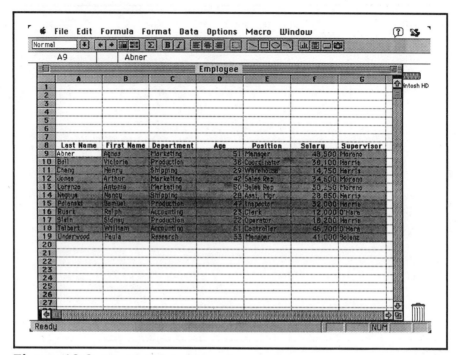

Figure 12.3: The sorted database

The program sorts varied contents of a field in the following order (provided the Ascending button is selected):

- Numbers
- Text
- Logical values
- Error values
- Blank cells

Capitalization is ignored.

FINDING DATA
WITH A CRITERIA RANGE

You can use a criteria range to find data that meets specific criteria. Try this feature now.

A criteria range is headed by *criteria names*: the exact names of fields that you want included in a search. You'll enter these names first, copying them through the clipboard to eliminate the possibility of typing errors.

1. Select cell F8, which contains the name of the Salary field.

2. Press ⌘-C to copy the field name to the clipboard.

3. Copy the field name to the criteria range. It's a good idea to place the criteria range above the database range. You'll find this a convenient location when you have to modify or change criteria. This placement can also keep the criteria range from being overwritten (see the next section, "Extracting Records"). To begin specifying the criteria range, select cell B2, which contains the field name Salary. Then press ⌘-V to paste the field name into that cell.

4. Select cell G8, which contains the field name Supervisor, and press ⌘-C to copy that field name too to the clipboard.

5. Select cell C2. Then press ⌘-V to paste the field name Supervisor into that cell.

6. You need to state the actual criteria to use in the sort. Assume that you want to locate employees with salaries greater than $28,000. Click B3 to select it and type the first criterion: **>28000**. Press Tab to enter this criterion and move to cell C3.

7. Add a second criterion. In C3, type the name **Harris**. (If the name were more complicated, you could use copy and paste techniques to eliminate typing errors.) Press Return.

You've completed the typing. Since the two criteria are on the same row, the criteria mean, "Find the first record for an employee who makes more than $28,000 a year *and* has Harris as supervisor.'' If you had placed the name Harris one cell lower (in C4), placing the two criteria on two separate rows, the criteria would have meant, ''Find the first record for an employee who makes more than $28,000 a year *or* has Harris as supervisor.''

Now you must identify the criteria range for Excel.

1. Drag to select the range B2:C3 (the criteria names plus the criteria themselves).
2. Pull down the Data menu and select Set Criteria. You have established both the database and search criteria. Your screen should resemble Figure 12.4.
3. Next try the Data Find command to see how the criteria work. Pull down the Data menu again and select the Find command. (Shortcut: Press ⌘-F.) Excel highlights the first record that matches the criteria: the record (or row) for Victoria Bell.

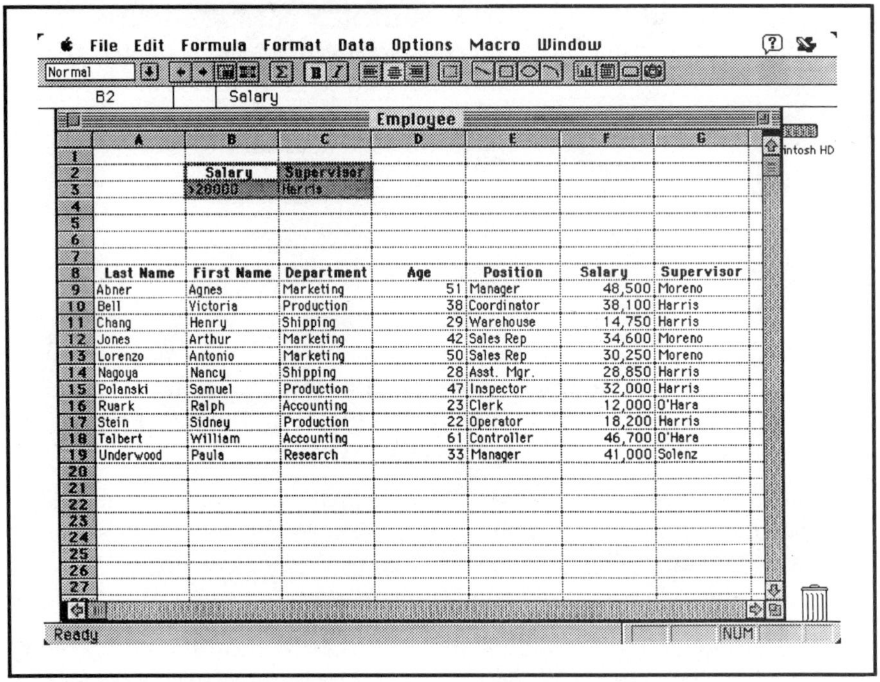
File Edit Formula Format Data Options Macro Window
Normal
B2 Salary
Employee
Salary Supervisor
>28000 Harris
Last Name First Name Department Age Position Salary Supervisor
Abner Agnes Marketing 51 Manager 48,500 Moreno
Bell Victoria Production 38 Coordinator 38,100 Harris
Chang Henry Shipping 29 Warehouse 14,750 Harris
Jones Arthur Marketing 42 Sales Rep 34,600 Moreno
Lorenzo Antonio Marketing 50 Sales Rep 30,250 Moreno
Nagoya Nancy Shipping 28 Asst. Mgr. 28,850 Harris
Polanski Samuel Production 47 Inspector 32,000 Harris
Ruark Ralph Accounting 23 Clerk 12,000 O'Hara
Stein Sidney Production 22 Operator 18,200 Harris
Talbert William Accounting 61 Controller 46,700 O'Hara
Underwood Paula Research 33 Manager 41,000 Solenz
Ready
NUM

Figure 12.4: The sorted database with a criteria range

4. To find the next record that matches the specifications, click the down arrow on the vertical scroll bar.

5. When no more records match the criteria, Excel activates whatever alert sound you specified in your Control Panel. Just click outside the database area to end the search, or click the up arrow on the scroll bar to search backward. (You might find searching backward convenient when the active record is at or near the end of the database, particularly if the database contains many records.) To terminate the search mode, click anywhere outside the database range.

CAUTION

If a cell within the database is active when you issue the Find command, Excel will search through only the records that follow that cell.

EXTRACTING RECORDS

Rather than having the program highlight records one at a time that match your criteria, you may prefer to extract the records so they appear together in a separate area of your worksheet. To accomplish this goal, you set up an extract range.

1. Drag to select the range A8:B8 and press ⌘-C to copy these field names to the clipboard.

2. To begin creating the extract range, select cell A21 and press ⌘-V to paste the names into cells A21 and A22.

3. Click cell F8 to select the field name Salary and press ⌘-C to copy the name to the clipboard.

4. Click cell C21 and press ⌘-V to paste the field name Salary into that cell.

5. Drag to select the range A21:C21, pull down the Data menu, and select the Set Extract command. The extract range is established.

6. Pull down the Data menu again and select the Extract... command. (Shortcut: Press ⌘-E.) You'll see the small Extract dialog box shown in Figure 12.5.

7. You could eliminate duplicate records in this dialog box to make Excel display only unique records—in other words, to show no exact duplicates. This precaution is not necessary in this case, so just click OK. Your screen will now resemble Figure 12.6.

8. Use the Save As... command to save this version of the worksheet as **Employee 2**. You'll continue to use this same version in the remainder of this chapter and in Chapter 13.

You've just extracted the records that match your criteria and placed them in a separate area of the database. However, since you headed the extract range with only three field names, the extraction procedure copied

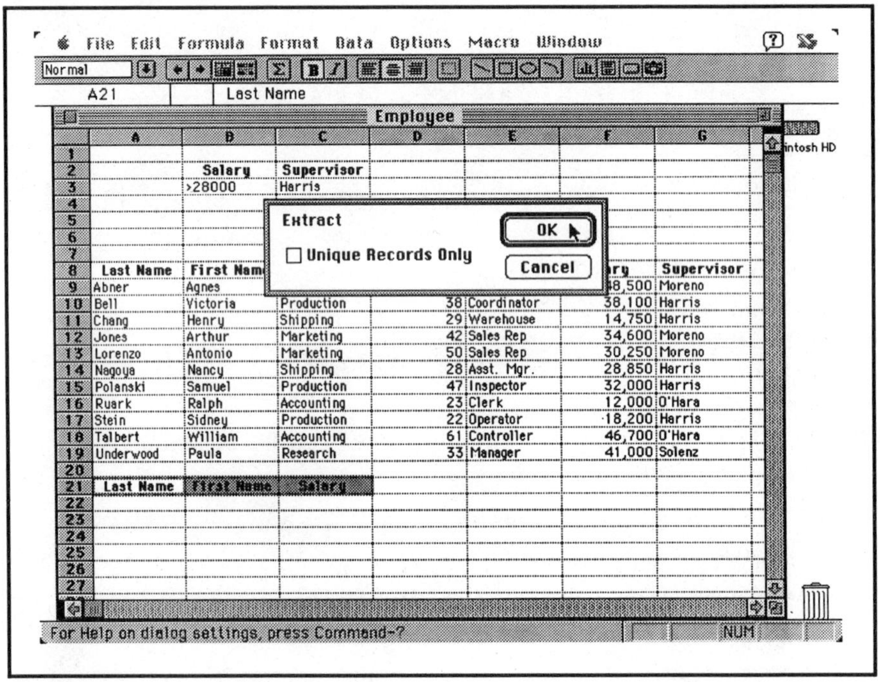

Figure 12.5: The Extract dialog box

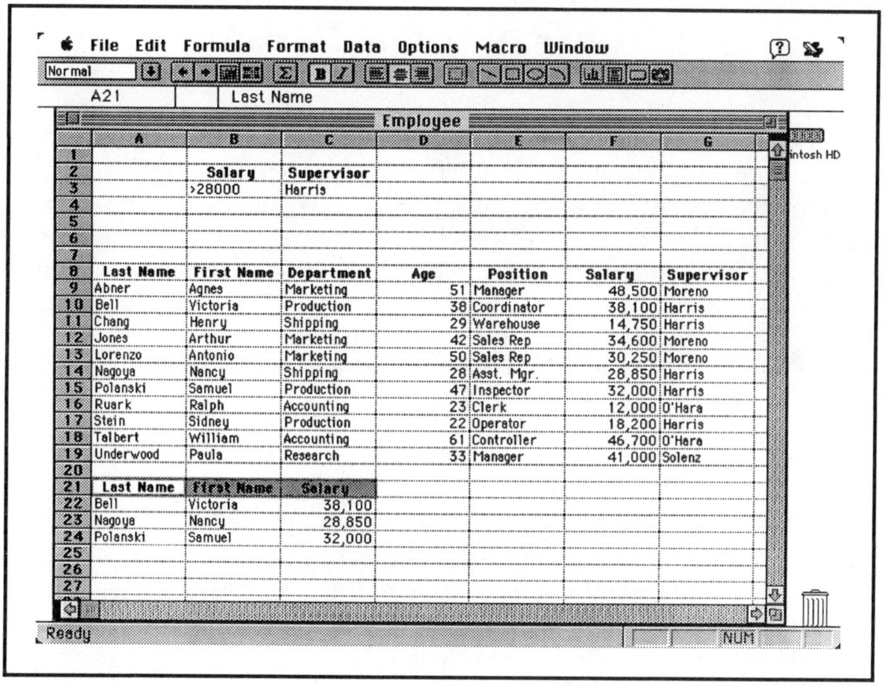

Figure 12.6: Database with extracted records

data for only those fields. The result is a handy list of the last names, first names, and salaries of all of the employees who have Harris as a supervisor and who make over $28,000 a year. For clarity, you could add a heading or note above the extract range explaining the nature of the data.

In this example, you listed only *headings* to define the extract range. You could also have dragged to set the *boundaries* for the entire range, including the data to be extracted.

CAUTION

When you include only headings in the extract range, Excel uses as many rows as it needs below those headings to display the records extracted, wiping out any data already in that area. This is a good reason for placing the extract range below the database range and, indeed, below any other data on the worksheet.

USING A DATA FORM

For users who have only limited knowledge of Excel, a convenient way to work with a database is to use the *data form* feature. You access this feature by issuing the Form... command from the Data menu. Excel displays one record at a time, with easy-to-understand buttons for establishing criteria and finding data, as well as for adding and deleting records. Using this feature, in a matter of minutes you could, for example, teach a temporary worker how to enter, retrieve, and update records.

When you use a data form, Excel ignores any criteria that you established in a criteria range on the worksheet.

Try the data form feature now:

1. Pull down the Data menu and select the Form... command. The form window shown in Figure 12.7 appears. The form window lists each field name in the database. A text box appears next to each field name for data entry or changes. If the database range of the worksheet had contained any protected cells (set up through the Cell Protection... command on the Format menu to prevent data entry) or calculated fields, no text box would appear beside those cell or field names, since direct data entry would not be possible.

2. Click the down arrow on the form's scroll bar. Excel displays the next record. The record number appears in the upper right corner of the form above a set of buttons that let you perform operations on the database. We'll discuss these buttons shortly.

3. For now, click the Criteria button. The contents of the second record disappear, and the text boxes become blank; they are ready for you to enter search criteria.

4. Click the Department text box to select it. Then type the letter **P**. When using a data form, you cannot enter a field name as a criterion with copy and paste commands; you must type the name. However, the program assumes that the wildcard asterisk (*) character follows any characters you type in a text box. Therefore, to specify the production department, all you have to do is enter the letter *P,* since no other department in the database starts with that letter. Excel will accept any characters whatsoever that follow the

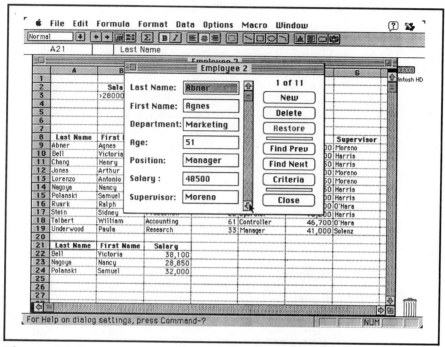

Figure 12.7: Data form for the Employee database

P as meeting the specification. Since Excel criteria are not case-sensitive, the program will also accept a lowercase *p* to select records pertaining to the production department.

5. Use the Tab key to move to the next field, **Age**. To have Excel look for any workers in the production department under 50 years of age, type **<50**. This completes the criteria. Your screen will resemble Figure 12.8.

6. Click the Find Next button to start the search. Excel retrieves the record for Victoria Bell, since she works in the production department and is 38 years old.

7. Continue to click the Find Next button. You'll discover that three people in the database under 50 years of age work in the production department. When Excel retrieves the last record that matches the criteria, your Macintosh alert sounds if you click Find Next again, signifying that the database contains no additional matching

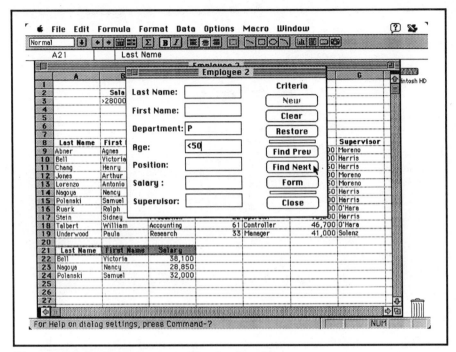

Figure 12.8: Criteria entered in the data form

records. The final record on your screen should be that for employee·Sidney Stein.

Let's experiment with more of the buttons at the right of the screen.

1. Click the First Name field after the *y* in the name *Sidney*. Backspace to delete letters until the name reads *Sid*. Observe that the Restore button, which had been dimmed, is now black again, signifying that the Restore option is available.

2. Click the Restore button. The record is restored to its previous condition, with the First Name field reading *Sidney*.

3. Suppose you want to check or change the search criteria. Click the Criteria button. The current record disappears from the data form window, and the window displays the criteria once more. The Criteria button is now labeled Form, meaning that you can click it to return to the display of records.

4. Click the Form button. The record for Sidney Stein reappears.

5. Click the Find Prev button. You'll see the previous record that matches the criteria. You could delete this or any other record on the screen by clicking the Delete button.

6. Click the Delete button now. You'll see the dialog box shown in Figure 12.9, warning that if you proceed with the command, the selected record will be deleted permanently.

7. Click the Cancel box to cancel the record deletion. Then click New to enter a new record. You'll see a blank record, ready for the entry of data in each field. Since the record hasn't been completed and therefore doesn't have a number yet, Excel identifies it as New Record.

8. Rather than actually entering a new record, click the Close button. This action closes the data form window and returns you to the worksheet.

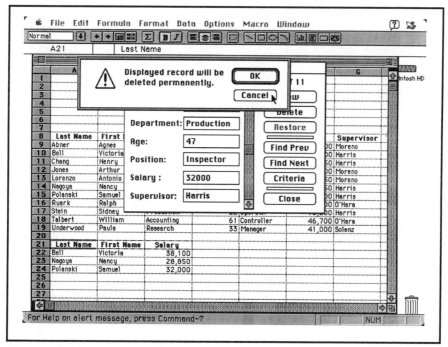

Figure 12.9: Alert box warning of record deletion

CAUTION

When you enter a new record or modify an existing record, you can make additional changes (or return the record to its previous condition by clicking the Restore button) only while that record is still displayed on the screen. You can press Tab to move from field to field for data entry. However, as soon as you press Return or Enter, the new record or change is entered in the database and cannot be restored.

To terminate the entry of new records, press Return or Enter to save the final new record to be entered. Then press Close. The dialog box closes, and you are returned to the worksheet.

A data form can display only as many field names and text boxes as will fit on your screen. You can't scroll the form to display additional fields. This means that you probably won't want to use the data form feature with a database that contains a large number of fields.

As you discovered previously, you can set up criteria directly on a worksheet to have Excel search for *either* one criterion *or* another criterion. You do this by placing the two criteria on separate rows. You can't perform that particular kind of search in a data form.

You also can't extract records through the data form window. You must perform this operation from the worksheet itself, as previously explained.

SUMMARY

In this chapter you learned how to set up a database on an Excel worksheet and to use criteria and extract ranges. You also learned how to set up and use a data form.

The next chapter discusses the use of database functions.

Chapter

13

Extracting Data
with Functions

Functions were introduced in Chapter 6. Excel has 12 functions that apply exclusively to databases. These specialized functions are the subject of this chapter. (Excel also offers similar functions that you can include in macros you can use with databases. Macros and macro functions are discussed in Chapters 15 through 18.)

You can apply database functions to any contiguous range of data with column headings—the range does not necessarily have to be formally defined as a database with the Set Database command. You can also designate any range as a criteria range for purposes of using the functions without using the Set Criteria command. Of course, the criteria range for a function must include one or more of the column headings (field names) already in the database.

Microsoft refers to the database functions collectively as *Dfunction( )*.

USING DATABASE FUNCTION ARGUMENTS

All database functions require these three arguments, in this same sequence: *(database,field,criteria)*.

Here is an explanation of the arguments:

- **The *database* argument.** To specify the database range, you can use cell addresses (such as A3:D10) or the name you've given to the range. Excel automatically gives the name *Database* to a database range established using the Set Database command. When using a database function, do not enclose the database name in quotation marks.

- **The *field* argument.** You can identify the field to be used with a database function in either of two ways: You can specify the field by its position in the database (for example, by entering the number 3 to denote the field that occupies the third column of the database) or by the field name (the title in the first row of the selected column). Unlike when entering a database name, you must surround a field name with double quotation marks.

- **The *criteria* argument.** You can identify a criteria range with cell addresses (such as B6:C8) or a range name. If you identify the criteria range through the Set Criteria command, Excel will automatically name the range *Criteria*. You do not surround a criteria range name with quotation marks. You can set up multiple criteria ranges on a worksheet, but you can use only one at a time.

THE DATABASE FUNCTIONS

Excel offers 12 database functions:

- **DAVERAGE(*database, field, criteria*).** This function finds the average of the numbers in the selected field column that match the criteria.

- **DCOUNT(*database, field, criteria*).** This function counts the cells in the field column that contain numbers that match the criteria. You can omit the *field* argument, in which case Excel counts all of the records in the entire database that match the criteria.

- **DCOUNTA(*database, field, criteria*).** This function counts cells in the field column that are not blank and that match the criteria. The cells counted can include data other than numbers.

- **DGET(*database, field, criteria*).** This function extracts from the field column the value in a single record that matches the criteria. If Excel doesn't find a record that matches the criteria, it returns the #VALUE! error value. If it finds more than one record that matches the criteria, it returns the #NUM! error value.

- **DMAX(*database, field, criteria*).** This function returns the largest number that matches the criteria from the column you designate as the field.

- **DMIN(*database, field, criteria*).** This function returns the smallest number that matches the criteria from the column you designate as the field.

- **DPRODUCT(*database, field, criteria*).** This function multiplies the values that match the criteria that Excel finds in the column you designate as the field.

- **DSTDEV(*database,field,criteria*).** This function uses the field column values that match the criteria to estimate the standard deviation of a population, assuming that the values in the field constitute only a sample of the population.

- **DSTDEVP(*database,field,criteria*).** This function uses the field column values that match the criteria to calculate the standard deviation of a population, assuming that the values in the field constitute the entire population.

- **DSUM(*database,field,criteria*).** This function adds the field column values that match the criteria.

- **DVAR(*database,field,criteria*).** This function uses the field column values that match the criteria to estimate the variance of a population, assuming that the values in the field constitute only a sample of the population.

- **DVARP(*database,field,criteria*).** This function uses the field column values that match the criteria to calculate the variance of a population, assuming that the values in the field constitute the entire population.

Note that nearly all of these database functions perform statistical operations.

USING DATABASE FUNCTIONS

To try some of these functions, load the Employee 2 database you created in Chapter 12.

TRYING THE DCOUNT( ) FUNCTION

Suppose that you're the personnel manager of the company with the Employee 2 database. In connection with a new insurance plan you're considering recommending to management, you need to know how many employees are over 40 years old.

To find the answer, you'll use the DCOUNT( ) function. You won't need to enter a *field* argument in this case, but you will have to use a field to set up the criteria range.

1. Click cell D8 (the heading for the Age field) to select it and press ⌘-C to copy it to the clipboard.

2. Click cell E2 to select it. Then press ⌘-V to paste the heading into this cell.

3. Press Return to select cell E3, type >40, and press Return again. This establishes a criterion of "any employee with an age greater than 40."

4. Cell E4 is now active. Pull down the Formula menu and select the Paste Function... command.

5. Scroll the list box until you see the DCOUNT( ) function. (Shortcut: Press the D key to move quickly to the first function starting with that letter.) Highlight this function to select it, deselect the Paste Arguments box to eliminate the argument placeholders, and click OK. The function appears in the formula bar.

6. You must add the necessary arguments within the parentheses. First you must define the area to be considered as the database. Drag to select the range A8:G19.

   As an alternative in this instance, you could pull down the Formula menu, select the Paste Name command, and from the Paste Name dialog box select the name Database, since this particular range of data is already included in the range named Database. The fact that the named range includes an extra blank row to facilitate the entry of new records doesn't matter, since the DCOUNT( ) function counts only records that contain data.

7. Next, enter *two* commas (,,). The first comma completes the entry of the range and separates the *database* argument from the argument to follow. You enter the second comma to represent the *field* argument, which you don't need here. When you omit the *field* argument, Excel counts all of the records that contain numbers and match the *criteria* argument—in other words, it counts the number of records in the database for employees over age 40. This operation gives you the information you want.

8. To add the *criteria* argument, drag to select the range E2:E3. Excel displays the formula = DCOUNT(A8:G19,,E2:E3)

9. Click the enter box in the formula bar to complete the formula.

The answer to your question appears in E4: The database contains records for five employees over the age of 40. Note that, although the criteria range you established in Chapter 12 still appears in the range B2:C3 of the worksheet (and is still, by default, named Criteria), the DCOUNT( ) function ignored that range and instead used the new range established in the formula. You could also have established an entirely different database range for the formula. Function criteria and ranges always take precedence over criteria and ranges established directly on the worksheet.

If you intend to use new database or criteria ranges frequently, you can give these ranges names of your own choosing to make them easier to select again in the future.

Your screen should now resemble Figure 13.1.

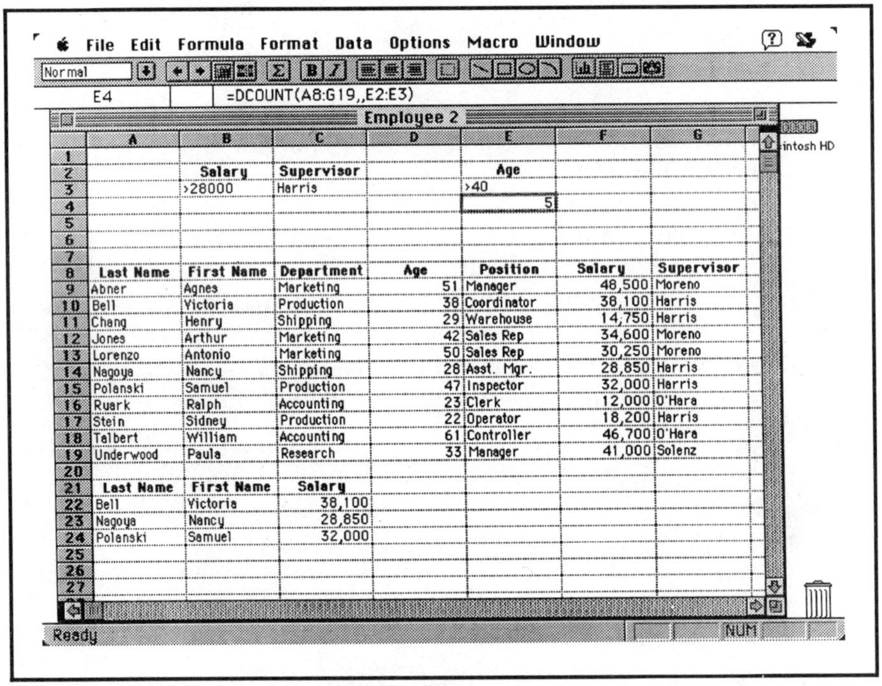

Figure 13.1: Using the DCOUNT( ) function

TRYING THE DGET( ) FUNCTION

Now try a text example. The goal here is to find the name of the inspector in the production department. Again start by setting up the criteria range.

1. Click cell E8 to select it. This cell contains the heading for the Position field. Press ⌘-C to copy the heading to the clipboard.

2. Click cell G2 to select it. Press ⌘-V to paste the Position heading into this new location. Then press Return.

3. In cell G3, now active, type the word **Inspector** and press Return. You've now created the criteria range. By selecting cells G2 and G3 as the range, you'll be telling Excel to look in the Position field for the text string *Inspector*. Cell G4 will now be active; you'll use the DGET( ) function in a formula in this cell.

4. Pull down the Formula menu, select the Paste Function... command, select the DGET( ) function, and click OK. The formula you're building appears in the formula bar.

5. Specify the *database* argument for the function by dragging to select the range A8:E19. This range excludes the last two fields—the Salary and Supervisor fields—of the original database from the database you're defining. There are two reasons for eliminating these two fields: (1) They're not needed for the data retrieval you have in mind, and (2) eliminating them demonstrates that you can redefine any database as many times as you like for use with functions without destroying its original boundaries.

6. Type a comma (,) to complete the entry of the *database* argument. Then, for the *field* argument, simply enter the number 1. This action specifies the first column or field of the database as the one in which Excel will display your answer. (As an alternative, you could have entered the field name "**Last Name**" enclosed in double quotation marks.)

7. Type another comma (,) to complete the *field* argument. Then drag to select the range G2:G3. These two cells constitute the criteria range. The formula appears as follows: = DGET(A8:E19,1,G2:G3).

8. Click the enter box in the formula bar to complete the formula. Immediately the answer appears in cell G4: the name Polanski.

Samuel Polanski is the employee in the database whose position is inspector.

Your worksheet should now resemble Figure 13.2.

The other database functions work in a fashion similar to the examples you've just tried.

You don't need to resave the Employee 2 worksheet unless you want to preserve the function examples.

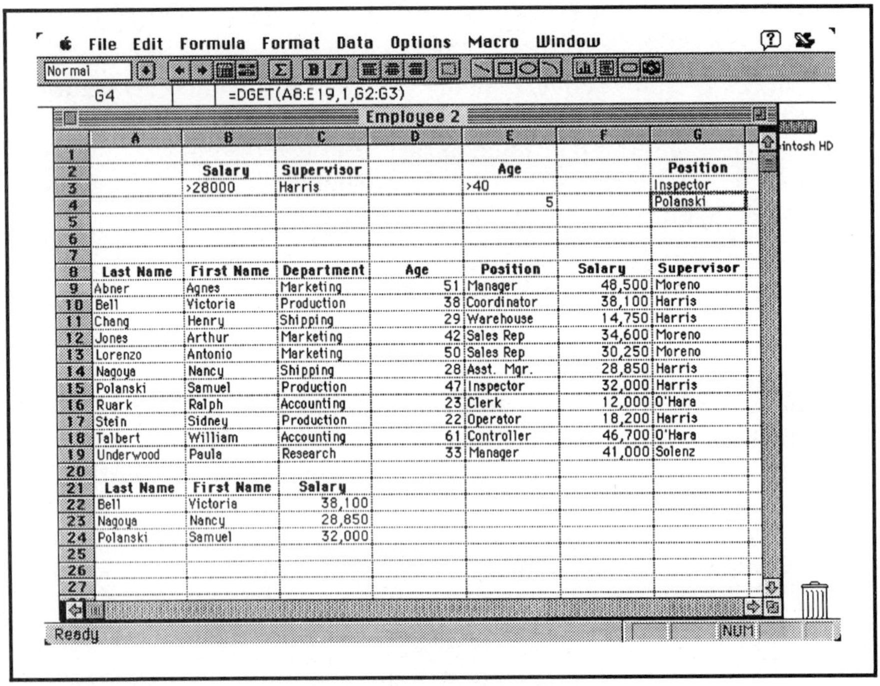

Figure 13.2: Using the DGET( ) function

SUMMARY

This chapter introduced you to Excel's 12 database functions. These functions can help you retrieve and analyze information from any range with column headings that you define as a database.

This chapter also showed how you can use database functions to utilize criteria range fields different from the field from which you extract the data.

In using functions, you can establish more than one database and criteria range on a single worksheet; however, you can use only one function at a time.

Part V

Printing
and Reporting

Chapter

14

Printing Worksheets,
Charts, and Reports

Excel offers you a great deal of flexibility in determining how your documents are printed. For example, you can print any selected portion of a worksheet. By default, Excel prints worksheets and charts with a header that lists the name of the file and a footer that lists the page number; you can change these elements, eliminate them from your printouts, or replace them with other information to produce precisely labeled reports. You can print or hide row and column headings (the numbers and letters of the alphabet that identify the rows and columns), resize your document, change margins, specify where page breaks occur, and make other refinements. Before you issue the Print... command, you can use the Print Preview command to see how your document will look, without wasting time and paper on actually printing the document.

This chapter discusses all of these features.

SETTING UP YOUR PRINTER

Before you can print anything on a Macintosh, your printer must be installed and selected according to the instructions in the manuals for the printer and the version of the Macintosh operating system you're using.

If your printer was made by Apple, this process should be easy. When the operating system was installed on your Macintosh, the installation utility should have automatically placed drivers into your System folder for all of the Macintosh printers sold by Apple.

If your printer was made by a company other than Apple, you can usually install its driver simply by dragging (and thereby copying) a printer icon into the System folder from a floppy disk supplied with the printer.

If you have more than one printer hooked up and available to your computer, before you print a document from any application, you must pull down the Apple menu, select the Chooser, and select the printer you want to use. If you have only one printer available, you have to perform these operations only once. Thereafter, you can continue to print with this printer month after month, or even year after year, without selecting the printer again.

Here are the basic steps you must follow in selecting a printer through the Chooser:

1. Be sure your printer is connected to your Macintosh and turned on.

2. Pull down the Apple menu and select Chooser. (You can do this either from the desktop or from within an application.) You will see the Chooser window. On the left, in a scrollable list box, the Chooser window displays the icons of printer types for which drivers have been installed and that are available for selection. (You may also see icons for devices other than printers that you can select as destinations for your files. For example, if you're running System 7.0 or a later version of the operating system, you can connect to a network file server through the AppleShare icon in the Chooser.)

3. Click the icon for your printer type to highlight and select it. Then follow the directions in step 4 or 5, depending on the kind of printer you have.

4. If your printer is a member of the Apple LaserWriter family, you will see the words *Select a LaserWriter* appear above the empty list box occupying the right half of the window. The name of your particular LaserWriter will appear within that list box. Click the name to select it. (If you're connected to a large network, you may see the names of several LaserWriters here; see Chapter 22 for a discussion of networking.) Since LaserWriters must be connected to your Macintosh through the AppleTalk network built into Macintosh systems, the AppleTalk Active button will also be selected automatically at the bottom of the window (the alternative button is Inactive).

   If you're using System 7, or if you're using MultiFinder under a previous version of the operating system, the Chooser window also includes buttons to turn background printing on or off; in either case, you can switch applications and continue working while files are printing in the background. Unless you're short of memory, using background printing is a good idea. If you're not using a LaserWriter, or if you're using a version of the operating system prior to System 7 and not running MultiFinder, this option will not appear in the window.

5. If your printer is a member of the Apple ImageWriter family, you will see only two options in the right half of the Chooser window.

You will see the option that lets you connect the printer to an AppleTalk network by clicking the Active or Inactive button, as with LaserWriters. Above the list box, instead of the words *Select a LaserWriter,* you will see the message, *Select a port.* Within the list box, you'll see two icons: one representing a *printer port* and displaying a drawing of a printer, and the other representing a *modem port* and displaying a drawing of a telephone receiver (see Figure 14.1). If you're using a free-standing Macintosh connected to an ImageWriter and not part of a network, the ImageWriter should be plugged into the printer port of your computer; therefore, select the printer port icon. On the other hand, if you're already connected to printers through a network and are adding an ImageWriter, the printer should be plugged into the modem port (so the new printer won't conflict with other printers on the network). In this case, select the modem port icon.

6. When your selections in the Chooser window are complete, click the close box to close the window and put the changes into effect.

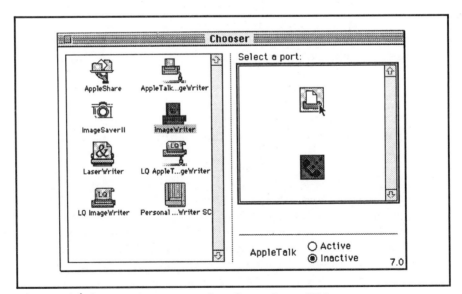

Figure 14.1: The Chooser window for an ImageWriter

INSTALLING FONTS

You must install any fonts you intend to use beyond those provided with the operating system. For this task you may be using a utility provided by the font maker, by Apple with the version of the operating system you're using, or by a third-party vendor of a font-management utility such as Suitcase II. These sources all provide step-by-step installation directions.

If you're using System 7.0 or a later version of the Macintosh operating system, you can install Macintosh True Type fonts simply by dragging their icons into the System folder icon when no application is active. Thereafter, as you work in your applications, Excel will create both screen and printer fonts instantly in the sizes you specify.

Unless you're a first-time Macintosh-user, you probably completed the necessary printer and font installation procedures for your system long ago.

CREATING FILES WITH PRINTING IN MIND

You can include or change many elements of worksheets and charts that affect the way they print.

CHANGING PRINTOUTS THROUGH FORMATTING

As you found in Chapters 3 and 10, you can easily alter the way a file prints by making formatting changes. Obviously, a heavier line, an alternate typeface, or a colored background will make a difference. However, in making such changes, you should observe two guidelines that could prevent problems:

- Never let fancy formatting make your worksheet or chart difficult to read or understand. Remember that your primary goal is to communicate—not, for instance, to show off all of the pretty type-faces you own.

- If your worksheet or chart will be printed on a system other than one on which it was created, make sure that the file will print properly on the new computer and printer. For example, the Macintosh connected to the other system may not have the same fonts installed. If your document is a very large worksheet, the other Macintosh may not have enough memory to run it. A lack of memory may occur even if both computers are running System 7, which supports the use of *virtual memory*, a technology that can temporarily store on disk portions of files that are too large for the computer's memory. If the other Macintosh doesn't have a 68030 processor or higher-numbered processor, it can't use the virtual memory feature.

CHANGING PRINTING FEATURES FROM WITHIN WORKSHEETS

In addition to formatting and typeface changes, you can make other changes in a worksheet itself that affect the way it prints.

Using Outlining Capabilities

Particularly if your printed worksheet will function as a report, you may wish to present prospective readers with only the highlights of the worksheet. You can do this by using Excel's outlining capabilities, discussed in Chapter 2. You can hide the detail in a worksheet and then print the top level of the outline as a summary or create a chart solely from the summary information.

Setting Page Breaks Manually

When you want to print all of a large worksheet, the printout can run several pages. In these circumstances, you may want to control exactly where page breaks occur, rather than accepting Excel's automatic divisions of the material.

For example, suppose you want all material relating to a particular regional office to appear on the same page, and you realize that you can accomplish this goal by preventing the information from starting at the bottom of the previous page. All you have to do is follow this simple procedure:

1. Select the first cell that you want to appear on the new page.

2. Pull down the Options menu and select the Set Page Break command, as shown in Figure 14.2.

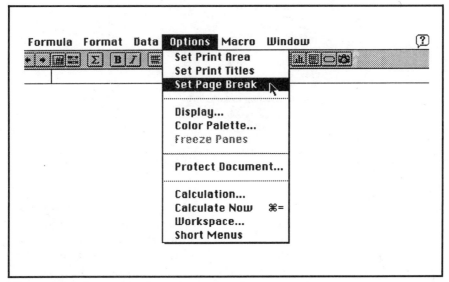

Figure 14.2: Issuing the Set Page Break command

You can easily distinguish manual page breaks in the worksheet because the lines marking them are darker than the lines indicating automatic page breaks. (Remember that Excel displays automatic page breaks only if you check the Automatic Page Breaks box in the Display dialog box, also accessed through the Options menu and shown in Figure 14.3.)

You can also see page breaks and judge their effect by using Excel's Page Preview feature, discussed later in this chapter.

Printing Row and Column Titles

When you print a worksheet with multiple pages, you may want the row and column titles you've created printed on each page so readers can identify the data easily. Here's how to print row and column titles.

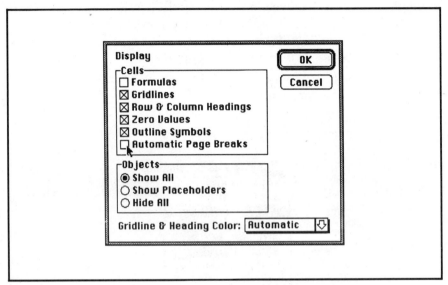

Figure 14.3: Displaying automatic page breaks

1. Select the row and column titles you want printed on each page by dragging across the areas. (If you want to select both row *and* column titles, you must drag to select the first range or group of titles—the column headings, for example—and then hold down the ⌘ key and drag across the second range—for example, the row headings. If you don't hold down the ⌘ key as you drag to select the second group of titles, the second group simply replaces the first group rather than being added to the first group.)

2. After the titles are selected, pull down the Options menu and select the Set Print Titles command.

3. Drag to select the area you want to print, without including the row and column titles. (If you include these titles in the area, the titles will be printed twice on the first page.)

4. Issue the Print command in the usual way. (See the sections that follow explaining the commands and procedures relating to the actual printing process.)

Printing Part of a Worksheet

You can print only a portion of a worksheet. This is the simple procedure:

1. Drag to select the area you want to print.

2. Pull down the Options menu and select the Set Print Area command.

3. Issue the normal command to print the document.

PAGE SETUP OPTIONS

The Excel dialog boxes that affect printing are slightly different for worksheets than they are for charts. Some options, such as the ability either to print or hide gridlines, are appropriate only for worksheet printing, while other options are appropriate only for charts.

USING PAGE SETUP OPTIONS WITH WORKSHEETS

You use the Page Setup dialog box to select several options related to printing any Macintosh document. However, the options displayed vary according to the particular printer you're using. In addition, publishers of specific applications often add items to the dialog box that are helpful to their users; this is what Microsoft has done with Excel.

Most of the Page Setup features are common to most Macintosh programs (you've probably used them many times if you've ever printed from your Macintosh). The Page Setup dialog box offers these options:

*   **Paper.** You can select the paper size you'll be using.

*   **Reduce or Enlarge.** You can reduce or enlarge the size of a printed file by specifying a percentage of its normal size.

*   **Orientation.** You can switch the orientation of the printed file between portrait (tall, with the paper printed vertically) and landscape (with the paper printed horizontally, or the wide way across the page).

You can also make adjustments specific to the type of printer. For example, a useful option for Excel users in an ImageWriter Page Setup dialog box is No Gaps Between Pages, which causes the printer to print across the perforations in tractor-feed paper. If you pick the icon for landscape printing and also select the No Gaps Between Pages option, you can print a worksheet with many columns sideways as one unit (except for rows that won't fit on one page) on one very wide sheet of paper.

Let's look at the options specific to Excel. Figure 14.4 shows the dialog box displayed when the active file is a worksheet and you select the Page Setup... command from the File menu. This figure shows the version of the dialog box seen if you're using a printer in the LaserWriter family; however, the Excel options are the same for any printer that works with a Macintosh. The Excel options start in the middle of the dialog box, where you see the word Header.

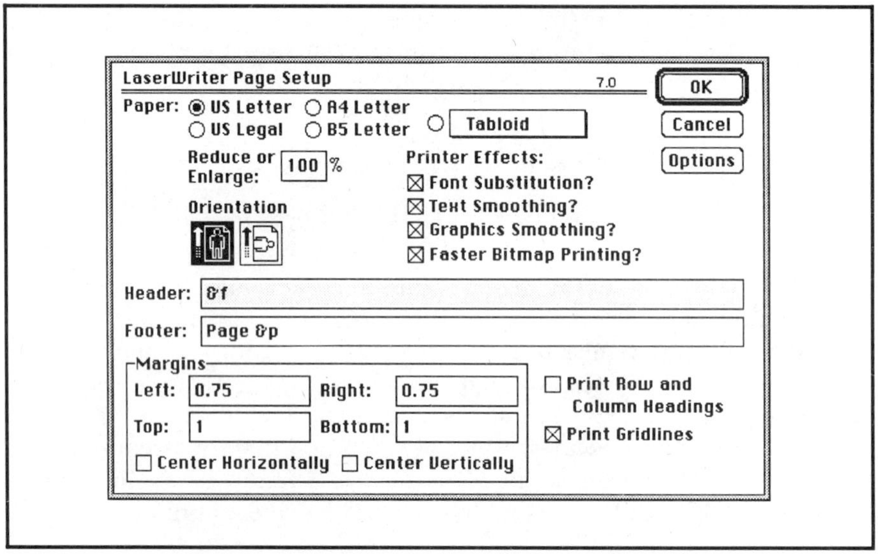

Figure 14.4: The LaserWriter worksheet Page Setup dialog box

- **Header.** You can add a header to every page of the worksheet printed (by default, the header consists of the file name).

- **Footer.** You can specify text that will appear at the bottom of every page of the worksheet (by default, the footer consists of the page number).

- **Margins.** You can set the width of the top, bottom, left, and right margins.

- **Center Horizontally/Vertically.** You can center a small worksheet on a page horizontally or vertically, or both.

- **Print Row and Column Headings.** This option lets you choose whether or not to print row numbers and column letters.

- **Print Gridlines.** This option lets you either print or suppress the worksheet gridlines.

These Page Setup options let you print your worksheet in the format that best meets your needs. For instance, you can use the Print Row and Column Headings and Print Gridlines options to suppress headings and gridlines and thus generate a report that lists items and totals without revealing that the report was created on a worksheet.

Using Header and Footer Codes

Note that if you don't want a header or footer on your printed worksheet, you can simply erase the default code entries in either the header or footer text box. The tricky part comes when you want to replace or add to the default codes. Table 14.1 lists the codes you can use in the Header and Footer boxes and what they mean. You can combine several of the codes in a single header or footer to print the text you've entered there in a particular typeface and style, complete with page numbering and date and time stamps.

USING PAGE SETUP OPTIONS WITH CHARTS

When the active Excel file is a chart, the Page Setup dialog box differs slightly from the one displayed for a worksheet. All of the differences are in the lower right corner of the dialog box. The chart version doesn't have boxes where you can choose to print row and column headings and gridlines. Instead, it provides an area headed Size. Here you can click a

Table 14.1: Header and Footer Codes

CODE	MEANING
&L	Left-align the following characters.
&C	Center the following characters.
&R	Right-align the following characters.
&B	Boldface the following characters.
&I	Italicize the following characters.
&U	Underline the following characters.
&S	Print the following characters with strikethrough.
&O	Print the following characters in outline style.
&H	Print the following characters in shadow style.
&D	Print the current date from the system clock.
&T	Print the current time from the system clock.
&F	Print the file name of the document.
&P	Print page numbers.
&P + *number*	Print the default page number, but add *number* to it. For example, entering **&P + 2** makes the first page number print as 3.
&P – *number*	Print the default page number minus *number.*
&&	Print a single ampersand (&).
&*"fontname"*	Print the following characters in the font specified by *"fontname"*. The name of the font must be enclosed in double quotation marks.
&*nn*	Print the following characters in the point size indicated by a two-digit number (*nn*).
&N	Print the total number of pages in the document. For example, if you type **Page &P of &N**, Excel prints this text and code combination on the first page of an eight-page document as Page 1 of 8.

To achieve the results you want, you can combine multiple codes with text in any header or footer.

button to select one of three choices:

- **Screen Size.** You can print a chart at the size displayed on the screen.

- **Fit to Page.** You can print a chart full page while retaining the original width-to-height ratio.

- **Full Page.** You can fill the page with a chart without attempting to maintain the width-to-height ratio.

USING PRINT PREVIEW

Before you print a document, you can see a preview of how it will look, including any header or footer. You can zoom in closer to examine how a selected portion of an Excel page will appear on paper, change the display to look at each page of a multipage document, and change the width of columns and the location of margins while you're in the preview mode.

Figure 14.5 shows the *Print Preview window.*. The figure shows the High Temperatures worksheet with its embedded 3-D area chart.

Here's how to use the preview feature:

1. Pull down the File menu and select Print Preview. This command displays the Print Preview window, which shows the entire first page of the current document.

   Alternatively, you can access the Print Preview window through the Print dialog box. Pull down the File menu and select the Print… command to display the Print dialog box. Then select the Print Preview box in that dialog box (shown in Figure 14.8 later in this chapter) and click the Print button (the OK button in versions of the operating system before 7.0). Excel will automatically display the Print Preview window before printing your document. When you're satisfied with the preview, you can click the Print button in the Print Preview window to print immediately, without bringing up the Print dialog box again.

2. In the Print Preview window, select the options you want. When you're finished, click the Print… button at the top of the window to proceed with printing or the Close button to close the window and return to the document.

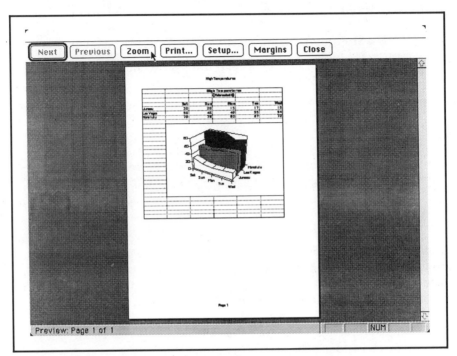

Figure 14.5: The Print Preview window

Here is a description of how to use the other buttons at the top of the window:

- **Margins**. Click this button to display lines representing the margins of the page, as in Figure 14.6. Drag one of the black handles on any of these lines to change a margin. At the top of the display, you'll also see handles representing column boundaries. Drag one of these handles to adjust the width of any column. When you're finished, click the Margins button again to hide the display of margin and column boundaries.

- **Next**. This option displays the next page of a multipage document.

- **Previous**. This option displays the previous page of a multipage document.

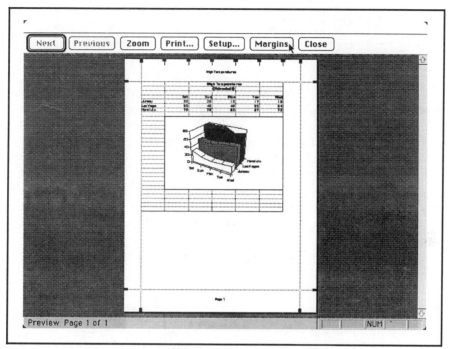

Figure 14.6: The Print Preview margins option

- **Zoom.** Click this button to enlarge the display so only a portion of the document is visible. You can use scroll bars to change the area displayed. You can also use the pointer to select an area to enlarge. When the pointer is positioned on the display of the document, it assumes the shape of a magnifying glass. You can then click the mouse button to enlarge the area under the pointer. To return to the display of a full page, either click the document again or click the Zoom button.

- **Print...** This option displays the standard Print dialog box unless you previously selected the Print Preview box in the Print dialog box. In that case, printing takes place immediately, from the Print Preview window.

- **Setup...** This option displays the standard Page Setup dialog box.

USING THE PRINT DIALOG BOX

When you pull down the File menu and issue the Print... command (or press ⌘-P, the shortcut to accomplish the same result), you'll see the Print dialog box. Its appearance and features depend on the application and printer you're using.

These differences are completely logical. For example, as you've already found, you can click a Print Preview box in the Excel Print dialog box to activate the preview feature before you print any Excel document. If you are working in some application other than Excel that does not have the Print Preview feature, this option will not appear. Similarly, if your printer doesn't use a paper cassette, the Paper Cassette option won't appear in the dialog box.

Figures 14.7 and 14.8 let you compare LaserWriter and ImageWriter print options for Excel.

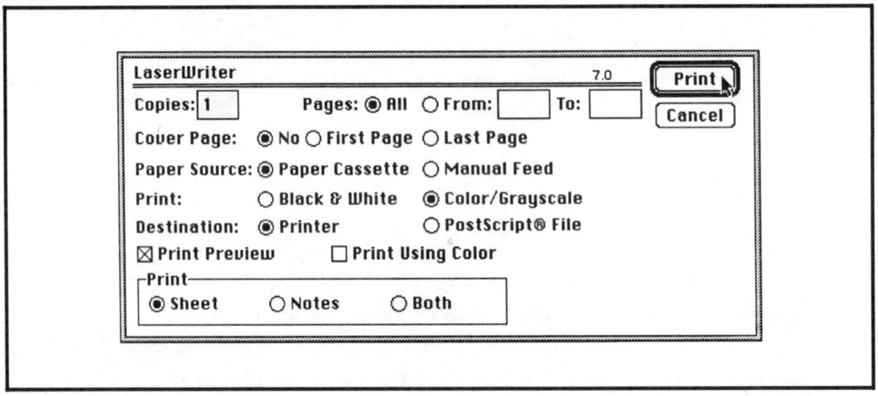

Figure 14.7: LaserWriter Print dialog box for Excel

PRINTING WITH POSTSCRIPT PRINTERS

Printers supporting the PostScript language, such as most Laser-Writers, have options relating to their specific capabilities. For example, if you are using a LaserWriter under System 7, you can click the PostScript File button to print a document to a PostScript file rather than to a printer

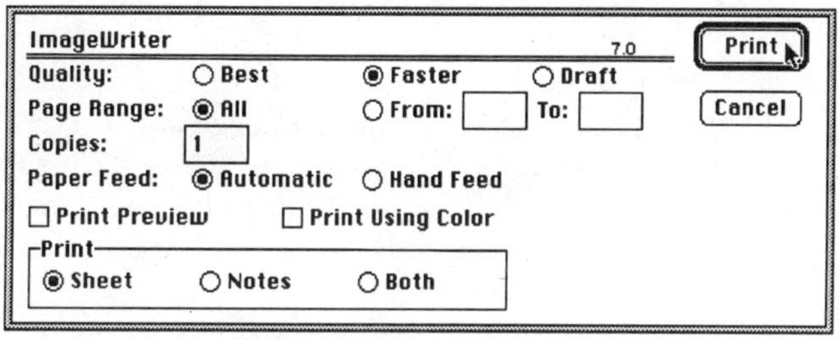

Figure 14.8: ImageWriter Print dialog box for Excel

(the default destination). The usual reason for printing to a PostScript file is to take that file to a production service for high-resolution printing, possibly as part of a professional publication.

System 7 and earlier versions of the Macintosh operating system alike offer a Cover Page option. A cover page is a list of basic information about a print job: the printer user, the application from which the document is being printed, the document name, the date and time, and the printer type. If you choose the No button (the default choice), Excel doesn't print a cover page. Choosing the First Page option causes the cover page to be printed before the document itself, and choosing the Last Page option prints the cover page after the document is printed. The Cover Page feature is useful mainly if a printer is connected to a network and is being fed by multiple computers. The statistics the feature provides help you determine which job belongs to which Macintosh on the network.

Some of the boxes and buttons in PostScript Print dialog boxes are found in most Print dialog boxes. You can specify the number of copies you want, which pages of a multiple-page document you want printed, whether the paper is to be fed manually or from the printer's cassette, and whether the document is to be printed in black and white or with color or gray-scale information.

Excel-specific options in PostScript Print dialog boxes are Print Preview (previously explained) and the Print options that let you print only the current worksheet or macro sheet, only notes attached to the worksheet or macro sheet, or both the worksheet or macro sheet and the notes.

PRINTING WITH IMAGEWRITERS PRINTERS

ImageWriter printers print with the Macintosh's built-in QuickDraw language, but do not support the PostScript language and are rarely fed by a group of computers on a network. Therefore, an ImageWriter Print dialog box does not include PostScript File or Cover Page options. This dialog box also doesn't offer a paper cassette option, but it does include Automatic and Hand Feed options.

The ImageWriter Print dialog box offers the usual Print dialog box options that control the number of copies and page range to be printed. In addition, it offers three Quality options: You can print slowly with the highest quality available on your printer by clicking the Best button; you can print more rapidly, with increasingly poorer quality, by clicking the Faster and Draft buttons.

From the ImageWriter Print dialog box, you can use the same Excel-specific print options as for the LaserWriter: You can activate the Print Preview option and the Sheet, Notes, and Both options.

TIP

You can print a group of worksheets or macro sheets at the same time simply by forming them into a workgroup, as described in Chapter 7. When you issue the command to print the workgroup, Excel will automatically print each file in the workgroup in turn.

USING EXCEL TO CREATE FORMS

Because Excel worksheets are composed of cells that can be labeled and easily adjusted in size, you can use these worksheets to create forms that involve no calculations at all. For example, you can print a blank form to be filled in by hand, such as the hotel valet-parking audit form shown in Figure 14.9.

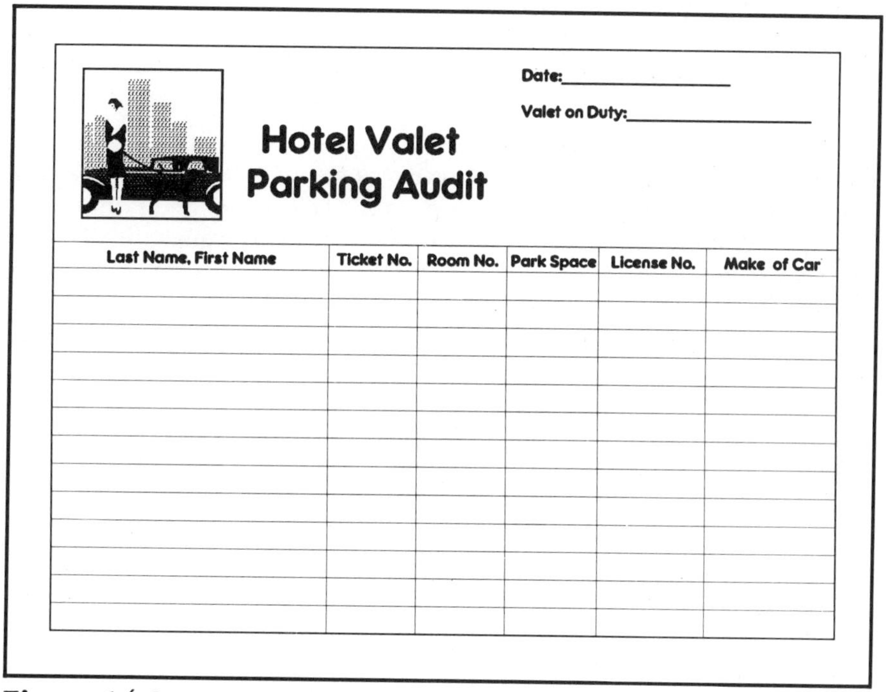

Date:_______________

Valet on Duty:_______________

Hotel Valet
Parking Audit

Last Name, First Name	Ticket No.	Room No.	Park Space	License No.	Make of Car

Figure 14.9: Creating a form

The heading of the form was created by overlapping two text notes, both formatted to appear without borders. The first note was stretched to fill the entire width of the worksheet. The second note positions the text in the upper right corner as a separate entity from the main title. The illustration is simply a piece of clip art from the Image Club library that was pasted into the worksheet through the clipboard. The typeface is Frankfurt, from Dubl-Click Software.

There is one trick to printing this form. By default, Excel prints only as much of a worksheet as is filled with data. Since the column titles constitute the bottom of the actual data in the form, normally none of the blank cells would be printed. All you have to do to make Excel print the blank cells is to place a period (or any other inconspicuous data) in the cell in the lower right corner of the range you want to include. The cell in the lower right corner here contains a period formatted to appear right-justified.

SUMMARY

This chapter described the options you can use to make Excel print your documents just the way you want them: selection and formatting options, Print Preview, and the options in the Page Setup and Print dialog boxes. In addition, you learned how to select a printer through the Chooser and how to create forms that take advantage of worksheet formatting and features.

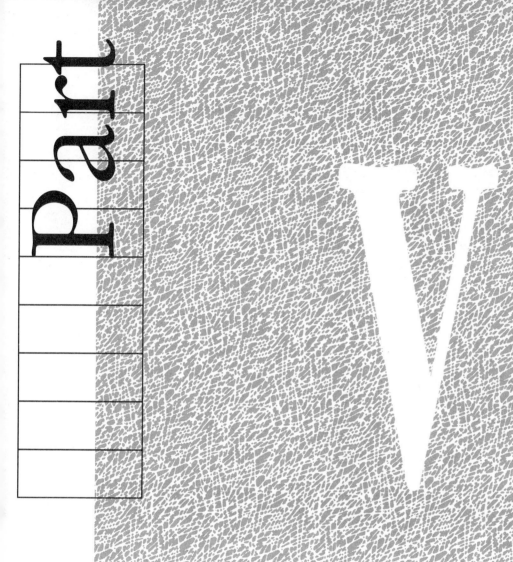

Part

VI

Automating
Your Work

Chapter

15

Recording Macros

Macros are small programs consisting of formulas that perform operations automatically. You can very easily record *command macros,* a series of mouse and keyboard actions saved for later playback.

This chapter discusses how to use Excel's time-saving macro recorder. Chapter 17 tells you how to *write* command macros. Chapter 18 explains how to write *function macros,* which add your own functions to those furnished with Excel.

USING THE MACRO RECORDER

Suppose you want to automate the saving of the three worksheets linked as a workgroup in Chapter 7. If you save these worksheets manually, you have to close each one separately, taking care to save any changes that have been made. The process would be easier if you could handle it with one command.

PLANNING THE
PROCEDURE TO AUTOMATE

Your first step is to select a method of saving the worksheets that *can* be accomplished automatically. For example, if you simply *close* the active worksheet by clicking the close box, your next step would be to close the next worksheet, provided no changes had been made. However, if changes had been made, the next step would be to respond to a prompt that asks if you want to *save* changes. Thus, a macro that starts by clicking the close box would often require human intervention and would therefore be a poor candidate for automation.

How else could you handle this task? The obvious solution is to save each worksheet automatically, regardless of whether or not changes had been made, and then to close the file. Let's set up a macro to do this.

The example macro you will create does not first save the *workspace* file. This is an unnecessary step here, since saving the individual worksheets preserves any changes to them. This example assumes that you are using the worksheets to analyze orders from regional offices, and that you ordinarily do not change the size or positioning of the separate worksheet windows. However, if changes in the proportions and arrangement of your worksheets are a common occurrence, you might want to start the macro by resaving the workspace too.

RECORDING THE PROCEDURE IN A MACRO

Follow these steps to record the close procedure in a macro:

1. Load the WORKSPACE EXERCISE file you saved at the end of Chapter 7. The three worksheets in the workgroup should appear on the screen as they do at the end of Chapter 7.

2. Pull down the Macro menu and select the Record... command. You'll see the Record Macro dialog box. In this box you're asked to provide a name for the macro and a shortcut key combination that can be used to run it.

3. As the name of the macro, type **SaveOrderGroup**. (Spaces are not allowed as part of a macro name.) Press Tab to enter the name and move to the Option + ⌘ box.

4. Enter the *shortcut key combination.* All of the shortcut key combinations dealing with macros involve pressing the ⌘ and Option keys simultaneously while also pressing a letter of the alphabet. Capital and lowercase letters are considered to be different characters for this purpose, so you can use any of the 26 lowercase letters and any of the 26 capital letters. Thus, you can assign shortcut kays to control a total of 52 possible macros in the same macro sheet. (You'll see a macro sheet shortly. These look much like worksheets and are used to store the macros you create.) For this macro, type the letter **s**, to remind yourself that the operation to be recorded is connected with saving files. Your screen should resemble Figure 15.1.

5. Click OK to close the dialog box and start recording the macro.

6. The Order Summary worksheet was active in the workspace when it was last saved and should therefore still be active. Press ⌘-S now to save that worksheet. Then click the close box to close the file.

7. The Chicago worksheet now becomes active. Repeat the actions in step 5: Press ⌘-S and click the close box to save and close the Chicago worksheet.

8. The New York worksheet becomes active. Press ⌘-S and click the close box to save and close the New York worksheet.

9. Pull down the Macro menu and select the Stop Recorder command to end the macro recording sequence.

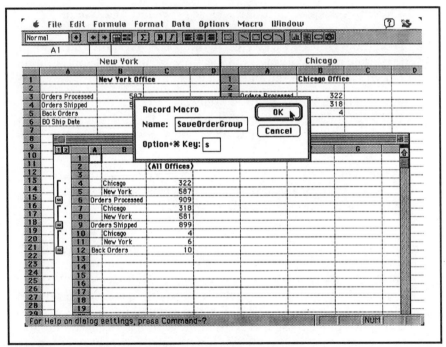

Figure 15.1: Recording a macro

THE MACRO SHEET

Your screen now displays a file you haven't seen before. It looks like a worksheet, and its title bar displays the name Macro1. This is a *macro sheet* (see Figure 15.2). Macros are stored on macro sheets. By default, macro sheets have wider columns than worksheets, to provide plenty of room for formulas. Also

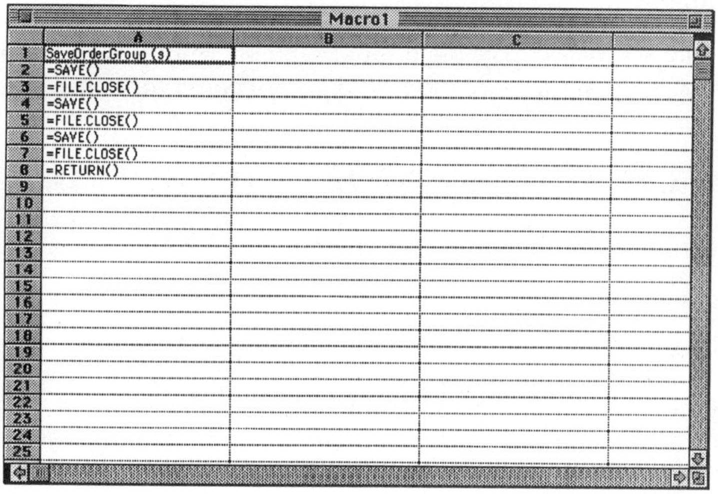

Figure 15.2: Macro sheet with the recorded macro

by default, the cells of macro sheets display the formulas themselves, rather than the results of the formulas normally seen in worksheets.

When you record a macro for the first time, Excel automatically creates a new macro sheet called Macro1. When you save the macro sheet, you can give it some other name, just as you can a worksheet called Worksheet1.

Once a macro has been recorded on a saved macro sheet, you must load the macro sheet into memory before you can run that macro or any other macro on the same macro sheet.

Look at the macro that you just created by recording the close procedure. In the first cell you'll see the name you gave the macro, followed in parentheses by the shortcut letter of the alphabet you assigned to the macro. (This is the letter you can type in combination with the ⌘ and Option keys to run the macro without using the Macro menu.)

Starting with the second row and continuing down column A, you'll see the macro functions recorded as a result of the commands you entered while the recorder was running. You repeated the same series of two commands three times (on three separate worksheets), so those commands are repeated on successive rows. Excel added the final command—=RETURN( )—automatically to complete the macro when you issued the Stop Recorder command.

If you had issued any command in error in recording the macro, you could easily edit that step of the macro simply by editing the relevant cell, using the same techniques you use to edit a worksheet formula.

SAVING AND RUNNING YOUR MACRO

Use the following sequence to save the macro you recorded and then to test it by running it.

1. Press ⌘-S to save the macro sheet. Since you haven't saved it before and therefore have had no opportunity to change the default name, Excel displays the Save As dialog box, shown in Figure 15.3. Click the Save button to save the sheet with the default name Macro1. (Remember that you can record many other macros on this same sheet, so assigning a name other than the default is less important than it is for a worksheet.)

2. Pull down the File menu again and select the WORKGROUP EXERCISE workspace file in which you saved the three worksheets. The worksheets reopen on your Excel desktop.

3. Since the Macro1 worksheet is still loaded into memory, you can now run the macro you recorded. Pull down the Macro menu and select the Run... command. You'll see the Run dialog box displayed in Figure 15.4.

4. Click OK to run the macro you created. Watch as Excel saves the worksheets one by one and then closes them, until only the macro sheet remains on your screen.

You could have used the shortcut key combination ⌘-Option-s to run the macro. We used the menu system instead to see the Run dialog box. Let's look at the Run... command options now.

Since you have so far defined only one macro, that macro is the only choice displayed in the Run list box. If you had multiple macro sheets open, each containing at least one macro, all of the macro names would appear.

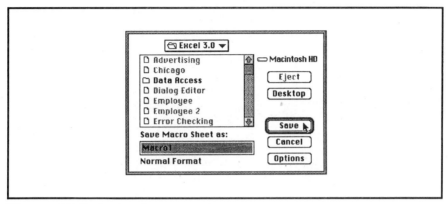

Figure 15.3: Saving the macro sheet

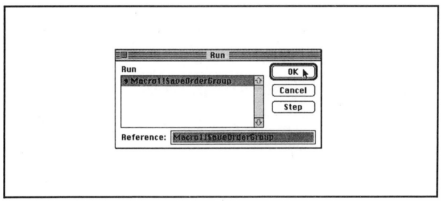

Figure 15.4: The Run dialog box

Note that, in addition to the usual OK and Cancel buttons, the Run dialog box also contains a Step button and a Reference text box.

Use the Step button to "step through" a macro function by function, usually to try to locate problems when the macro is not working properly. When you use the Step button, the macro runs in stages, one cell at a time, thus providing a handy debugging capability.

The Reference text box works in conjunction with the Step button. If you don't want to start the macro at its beginning, you can enter in the text box the address of the cell at which you want to start. Click the cell at which you want to start. The address appears in the text box, and you can click OK to run the macro starting at that point.

Incidentally, by default Excel records all cell addresses in macros as absolute references. If you want to make these addresses relative instead, pull down the Macro menu and select the Relative Record command before recording the macro.

ASSIGNING MACROS TO OBJECTS

As you've just learned, you can run a macro by selecting a command from the Macro menu or by using a keyboard shortcut. You can also use two additional methods to run a macro: You can create a button a user can click to run the macro, or you can assign the macro to a graphic object such as a drawing or clip art cartoon that a user can click to start the macro.

When you create a button or graphic object, you can make it any size you want, have it display any text you want, and format the text with any style attributes you desire (such as boldface or italics), using any typefaces installed on your system.

ASSIGNING A MACRO TO A BUTTON

Let's create a button to close the three worksheets without using the Macro menu or the keyboard shortcut.

1. Click the button tool on the Toolbar. (The button tool is the icon at the right end of the Toolbar, just to the left of the camera tool. It looks like a rectangle with rounded corners, like a Macintosh button.)

2. Place the pointer on the Order Summary worksheet at the location where you want one corner of the button to appear.

3. Drag to make the button the size and shape you want. (If you want the button to be square, hold down the Shift key as you drag. To align the button to the cell grid, hold down the ⌘ key.) The Assign Macro dialog box appears, as shown in Figure 15.5. At the same time, the text *Button 1* appears inside the button.

4. In the Assign Macro dialog box, highlight the SaveOrderGroup macro and click OK. (If you want to select a macro from a macro

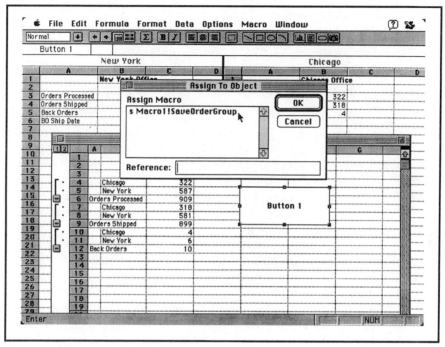

Figure 15.5: The Assign Macro dialog box

sheet that is not open and therefore does not appear in the list box, you type the name or a cell reference for the macro in the Reference text box.) The button area is now ready for text entry. You will replace the placeholder text *Button 1* with the text you will actually use.

5. Type the text to be displayed in the button. Type **CLICK HERE**, press Return, type **to**, press Return again, type **Save & Close**, press Return again, and type **Worksheets**. By default, Excel centers each of the four lines automatically.

6. Drag across the first line of text (the line that says *CLICK HERE*) to select it for formatting.

7. Pull down the Format menu and select the Font... command. The Font dialog box appears.

8. In the Font dialog box, select the typeface, size, and style you want for that first line of text. Select from among the typefaces currently

installed on your Macintosh. Choose an easy-to-read font that calls attention to the button.

9. Drag to select the remainder of the text you typed for the button (*to Save & Close Worksheets*) and format this text using a font that is a slightly smaller size than the one you picked for the first line.

10. Click outside the button area to complete the text formatting and deselect the button.

If some of the text in the button is hidden from view because a font size you selected was too large, you can drag one of the handles on the button to resize or reshape it. However, if you click the button to reselect it, the action of clicking will execute the macro and save and close all of the worksheets, rather than reselect the button. The Excel programmers have anticipated this problem. To reselect the button without executing the macro, simply hold down the ⌘ key as you click.

Your screen should now resemble Figure 15.6. The typefaces used for the button in this figure are 14-point Gill Sans Ultra Bold for the first line of text and 13-point Gill Sans Extra Bold for the remainder.

Incidentally, any time you move the pointer over the area of the completed button, the pointer will assume the shape of a hand with a pointing or pressing finger.

You can easily drag a macro button to another location on your worksheet. Here's how:

1. Select the button by holding down the ⌘ key as you click the button.

2. Pull down the Format menu and select the Object Placement... command. You'll see the Object Placement dialog box displayed in Figure 15.7.

3. Click a button in the dialog box to tell Excel to move and size the button when cells are moved or resized; to move the button when cells are moved, but not to size it when cells are resized; or not to move *or* size the button in relation to cells—in other words, to let it move independently over the surface of the worksheet. For Figure 15.7, we chose the third option in the dialog box: to keep the button independent.

4. Click OK to close the dialog box, hold down the ⌘ key and drag the selected button to its new position, and then click outside the button area to deselect the button.

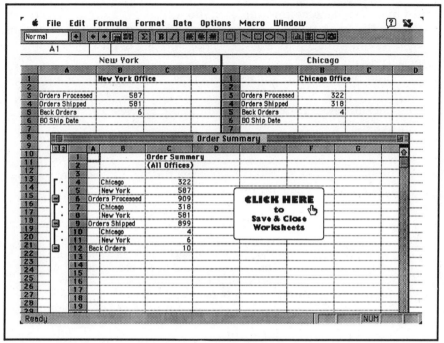

Figure 15.6: The completed macro button

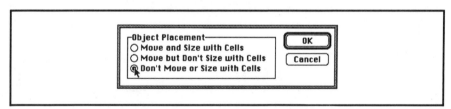

Figure 15.7: The Object Placement dialog box

ASSIGNING A MACRO TO A GRAPHIC OBJECT

You can assign a macro to any graphic object, whether it's a drawing you've created yourself, a scanned image such as a photo, or a piece of clip art you've bought from a graphic art library.

In choosing a graphic object, either select an object that clearly indicates by its appearance that the user should click it to run a macro (for instance, use a sketch of a man running), or clearly label the object. In most instances, you will want to place a text box adjacent to the object telling the user what to do.

This is the procedure for assigning a macro to a graphic object:

1. Click the graphic object you want to use to select it.

2. Pull down the Macro menu and select the Assign to Object... command.

3. In the Assign Macro dialog box, select the macro you want to assign to the graphic and click OK.

TIP

At any time you can assign a different macro to either a button or a graphic object simply by selecting the object (holding down the ⌘ key while doing so, as explained earlier) and using the Assign to Object... command again to choose another macro.

Even though you have a macro assigned to an object, you can still run that macro by using the Macro menu or the keyboard shortcut assigned to the macro.

SUMMARY

You've learned to record and run macros, and you've been introduced to macro sheets. In addition, you've created a custom button that can be clicked to run a macro.

In the next chapter you learn how to use some sophisticated, ready-to-run macros that Excel provides for you.

Chapter

16

Using Library
Templates
and Macros

In Chapter 15 you learned how to record macros. Excel also lets you *write* macros, using a macro language composed of over 300 specific macro functions. Why would you want to write a macro when you could simply record it by capturing keystrokes and mouse movements? The reason is that written macros can include complex procedures that would be impossible to create by recording.

For example, in a written macro you could use a function macro called IF(logical_test) to construct a routine dealing with employee benefits. The macro would branch and call any one of four different subroutines, based on the data entered in a Date Hired cell. Suppose, for instance, that if an employee has been with the company less than six months, the person is not eligible for any vacation time. If the length of time employed is over six months but less than a year, the employee is entitled to one week of vacation. If the employee has been with the company more than a year but less than five years, the person is entitled to two weeks of vacation. If the employee has been with the company more than five years, the person is entitled to three weeks of vacation. Each subroutine would allocate the appropriate vacation time, keep track of how much time the employee used and when, and even control the issuance of vacation payroll checks without requiring the usual input of hours worked derived from time clock records.

However, writing complicated macros can require considerable programming knowledge. Fortunately, Excel provides a number of completed macros you can use that perform complex operations and require no programming. This chapter discusses these macros.

In addition, Excel furnishes several models, or templates. These are complete worksheets that include macros. You can use these templates as they are or easily modify them to suit your particular needs. Each template is a specially configured worksheet that is protected so that you automatically save only a copy of the worksheet after you make your changes—leaving the original for use again and again.

USING THE MACRO LIBRARY

Both the templates and the predefined macros furnished with Excel are located in a folder called Macro Library, found inside the main Excel folder.

Unfortunately, templates and macros are mixed together in this folder: The Open Document dialog box lists them all in the same box and labels them only with their names and without any clue as to whether they're templates or macros.

For example, look at Figure 16.1. Amortization Table, Annual Budget, and Bill Template are all templates—yet only Bill Template is identified by its name as a template.

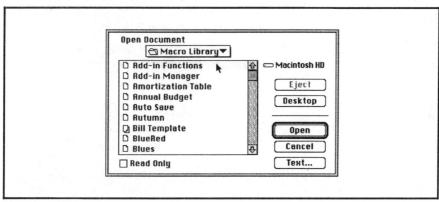

Figure 16.1: Listing models and macros

Shortly, we'll discuss the names and purposes of specific templates and macros, so you'll know not only which is which, but also know what tasks each accomplishes.

AN EXAMPLE MACRO SHEET

Let's look at an example of the type of macro sheet Excel provides.

Examine Figure 16.2. This figure shows a small portion of the macro sheet for one macro: Multiple Sheet Aide. This macro performs two seemingly straightforward tasks: It arranges a group of worksheets in separate windows so that the user can view a horizontal portion of each, and it selects and displays a range in an external worksheet or macro sheet that is referenced in the current sheet. Yet the macro is so complicated that it occupies 125 rows on its macro sheet!

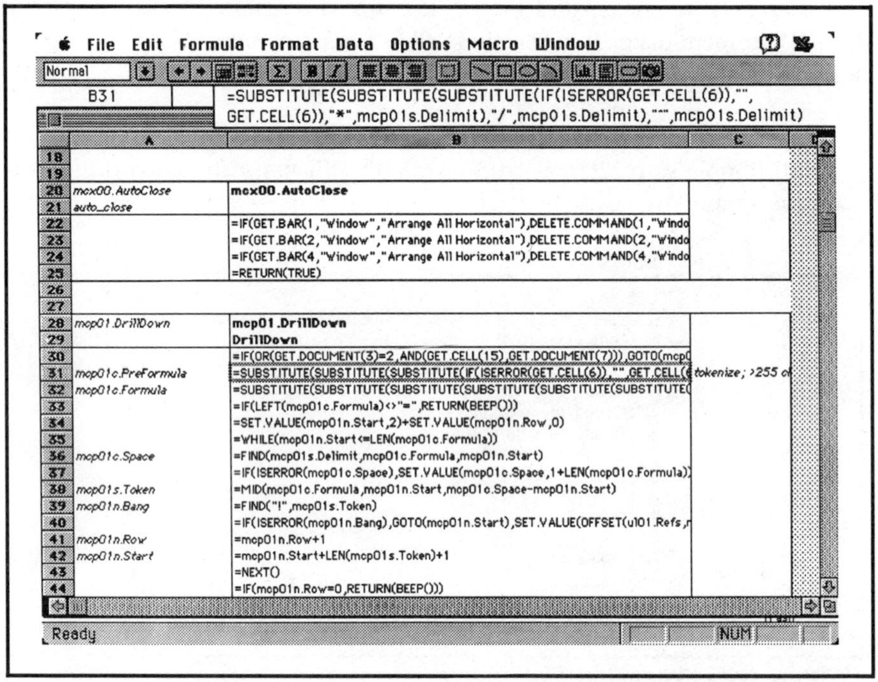

Figure 16.2: A portion of the Multiple Sheet Aide macro

To see an example of the complexity of just one cell of the multiple sheet aide macro, look at an active cell. In Figure 16.2, cell B31 of the sheet is active. Look at the full formula for that cell, displayed in the formula bar. You can see that, like many other formulas in this macro, it is so long that the cell cannot display all of it, even though column B is exceptionally wide. Regardless of its complexity, however, you can use the Multiple Sheet Aide macro, like all of the other macros Excel provides, with no knowledge whatsoever of how the intricate macro was programmed.

AN EXAMPLE TEMPLATE

Figure 16.3 shows a typical Excel template: Break-Even Analysis. Because the gridlines have been hidden (an easy task to accomplish using the Display... command on the Options menu), the display, at first glance, bears little resemblance to a worksheet.

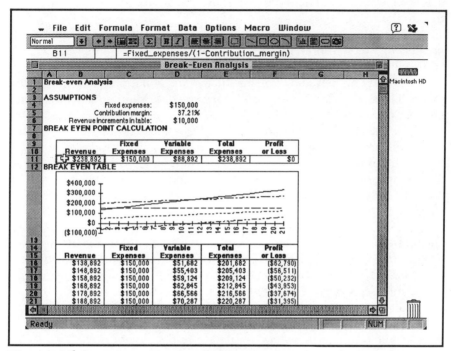

Figure 16.3: The Break-Even Analysis Template

This template includes an embedded chart, programmed so that values you enter in the Assumptions area affect the analysis depicted on the chart. The purpose of the model is to help a company determine, by entering assumptions, how much revenue it must earn to avoid losses—in other words, to reach a break-even point.

THE MACROS

The macro files Excel provides are *add-in macros*; if you haven't loaded a particular macro, you won't see its command on the applicable menu. You use the macros by selecting options added to Excel menus when the macros are loaded into memory. By default, Excel opens the *macro sheets* for the macros without displaying them. To display and edit an add-in macro sheet, you must hold down the Shift key as you click the Open button to load the file.

Selecting a menu command for an Excel-supplied macro usually brings up a dialog box that presents clearly defined options. On-line help screens add additional detail.

This section lists and explains the macros you'll probably find in the Macro Library folder. We say *probably* because Microsoft occasionally changes the contents of this folder.

The file names in the folder with color-related names (Autumn, Reds, and so on) are alternate color palettes, as explained in Chapter 24.

You can make any add-in macro load automatically when Excel starts. Simply drag the macro file into the Excel Startup Folder, located inside the Macintosh System folder. For details, see the instructions at the end of Chapter 18.

- **Add-in Functions.** This macro provides six additional mathematical functions that can be used in worksheets: BASE (which converts a base-10 number to another base), DEGREES (which converts radians into degrees), FASTMATCH (which returns the relative position of an element in an array that matches a specified value), RADIANS (which converts degrees into radians), RANDBETWEEN (which returns a random integer within a specified range), and SUMSQUARES (which returns the sum of the squares of all of the numbers in a specified contiguous range of cells). To use these functions with the current worksheet, simply load the Add-in Functions macro sheet. The functions will be added automatically to those displayed through the Paste Function... command. As with other functions, when you highlight one of these functions in the Paste Function dialog box, Excel displays the arguments that are required to use it.

- **Add-in Manager.** This macro lets you select a set of add-in macros that Add-in Manager can load automatically for use with your worksheet. The set can include add-in macros you have written or recorded yourself. Once you've loaded the Add-in Manager, you use it by selecting the Add-Ins... command that then appears on the Options menu.

- **Auto Save.** This macro guards against data loss by automatically saving Excel files at preset intervals as you work. After you've loaded the macro, you make your settings through the AutoSave... command that then appears on the Options menu.

- **Crosstabs.** This macro summarizes records from a defined database in a two-dimensional table. When this macro is loaded, the Crosstabs command to execute it appears on the Data menu.

- **Document Summary.** Use this macro to store information about a worksheet so you can determine later who created it, the date it was created, the subject, and the number of revisions. This macro also stores any comments that the worksheet contains. Once you've loaded this macro, you enter or view information in the summary by selecting the Summary Info... command from the Edit menu. This command appears only if the macro has been loaded.

- **File Functions.** This macro loads a series of macros that creates folders, deletes folders, tests for the existence of a file or folder, and lists all folders within a current folder.

- **Flat File.** Use this macro to transfer data between flat text files (files in which data is not separated by tabs) and worksheet cell ranges. You can either export a cell range to a text file or import and distribute values from a text file into worksheet columns. Separate the values from one another with a space, a slash, or some other symbol you designate. The export and import operations in this macro are handled by two commands that appear on the Data menu if the macro is loaded: the Export... and Smart Parse... commands.

- **Glossary.** This macro can save formulas and cell contents in glossary entries you can paste as often as you like into worksheets or macro sheets. Loading the macro adds the Glossary... command to the Edit menu.

- **Macro Debugger.** This macro lets you debug macros you've written. You can set tracepoints and breakpoints at designated cells. Loading the macro adds the Debug command to the Macro menu.

- **Multiple Sheet Aide.** When you load this macro, three new commands appear on the Window menu. These commands rearrange the display of multiple open worksheets. You can choose the arrangement that you find most convenient. The macro also performs a second task: When you press ⌘-Option-D from within a cell that contains a reference to another worksheet or macro sheet, the macro selects and displays the range in question in the other sheet. If the other sheet is not open, you will even be asked if you want to open it.

- **Name Changer.** This macro changes every reference to a designated name in a worksheet to a new name. You can also use this macro to delete a name. Loading the macro adds the Change Name... command to the Formula menu.

- **Slide Show.** This macro lets you create a "slide show" of Excel charts and worksheets and display it using the sequence and timing you specify on the screen. Loading the macro adds the Slide Show... command to the Macro menu.

- **Sound Notes.** This macro lets you add sound notes to cells. This feature is explained at the end of this chapter.

- **What If.** This macro adds a What If... command to the Formula menu, through which you can enter a series of input values for one or more independent variables. The macro cycles through the results yielded by each of the possible combinations.

- **Worksheet Auditor.** This macro adds the Worksheet Auditor... command to the Formula menu. With this command you can display a list of potential errors in a worksheet, generate a map of the worksheet contents (formulas, text, values, and so on), trace cell dependencies to help determine data flow, and generate summary information about the worksheet.

- **Worksheet Comparison.** This macro adds a Compare... command to the Formula menu. Use this command to obtain a list of differences between two worksheets (handy in determining whether changes have been made in some version or copy of a particular worksheet).

THE TEMPLATES

You should find the following worksheet templates in the Macro Library folder. The instructions for using the templates appear on the templates themselves.

- **Amortization Table.** This template contains an amortization table that calculates the beginning balance, interest, principal payments, and ending balance for any 24-month consecutive payment periods of a loan. This template can also calculate the amount of a periodic payment.

- **Annual Budget.** Use this template in budgeting the operations of a company. The template uses the outlining capabilities of Excel, enabling you to hide or show levels of detail. You must alter this template to include the categories required for a specific company.

- **Bill Template.** This template provides a sample worksheet you can alter to fit the circumstances of your own business and use to bill customers. It contains appropriate bill formatting and formulas.

- **Break-Even Analysis.** This template helps determine the break-even point for a company, using user-provided assumptions.

- **College Expenses.** This template works in conjunction with the College Helper macro sheet, which is loaded automatically when you open the worksheet. This template lets you enter investment assumptions and determine whether or not the contemplated investments will result in sufficient return to fund college education for one or more children.

- **Sales Tracking.** This model consists of two templates—Sales Database and Sales Analyzer—plus a macro sheet called Sales Analyzer Macro. All are loaded automatically when you select Sales Tracking in the Macro Library folder. In combination, these files provide analysis and projections based on sales figures you enter.

- **Structured Macro Template.** This template helps debug macros.

TRYING THE
WORKSHEET AUDITOR MACRO

To see how to use the macros in the library, open the Error Checking worksheet that you used in Chapter 8. Recall that you changed cell D13 in that worksheet so that it no longer contains a formula; instead, it contains the result of a formula. You also added a note to cell E11.

Let's load the Worksheet Auditor macro and try out its features on the Error Checking worksheet.

If you're accustomed to using macros that perform one simple task—such as printing a weekly report—a macro such as the Worksheet Auditor can be a real eye-opener. Like some of the other macros in the Macro Library, it has so many features that it could really serve as a stand-alone program.

MAPPING THE WORKSHEET

First you'll generate a map of the worksheet.

1. With the Error Checking worksheet already open, issue the file opening command again. (Pull down the File menu and select the Open... command. Shortcut: Press ⌘-O.)

2. In the list box of the resulting Open Document dialog box, scroll until you see the Macro Library folder listed. Double-click the name to open the folder.

3. The list box now shows the contents of the Macro Library folder. Scroll the list box until you see the Worksheet Auditor file. Double-click the name to open the macro sheet for that macro.

4. Pull down the Formula menu and select the Worksheet Auditor command, which Excel added to the menu when you loaded the macro sheet. You'll now see the Worksheet Auditor dialog box shown in Figure 16.4. The dialog box contains four buttons, each of which can be selected to perform some kind of analysis on the worksheet. You'll try all of the buttons.

5. Click the Map Worksheet button. Excel displays the map shown in Figure 16.5.

If you're not accustomed to seeing the type of analysis used in the worksheet map, this tabular representation may seem strange and incomprehensible. However, take a closer look.

This map is actually a bird's-eye view of how the worksheet is organized. The map shows the row and column headings that are active in this particular worksheet. It also displays a single-character code in each cell to show the kind of data in each cell. As the legend at the right of the map shows, the letter T indicates text such as a label, the letter F indicates a formula, the number 9 indicates a number, the letter an L indicates a logical

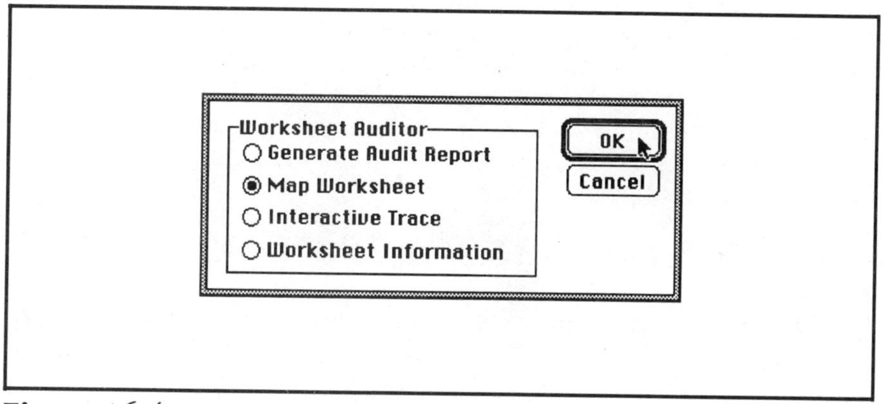

Figure 16.4: The Worksheet Auditor dialog box

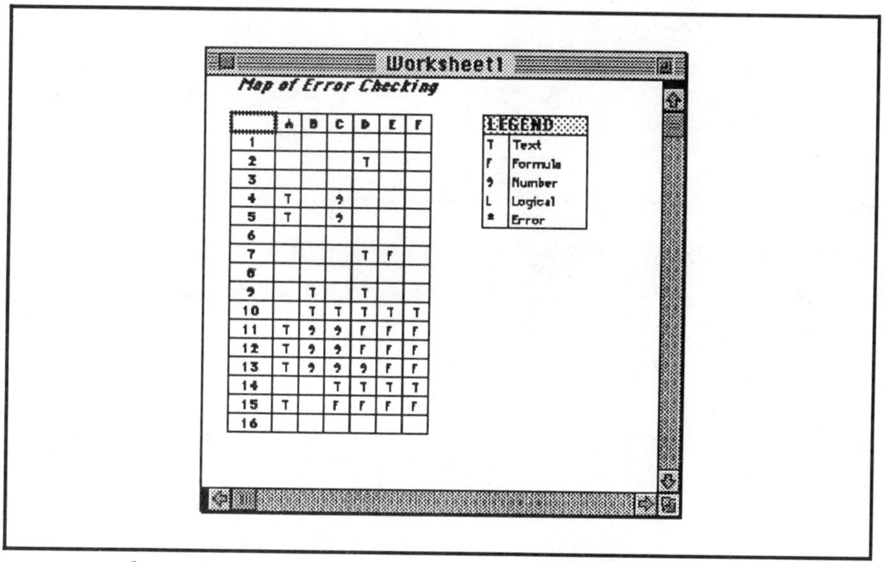

Figure 16.5: A map of the Error Checking worksheet

value (TRUE or FALSE), and an asterisk (∗) indicates an error value. (This particular worksheet in its current form contains no logical values or error values.)

For example, cell D13 displays 9, indicating a number, because, as mentioned a few paragraphs ago, in Chapter 8 you replaced the formula in that cell with its result. The cells above and below D3 contain other kinds of data.

A map of the worksheet organization can be particularly helpful in two circumstances: when you're trying to find the cause of a problem in a worksheet, and when you're trying to learn the structure of a large worksheet created by someone else.

Click the close box to close the worksheet containing the map. Click the No button when asked if you want to save any changes.

OBTAINING WORKSHEET INFORMATION

The Worksheet Information option on the Worksheet Auditor menu produces a quick summary of facts about the current worksheet. Try this button next.

1. Pull down the Formula menu and select the Worksheet Auditor command again.

2. In the Worksheet Auditor dialog box, click the Worksheet Information button. Then click OK. Excel creates another worksheet, this time showing the information displayed in Figure 16.6.

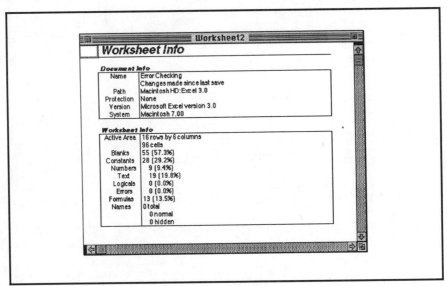

Figure 16.6: A Worksheet Information worksheet

As you can see, the Worksheet Information option provides you with data about the file: its name, the folder it's in, any security protection in effect, the version of Excel being used, and the version of the Macintosh operating system being used. More important, it gives you information about the worksheet itself: the size of the active area, the number of blank cells, the number of *constants* (data of any kind, except formulas, entered directly into cells), the number of cells occupied by numbers, the number of cells filled with text, the number of logical and error values, the number of formulas, and the number of cell and range names used (including both displayed and hidden names).

When you're finished viewing the Worksheet Information worksheet, close it without saving it.

GENERATING AN AUDIT REPORT

The Worksheet Auditor macro's Audit Report feature produces a list of cells with possible problems. Select this option now.

1. Pull down the Formula menu and select the Worksheet Auditor command.

2. In the Worksheet Auditor dialog box, click the Generate Audit Report button. This action brings up an Audit Report dialog box (see Figure 16.7), where you can click boxes to display any or all of the following information: lists of cells that contain error values,

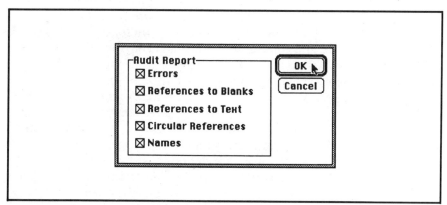

Figure 16.7: The Audit Report dialog box

formula references to blank cells, formula references to cells that contain text, *circular references* (cells involved in formulas that refer to themselves), questionable names, and names defined but not used.

3. By default, all possible report information is selected. However, if your worksheet is very large and you're interested only in one or two specific audit items, you'll save time and paper by deselecting some of the boxes. For this example, leave all options selected and click OK. Figure 16.8 shows the report that will be produced.

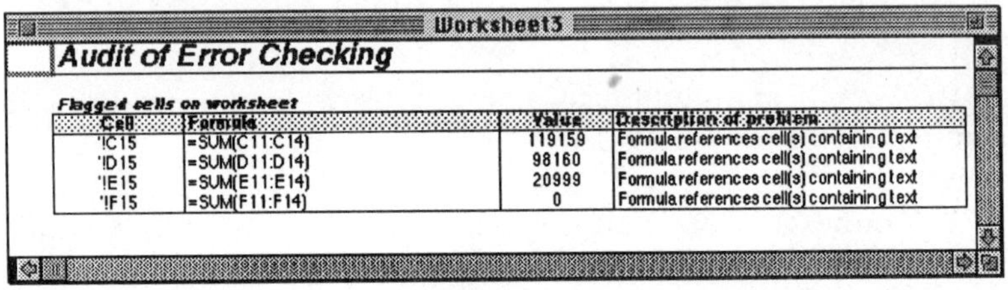

Figure 16.8: Audit report of the Error Checking worksheet

As you can see, only four cells are questioned. The potential problem with each is listed as *Formula references cell(s) containing text.*

Is this a real problem? Note the formulas shown for each cell. They're summation formulas, and you entered them when you originally created the Error Checking worksheet as the Performance Report worksheet in Chapter 4. At that time you clicked the auto-sum button on the Toolbar to total the contents of the range of cells immediately above an active cell in row 15. This range contained a line of dashes in row 14 to separate the data from the total. These cells with dashes in row 14 are technically text and are therefore ignored by Excel in adding the values in the range. Since they don't affect the accuracy of the formulas, they're no cause for concern.

Nevertheless, the flagging of these cells in the Audit Report worksheet indicates how thoroughly this macro option examines the current worksheet.

Close the Audit Report worksheet without saving it.

CONDUCTING AN INTERACTIVE TRACE

Using the remaining Worksheet Auditor macro feature, Interactive Trace, you can trace the data path leading to or emanating from a selected cell, following any branches in the path that you wish.

1. Select cell E11 in the Error Checking worksheet. This is the cell to which you attached a note.

2. Pull down the Formula menu and select the Worksheet Auditor command a final time.

3. In the Worksheet Auditor dialog box, click the Interactive Trace button. Then click OK. You'll see the screen displayed in Figure 16.9.

At the upper left of the Interactive Trace worksheet, you'll see a complete analysis of cell E11: the formula it contains, the value produced by the formula, any cell or range names used, and the text of the attached note.

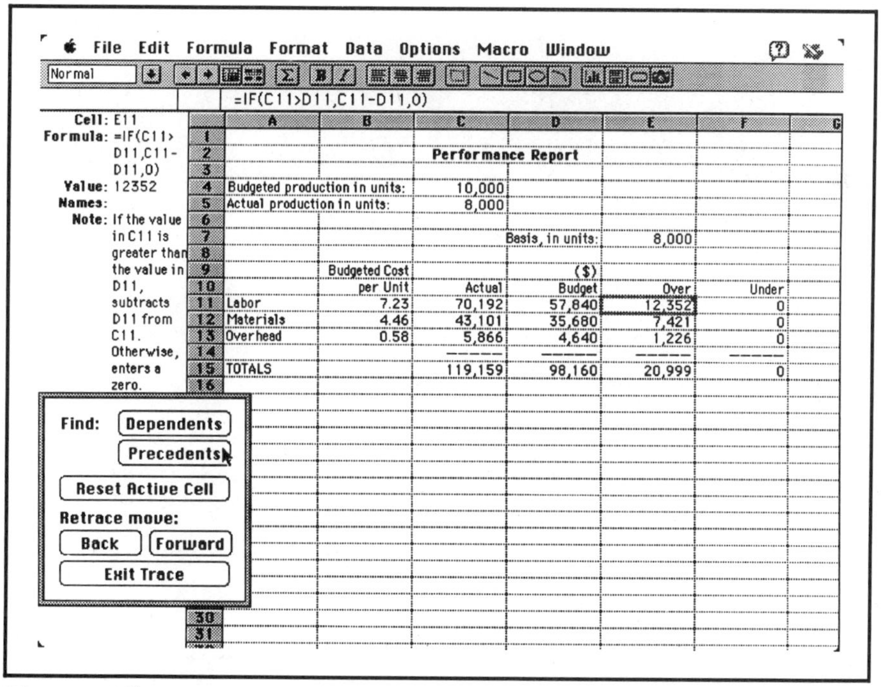

Figure 16.9: Running an interactive trace

Below this information is a small box where you can click buttons to trace the dependents or precedents (see Chapter 8) of the active cell, reset the active cell to some other cell, move backward or forward in the tracing hierarchy, and exit the Trace module.

Experiment with these options if you like. Click the Exit Trace button when you're finished. Finally, close the Error Checking worksheet without saving it.

TRYING THE AMORTIZATION TEMPLATE

To see how the worksheet templates included with Excel work, load the template in the Macro Library folder called Amortization Table.

As Figure 16.10 shows, the instructions displayed on the worksheet indicate that you won't need any new menu options to use the Amortization

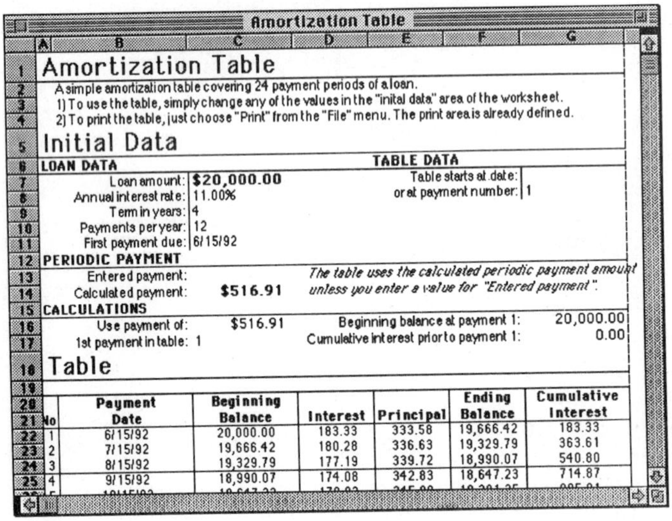

Figure 16.10: The Amortization Table model

Table template. All you have to do is change one or more of the sample values in the Initial Data section of the worksheet to conform with the details of a current or contemplated loan about which you'd like information. The data in the Table section of the worksheet will change instantly to reflect the new data set.

Experiment with the worksheet, using your own data. When you have a group of values for which you'd like to see an amortization table, scroll the worksheet to analyze the results. If you want to print the table, just issue the usual Print... command from the File menu. (Shortcut: Press ⌘-P.) Then click the Print button in the Print dialog box. (Click OK instead if your computer is running under a version of the operating system earlier than System 7.)

'If you want to save the Amortization Table model, do so under another name. Otherwise, in this particular case, you will overwrite the original model and no longer have it available for use.

CREATING A TEMPLATE

You can also create your own templates. For instance, you can construct a standard worksheet to be used by branch offices for figuring monthly budgets. As a template, the worksheet can be used repeatedly by each branch office without damage or alteration to the model.

These are the steps to follow:

1. Construct a worksheet in the usual way.

2. Pull down the File menu and select the Save As... command. You'll see the Save As dialog box.

3. In this dialog box, type a name for the template, such as **Budget Template**.

4. Click the Options button. You'll see the Options dialog box.

5. Press the down arrow at the right of the File Format box to see the drop-down menu of available file formats for saving a worksheet (see Figure 16.11).

6. Select Template as the format.

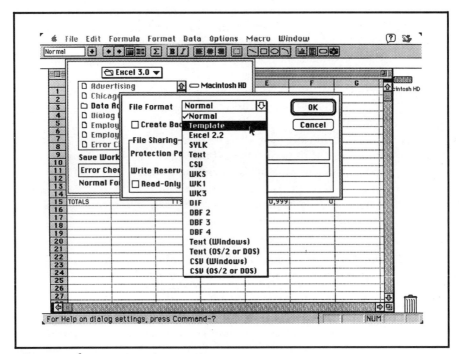

Figure 16.11: Saving a worksheet as a template

7. Click OK to close the Options dialog box. Then click the Save button to save the template and close the Save As... dialog box.

TIP

As mentioned earlier, when you open a template, you automatically open a copy of the template, which you will give a new name when you save it. However, if you want to edit an *original* template file, you can open the original instead of a copy simply by holding down the Shift key as you click the Open button to load the file. You will see a warning that the template is a "stationery pad"—another term for a template. Click OK to proceed and edit the original file.

RECORDING SOUND NOTES FOR WORKSHEETS AND MACRO SHEETS

All Macintoshes can reproduce sounds, ranging from an alert beep to the elaborate recorded music, voices, and sound effects found in many game programs. However, you can also *record* sound on some Macintoshes. When you work in Excel, this capability means that, instead of adding visual notes to worksheets and macro sheets (explained in Chapter 8), you can actually record notes in your own voice and attach them to specific cells. The presence of these sound notes is marked by the same small symbol that appears in the upper right corner of cells containing visual notes.

You accomplish this audio annotation of cells through an add-in macro included in the macro library. We have waited until the very end of the chapter to discuss this feature, since most Macintoshes do not record sound. However, Apple now regularly sells computers with this capacity. The first models were the Macintosh LC and the Macintosh IIsi, both introduced late in 1990. Some third-party vendors manufacture accessories that add sound recording to existing Macintoshes.

Starting with version 6.0.7 of the Macintosh operating system, Apple provides a recording feature as part of the Sound control panel device.

DETERMINING WHETHER YOUR MACINTOSH CAN RECORD

Here's a quick way to find out if the Macintosh you're using can record:

1. Pull down the Apple menu and select Control Panels (or Control Panel, if you're not running System 7).

2. Locate the Sound icon and double-click to open it. If the Sound panel displays one or more microphone icons at the bottom of the window, your Macintosh can record sound. Some recording devices have special features you can select or adjust by clicking the Options... button in this panel. Figure 16.12 shows the Sound control panel for a Macintosh IIsi. On this panel you can choose a

sound from those listed to be played when your Macintosh displays Alert messages. Also, you can drag the Speaker Volume bar to adjust the volume of your built-in speaker.

3. Click the Add... button to open the Record dialog box (see Figure 16.13). Here you can control the recording of sounds or voice messages to be used as alternative Alert sounds. To accomplish this, you must also have a recording device attached to the sound input port at the back of your computer: a microphone or (through an adapter plug) a device such as a tape recorder.

4. Click the Record icon to start recording. Through other clearly labeled icons, you can end the recording, pause, cancel the operation, and save the result under a name of your choosing. The name you type will thereafter appear in the Sound panel (unless you highlight the name and click the Remove button to delete the file).

The bar at the bottom of the Record dialog box shows how long you've been recording; you cannot record a message more than 10 seconds long. There is no built-in recording-volume control; you must provide this control yourself: by speaking louder or more softly, by changing your distance

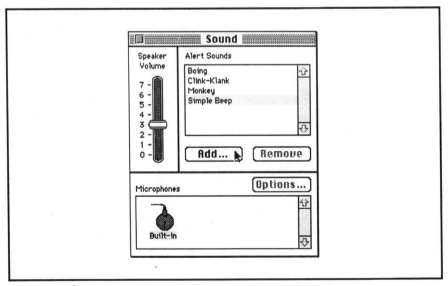

Figure 16.12: The Macintosh IIsi Sound control panel

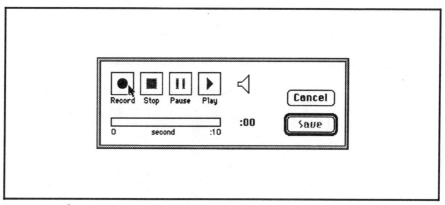

Figure 16.13: The Record dialog box

from the microphone, or by adjusting the playback volume on some other device attached to the sound input port.

Excel uses this same Record dialog box for recording worksheet and macro sheet sound notes. The next section describes the additional elements and procedures required.

ADDING EXCEL SOUND NOTES

Use the following steps to activate Excel's Sound Notes macro and add recorded notes to worksheets or macro sheets. (You cannot add sound notes to chart files.)

1. Scroll the list box in the Macro Library folder until you see Sound Notes (as shown in Figure 16.14). Double-click the name to load the Sound Notes add-in macro.

2. Open a worksheet or macro sheet to which you'd like to add notes.

3. Select a cell to annotate.

4. Pull down the Formula menu and select the Sound Note... command, which will have been added to that menu (see Figure 16.15). The Cell Sound Note dialog box will appear (see Figure 16.16).

5. If you want to change the recording quality, place the pointer on the arrow beside the drop-down menu labeled Recording Quality

and hold down the mouse button to see the available selections. Your choices are Good (the default setting), Better, and Best. When you specify higher quality, your recordings will be saved as larger

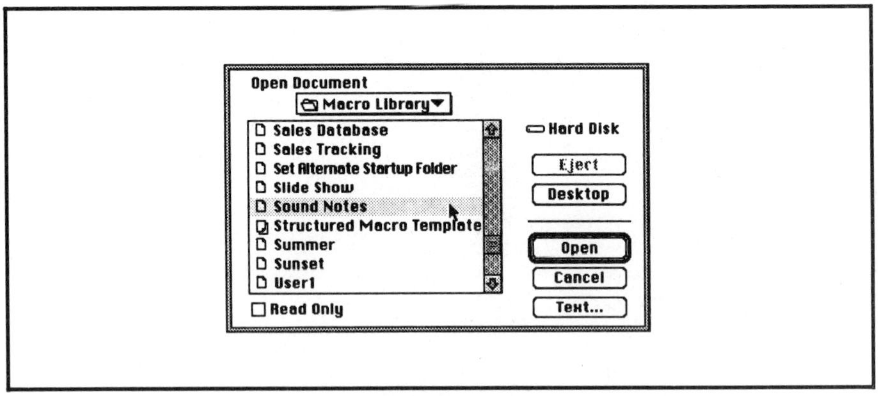

Figure 16.14: Loading the Sound Notes macro

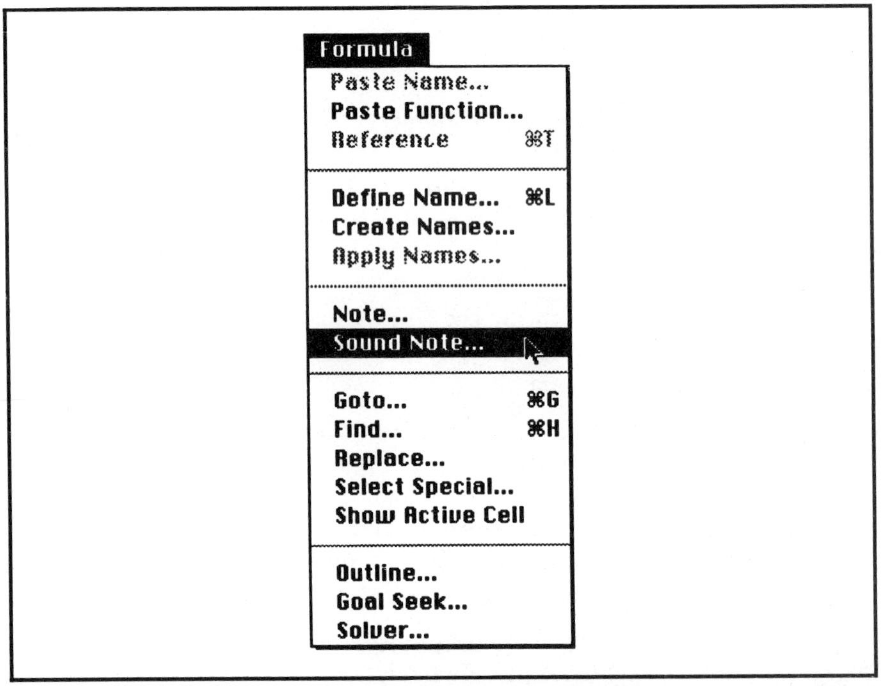

Figure 16.15: Selecting the Sound Note... command

files, requiring more available disk storage space and more memory to run.

6. To proceed with recording, click the Record... button. The same Record dialog box that you access through the Sound control panel will appear. The operation is the same too, except that since the note will be attached to a previously selected cell, you will not be asked to name the sound when you save it.

Figure 16.17 shows the appearance of the Record dialog box during an actual recording. The dialog box gauge and the displayed value both indicate that the recording proceeded for 6 seconds.

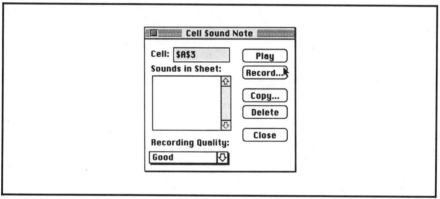

Figure 16.16: The Cell Sound Note dialog box

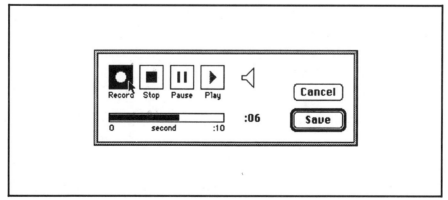

Figure 16.17: Recording a sound note

As Figure 16.18 shows, you can play any sound attached to a sheet by highlighting the sound's cell address in the list box and then pressing the Play button. Of course, this feature works only if the Sound Notes macro is loaded in memory.

Copy a sound from one cell to another by clicking the Copy... button. The Copy Sound dialog box will appear (see Figure 16.19). Click the cell to which you want the sound copied. Then click OK. You cannot copy sounds through the Excel Edit menu.

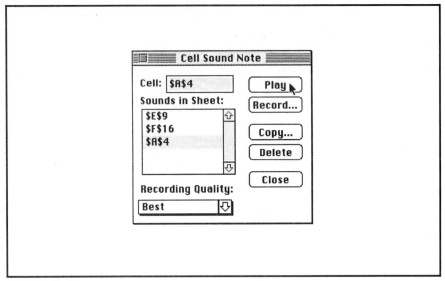

Figure 16.18: Playing a previously recorded sound note

SUMMARY

Chapter 16 introduced you to the macros and templates included in Excel's Macro Library folder. You also learned how to create your own templates. Finally, you learned how to record sound notes, if your computer has this capability.

In Chapter 15 you learned how to record macros. In Chapter 17, you'll discover how to write macros.

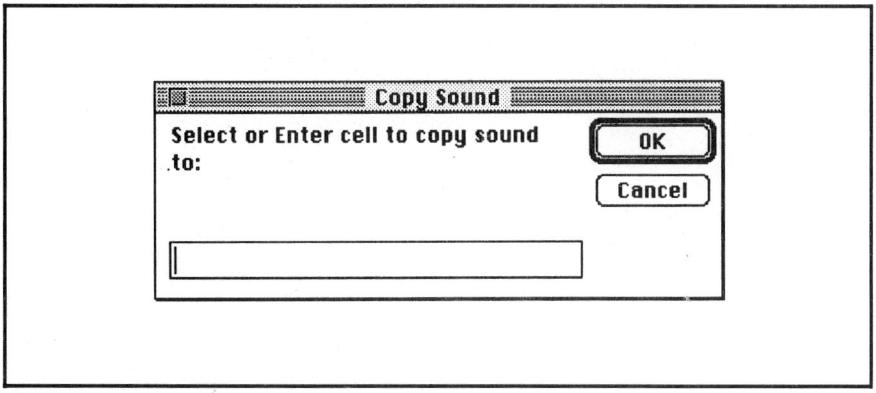

Figure 16.19: Copying a sound note to another cell

Chapter

17

Writing Command
Macros

The main reason for *writing* a command macro instead of *recording* it is to include features that cannot be realized by merely capturing keystrokes and mouse movements.

When you write a macro, you're really acting as a programmer—laying out a series of actions for Excel to follow to achieve a goal you've established. Through Excel's *macro language* (actually a series of functions), you can use many of the techniques that are familiar to programmers. For example, you can make the macro branch to perform different subroutines, depending on circumstances. You can repeat actions through loops. You can make the macro pause for user input, and you can provide on-screen instructions regarding the type of input required.

These feats may sound difficult and beyond the capabilities of a mere computer user. It's true that a professional programmer can write complex applications with Excel's macro language; you saw some evidence of this in the Macro Library files introduced in Chapter 16. However, you don't have to be a programmer to write useful command macros. In this chapter you learn the basic skills required.

WRITING A PRINTING MACRO

Let's create a macro to save and print a worksheet. In preparation for this macro exercise, follow these steps:

1. Load the Error Checking worksheet again.

2. Pull down the File menu and use the Save As... command to make a copy of the worksheet.

3. In the Save As dialog box, type **Budget** as the name of the worksheet and click the Save button. The title bar in the active window changes to display the new name.

PLANNING THE MACRO

The purpose of this macro will be to save and print the Budget worksheet, with the number of copies varying according to circumstances.

You originally created this worksheet as Performance Report in Chapter 4. The intent was to show whether or not production runs of a product were over or under budget, considering costs in three categories: labor, materials, and overhead.

Let's assume that the manufacturing company involved has become very concerned about costs at the facility that produces the product. Although the report generated after each production run by revising and printing the worksheet is usually seen only by management within the plant, an order has been issued from headquarters that a copy of any report showing cost overruns will also be sent to the corporate office. The macro you'll create will print one copy of the report if production is within or under budget, but will automatically print an extra copy for headquarters if overruns occur.

Planning is essential to the successful writing of most macros. You should follow this procedure:

1. Set an exact purpose for the macro: for example, ''Alert headquarters whenever cost overruns occur'' (not ''Do something about staying within the budget'').

2. Determine the precise method of accomplishing the goal: for example, ''Make an extra copy of the Performance Report for headquarters whenever a production run is over budget.''

3. Map out step-by-step what the macro must do to achieve the goal.

4. Use *subroutine macros* (short macros within the main macro) to accomplish specific tasks. Short macros are easier to write and debug.

5. Determine which, if any, portions of the macro you can record. Recording, rather than writing, macros can save you time.

6. Write the macro, incorporating any recorded elements.

7. Test the completed macro to make certain that it works.

8. Debug problem areas, if necessary, and test the macro again, until it is correct.

9. Document the macro so you or others will understand later what it does and the functions of its various elements. You can do this by using the text box tool on the Toolbar (which you used in Chapter 2) or the Note... command on the Formula menu (which you used in Chapter 8). However, since Excel simply passes over cells

on macro sheets that contain text, a better way is merely to enter the documentation directly into cells in the column to the right of the macro. Then you will be able to see explanations displayed next to the cells to which they refer. (Figure 17.6 later in this chapter shows such documentation.)

In the example macro we'll create here, the easiest way of making the macro check the worksheet for overruns is to have it look for a value greater than zero in the cell that totals the items that exceed their budgets. This cell is E15, in the column with the heading Over.

Next the macro can call either of two subroutine macros that will save the latest changes to the worksheet and print either two copies if E15 contains a value other than zero, or one copy if the value in the cell is zero. You can easily record these subroutine macros rather than writing them.

You'll need to use three Excel macro functions in the main macro. The first function is form 2 of the IF function, which can be used only on macro sheets. (You're already familiar with form 1, which can also be used with worksheets; it appears several times in the Budget worksheet.) To use form 2 of the function, you must enclose in parentheses a logical test you want performed—in other words, a test that can be answered TRUE or FALSE. In this case, the test will be whether E15 contains a value greater than zero. If the answer is yes, the result is TRUE; otherwise, the result is FALSE.

You'll use the IF( ) function in conjunction with ELSE( ) and END.IF( ). The ELSE( ) function specifies what happens if the result of the logical test is FALSE. The END.IF( ) function ends the IF/ELSE sequence.

Usually, you end a macro with yet another function: RETURN( ). This function tells Excel that the macro is completed. In some other programs such as Lotus 1-2-3, reaching a blank cell terminates a macro. However, Excel ignores blank cells. Therefore, you can use blank cells to visually separate parts of a macro without affecting its performance.

However, you don't want to use the RETURN( ) function to end the main macro you're about to create, since the presence of the function at this point would keep Excel from continuing down the column of the macro sheet and finding the two subroutine macros. Instead, you will use the RETURN( ) function to end each of the subroutine macros.

RECORDING THE SUBROUTINE MACROS

Let's begin to create the macro. First, use the recorder to create the subroutine macros.

1. With the Budget worksheet active, pull down the Macro menu and select the Record... command. The Record Macro dialog box appears.

2. Type a name for the macro: **Print1**.

3. Accept the default shortcut Option-⌘ key combination for executing the macro, which will be called *a*, and click OK to start recording.

4. Pull down the File menu and select the Save command, which, when the macro is run later, will save changes to the worksheet. (Shortcut: Press ⌘-S.)

5. Pull down the File menu again and select the Print... command. (Shortcut: Press ⌘-P.) The Print dialog box appears.

6. This subroutine macro will be the one that prints only one copy of the worksheet (if there are no cost overruns), so accept the default settings and click the Print button. (Click the OK button for versions of the operating system before System 7.0.)

7. Pull down the Macro menu and select the Stop Recorder command. (This command appears just below the Run... command when a macro is running.) This action completes the macro.

8. Repeat steps 1 through 7 to record the second subroutine macro, with these changes: In step 2, name the second macro **Print2**. In step 6, before you click the Print or OK button, type the number **2** so that Excel will print two copies of the worksheet. (This macro will run if cost overruns appear on the worksheet so that an extra copy can be sent to headquarters.)

9. Pull down the Window menu and select Macro1 to view the macro sheet (or click somewhere on the macro sheet itself if some portion of it is visible behind the worksheet). Your screen should resemble Figure 17.1. The lowercase letter in parentheses after the name of each macro is the letter selected (by default, in this case) for use with the Option-⌘ shortcut key combination.

10. Pull down the File menu and select the Save As... command. The Save As dialog box appears.

11. Type **Budget Macro** as the name for the macro sheet and click the Save button.

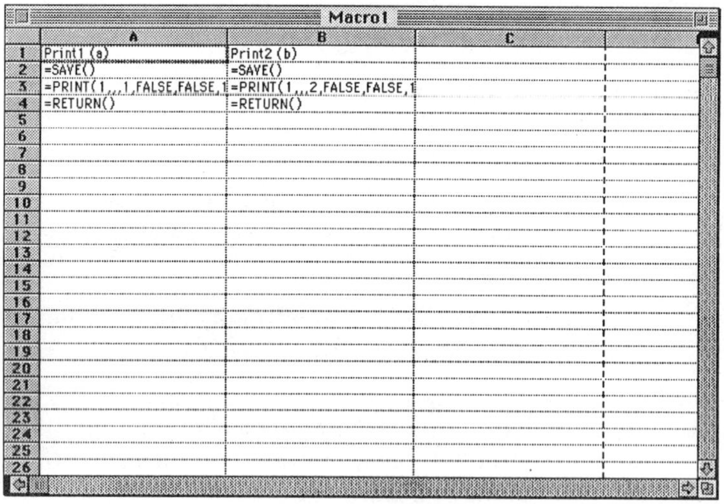

Figure 17.1: Recorded subroutine macros

You've now completed the recording of both subroutine macros.

In row 3 of each of these macros, you'll see a long entry that has been truncated because the text is too long to fit in the cell. The full entry for cell B3, for example, is actually = PRINT(1,,,2,FALSE,FALSE,1,FALSE,1). This entry automatically lists (in terms Excel can understand) the settings you've either made or accepted in the Print dialog box.

Note that each line of each macro, except for the first cell that contains the macro name, begins with an equal sign (=), since these lines really constitute formulas within the macros.

WRITING THE MAIN MACRO

Now it's time to write the main macro.

1. To make room for the macro you're going to write, drag to select the range A1:A4 (the Print1 macro).

2. Pull down the Edit menu and select the Cut command. (Shortcut: Press ⌘-X.)

3. Click cell B6 to select it. Then pull down the Edit menu again and select the Paste command. (Shortcut: Press ⌘-V.) Both recorded macros are now stored in column B of the macro sheet, and column A is available for the macro you'll write.

4. Click cell A1 (now blank) and type the name for the main macro: **Budget_Info**. The two words are connected with an underline because spaces are not permitted in macro names. Click the enter box in the formula bar to enter the name.

5. Pull down the Formula menu and select the Define Name... command to identify the macro for Excel. (The names you entered for the recorded subroutine macros were automatically defined as macro names by Excel. However, you must use a menu option to accomplish this step for any macro you write. Otherwise, Excel will not recognize your macro as such on the macro sheet, and your macro will not appear on the Macro menu.)

6. In the Define Name dialog box, click the Command button to indicate that you're creating a name for a command macro. Budget_Info will already appear as the suggested name for the macro; Excel picked up this name from the active cell, A1. Below the Name box, A1 (cell A1 as an absolute reference) is proposed as the reference for the name. These are the entries you want, so don't change them.

7. Click the Option-⌘ Key text box (to the right of the Command button) to activate it. Type i (a lowercase *i*) as the shortcut key to start the macro (since Info starts with an *i* and the *b* in Budget_Info is already used for the second macro you recorded). The dialog box on your screen should now resemble Figure 17.2.

8. Click OK to complete the name-definition process and close the dialog box. Now enter a function in the cell below.

9. Click cell A2 to select it. Then pull down the Formula menu and select the Paste Function... command. The Paste Function dialog box appears.

10. Scroll the list box to find and select the IF( ) function. Click the Paste Arguments box to deselect the Paste Arguments option. Then click OK.

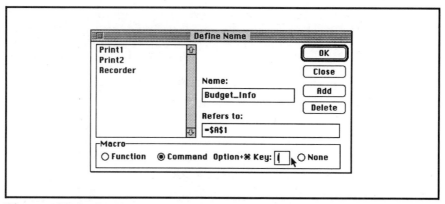

Figure 17.2: Naming a command macro

11. Supply the logical-test argument to complete this formula: Add the necessary text between the parentheses to make cell A2 read **= IF(Budget!E15 > 0).** The formula in this cell now says, "If cell E15 on the Budget worksheet contains a value greater than zero...." (An important programming consideration is at work here. If you don't include a reference to the worksheet by name, as well as the cell address, Excel will look at cell E15 on the *macro sheet* to see if it contains a value greater than zero. Since this cell on the macro sheet is empty, the main macro will always find no value greater than zero in the cell. In other words, Excel will always evaluate the logical test as FALSE, and the macro will always print only one copy of the worksheet, regardless of any actual budget overruns. Remember also to use an exclamation point (!) to separate a reference to an external file—the worksheet—from the cell reference. This subject was discussed in Chapter 7.)

12. Press Return to enter the formula and make A3 the active cell. In A3, type an equal sign (=), five spaces, and the name of the second subroutine macro: **Print2**. This entry tells Excel to start the Print2 macro if the logical test is evaluated as TRUE. (The insertion of the five spaces indents the contents of this cell to make the macro easier to understand. The indentation shows that this cell is related to the IF( ) function in the preceding cell. The macro would operate just the same without the spaces.)

13. Press Return to enter the formula and make A4 the active cell. Pull down the Formula menu and select the Paste Function... command. The Paste Function dialog box appears again.

14. Scroll the list box to select the ELSE( ) function. Then click OK.

15. Press Return to enter the formula and make A5 the active cell. Now you must tell Excel what to do if the result of the logical test in A2 is FALSE. Type an equal sign (=) followed by five spaces. Then type **Print1** to indicate that Excel is to run the Print1 macro if the production costs do not exceed the budget.

16. Press Return to enter the formula and make A6 the active cell. Pull down the Formula menu and select the Paste Function command once more. The Paste Function dialog box appears.

17. Scroll the list box to select the END.IF( ) function. The END.IF( ) function is required to end an IF/ELSE sequence. Click OK. Press Return to complete the cell entry. You've now completed the writing of the main macro. (Wasn't that easy?)

18. Now you must place the subroutine macros in position so they follow the main macro on the macro sheet. Drag to select the range B1:B9, thereby highlighting both the Print2 and Print1 macros.

19. Press ⌘-X to move the macros to the clipboard.

20. Click cell A8 and press ⌘-V to paste the subroutine macros into column A, just below the main macro.

21. Press ⌘-S to save the additions to the macro sheet.

The job is finished (although you must still test and document the Budget_Info macro). Your macro sheet should resemble Figure 17.3. (By dragging the boundary between the headings for columns A and B to the right, column A in Figure 17.3 has been widened to display the complete formulas in cells A10 and A15.)

Because you moved Print1 out of column A before you started the main macro, Print1 now appears below Print2 on the macro sheet. That's exactly where you want it. In fact, the macro sequence wouldn't work if the two subroutine macros didn't appear in their present order and below the main Budget_Info macro. Subroutine macros must appear in the same order in which they're mentioned in the main macro.

```
┌────────────────────────────────────────────────────────────┐
│                        Budget Macro                         │
│         A                    B                 C            │
│ 1  Budget_Info                                              │
│ 2  =IF(Budget!E15>0)                                        │
│ 3  =    Print2                                             │
│ 4  =ELSE()                                                  │
│ 5  =    Print1                                            │
│ 6  =END.IF()                                                │
│ 7                                                          │
│ 8  Print2 (b)                                              │
│ 9  =SAVE()                                                 │
│ 10 =PRINT(1,,,2,FALSE,FALSE,1,FALSE,1)                     │
│ 11 =RETURN()                                               │
│ 12                                                         │
│ 13 Print1 (a)                                             │
│ 14 =SAVE()                                                 │
│ 15 =PRINT(1,,,1,FALSE,FALSE,1,FALSE,1)                    │
│ 16 =RETURN()                                              │
│ 17                                                         │
│ 18                                                         │
│ 19                                                         │
│ 20                                                         │
│ 21                                                         │
│ 22                                                         │
│ 23                                                         │
└────────────────────────────────────────────────────────────┘
```

Figure 17.3: The completed Budget_Info macro

(After you've tested the Budget_Info macro—your next step—you might want to experiment by switching the positions of Print1 and Print2. You'll find that, with Print1 entered first below the Budget_Info macro, the Budget_Info macro will always select Print1 and print only one copy of the Budget worksheet, regardless of whether cell E15 in the worksheet shows that the production run is over budget. The Print2 macro will be ignored.)

TESTING THE MAIN MACRO

Now test your work.

1. Click a visible portion of the Budget worksheet to select it and bring its window to the foreground (or pull down the Window menu and select Budget).

2. Pull down the Macro menu and select the Run... command. The Run dialog box appears, as shown in Figure 17.4. Note that this dialog box lists all three of the macros on the Budget Macro macro sheet.

3. Highlight the main macro (Budget_Info) and click OK. The macro will run. (Shortcut: Instead of following steps 1 and 2, press Option-⌘-i to start the macro.)

If you've correctly followed all of the steps required to create these macros (and haven't changed the data on the Budget worksheet), Excel will execute the Budget_Info macro by resaving the worksheet and then printing two copies of it.

NOTE

Don't forget that you can't run any macro unless the macro sheet that contains it has been loaded into memory.

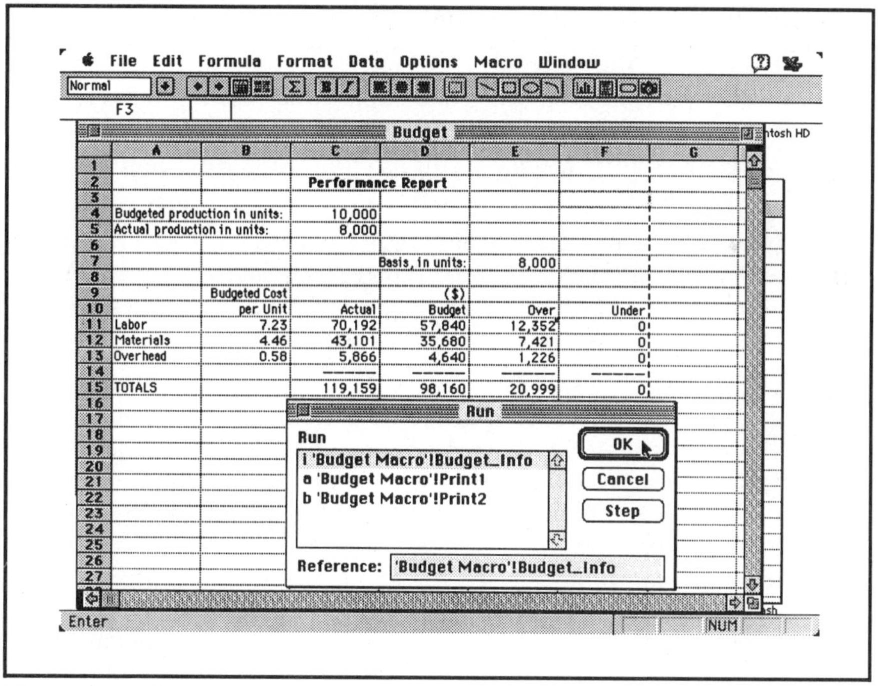

Figure 17.4: Running the Budget_Info macro

DEBUGGING THE MACROS

In the Run dialog box, at the lower right, is a button labeled Step. You can use this button to step through a macro one cell at a time to find any problems. Try this feature now.

1. Pull down the Macro menu and select the Run command. The Run dialog box appears. (You can drag the title bar at any time to move the dialog box if it obstructs your view.)

2. Select the Budget_Info macro and click the Step button. You'll see another dialog box, titled Single Step. The main area of the dialog box shows which cell of the macro is active at any time, plus either the formula that the cell contains or how that formula is being evaluated. At the right side of the dialog box are four buttons: Step (to execute the next step), Evaluate (to show the result of the formula currently displayed), Halt (to stop the debugging process), and Continue (to terminate the Single Step feature and run the remainder of the macro without interruption, unless a bug in the macro stops it, of course).

3. Initially, the Single Step dialog box displays the contents of the cell that contains the title of the macro. Click the Evaluate button. Since there's nothing to evaluate in the title, the macro moves on to its second cell, and the dialog box displays the formula in the second cell.

4. Click the Evaluate button again. Excel evaluates the formula in the second cell, and the dialog box displays the result of the formula in italics: = *IF(TRUE)*. This result means that Excel evaluated the logical test as TRUE and will proceed to start the Print2 macro instead of Print1. (See Figure 17.5.)

5. Continue to step through the macro by clicking the Evaluate button to observe how the Single Step option handles the remainder of the active macros. Note that Single Step moves from the Budget_Info macro to the Print2 macro, because the logical test was evaluated as TRUE. (If worksheet had not shown any cost overruns, the evaluation of cell A2 would have read = *IF(FALSE)*, and the Budget_Info macro would have started the Print1 macro. If the Print1 macro had been moved to appear above the Print2 macro on the worksheet

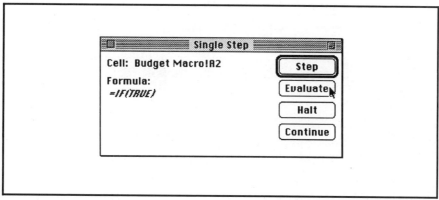

Figure 17.5: Stepping through the macros

(but below the Budget_Info macro, of course), the Budget_Info macro would have started the Print1 macro every time, regardless of the information contained on the worksheet. As indicated earlier, Excel would have ignored Print2 completely.)

DOCUMENTING THE MACROS

As already mentioned, you should always document macros, both so you will later remember exactly what each formula accomplishes, and so others can understand how you constructed the macros.

Figure 17.6 illustrates how you could document these macros, with column B widened to accommodate the comments.

MORE ABOUT WRITING MACROS

Appendix B lists the functions you can use in macros.

You can use the FOR( ) function to create *loops*: subroutines that make a macro repeat actions or calculations. The FOR.CELL( ) function repeats an operation for each cell you specify. The NEXT( ) function restarts a loop. The WHILE( ) function continues a loop so long as a specified condition is TRUE.

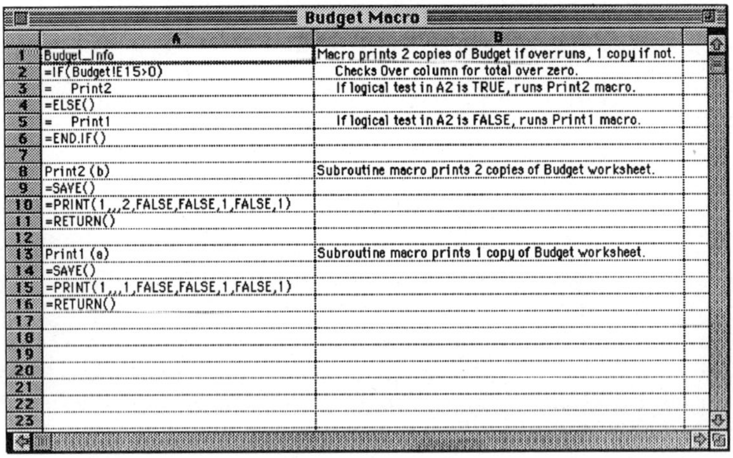

	A	B
	Budget Macro	
1	Budget__Info	Macro prints 2 copies of Budget if overruns, 1 copy if not.
2	=IF(Budget!E15>0)	Checks Over column for total over zero.
3	= Print2	If logical test in A2 is TRUE, runs Print2 macro.
4	=ELSE()	
5	= Print1	If logical test in A2 is FALSE, runs Print1 macro.
6	=END.IF()	
7		
8	Print2 (b)	Subroutine macro prints 2 copies of Budget worksheet.
9	=SAVE()	
10	=PRINT(1,,,2,FALSE,FALSE,1,FALSE,1)	
11	=RETURN()	
12		
13	Print1 (a)	Subroutine macro prints 1 copy of Budget worksheet.
14	=SAVE()	
15	=PRINT(1,,,1,FALSE,FALSE,1,FALSE,1)	
16	=RETURN()	
17		
18		
19		
20		
21		
22		
23		

Figure 17.6: Documenting the macros

You can use the INPUT( ) function to allow user input in a macro. A message argument tells the user what input is required.

The ALERT( ) function stops the execution of a macro, displays whatever message you desire, and then continues when the user selects a button.

Some spreadsheet programs use a method of designating cells called the *R1C1 reference style*. For example, with this style, instead of referring to a cell as D12, you might call it R[2]C[3]. This reference means "the cell two rows down and three columns to the right of the current cell." If you're accustomed to using this reference style in writing macros or formulas, you can use it in Excel too. Simply pull down the Options menu and select the Workspace... command. Then, in the Workspace dialog box, click the R1C1 box to select it and click OK. You can switch back again to the normal A1 reference style in the same manner.

SUMMARY

This chapter explained the basics of writing your own command macros. You can easily record many macros or parts of macros to reduce the writing time and skill that would otherwise be required.

You also learned that you should always test and debug the macros you write and document them for future reference.

Chapter

18

Creating Custom Macros

$\mathbf{Y}$ou can create your own functions. Custom functions have the same advantage as the functions included with Excel: They can perform complex calculations, yet occupy little space in but a single cell of a worksheet.

Obviously, custom functions have another advantage. They can accomplish a task specific to your own needs or business in exactly the way you'd like and using formulas you've specified or written.

Once you've completed a custom function, you access it with the same menu option that displays other functions: the Paste Function... command on the Formula menu.

BUILDING A NEW FUNCTION

You create custom functions on macro sheets. Custom functions are composed of a combination of standard Excel macro functions and formulas you write yourself. You cannot record a function.

You'll create a function now that would be very useful to any company that advertises or to an advertising agency or its suppliers.

Customarily, an advertising agency obtains most of its revenues by retaining a 15 percent commission that has been added to advertising placed or services purchased on behalf of its clients. You might think that you figure the markup on, say, $1,000 simply by adding 15 percent, or $150, to the invoice, for a total of $1,150. Not so. The reason is that if an advertising agency deducts 15 percent from $1,150, the result is not the original $1,000. Try it! The answer is $977.50.

To obtain a *true* 15 percent markup, it's necessary to multiply the amount in question by .1765. That's what the function you'll create will do. (This is a standard calculation in the advertising industry.)

1. Pull down the File menu and select the New... command. (Shortcut: Press ⌘-N.)

2. In the New dialog box, highlight the line that says Macro Sheet and click OK to create a new macro sheet.

3. Give the macro sheet a name. Pull down the File menu and select the Save As... command. Type the name **Adv M** and click the Save

button. The title bar of the macro sheet now displays the new name.

(The letters *Adv* were selected because the macro sheet relates to advertising; the letter *M* was added to indicate on a list of files that this file is a macro sheet. You should choose a short name for a macro sheet that will contain functions, because the name of the macro sheet will precede the name of each function on its line in the Paste Function dialog box. If the name of the macro sheet is too long, there won't be room on the line to display the name of the function itself.)

4. Click cell A1 and type **MARKUP** (in capital letters) as the function name. Press Return to enter the name and activate cell A2.

5. In A2, pull down the Formula menu and select the Paste Function... command. The Paste Function dialog box appears. By default, it displays a Paste Arguments box containing an X to indicate that it is selected. In previous exercises, you clicked the Paste Arguments box to *deselect* it. However, in this exercise, accept the default choice and leave the box selected. Placeholders for arguments will now be pasted into cells along with the functions themselves. You will later replace these placeholders with the actual arguments required.

6. In the Paste Function dialog box, scroll the list box and highlight the RESULT( ) function. Click OK to paste the function into cell A2. RESULT( ) will cause your custom function to accept only a certain type of data as its result. In this case, you want the result to be a number. Although including RESULT( ) is optional, when this function is used, it must appear in the first cell below the name of the custom function.

7. In the formula bar you'll see highlighted the required argument for RESULT( ): *type_num*. You must enter a value that tells Excel the type of data to accept. As you can see by scanning Table 18.1, which lists the data types and their codes, you will want to enter 1. Type 1. This value replaces the argument placeholder *type_num* between the parentheses. (You can add data-type codes together to allow additional kinds of data in a user response. For example, to accept a number or text or a logical value, you could enter 7, the total of the codes for those three data types.) Press Return to complete the entry and move to cell A3.

8. Now define a new argument for your custom function. Such arguments must appear at the top of the formulas used in the custom function, preceded only by the RESULT( ) function (if this function is used). Pull down the Formula menu again, select the Paste Function... command, and select the ARGUMENT( ) function. A special Select Arguments dialog box appears in which you can choose between two sets of arguments. The first set (*name_text,data_type_num*) is the one you want. The first argument in this set (*name_text*) specifies the name of the argument; the second argument (*data_type_num*) specifies the type code for the kind of data you want entered from the list in Table 18.1. The alternate data set adds one additional argument (*reference*), which specifies a cell or range from which Excel obtains the argument value.

Table 18.1: Argument Data Types Used in Custom Functions

VALUE	DATA TYPE
1	Number
2	Text
4	Logical
8	Reference
16	Error
64	Array

9. Click OK to accept the first argument set. The ARGUMENT( ) function is pasted into cell A3.

10. In the formula bar, the placeholder for the first argument (*name_text*) is highlighted. Replace this placeholder by typing "**Total_Cost**" (be sure to include the opening and closing double quotation marks and the underline between the two words; no spaces are allowed in arguments).

11. Still in the formula bar, replace the second placeholder by typing the number **1** (you want the argument to accept only numbers).

12. Press Return to complete the entry and activate cell A4.

13. In A4, enter a formula that includes the argument you just defined. Type = **Total_Cost**∗**0.1765**. (Now that the argument Total_Cost has

been defined, you don't have to enclose it in quotation marks.) This formula multiplies a number entered as the total cost of an advertising expense by .1765 to provide the true 15 percent markup, as discussed earlier. Press Return to enter the formula and activate cell A5.

14. End your custom function with the RETURN( ) function you used in Chapter 17 to end macros. Pull down the Formula menu again, select the Paste Function... command, and select the RETURN( ) function. Excel pastes RETURN( ) into A5. When used in writing a custom function, the RETURN( ) function can have an additional purpose: determining what is to appear in the worksheet cell that contains the custom function. In this case, you want to display the result of the formula you just entered into cell A4. Specify this result by typing **A4** in the formula bar to replace the placeholder *value*. Click the enter box in the formula bar to complete the formula.

15. The custom function is now ready for use, with one exception. You must tell Excel that it is a custom function. You do this by using the Define Name... command you used in writing your command macro in Chapter 17. However, you choose a different option from the dialog box. First click the cell that contains the title of your function, A1. Your screen should now resemble Figure 18.1.

16. Pull down the Formula menu and select the Define Name... command.

17. In the Define Name dialog box, click the Function button in the lower left corner. Then click OK. The dialog box closes. Excel will now recognize your macro as a custom function.

USING THE CUSTOM FUNCTION

It's time now to test the new function.

1. Activate a new worksheet with cell A1 selected.

2. Pull down the Formula menu and select the Paste Function... command.

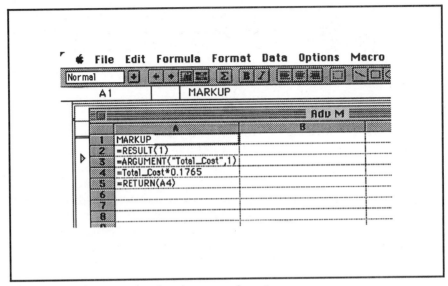

Figure 18.1: The completed custom function

3. Scroll to the end of the functions shown in the list box. The last Excel-provided function alphabetically is YEAR( ), which enters the current year in a cell. Custom functions appear after YEAR( ), following the alphabetical listing.

4. The last function listed now is 'Adv M'!MARKUP( ), as illustrated in Figure 18.2. This listing indicates that the new function is located on the ADV M macro sheet. (Remember that the function name appears only if the Adv M macro sheet has been loaded into memory.)

5. Select your new function and click OK. Excel pastes the function into cell A1, although column A is not wide enough to display all of the function. However, you can see the complete function in the formula bar, as shown in Figure 18.3. Note that the placeholder Total_Cost (the argument you defined) is highlighted, ready for you to enter an actual figure.

6. Assume that the total cost of some advertising expense is $5,260. Type as the argument the number **5260** and click the enter box in

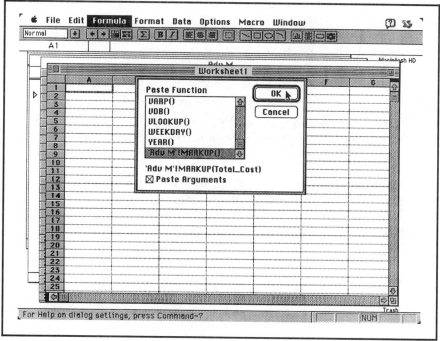

Figure 18.2: Selecting the new function in the Paste Function dialog box

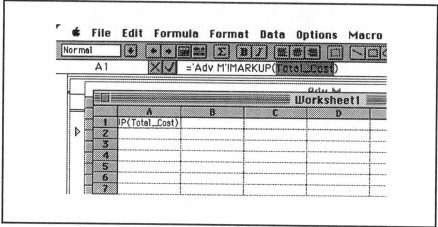

Figure 18.3: The new function pasted into cell A1

the formula bar. The number 928.39 appears in cell A1, as shown in Figure 18.4. Your function multiplied 5260 by .1765 to determine the markup that must be added to $5,260 to obtain a true 15 percent commission—$928.39.

CREATING AN ADD-IN FUNCTION

You can make your new function appear as an integral part of the Excel functions displayed in the Paste Function list box, integrated into the normal alphabetical order. You do this by defining the macro sheet as an *add-in*.

Since a custom function appears at the bottom of the list anyway (provided the macro sheet has been loaded into memory), you may not want to make the macro sheet an add-in, unless you repeatedly use functions on the sheet. There are two reasons.

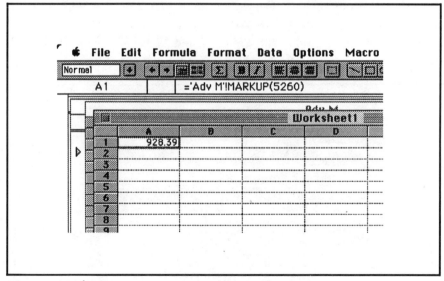

Figure 18.4: The result calculated by the function

First, after you close a macro sheet you've defined as an add-in, it will not be displayed when you load it again (although it will operate properly). To make it visible for editing, you will have to hold down the Shift key as you click OK to open the sheet. (Of course, if your macro sheet is to be used by others, you may want the sheet hidden from view to prevent tampering.) A macro sheet that is not defined as an add-in is always displayed (unless it's covered by another window)—providing a temptation to experimenters.

The second potential reason for not creating an add-in macro sheet is that any command macros you have defined on the same sheet will be hidden too—they will not even appear in the Macro Run dialog box. The exception is a macro that has been defined as an add-in macro so that it appears on regular menus. (You used Excel's library of add-in macros in Chapter 16. Defining your own add-in command macros is a more complicated procedure, as you will learn in Chapter 19.)

To solve the problem of hidden macros on an add-in macro sheet, don't define any macros on a macro sheet that contains custom functions.

Here's how you save a macro sheet as an add-in:

1. Pull down the File menu and select the Save As... command.

2. In the Save As dialog box, click the Options button at the lower right corner. The Options dialog box shows that the default file format in which the macro sheet is saved is called Normal.

3. Place the pointer on the down arrow located to the right of the File Format box while holding down the mouse button. A list of alternate file formats drops down for selection.

4. As shown in Figure 18.5, select the Add-In option. Then click OK. The Options dialog box closes.

5. In the Save As dialog box, the words *Add-In Format* appear below the text box that displays the macro sheet name. Click the Save button to complete the sequence and close the dialog box. Your custom function instantly becomes available for viewing as part of the regular alphabetical list of functions in the Paste Function dialog box. The function is no longer preceded by the name of the macro sheet where it's stored, nor by the exclamation point that previously separated the name of the sheet from the name of the function.

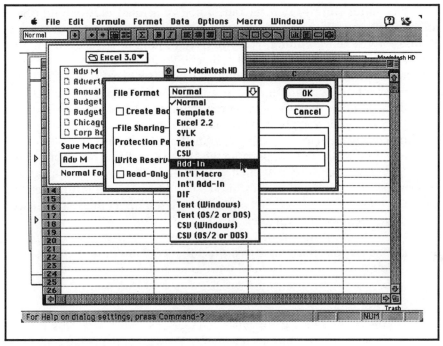

Figure 18.5: Saving a macro sheet as an add-in

OPENING FILES AUTOMATICALLY

As you've been cautioned, neither macros nor custom functions appear on menus nor are available for use unless the macro sheet containing them has been opened. If you want to use certain macros or custom functions frequently, you may want the sheets containing them to be loaded into memory automatically every time you open Excel.

You can easily accomplish this. As mentioned in Chapter 16, you will find the Excel Startup Folder inside the Macintosh System folder. This folder was placed in the System folder during the Excel installation process. Any Excel file you drag into the Excel Startup Folder will thereafter be opened automatically when you start the program.

If your Macintosh is running under System 7, you can leave the original file undisturbed and drag an *alias* of the file into the Excel Startup Folder. An alias is a tiny file that serves as a stand-in for the original. To create the alias, simply select the original file and then pull down the File menu and choose the Make Alias command. A copy of the file will appear, with *alias* appended to the name. Drag the alias icon into the Excel Startup Folder.

SUMMARY

You've found that you can create custom functions by using a combination of macro functions and formulas and then saving the result as a function.

You cannot record functions. However, you can have them loaded automatically when you start Excel, and you can integrate them into the menu listing of Excel's own functions.

In Chapter 19, you integrate what you've learned in Chapters 16, 17, and 18 to create custom Excel applications.

Chapter

19

Designing Custom
Applications

You can create your own Excel applications, even using custom menus and dialog boxes. For example, you might want a simplified program that could be used by temporary employees to enter sales data. You could design this application to load automatically when Excel is opened (or even at the moment the computer is turned on), displaying only special menus related to the job at hand. Inexperienced workers could not become confused by choosing the wrong Excel menu or the wrong file or the wrong command from a list of 15 on some menu. They would see only the few commands you have developed or selected for their specific assignment. You could even provide custom Help screens.

You should plan a custom application carefully before you begin to construct it. You can then create custom commands, macros, or functions, along with any new menus or dialog boxes required. New menus and dialog boxes are discussed in Chapter 20. This chapter explains how to run macros automatically and add new commands to existing menus.

RUNNING A MACRO AUTOMATICALLY

If your goal is to create an application that shields the user from the normal Excel procedures, you may want certain macros to run automatically when a stipulated document is opened or closed, or upon the occurrence of some other specified event, such as the opening of a particular Excel window.

You can accomplish these objectives in some cases by using the Define Name command and in others by using functions that trigger the running of a macro when an event occurs.

STARTING MACROS ON DOCUMENT OPENING OR CLOSING

Follow this procedure to make a macro run when a specific document is opened or closed:

1. With the document active, pull down the Formula menu and select the Define Name... command. (Shortcut: Press ⌘-L.) You'll see the Define Name dialog box.

2. In the Name box, type any short name that starts with **Auto_Open** if you want the macro to run when the document is opened. Type a name that starts with **Auto_Close** if you want the macro to run when the document is closed. In either case, be sure you use an underline and not a space between elements in the name.

3. When you defined names previously, the Refers To box referred to the cell containing the name of a macro you were creating. In this case, you enter into the Refers To box the name or reference address of a macro that you want to run when the specified document is opened or closed. The macro can be on either an active or inactive macro sheet; if you use a reference to an inactive macro sheet, Excel will automatically open the sheet before it runs the macro. Instead of typing a reference to the macro, you can click the cell where the macro starts, provided the macro sheet for the macro is visible.

4. Click OK to complete the naming sequence and close the dialog box.

HIDING AUTOMATIC MACRO NAMES

You can define automatic macro names so they are hidden, so that they will not be listed on menus and accidentally be selected directly by a user. To accomplish this, you must use the DEFINE.NAME macro function instead of the equivalent command. Here is the function with its sequence of arguments:

DEFINE.NAME(*name_text,refers_to,macro_type, shortcut_text,hidden*)

The following paragraphs explain the arguments in this function.

- The *name_text* argument indicates the Auto_Open or Auto_Close name you want to provide. This argument is equivalent to the Name box in the Define Name dialog box.

- The *refers_to* argument is equivalent to the Refers To box in the dialog box. Here is where you refer to the macro you want to run.

- The *macro_type* argument is a reference to the name you entered in the *name_text* argument. Enter **1** if the name refers to a custom function, **2** if the name refers to a command macro, or **3** if the name does not refer to a macro. In the example, the name in *name_text* does not refer directly to a macro, so you would type **3**.

- The *shortcut_text* **argument** indicates the shortcut letter of the alphabet to be used in running the macro. In the example, you want the macro to be actuated only by opening or closing the document, so you'll want to skip this argument. Nevertheless, remember that you must include the comma for the argument, as a placeholder.

- The *hidden* **argument** is the final argument for the DEFINE.NAME function. When the function is used for other purposes, you can eliminate this argument from the series. In the example, however, type the number **1** to hide the name from view. If you enter a zero (0) instead, or omit this argument, the name will be displayed on menus.

STARTING MACROS AFTER SPECIFIC EVENTS

Excel provides a group of functions that you can use to make a macro run after a specific event occurs. They are listed in Table 19.1.

Table 19.1: Functions that Start Macros When Specific Events Occur

FUNCTION	EVENT THAT STARTS MACRO
CANCEL.KEY	Cancellation of an operation or macro
ERROR	Error in a running macro
ON.TIME	Reaching of a specified time
ON.WINDOW	Activation of a specified window
ON.KEY	Pressing of a specified key
ON.DATA	Receipt of data by Excel from another application through dynamic data exchange
ON.RECALC	Recalculation of a specified worksheet

ADDING COMMANDS
TO EXCEL MENUS

You can add your own commands to Excel menus. These commands are actually the same command macros you learned to create in Chapter 17. However, to make one of these commands appear on a menu, you must enter the command in a five-column *command table* on a macro sheet. In addition, you use a macro function called ADD.COMMAND, which specifies the menu on which you want the command displayed, as well as the exact position of the command on that menu.

You'll follow these steps to run the Budget_Info macro you created in Chapter 17 by means of a new command you'll add to the File menu.

CREATING A COMMAND TABLE

The following paragraphs describe the columns required in a command table (from left to right) and the data to be entered in each column. You can place the table in any convenient area of a macro sheet.

- **Command name**. In this first column, type the name you want to appear on the menu. You can also place a single hyphen in this column to display only a horizontal line running the full width of the menu at the column position—a handy technique if you want to separate added commands from commands already on the menu. If you precede a character with an ampersand (**&**), the character can be used as an access key for the command.

- **Command macro name**. In the second column, type the name of the command macro to be run when the menu name is selected. If you entered a hyphen in the first column, leave this column blank.

- **Shortcut key**. In the third column, type a shortcut key to be displayed on the menu to the right of the command name. When a user presses this key in combination with the ⌘ key, the command will be selected without the menu appearing. This can be any letter of the alphabet. An entry in this column is optional. If you select a letter that is already in use for a macro, Excel will run the first command using this letter that is displayed in the Macro Run dialog box. If a built-in command uses the same key, Excel runs your custom command instead of the built-in command. If you entered a hyphen in the first column, leave this column blank.

- **Status message**. The fourth column is optional. It displays a message in the status bar at the bottom of the screen when the command name is selected.

- **Help topic**. The fifth column is optional too. It displays a custom help topic when a user asks for help with the new command. You create the help topic by saving in a plain-text format a file that consists of a one-line header followed by a short paragraph containing the help message. The header must begin with an asterisk, and the asterisk must be followed by a topic number you assign to the item (such as 28) and the subject covered. For example, you might type **∗28 Printing Budget Reports** as the header, type the help message below this header, and save the file under the name **Print Budget Help**. To use this help screen, in the fifth column of the command table you would type **Print Budget Help!28**, which identifies the file name and topic number and so tells Excel where to find the help message for this command.

Create a command table now for the Budget_Info macro.

1. Load the Budget worksheet and then the Budget Macro macro sheet.

2. On the Budget Macro sheet, scroll right until you can see column C (which is empty).

3. Click cell C10 to select it and type a hyphen (-). This entry places a horizontal line on the menu above the command you'll add.

4. Click the enter box in the formula bar to complete the entry. Then click cell C11 to select it.

5. In C11, type **Report** (the command name you want to display on the menu). Press Tab to complete the entry and move to the right, activating cell D11.

6. In D11, type **Budget_Info** (the name of the command macro). Make sure you place an underline symbol—not a space—between the two elements of the name. Press Tab to complete the entry and move to cell E11.

7. In E11, enter only the letter **J** (this will be your shortcut letter; it is not used by the built-in commands on Excel menus). Press Tab to move to cell F11.

8. In F11, type a message to appear on the status bar: **Prints 1 Budget report if no overruns, otherwise 2**

9. Click the enter box on the formula bar to complete the entry.

10. Drag the boundaries between the column headings to adjust the column widths until the Budget Macro window resembles Figure 19.1. (You'll soon enter a new macro in the blank area at the top of column C.)

You won't add a help message, so you've now finished the command table.

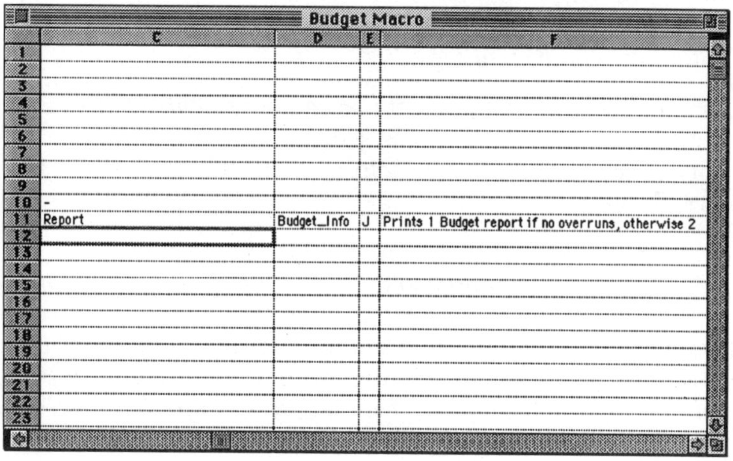

Figure 19.1: The completed command table

WRITING A MACRO WITH THE ADD.COMMAND FUNCTION

The next step is creating a macro that will run the ADD.COMMAND function, to place the new command on the File menu whenever the Budget worksheet is opened.

1. Click cell C1 and type a name for the macro: **Add_to_Menu** (remember to use underlines—not spaces—between words).

2. Press Return to complete the entry and activate cell C2.

3. In C2, pull down the Formula menu and select the Paste Function... command.

4. Scroll to highlight the function ADD.COMMAND( ) and click OK.

5. In the formula bar, replace the first argument placeholder (*bar_num*) by typing the number **1**, the Excel code specifying that you want to add the new command to the worksheet menu bar displayed when *full menus* are selected. (Excel provides six codes in all, only two of which will be used in this macro. Table 19.2 shows the complete list.)

6. Replace the second argument placeholder (*menu*) in the formula bar with the name of the menu on which the new command will appear. The name must be enclosed in double quotation marks. Type **"File"**.

7. Replace the third argument placeholder (*command_ref*) in the formula bar with a reference to the range occupied by the first command entry in the command table you just created. Your first entry in the table was not really a command at all—just a hyphen that caused a line to be drawn on the menu. However, you must include the entry in the formula so that the line will appear on the menu. Furthermore, each reference to the command table must include at least two columns. Therefore, even though cell D11 is empty, type the range **C10:D10**.

8. Skip the last argument, which is optional, and click the enter box in the formula bar to complete the formula. (The last argument, *position*, lets you specify exactly where on the designated menu your

command will appear. If you omit the argument, the command will appear at the bottom of the menu, exactly where we want it in this example. To specify a position, you would enter either the name of the command that is displayed immediately above the position where you want your command, or the number of the position on the menu to be occupied by your command, counting the first command at the top of the menu as number 1. When omitting the *position* argument, be sure to delete its placeholder.)

9. You've just caused a horizontal line to be added to the worksheet menu bar when full menus are selected. Now you must go through the sequence again to add the horizontal line to the menu bar when short menus are selected. Click cell C3 to select it and repeat steps 3 through 8, with one difference: Replace the first argument placeholder by typing **5** instead of 1; 5 is the code for the worksheet menu bar when short menus are selected. (Shortcut: Copy C2 to the clipboard, paste the copy into C3, and change the number 1 to a 5.)

10. Now that you've completed the formulas dealing with the horizontal line on both full and short menus, repeat the steps again to tell Excel where on the command table it can find the information for the actual command that will be called Report. Click cell C4 to select that cell and repeat steps 3 through 8, with these changes: Type **1** for the first argument again (for full menus) and change the range referenced on the command table by typing **C11:F11**. This range includes the columns containing the command name, the command macro name, the shortcut key, and the status message. (Shortcut: For both steps 10 and 11, you can copy, paste, and edit to create the contents of C4 and C5 shown in Figure 19.2.)

11. Press Return to complete the formula and activate cell C5. Paste in the macro function one final time, making the first argument **5** (for short menus) and repeating the other argument entries you completed in step 10, including the designation of the range as **C11:F11**.

12. Press Return to complete the formula and activate cell A6. Now end the macro. Pull down the Formula menu and select the RETURN( ) formula. Delete the argument placeholder in the formula bar, retaining only the name of the function and the parentheses.

13. Click the enter box in the formula bar to complete the formula and the macro.

14. You must tell Excel that these formulas constitute a macro. Select cell C1. Then pull down the Formula menu and select the Define Name... command. (Shortcut: Press ⌘-L.)

15. The Define Name dialog box proposes Add_to_Menu as the name for the macro. Click the Command button to enter the name as a command macro. Then click OK to close the dialog box. Your Budget Macro window should now resemble Figure 19.2.

Table 19.2: Menu Bar Identification Numbers Used with Functions in Customizing Menus

MENU BAR	SHORT MENUS	FULL MENUS
Worksheet	5	1
Chart	6	2
Null (no document open)	3	3
Info Window open	4	4

RUNNING THE NEW MACRO AUTOMATICALLY

The macro you've just completed places a horizontal line at the bottom of the File menu. Below that line, it displays a new command: Report. However, none of this will happen unless the new macro is run.

To run the new macro, you must use a name starting with Auto_Run, an option discussed earlier in this chapter. To make the new macro start automatically when the Budget worksheet is opened, follow these steps:

1. Activate the Budget worksheet.

2. Pull down the Formula Menu and select the Define Name... command. (Shortcut: Press ⌘-L.) The Define Name dialog box appears.

3. In the Name box, type **Auto_Open_AddMenu** (no spaces).

4. In the Refers To box, type = **'Budget Macro'!C1** (using a space between the two words, *single* quotation marks, and an exclamation point). Click OK. This entry makes the Auto_Open_AddMenu

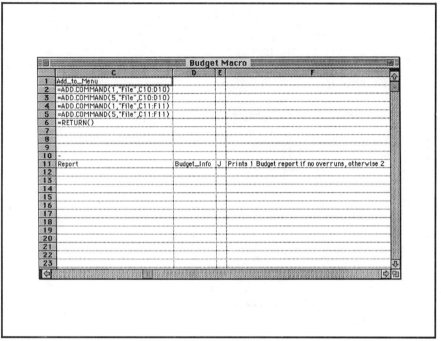

Figure 19.2: Budget Macro sheet with completed Add_to_Menu formula

name refer to cell C1 of the Budget Macro macro sheet, where the Add_to_Menu macro starts.

The macro will now run automatically every time the Budget worksheet is opened. In fact, if the Budget Macro macro sheet is not open, the sheet will be loaded into memory automatically too.

The entry in the Define Name dialog box should now resemble Figure 19.3.

TESTING THE NEW MACRO

Now test your work:

1. Save and then close the Budget worksheet and the Budget Macro macro sheet.

2. Reopen only the Budget worksheet. Excel also opens the Budget Macro sheet without any additional action on your part.

3. Pull down the File menu. The new Report command should appear at the bottom of the menu, beneath a new horizontal line, as shown in Figure 19.4. Note that the message text you typed appears in the status bar.

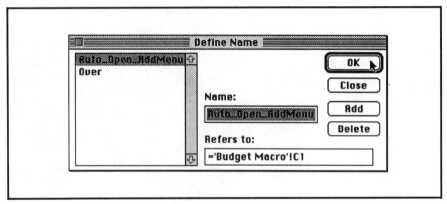

Figure 19.3: Using an Auto_Open name

USING AUTO-CLOSE

If users will be working only with the Budget worksheet, you don't have to worry about removing the Report command from the File menu when the worksheet is closed. However, if users will be accessing other files as well, you may want to remove the Report command from those other files, since the command functions only with the Budget worksheet.

You can delete the Report command every time the Budget worksheet is closed by creating a macro accessed by a name starting with Auto_Close instead of Auto_Open. The procedure is exactly the same, except that the featured macro function would not be ADD.COMMAND; it would be DELETE.COMMAND. The arguments for this function are the menu bar number (*bar_num*), the name of the menu containing the command to be removed (*menu*), and the name or position of the command itself (*command*).

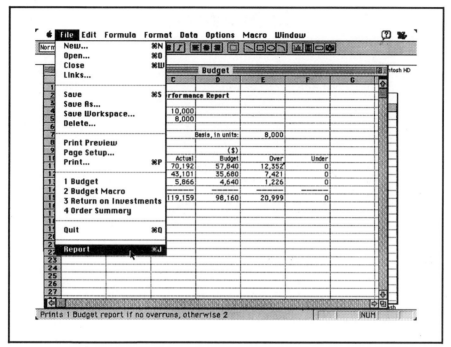

Figure 19.4: Report command added to the File menu

ADDING A FILE ALIAS

Remember that you can open a document automatically every time you start Excel by merely dragging the file into the folder named Excel Startup Folder, located in your Macintosh System folder.

If you're using System 7, you can even open Excel and an Excel document automatically every time you turn on your Macintosh. Simply drag the Excel document you created into the Startup Items folder within the System folder. The next time you start the computer, both Excel and the file will load.

Under System 7, you can load a file *alias* instead, if you prefer, as described at the end of Chapter 18.

SUMMARY

You've learned how to run macros automatically and to modify Excel menus by adding or deleting commands.

In Chapter 20, you build on this knowledge to craft custom menus and dialog boxes.

Chapter 20

Making Custom Menus and Dialog Boxes

In Chapter 19 you found that you can add commands to Excel menus and delete commands from Excel menus. In addition, you can make macros run automatically when your Macintosh is started, when Excel is started, or when a particular document is activated. You can even create your own functions and help screens. Using these techniques, you can create a customized application that shows only the worksheets and menu items needed to handle a certain task—very helpful if a novice computer user must perform the task. With this much control exerted, the user will have little opportunity to get into trouble by selecting the wrong command, worksheet, or application.

Nevertheless, you can go further. You can also create and name entire new menus and design custom dialog boxes. This chapter tells you how.

CREATING CUSTOM MENUS

Making a custom menu requires little additional knowledge beyond what you learned in creating a custom command. Most of the procedures are similar or identical.

In Chapter 19 you set up a command table as part of the process of adding your own command to an existing menu. To create a custom menu, you need to build a *menu table*.

BUILDING A MENU TABLE

Like a command table, a menu table occupies five contiguous columns on a macro sheet, and the content of each column is almost identical to that in a command table. Menu table columns include the following items:

- **Menu and command names.** Type the name of the menu in the first cell of the first column. Below that, type the names of commands to appear on the menu. As with a command table, to separate items you can enter a hyphen (-) in a cell of this column to cause Excel to draw a horizontal line across the width of the menu. You can also enter an ampersand (&) before a character to designate that character as an access key for a command.

- **Command macro names.** In the second column, type the name of the command macro that you want run when a command name to the left is selected.

- **Shortcut key.** As with a command table, you can use the third column to assign an optional shortcut key that will run the command.

- **Status message.** Again following the format of a command table, you can enter an optional message in the fourth column that will appear in the status bar at the bottom of the screen when the command is highlighted on the menu.

- **Help topic.** You can use the same instructions given in Chapter 19 to provide a help screen for the command.

USING THE ADD.MENU FUNCTION

To make Excel display the new menu, you run a macro that contains the ADD.MENU macro function. The procedure is equivalent to that used in Chapter 19, where you employed the ADD.COMMAND function to add a command to an existing menu.

Here is the ADD.MENU function with its arguments:

ADD.MENU(*bar_num,menu_ref,position*)

This is what the arguments mean:

- **The *bar_num* argument** indicates the number of the menu bar to which you want to add the menu. The menu bar numbers were listed in Chapter 19, in Figure 19.6.

- **The *menu_ref* argument** indicates the name of the menu table created through the Define Name... command. If you haven't defined a name, you can instead specify the range where the menu table is located.

- **The *position* argument** indicates the name or reference position of the existing menu to the left of the location where you want the new menu to appear. The reference position is obtained by simply counting the existing menus, starting with 1 as the position of the menu on the extreme left. If you omit this argument, the new menu will appear to the right of all existing menus.

USING THE DELETE.MENU FUNCTION

Just as you may want a custom command to disappear from a menu when the worksheet to which it applies is closed, you may want a custom menu displayed only under certain circumstances. To terminate the display of a custom menu, you use the DELETE.MENU macro function. This function has the following format:

DELETE.MENU(*bar_num,menu*)

Here is an explanation of the two DELETE.MENU arguments:

- The *bar_num* **argument** indicates the number of the menu bar that contains the menu to be deleted (from the codes listed in Figure 19.6).

- The *menu* **argument** indicates the name or number of the menu to be deleted.

ANALYZING A SAMPLE CUSTOM MENU

Figure 20.1 shows a macro sheet created to produce a special menu, called the Graph menu. Options on this menu graph the sales achieved by any of three regional offices of a mythical company or the combined sales of all three offices.

ADD.MENU Arguments

Cell A1 contains a macro named AddMenu. This is the macro required to display the new menu on the menu bar. It's very short, since the third argument for the ADD.MENU function has been eliminated—the argument that would specify an exact position on the menu bar for the added menu. Because the third argument is missing, this custom menu will appear to the right of the usual Excel menus.

The first argument is the number 1, a code from the list in Figure 19.6 specifying that the menu will be added to the Worksheet Full Menus menu bar. The second argument identifies the range on the macro sheet where the menu table is located.

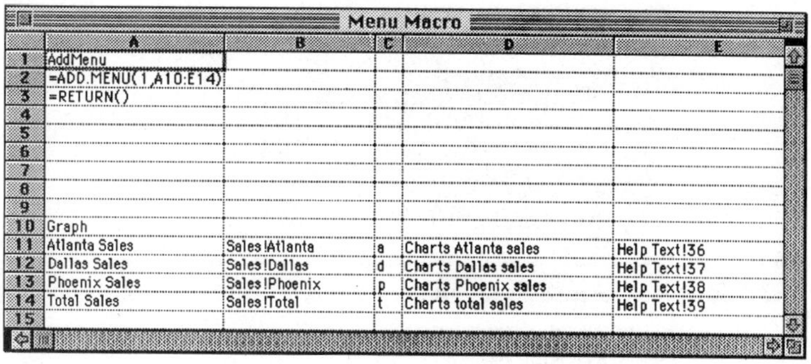

Figure 20.1: A macro sheet to create a special menu

The RETURN( ) function is required to end the macro.

You make the macro run automatically by specifying a name starting with the prefix Auto_Open in the Define Name... command, as described in Chapter 19. You can make the macro run every time a Monthly Sales worksheet is loaded.

The Menu Table

The first cell of the menu table (A10) contains the name of the menu to be added: Graph. Directly under this cell are the names of the commands that will appear on the menu.

The second column of the menu table provides the name of the command macro that will run when a command name in column A is selected. In this case, all of the macros are located on a macro sheet named Sales, so the name of each macro is preceded by the word *Sales*, followed by an exclamation point (!). Of course, if you were really creating such an application, you would have to write or record these macros to make the commands work, using the skills you acquired in previous chapters.

The third column lists the shortcut keys assigned to appear on the menu for each command. The fourth column lists the status bar messages to be displayed for each command. The last column pinpoints the location of help messages for each command (in a text file named Help Text).

These are the only elements needed to create and display the new menu. Figure 20.2 shows the resulting Graph menu in use.

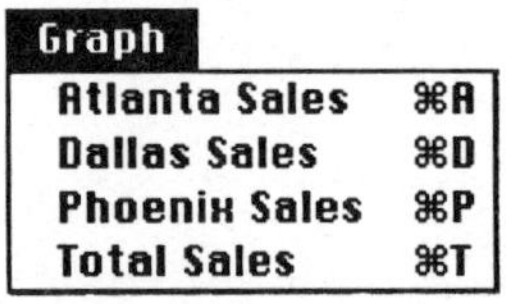

Figure 20.2: The contents of the custom Graph menu

CREATING CUSTOM DIALOG BOXES

To create a custom dialog box, you use a special utility included in your Excel folder: the *Dialog Editor*. As you use the utility's menus to select items for inclusion in a dialog box and then arrange those items within a representation of the dialog box you're building, Excel automatically generates a *dialog box definition*: code that you can copy through the clipboard to a macro sheet. To display the completed dialog box within an application, you write and run a macro that includes this definition.

You can compare the Dialog Editor to Excel's macro recorder. Both are aids that help you compose macros. In both cases, if you know enough about writing macros, you can skip using the utility and enter the required information directly into a macro sheet.

BECOMING FAMILIAR WITH THE DIALOG EDITOR

Before you start creating a dialog box, you should become familiar with the menus and general features of the Dialog Editor. Take a look now.

1. Close any Excel files you may have open.

2. If you're using a version of the Macintosh operating system earlier than System 7.0 and are not using the MultiFinder, exit the Excel program as well. Otherwise, simply hide Excel by using the System 7 Application menu or (under MultiFinder) by clicking the MultiFinder icon in the upper right corner of your screen.

3. In the Excel folder, double-click the icon for the Dialog Editor to open the utility.

With the Dialog Editor loaded, very few items are displayed. A large frame occupies the center of the screen. You'll create your dialog box inside this frame.

The upper left corner of the screen displays the familiar icon for the Macintosh Apple menu. Next to it are the three Dialog Editor menus: File, Edit, and Item.

Using the File Menu

Pull down the File menu and look at it now. It contains only two commands: New and Quit. You use the New command to start a new dialog box and the Quit command to leave the Dialog Editor.

Note that there is no Save command. That's because you don't save completed dialog boxes to disk files; you copy them to the clipboard, for pasting into a macro sheet.

Using the Edit Menu

Next, pull down the Edit menu. As Figure 20.3 shows, this menu displays several standard Macintosh commands: Undo, Cut, Copy, Paste, Clear, and Duplicate. All of these commands have shortcut key combinations, listed beside each command, and operate in the usual way.

Below these commands are five other commands that warrant special comment:

- **Info...** This command is an important part of the Dialog Editor. The command brings up the Info dialog box, through which you can control several display options relating to a selected item in a dialog box under construction. You'll use this feature shortly.

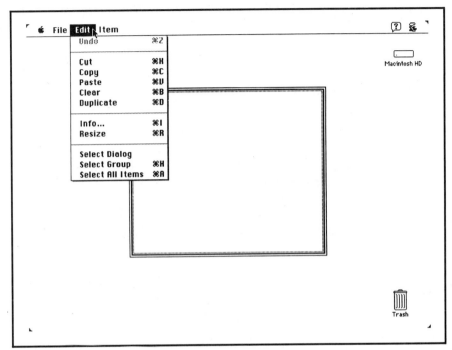

Figure 20.3: The Dialog Editor Edit menu

- **Resize.** Use this command to shrink your custom dialog box automatically so that its borders enclose the items within it without displaying empty areas.

- **Select Dialog.** Use this command to select the custom dialog box itself, rather than any of its components.

- **Select Group.** Use this command to select items that have been previously entered as a group.

- **Select All Items.** Use this command to select all items within the dialog box.

Using the Item Menu

Finally, pull down the Item menu. As shown in Figure 20.4, this menu includes six commands, four of which have related dialog boxes. Here is where you select items to add to a custom dialog box: a button, text, an edit

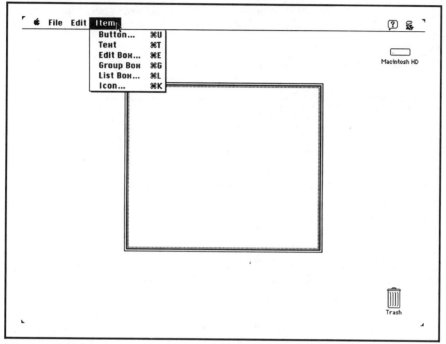

Figure 20.4: The Dialog Editor Item menu

box, a group box, a list box, or an icon. As you'll find as you use these commands, Excel furnishes a variety of options for each. For example, select the List Box... command, and you'll be offered a selection of four different kinds of list boxes you could add to a custom dialog box.

Designing a Dialog Box

In Chapter 17, you created a macro called Budget_Info, which printed either one copy of a Budget worksheet, if there were no production budget overruns, or two copies (an additional copy to send to corporate headquarters), if the worksheet showed one or more items as over budget. You saved this macro on a macro sheet named Budget Macro. The macro incorporated two additional macros you recorded to save any changes to the Budget worksheet and then print either one or two copies. You named these subsidiary macros Print1 and Print2. You'll use these recorded macros in a dialog box you'll create now.

The purpose of your dialog box will be to allow the user to *choose* whether to save and print one or two copies of the worksheet, rather than having the decision made automatically by Excel based on the content of the worksheet.

Let's get started.

Adding a Name and Standard Buttons

1. With the Dialog Editor loaded, pull down its Item menu and select the Text command. (Shortcut: Press ⌘-T.) As Figure 20.5 shows, the word *Text* appears in the upper left corner of the frame within which you'll create the dialog box; the word is surrounded by a border of dotted lines.

2. Type the words **Report Options**. This text appears within the dialog box as the dialog box name. Click outside the text area to complete the entry.

3. Pull down the Item menu again and select the Button... command. (Shortcut: Press ⌘-V.) You'll see the Button dialog box shown in Figure 20.6. OK is selected by default. Since you need an OK button in your dialog box, click OK to accept the default selection. The OK button is added to your dialog box.

4. Drag the OK button to the upper right corner of the dialog box.

5. Since a Cancel button usually accompanies an OK button, Excel has provided a quick means of adding the Cancel button. Simply press Return, and a Cancel button appears below the OK button.

6. The Cancel button is surrounded by a dotted line, ready for you to move it if you so desire. Click outside the Cancel button area of the dialog box to accept the default positioning.

Adding a Group Box with Option Buttons

Now you need to add *option buttons* the user can click to save and print either one or two copies of the Budget worksheet. Many Macintosh users know buttons of this type as *radio buttons*. As explained in an earlier chapter, these buttons are called radio buttons because you can select only

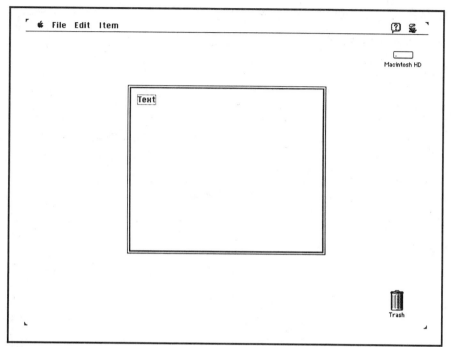

Figure 20.5: Adding text to a dialog box

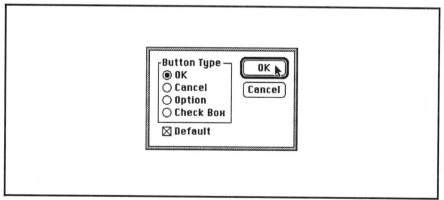

Figure 20.6: The Button dialog box

one button in a group at a time. Selecting any button automatically deselects any other in the group, making the feature function like the station-selection buttons on a pushbutton radio.

The first step in adding option buttons is to establish a group to contain the buttons:

1. Pull down the Item menu again and select the Group Box command. (Shortcut: Press ⌘-G.) A group box appears in your custom dialog box, directly under the Cancel button. (By default, a new item appears under the item that was last added or positioned.)

2. Drag the group box to the left, well below the Report Options title. Your screen should now resemble Figure 20.7.

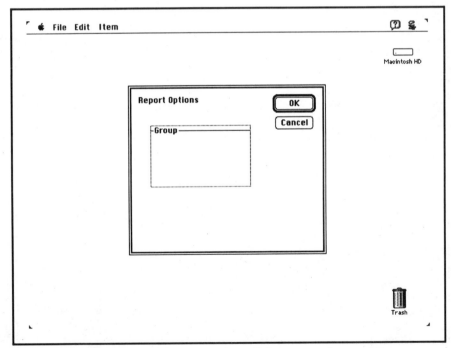

Figure 20.7: A custom dialog box with title, OK, and Cancel buttons and a repositioned Group box

You can quickly add the option buttons you need through another shortcut. But first, let's rename the Group box to something more helpful to the user.

1. Pull down the Edit menu and select the Info... command. You'll see the Group Info dialog box shown in Figure 20.8. Info dialog boxes have several positioning and display options that we'll discuss after you complete the group box.

2. Right now, change the current name by clicking the Text box, deleting the name *Group*, and typing the words **Save and Print**.

3. Click OK to close the box. The group box is now headed Save and Print, the new name you just entered.

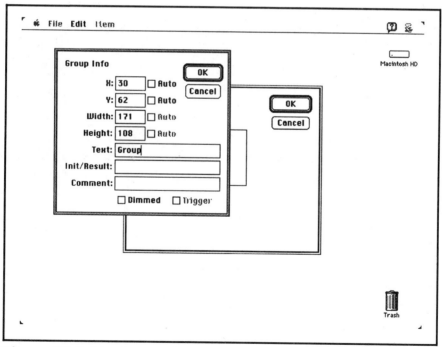

Figure 20.8: The Group Info dialog box

4. Now for that option button shortcut. Before you take any other action, simply press Return to add an option button to the group box.

5. Type **One copy**. These words become the label for the button.

6. Press Return again to add a second option button. Your screen should now resemble Figure 20.9.

7. Type **Two copies** as the label for the second button.

8. Click anywhere outside the group box to complete the entry of the text for the second button without adding a third button.

9. Click the border of the group box to select it. Place the pointer at the lower right corner of the group box until the pointer assumes the shape of a thick diagonal line with arrows at each end. Drag the corner of the box to reduce its size until you eliminate excess white space below and to the right of the buttons. (Alternatively, you can

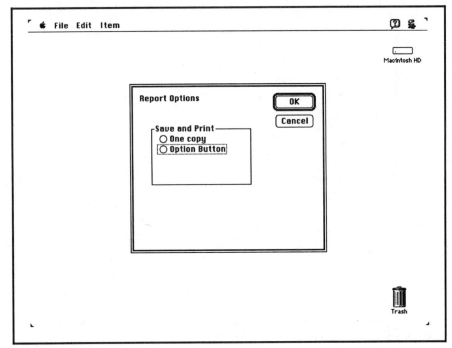

Figure 20.9: Adding option buttons

click the border of the group box to select it, pull down the Edit menu, and select Resize. This command will remove excess white space automatically, but you may not be as pleased esthetically with the results since the command gives you no control over the exact framing of elements.)

10. Resize the custom dialog box itself by clicking a border to select the box and then using either of the techniques just explained in step 9. Your screen should now resemble Figure 20.10.

You've completed your work in the Dialog Editor that is required for this particular dialog box. Soon you'll copy the dialog box to the clipboard and paste it into a macro sheet. However, first let's explore the options in the Info dialog box and Item menu that you didn't use this time but may need in the future.

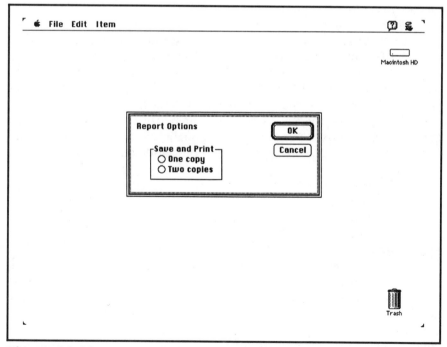

Figure 20.10: The completed dialog box

Info Dialog Box Options

You can pull down the Edit menu and issue the Info... command to display an Info dialog box for any selected element of a custom dialog box. The Info dialog box always resembles the example reproduced in Figure 20.8.

At the top of an Info dialog box are entry boxes labeled X, Y, Width, and Height. These entry boxes relate to the location or dimensions of the item in your custom dialog box. If you move the item to a new position or drag to resize it, any numbers shown will change automatically to reflect your modifications.

The X number represents the location of the left edge of the item, measured from the left edge of the custom dialog box, in *horizontal screen units*. One horizontal screen unit represents one-eighth of the width of an average character in the system font.

The Y number represents the location of the top edge of the item, measured from the top edge of the custom dialog box, in *vertical screen units*. One vertical screen unit represents one-twelfth of the height of one character in the system font.

The Width is the width of the selected item in horizontal screen units.

The Height is the height of the selected item in vertical screen units.

To the right of each of the entry boxes for these four elements of an Info dialog box is a small check box labeled Auto. If this box is selected, you may not be able to move or resize the item until you click the box to deselect it.

You can make changes by typing a number of your own choosing in any of these four boxes. For example, you might want to enter an X number for an item so it will line up horizontally under another item with the same X measurement.

The Text box contains the heading or label text for the selected item. To change the text displayed, type new text as you did for the Group box title.

The Init/Result box is where you can enter an initial value for items that support the Init/Result feature. For example, to have the third item in a list box displayed by default, you'd enter the number 3 here. Then, when you copied the completed dialog box from the Dialog Editor into a macro sheet, the number would be transferred automatically to the row for the list box in the Init/Result column of the definition (the seventh column of the table). This initial value would later be replaced in the column by the number of the item actually selected by a user—the result. This is why the column is named Init/Result: It displays both an optional initial value and the result of a user entry.

Use the Comment text box in an Info dialog box to add an optional programming comment. When the custom dialog box definition is copied to a macro sheet, the eighth column of the definition area will display any comments.

The two remaining options in the Info dialog box are Dimmed and Trigger. A *trigger* item causes a result to be entered in the definition but leaves the custom dialog box displayed so further choices can be made, perhaps from option buttons in other groups. A *dimmed* item appears dimmed in the custom dialog box—in other words, not available for selection until some other function is performed. Custom dialog boxes that change their appearance based on user actions are called *dynamic dialog boxes*.

Other Item Menu Dialog Boxes

You can select commands on the Item menu that display three additional dialog boxes with which you should be familiar: the Edit Box, List Box, and Icon dialog box.

Let's look first at the Edit Box options.

Dialog boxes often contain *edit boxes* for user entry of data. You add one of these boxes by choosing the Edit Box... command. (Shortcut: Press ⌘-E.) The resulting dialog box, shown in Figure 20.11, lets you select the type of data that the edit box will accept.

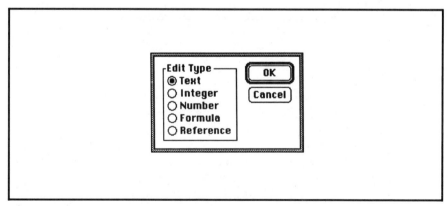

Figure 20.11: The Edit Box dialog box

These are the edit box data options:

- **Text** permits the entry of text.

- **Integer** permits the entry of whole numbers.

- **Number** permits the entry of any number, including a number with a decimal point.

- **Formula** permits the entry of a formula.

- **Reference** permits the entry of a cell or range address.

You can also choose among four List Box options. The dialog box for the Dialog Editor's List Box... command lets you select the type of list box you want added to a custom dialog box. The four choices are Standard, Combination, Dropdown, and Combination Dropdown (see Figure 20.12).

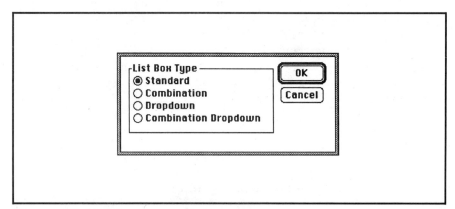

Figure 20.12: The List Box dialog box

The shortcut key combination for this command is ⌘-L.
Here is an explanation of each kind of list box:

- **Standard.** A dialog box that contains a standard Excel list box displays a list of choices in a small window area accompanied by a vertical scroll bar for scrolling through the choices. An example is the familiar Paste Function dialog box, displayed through the Paste Function... command on Excel's Formula menu.

- **Combination.** A standard list box accompanied by an edit box, where the user can enter data or where a choice is displayed, is called a combination list box. An example is the Save As... dialog box.

- **Dropdown.** A list box in a dropdown format displays one item with a downward-pointing arrow that the user can click to display a list of other options. An example is the Patterns dialog box, displayed through the Patterns... command on Excel's Format menu.

- **Combination Dropdown.** A combination dropdown list box combines a dropdown list box with an accompanying edit box. An example is Excel's Font dialog box, displayed through the Font... command on the Format menu.

The Icon options lets you add three types of icons to a custom dialog box: alert, information, and warning. Use the alert icon to alert users to a choice that must be made, the information icon to indicate that the dialog box merely contains information, and the warning icon to inform users of an error or problem. The types are displayed in the Icon dialog box, displayed through the Icon... command on the Dialog Editor's Item menu (see Figure 20.13). The shortcut key combination for this command is ⌘-K.

You can move or resize an icon after selecting it for a custom dialog box. However, you may have to deselect one or more Auto boxes in the item's Info dialog box to turn off the Dialog Editor's automatic placement and sizing features.

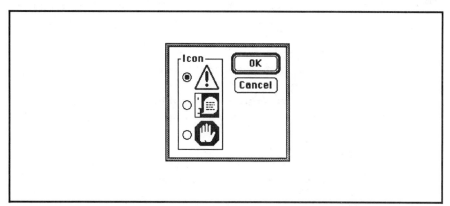

Figure 20.13: The Icon dialog box

COPYING THE DEFINITION TO A MACRO SHEET

With your completed custom dialog box still displayed in the Dialog Editor, follow these steps to transfer the definition of the dialog box to a macro sheet:

1. Pull down the Edit menu and pick the Select Dialog command.

2. Now that your new dialog box is selected, pull down the Edit menu again and select the Copy command. (Shortcut: Press ⌘-C.) This action copies the dialog box definition to the clipboard.

3. Switch to Excel and press ⌘-N to open a new file. Then, from the resulting New dialog box, click Macro Sheet to select that option and click OK. A blank macro sheet appears.

4. Click A20 on the macro sheet to select this cell for the beginning of the first column of the dialog box definition. Selecting cell A20 leaves space above the definition for macros you also need to enter before you can use the dialog box.

5. Press ⌘-V to paste the definition from the clipboard into the macro sheet. Your screen should now resemble Figure 20.14.

This figure shows the first four columns of the definition the Dialog Editor created for your custom dialog box. Actually, the definition includes seven columns in all; you can see the remaining columns displayed in Figure 20.17 later in this chapter. (If you had added comments to any item, they would have been displayed in an eighth column.)

Here is an explanation of the contents of each column:

- **Column 1** contains an identification number for the kind of item described in each row. For example, the number 12 designates an option button. The first column of the first row of the definition is empty because the first row contains (in other columns) location and size specifications for the dialog box itself; the dialog box is not an item and therefore has no item identification number.

- **Column 2** provides the X position of the upper left corner of an item (measured in horizontal screen units) in relation to the left

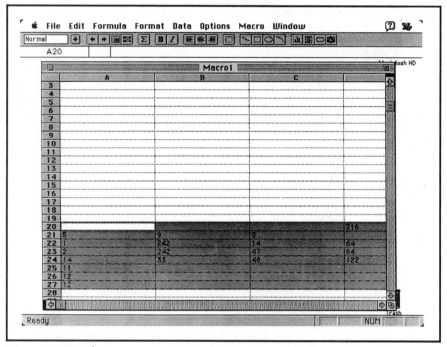

Figure 20.14: Pasting the dialog box definition into a macro sheet

edge of the dialog box. Again, the first row in column 2 is empty because the first row of the definition refers to the dialog box itself.

- **Column 3** provides the Y position of the upper left corner of an item (measured in vertical screen units) in relation to the top edge of the dialog box. The first row in column 3 is empty too because the first row of the definition refers to the dialog box itself.

- **Column 4** provides the width of the item measured in screen units. (In the first row, column 4 provides the width of the dialog box itself.)

- **Column 5** provides the height of the item measured in screen units. (In the first row, column 5 provides the height of the dialog box itself.)

- **Column 6** provides any text to be displayed in conjunction with an item, such as the label for an option button.

- **Column 7** displays the initial value or result of an item (as explained earlier in this chapter in the discussion of the Init/Result box). You must include this column in any range or name reference to the definition, even when the column is empty.

- **Column 8** is for comments and can be ignored if you haven't added comments.

Remember that you can write dialog box definitions directly on a macro sheet without using the Dialog Editor. However, in most cases, the use of the editor does speed up the process.

Table 20.1 lists the identification numbers you must enter in column 1 when you write your own definitions.

Now, while the range that includes the dialog box definition is still selected, let's name it:

1. Pull down the Formula menu and select the Define Name... command. (Shortcut: Press ⌘-L.)

2. Type the name **Report_Options**. (Be sure to type an underline between the two words instead of a space). Leave the None button selected in the Macro section of the Define Name dialog box, as shown in Figure 20.15.

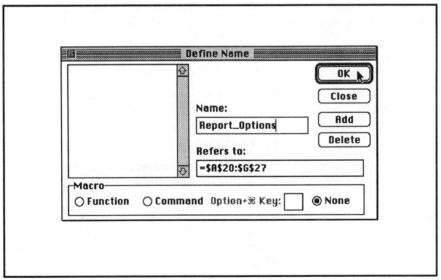

Figure 20.15: Entering a name for the dialog box definition

Table 20.1: Dialog Box Item Identification Numbers

ID NUMBER	MEANING
1	Indicates the default OK button.
2	Indicates an alternate Cancel button (with a lighter border).
3	Indicates an alternate OK button (with a lighter border).
4	Indicates the default Cancel button.
5	Indicates text not attached to a specific item in a dialog box (such as the name you give the dialog box itself).
6	Indicates a text edit box.
7	Indicates an integer edit box.
8	Indicates a number edit box.
9	Indicates a formula edit box.
10	Indicates a reference edit box.
11	Indicates an option button group.
12	Indicates an option button.
13	Indicates a check box.
14	Indicates a group box.
15	Indicates a list box.
16	Indicates a linked list box. (When preceded by a text edit box, displays in the text box the item chosen from the list.)
17	Indicates an icon. (Enter 1 in the text box of the row to display an alert icon, 2 to display an information icon, or 3 to display a warning icon.)
18	Not used in the Macintosh version of Excel.
19	Not used in the Macintosh version of Excel.
20	Displays the name of the current folder.
21	Indicates a drop-down list box.
22	Indicates a drop-down combination edit/list box.

3. Click OK to complete the entry of the name. In the future you can use this name instead of a cell range in formulas as you refer to the definition.

4. Save the macro sheet by pressing ⌘-S and entering the file name **Report Dialog Macros**. After saving the macro sheet, leave it displayed on your screen.

USING A CUSTOM DIALOG BOX

You can easily create a macro that displays the new dialog box. However, making it work requires a little more effort.

You first write a macro to add a command to a menu through which a user can to display the dialog box. To accomplish this, you employ the techniques you learned in Chapters 17 and 19.

You must name the new command—for example, you could call it Report Options—and then add it to the File menu with a macro stored on the Budget Macro macro sheet. If you begin the macro name with the prefix Auto_Open, this macro could start automatically when the Budget worksheet is opened.

Next you must write the additional macro to be called by the macro that provides the new Report Options command. This second macro actually does the work of displaying the dialog box and making it function as it should, running either the Print1 or Print2 recorded macros according to the selection made in the dialog box.

Since you have already completed step-by-step exercises through which you've learned how to add a command to a menu, you don't need to repeat these steps now. However, you will create the new macro that makes the dialog box operational.

DISPLAYING THE NEW DIALOG BOX

First, let's see how easily you can display the dialog box. You could simply enter the following macro in the Report Dialog Macros macro sheet:

```
= DIALOG.BOX(Report_Options)
= RETURN( )
```

The DIALOG.BOX macro function is intended for just this purpose: to display the specified dialog box. To enter its one argument, all you have to do is type between the parentheses the name of the definition or the range the definition occupies.

You must then use the Define Name... command to name the macro and tell Excel that the two lines constitute a command macro.

Finally, you must pull down the Macro menu, select the Run... command, select the newly added macro by name, and click OK. The dialog box will be displayed.

Of course, since all this two-line macro does is display the dialog box, it is useful for test purposes only.

Figure 20.16 shows the completed dialog box displayed over the Budget worksheet with which it would be used.

Suppose you now click the One Copy or Two Copies option button and then click OK. What would happen? Some functionality is provided within the dialog box definition itself. The definition will record which

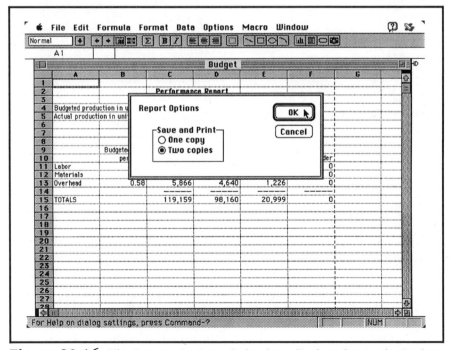

Figure 20.16: The Report Options dialog box displayed over the Budget worksheet

button was selected, and the dialog box will close when you click OK—indicating that the OK button is already functional.

Figure 20.17 illustrates how the final four columns of the dialog box definition appear after a user clicks the button for Two Copies and then clicks OK. (The definition has no eighth column because you added no comments.) Note that the seventh column (column G) contains only one entry: the number 2. This number appears in the line of the definition relating to the option button group and records the *result* of selecting the second option, Two copies.

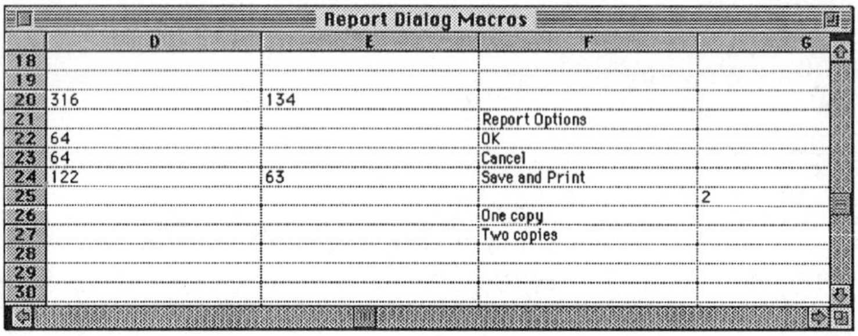

	D	E	F	G
18				
19				
20	316	134		
21			Report Options	
22	64		OK	
23	64		Cancel	
24	122	63	Save and Print	
25				2
26			One copy	
27			Two copies	
28				
29				
30				

Figure 20.17: The last four columns of the dialog box definition, showing that the second option button was selected

However, in order to have the number 2 actuate the printing of two copies of the Budget worksheet, you need more than a two-line macro. In fact, the two-line macro doesn't provide for what should happen if a user selects the Cancel button either.

MAKING THE DIALOG BOX WORK

To make the dialog box fully functional, you must write a macro similar to the one shown at the top of column A in Figure 20.18. In that figure,

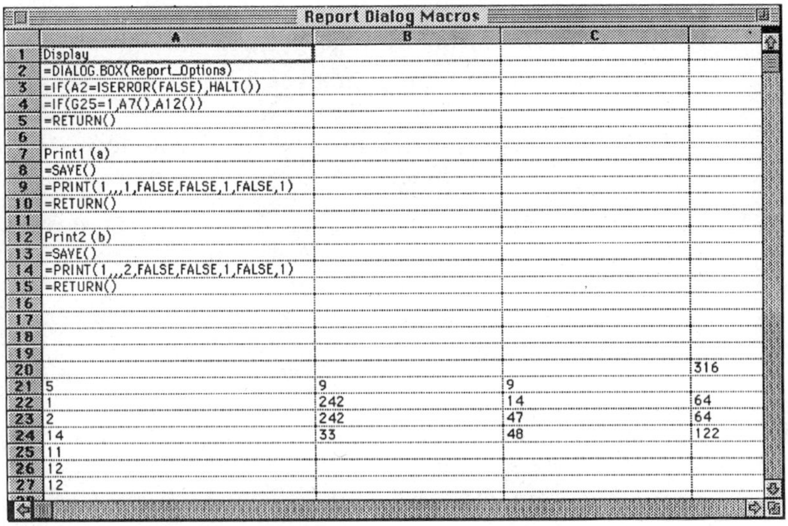

Figure 20.18: Macros that make the dialog box functional

the macro is followed by the Print1 and Print2 macros, copied from the Budget Macro macro sheet through the clipboard so you can see all three of these related macros together.

You could also use the Print1 and Print2 macros by referring to them in their original positions on the Budget Macro macro sheet.

Follow these steps:

1. Open the Budget worksheet. Because of programming you did previously, this action automatically opens the Budget Macro macro sheet too. (You need the Budget worksheet open to test the macro you'll create.)

2. Activate the Budget Macro macro sheet. Copy the Print1 and Print2 macros from this sheet through the clipboard to the positions shown on the Report Dialog Macros macro sheet.

3. Type **Display** in cell A1 of the Report Dialog Macros worksheet, to serve as a title for the new macro. Press Return.

4. In cell A2, type the formula = **DIALOG.BOX(Report_Options)** and press Return. This line displays the custom dialog box.

5. In cell A3, type = **IF(A2 = ISERROR(FALSE),HALT( ))**. This formula causes the macro to end and the dialog box to close if a user clicks the Cancel button. (FALSE is the value returned to A2 by the DIALOG.BOX function when Cancel is chosen. The ISERROR function determines what happens if the program encounters an error such as FALSE. The HALT function terminates any running macro.)

6. In cell A4, type = **IF(G25 = 1,A7( ),A12( ))**. This formula states that if cell G25 in the dialog box definition reads 1 (the result returned if a user clicks the One Copy button), Excel is to run the macro that starts in A7; otherwise, Excel is to run the macro that starts in A12. A7 is the cell where Print1 starts on this macro sheet; A12 is the cell where Print2 starts.

7. In cell A5, type = **RETURN( )** to end the macro. In this instance, if you don't enter the RETURN macro function here, Excel will double back after executing the Print1 or Print2 macro (whichever is selected) and print one additional copy of the worksheet.

8. Now you must define the cells as a macro. Start with A1. Select A1 and press ⌘-L to bring up the Define Name dialog box. Since the cell selected contains the word *Display,* the text box proposes that word as the name for the macro. This name is what you want, so don't change it.

9. Click the Command button to define the name as a command macro. Then click OK to complete the entry and close the Define Name dialog box.

10. Press ⌘-S to save the changes to the Report Dialog Macros macro sheet.

11. To test your work, activate the Budget worksheet (without closing any files) and select the new Display macro through the Run... command on the Macro menu.

You can now test the new dialog box by selecting any of its options (provided your printer is turned on and is online). You'll find that the dialog box is fully operational so long as the worksheet is selected and the macro sheets remain in memory.

Remember that, for an actual application, you should also write and name (with an Auto_Open prefix) the macro on the Budget Macro macro sheet that places the Report Options command on the File menu and then starts the Display macro on the other macro sheet when a user selects the command. With this command-generating macro in place, you would no longer need to use the Run... command to start the Display macro.

As you develop your own applications, you can include all of your macros and tables on one macro sheet if you prefer. Merely to avoid possible confusion, we used a second sheet in this example to separate the definition table and macros relating to the custom dialog box from the menu table and annotated macros used in previous chapters.

SUMMARY

In this chapter, you learned how to add both custom menus and dialog boxes to Excel. With these capabilities, you can create many useful applications.

However, think twice about incorporating entirely new menus; they do take up space on a menu bar. For example, suppose you create an application on a Macintosh IIsi, using a 13-inch monitor, and a user tries to run that application on a Macintosh Classic with its 9-inch screen. Because the smaller menu bar of the Classic does not have enough room to display the added menus, the user could not access them unless you temporarily deleted one or more standard menus.

Custom dialog boxes do not present this kind of problem, since you can make them small enough to pop up on the screen of any Macintosh. Still, they do present potential pitfalls. Check and double-check related macros to make certain the dialog boxes always function properly, no matter what actions the user takes.

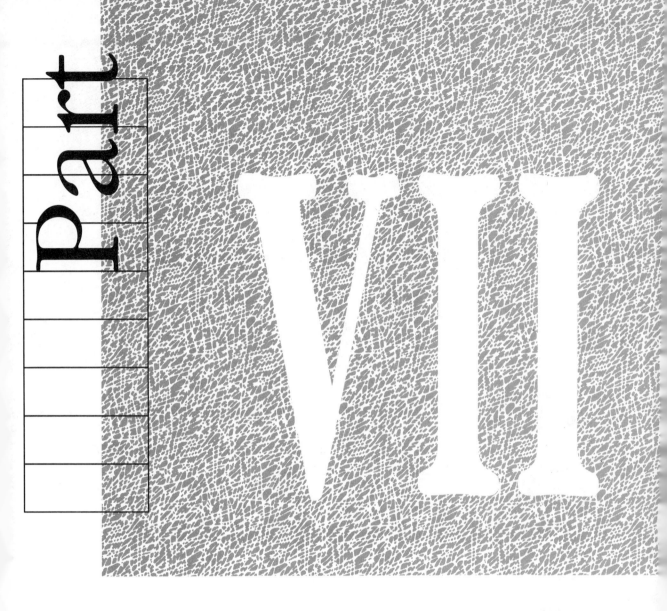

Part VII

More Advanced Topics

Chapter

21

Protecting
Your Data

In Part 6, you learned that you can keep inexperienced users of your Macintosh from accessing menus, commands, or files not related to their work. You can do this by causing only certain files to be loaded and only necessary commands to be displayed.

In addition, in Chapter 4 you found that you can protect all or part of a worksheet so that the user cannot change the data stored there without providing specified password. In fact, you can prevent even the opening of a file without the proper password.

If a particular file format will be used repeatedly, you can save the master file as a template; then the user will always open and work with a copy of the file, thereby protecting the original. Chapter 2 discussed this feature.

Excel offers still other ways of restricting a user to necessary operations and preventing accidental or intentional alteration of files. These techniques are the subject of this chapter.

RESTRICTING THE WORKSPACE

You first used the File menu's Save Workspace... command in Chapter 7—to save a working environment so you could return to it exactly as you left it, with the same files open in the same relationships. You can also take advantage of this command to structure the workspace so that the user's options are restricted by far more than the specific commands the menus display.

HIDING FILE WINDOWS

You can load a file necessary to the proper operation of an application without displaying that file. This action reduces the probability of a user making unwanted changes to the file. Once you've hidden a file and then saved your workspace, the file will remain hidden when the workspace file is subsequently reopened.

You've already learned that you can cause a designated file to open automatically when Excel is loaded. That file can be a workspace file, so you can decree that Excel automatically open and arrange an entire group of files, including one or more files that you want to keep hidden—all without any action on the part of the user.

Examples of useful hidden files are lookup tables and databases that a user needs to access only indirectly.

Here's all you have to do to hide a file:

1. Make the file the active window.

2. Pull down the Window menu and select the Hide command, as illustrated in Figure 21.1.

3. When you have arranged the remainder of the workspace and its files to your liking, pull down the File menu and select the Save Workspace... command.

4. In the Save Workspace dialog box, give the workspace an appropriate name (if you haven't already named it in a previous session). Remember that this book suggests typing a workspace file name in capital letters so you can easily distinguish the file later from individual worksheet, chart, and macro sheet files.

The file will be hidden.

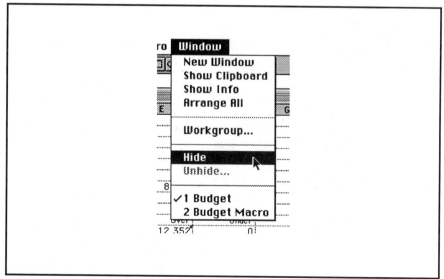

Figure 21.1: Hiding a file window

To make a file visible again, follow this procedure:

1. Pull down the Window menu and select the Unhide... command. The Unhide dialog box appears, displaying the names of all currently open, but hidden, files.

2. Scroll if necessary to highlight the name of the file you want to "unhide."

3. Click OK to close the dialog box. The file will be displayed again.

HIDING ROWS AND COLUMNS

As discussed in Chapter 5, you can hide selected rows and columns. The easiest way to hide a single row or column is to use the same dragging technique you would use for resizing, as explained in Chapter 5. Drag the boundary between the heading of the row or column you want to hide and an adjacent row or column until the dragged boundary covers the other boundary of the row or column you want to hide. In effect, you reduce the row height or column width to zero, thereby hiding the data that the row or column contains.

If you want to hide a group of rows or columns, it's faster to use the menu system:

1. Drag across the rows or columns you want to hide, to select and highlight them.

2. Pull down the Format menu and select either the Row Height... or Column Width... command, as appropriate. When you issue one of these commands, a dialog box appears in which you can specify an exact row height (in points) or column width (in number of characters displayed). The dialog box also contains a box you can click to restore the selected rows or columns to their default sizes. At the bottom of the dialog box are buttons you can click to hide or unhide the selection.

3. Click the Hide button, as shown in Figure 21.2. Then click OK. The selected rows or columns are reduced in height or width to zero and remain hidden until restored through the same dialog box, as described next.

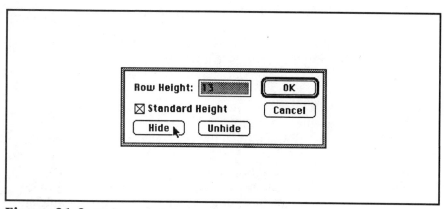

Figure 21.2: Hiding worksheet rows

To restore hidden rows or columns, follow this procedure:

1. Drag across the area involved, selecting either a group of cells or the headings on either side of the hidden area.

2. Pull down the Format menu and select the Row Height... or Column Width... command.

3. In the resulting dialog box, click the Unhide button and then click OK. The hidden area will reappear.

CHANGING WORKSPACE FEATURES

You can change various aspects of your workspace, even hiding some features to keep the user from performing unwanted actions in working with your application.

For example, if you hide the scroll bars, a user will be less tempted to look at worksheet areas not initially displayed.

Here's how to hide the scroll bars and make several other adjustments.

1. Pull down the Options menu and select the Workspace... command. The Workspace dialog box appears.

2. Turn one or more options in this dialog box on or off by clicking the box for the feature to be changed.

3. Click the OK button to implement the changes and close the dialog box.

Figure 21.3 shows the Workspace dialog box.
Following is an explanation of the options in this dialog box.

- **Fixed Decimal**. When this option is selected, Excel automatically inserts a decimal point in numbers. Excel inserts the decimal point immediately to the left of the number of decimal places selected in this section of the dialog box. Using this feature can speed up data entry for individuals entering amounts as currency. For example, with the Fixed Decimal option on and Places set to 2, Excel enters 2398 as 23.98. You might want to use this option when setting up an application for data entry operators.

- **R1C1**. This option provides an alternate method of indicating cell relationships. It numbers both rows and columns and refers to cell locations in formulas by their positions on the worksheet rather than by their specific addresses. For example, the designation R4C8 refers to the cell 4 rows (R4) down and 8 columns (C8) to the right of a cell previously mentioned. Activate this option if the people

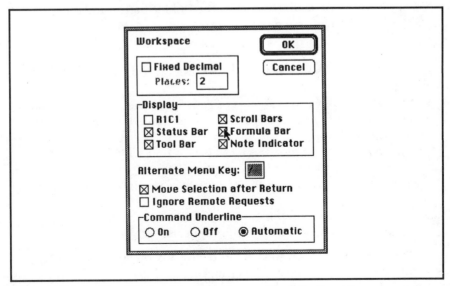

Figure 21.3: The Workspace dialog box with default settings

who will be using your application prefer this cell-designation system to the default representation, wherein rows are numbered and columns are designated by letters of the alphabet.

- **Status Bar**. If you deselect this item, Excel will no longer display status messages at the bottom of the screen. In certain applications, you might feel that these messages could confuse the user.

- **Toolbar**. When the Toolbar is displayed, a worksheet user could cause problems by accidentally clicking one of the tools. Deselect this option if you feel it might be a hazard.

- **Scroll Bars**. As previously mentioned, removing the display of the scroll bars can discourage the user from scrolling the file currently displayed. (However, even without scroll bars, a worksheet still can be scrolled. For example, if the user has a Macintosh with an extended keyboard that includes PageUp and PageDown keys, pressing one of these keys scrolls the worksheet vertically.)

- **Formula Bar**. You can hide the formula bar by deselecting this option, thereby preventing the user from changing the contents of cells.

- **Note Indicator**. This option merely controls whether or not cells that have been annotated display a symbol indicating the presence of a note. Deselect this option if you don't want the user to be aware of cell notes in a worksheet.

- **Alternate Menu Key**. By default, you can access menus by using the keyboard as well as the mouse. To use the keyboard alone, you press the slash (/) key (the same key that provides a question mark when pressed in conjunction with the Shift key) followed by a character underlined on the menu bar. If you then press an additional character also underlined on the menu, you can issue a command without using the mouse at all. For example, you can press /-M-C to start recording a macro. If you want to use a key other than the slash to display the character underlines and to access the menus, you use the Alternate Menu Key option. You might want to suggest the keyboard alternative to a data entry operator either unfamiliar with the operation of a mouse or accustomed to issuing commands through a keyboard-only version of a spreadsheet program such as Lotus 1-2-3, which uses the slash key to display menus. (Also see the discussion of the Command Underline option that follows.)

- **Move Selection after Return**. This option is normally selected. It causes the pointer to move from the current cell to the cell immediately below when you press Return to complete data entry in a cell. If you deselect the option, the current cell remains selected after data has been entered. You might want to use this option in a situation where special formatting is required for each cell after data entry is completed.

- **Ignore Remote Requests**. When you select this option, you block remote access to your workspace.

- **Command Underline**. This option works in conjunction with the Alternate Menu Key option, explained previously. You use the Command Underline option to specify when characters for accessing menus and commands from the keyboard are underlined on the screen. You can have the characters underlined all the time (On), never underlined (Off), or underlined only after the alternate menu key is pressed (Automatic). You might want to select the On option if you want a user always to enter data without using the mouse.

  Figure 21.4 shows the Formula menu with command underline characters displayed. Note that, to avoid conflicts caused by using

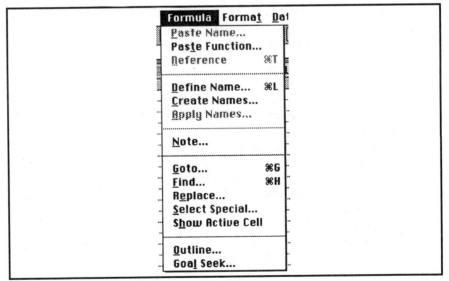

Figure 21.4: The Formula menu with keyboard command options underlined

the same key twice, you select some commands through the keyboard by pressing unlikely characters. For example, you must press *t* to select the Paste Function... command.

USING PROTECTION COMMANDS

In Chapter 4 you protected areas of data on a worksheet from accidental changes by using the Cell Protection... command on the Format menu in conjunction with the Protect Document... command on the Options menu.
This is the sequence you followed:

1. Select the entire data area of the worksheet.

2. Pull down the Format menu and use the Cell Protection... command to protect the selected area.

3. Select the cells within the data area that you want to exempt from cell protection—in other words, the cells in which you want to permit data entry.

4. Pull down the Format menu and use the Cell Protection... command again to remove protection from the selected cells.

5. Pull down the Options menu and use the Protect Document... command to put the protection into effect. You can assign a password so that only someone who provides the password can change the protection status of the document.

Protecting specific areas can help you maintain the integrity of a worksheet.

PROTECTING CHARTS

You can protect charts in a similar manner. However, when you select an embedded chart on a worksheet, the Format menu won't display the Cell Protection Command. Instead, the menu will display the Object Protection... command. Select this command, and you'll bring up the Object Protection dialog box shown in Figure 21.5.

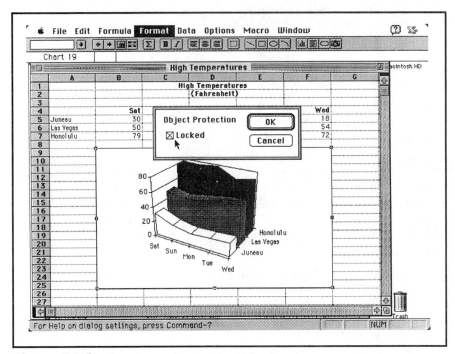

Figure 21.5: The Object Protection dialog box

After you lock a selected chart, the user can't change it. As with the Cell Protection... command, you must pull down the Options menu and choose the Protect Document... command to put the protection in effect.

To protect an independent chart (a chart not part of a worksheet), you must pull down the Chart menu and select the Protect Document... command. You'll see the Protect Document dialog box shown in Figure 21.6. Using this dialog box, you can specify a password that protects only the chart or both the chart and the open windows.

Protected windows do not display either a close box or a zoom box. An individual without the password cannot resize or move the protected window, nor open or close it. You would use this option in a situation in which the protected window is displayed automatically, and you do not want others to alter that display in any way.

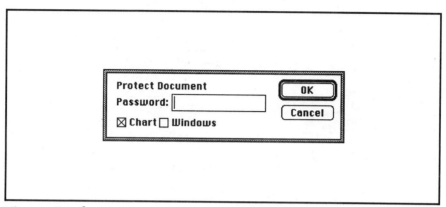

Figure 21.6: The Chart Protect Document dialog box

PROTECTING FILES
WITH FILE MENU OPTIONS

You have access to additional file protection options through the Save As... command on the File menu. We'll discuss the individual options in a moment. Follow these steps to select any of the options:

1. Pull down the File menu and select the Save As... command. The Save As dialog box appears.

2. Click the Options button at the bottom of the dialog box. This action brings up the Options dialog box shown in Figure 21.7.

3. Select the options you want and enter passwords if you want them used.

4. Click OK to save your changes. The Options dialog box closes, and you return to the Save As dialog box.

5. Change the name of the file if you wish. Then click the Save button to enter the changes and close the dialog box.

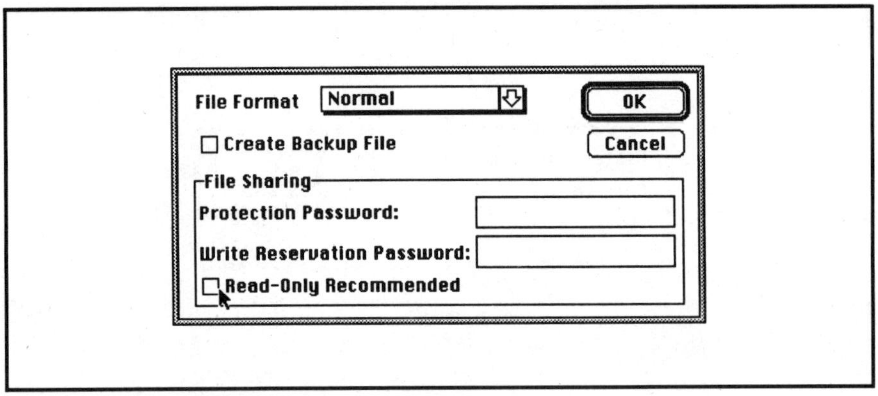

Figure 21.7: The File Options dialog box

Here is an explanation of the options in the File Options dialog box:

- **File Format**. Here you can press the downward-pointing arrow to see a list of file formats you can use to save the file in some format other than the standard Excel format. After you highlight a format name to select it, it will appear in the text box instead of the default word, Normal.

- **Create Backup File**. If you select this box, Excel will automatically create a backup copy of the previously saved version of the document before saving the latest version. The backup file will carry the same name as the the regular file, except that the name will be preceded by the words *Backup of.* Obviously, an excellent way to protect data is to make backup files—if you have sufficient disk space available.

- **Protection Password**. If you enter a password in this box, no one will be able to open the file without knowing the password. When you enter the password, an asterisk will appear in the text box to represent each character you type. After you've completed the password, you'll be asked to enter it once more, to make certain that you haven't typed any characters in error.

- **Write Reservation Password**. You enter a password in this box following the same procedure as for the Protection Password option. However, this option does not prevent access to the document, but rather prevents the user from saving changes under the same name as the current document.

- **Read-Only Recommended.** If you select this box, any user subsequently opening the document will see the warning displayed in Figure 21.8, which recommends that the file be opened as a read-only file. Obviously, this form of protection is less stringent than the others previously mentioned. The user is merely cautioned that the file should be opened in read-only mode unless the saving of changes is absolutely necessary.

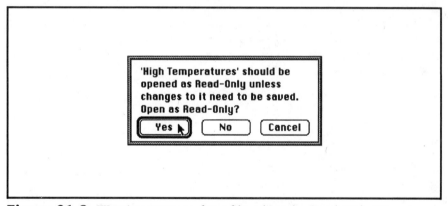

Figure 21.8: Warning message for a file when the Read-Only Recommended option is in effect

---

SUMMARY

You've learned that you can protect files and data in several ways: You can use templates; make backup files; invoke cell protection; hide windows and cells; hide options that alter data or the user environment; and use passwords to prevent access to, or the overwriting of, files.

These techniques are intended to prevent alteration or loss of data when someone else uses your computer. Needless to say, you should be vigilant when *you* use the computer too—carefully checking formulas and procedures to make sure they do not corrupt data, and that they produce the results you want.

Chapter

Using a
Network

You've already learned many Excel skills that are handy in networking. For example, you know how to link and consolidate files, how to hide certain features to avoid confusing users or to maintain confidentiality, and how to control file access by assigning passwords. With these skills, you can easily share Excel data with other applications and with other users of your computer.

This chapter shows you how to take Excel a step further: to share data with the users of other computers.

UNDERSTANDING KINDS OF NETWORKS

Your Macintosh can operate as part of a network in any of several ways. For example, if you use a Macintosh that is not linked to any other computer but is connected to a printer in the LaserWriter family, you're already using the *AppleTalk* networking capability that is built in to every Macintosh and every LaserWriter.

Why would this be called networking? The answer is that networking is really *sharing*. By simply adding more AppleTalk cables, you can connect additional Macintosh computers so all of them can share the same printer. The AppleTalk system even queues files from the different computers automatically so that each document is printed in the order in which the user issued the Print command to enter the document into the system.

You may be using a computer in an organization where a network is already set up so that more elaborate methods of sharing can be accomplished. Instead of being limited to printing on one printer, you may have access through your network to several printers of different types. This means you might be able to choose between options such as a high-resolution printer for work to be reproduced by a professional printshop, a standard laser printer for letters and reports, and a dot-matrix printer for large worksheets printed on tractor-feed paper.

In addition, a professional network usually lets you share files between computers. You may be able to work with applications stored on other computers and to store your own files on some other computer with large storage capacity that is being used as a *file server*. (A file server is a computer functioning as a repository for programs and files used by members of a network.)

You connect to a network from your own computer through the Chooser option on the Apple menu. However, instead of using the Chooser to select the icon for a printer attached to your own Macintosh, you can select a network icon or the icon for one of a variety of printers that may be listed for use through the network.

Figure 22.1 shows the *AppleShare* icon, which you can select to connect to another Macintosh functioning as a file server. The figure also indicates (in the lower right corner) that AppleTalk is active on this computer.

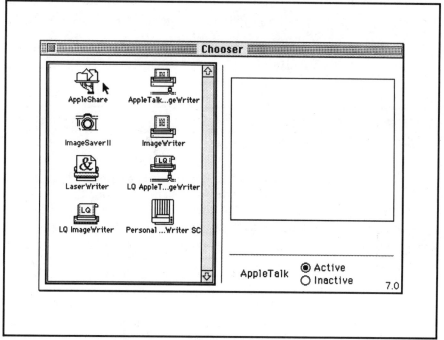

Figure 22.1: The Chooser, showing the AppleShare icon

You can use three different kinds of AppleTalk networks:

- **LocalTalk** is the name applied to an AppleTalk network consisting only of the basic cables, connectors, and software provided with all Macintosh computers.

- **EtherTalk** is a more sophisticated system that lets you connect to *Ethernet* networks. Ethernet is a popular networking standard that permits high-speed data transmission. EtherTalk requires the installation of EtherTalk expansion cards, sold by Apple and other companies.

- **TokenTalk** is an alternative system that lets you connect to *token ring* networks. A token ring network employs devices interconnected in a closed loop. In this type of network, a sequence of bits called a token is used to determine which device can transmit data. TokenTalk requires the installation of TokenTalk expansion cards, sold by Apple and other companies.

To install an expansion card, you must open your computer and install the card in a free slot. Some computers, such as the Macintosh Classic, do not have expansion slots.

Later in this chapter you'll learn the procedures required for connecting to an AppleTalk network.

SYSTEM 7 NETWORKING OPTIONS

With the System 7 version of the Macintosh operating system, Apple introduced many added networking features. If you're operating under an older version of the operating system, you will not be able to use these features, and they will not appear on your menus.

USING PUBLISHERS AND SUBSCRIBERS

You can use System 7's publisher and subscriber feature as a convenient new way to use all or part of an Excel document in other Excel files or in other applications. The feature provides automatic updating.

The publisher and subscriber feature has the following advantages over the linking option you used in Chapter 7:

- You can share material with files and applications running on other computers, not merely on your own computer.

- You don't have to write formulas.

- You can use the publisher and subscriber feature with most applications running under System 7. (Although you don't need System 7 to use linking, few applications support linking at all.)

- All users can see a visual representation of the material involved before deciding to share it or receive it.

- Once you have made material available, any user of your computer or your network can choose to receive the material (with the automatic updating) by making simple menu choices, with no further action required on your part.

Here is an explanation of the basic terms involved in publishing files:

- **Publisher.** A *publisher* is any material you decide to share for automatic updating. As already mentioned, this material can be all, or any part, of a file.

- **Edition.** An *edition* is a special file that holds the selected material.

- **Subscriber.** A *subscriber* is the name given to the material inserted into another document (which may have been created in an application different from the original application). An edition can have many subscribers: either files residing in applications on the same computer or files in applications stored on other computers within the network.

The edition file updates the subscriber files automatically by copying the latest information from the publisher file. You can make changes in the material only by revising the publisher file; you cannot edit the edition file directly.

Designating a Publisher

If your Macintosh is operating under System 7, you'll see Create Publisher... and Subscribe To... commands on the Excel Edit menu (but only with Full Menus selected). This is the procedure for establishing a publisher:

1. Open the file from which you want to publish data. The figures accompanying this chapter use the Performance Report worksheet as an example. (If you want to try these procedures using the same sample file, make a copy of this worksheet first and title the copy **Optimize Budget**. You'll need the Optimize Budget worksheet to complete the exercises in Chapter 23. However, use the Performance Report worksheet here in Chapter 22, not the new copy.)

2. Drag to select the portion of the file you want published.

3. Pull down the Edit menu and select the Create Publisher... command, shown in Figure 22.2. You'll see the Publisher dialog box displayed in Figure 22.3. A Preview area appears at the left side of this dialog box; Preview displays a small reproduction of the range you selected for publishing.

4. Click the New button if you want to create a new folder to store the edition file that will be generated from your selections in the Publisher dialog box. If you choose New, a smaller dialog box will pop up in which you can type a name for the folder. When you're finished typing, click the Create button to create the folder under that name and return to the main Publisher dialog box. (Although a separate folder for edition files makes for tidy housekeeping, System 7 lets you store these files anywhere you like.)

5. If you want to publish the area you've selected so that it will appear in subscriber documents as printed, click the Options button to bring up the Publisher Options dialog box shown in Figure 22.4. In this dialog box, click the button labeled As Shown when Printed. Then click OK to return again to the main Publisher dialog box. If you don't access this Options dialog box, the edition you create will show the selected area as displayed on the screen (the default setting). A typical reason for selecting the As Shown when Printed option is to display a worksheet area without gridlines, a choice you would normally make in the Excel Page Setup dialog box before printing (see Chapter 14).

6. In the main Publisher dialog box, click the Publish button to publish the edition.

7. To save the publisher you've created, you must save the document from which you're publishing. System 7 saves the publishing information with the file. If you try to close the document without saving it, the dialog box shown in Figure 22.5 appears, reminding you to save it.

You can create multiple editions from a single document if you like. For example, you might want to select different areas of a large worksheet for insertion into a variety of other files. To create multiple editions, simply repeat steps 1 to 7.

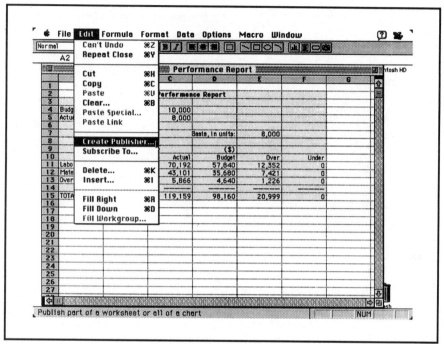

Figure 22.2: Creating a publisher

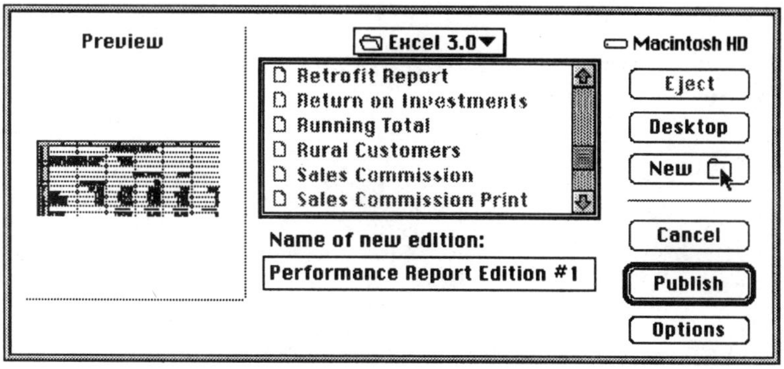

Figure 22.3: The Publisher dialog box

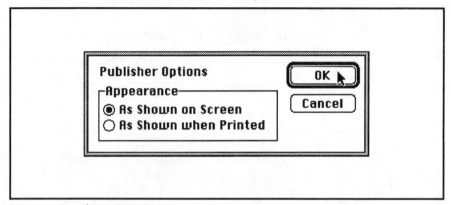

Figure 22.4: The Publisher Options dialog box

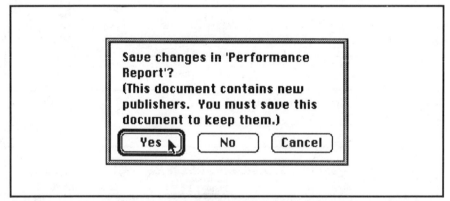

Figure 22.5: Message reminding the user to save a file with a publisher

Subscribing to an Edition

You subscribe to an edition by using the Subscribe To… command on the Edit menu. Here's how to do it:

1. Open the document (and application, if necessary) in which you want to insert the subscriber.

2. Click to select the location in the document where you want the upper left corner of the subscriber to appear.

3. Pull down the Edit menu and select the Subscribe To... command. You'll see the Subscriber dialog box.

4. Change folders and drives as necessary to select the edition to which you want to subscribe. Once you've highlighted an edition file name, the Preview area of the dialog box displays a small reproduction of the contents of the edition, to help you make sure you've selected the right file (see Figure 22.6).

5. Click the Subscribe button to complete the subscription process and close the dialog box.

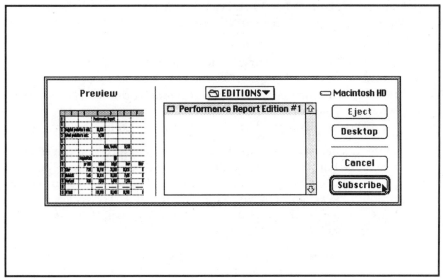

Figure 22.6: The Subscriber dialog box

CONNECTING TO
AN APPLETALK NETWORK

You use network-related control panels, reached through the Apple menu, to connect your computer to an AppleTalk network. Within these control panels, you can determine which users of your computer can access particular folders or applications, either individually or as members of groups you can establish. You can assign passwords and, if you like, keep them from being changed by the users.

Follow these steps to connect your computer:

1. Pull down the Apple menu and select Control Panels. The Control Panels window will appear. It will resemble Figure 22.7, although the icons on your Macintosh may be arranged in a different order, and you may see additional icons representing third-party products that have been installed in your system.

2. Scroll if necessary to locate the Sharing Setup icon and double-click to open it. This action brings up the Sharing Setup control panel shown in Figure 22.8. As you can see, this control panel is divided into three sections, headed Network Identity, File Sharing, and Program Linking.

3. In the top section, you first identify the owner of your computer—meaning the person responsible for setting up its users and its relationship with the network. If you're handling the setup, this name would be your own. Type the appropriate name in the Owner Name text box and press Tab to move to the text box below.

4. In the Owner Password text box, enter a password you can remember easily, but that others would have difficulty guessing. The password cannot contain more than eight characters. When you're finished, press Tab to move to the next text box. For security reasons, the characters constituting the password will hereafter be displayed as a series of bullets (small black circles).

5. In the Macintosh Name text box, type a name for the computer itself. This name can be anything you wish: for example, the Macintosh model or, in a large organization, a location reference such as Personnel Department #2.

6. To allow other users to access folders you designate as shared, click the Start button in the File Sharing section of the control panel. Immediately, you will see a message stating that file sharing is starting up. The Start button will become a Cancel button, with which you can abort the startup procedure. As soon as the procedure is completed, the Cancel button will become a Stop button (see Figure 22.9). File sharing is then active, and you can reenter the control panel and click this Stop button at any time to terminate file sharing. You will be asked, *How many minutes until file sharing is*

disabled? The default time is 10 minutes, to allow current users time to finish their work. However, you can type some other number. Click OK to start the countdown until the time when file sharing will cease.

7. In the Program Linking section of the control panel, click the Start button to let other users link to programs you wish to share. When you click this button, it changes almost instantly to a Stop button, and program linking is activated. For the linking feature to function, the programs involved must support the special linking capabilities of System 7. Consult the manuals for any programs you wish to link to make certain they include this kind of linking and to determine exactly how they implement the procedure.

8. When you have finished modifying to the Sharing Setup control panel, click the close box to close it.

Once you have used the Sharing Setup control panel to specify that you "own" your computer, you can control access to it by assigning passwords and privileges to individual users on the network. You can also specify which folders are available for sharing with these users.

The next section explains how to set up user access.

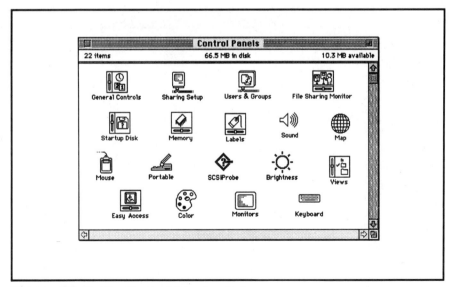

Figure 22.7: The Control Panels window

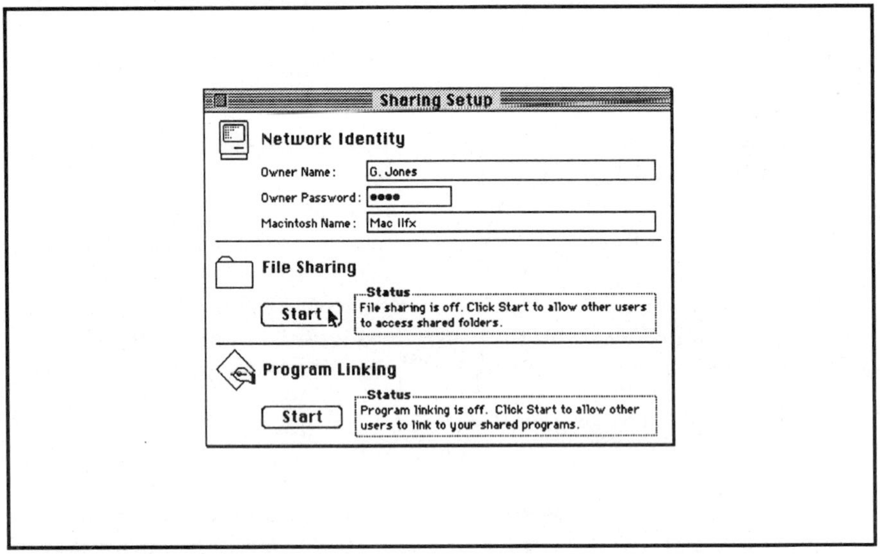

Figure 22.8: The Sharing Setup control panel

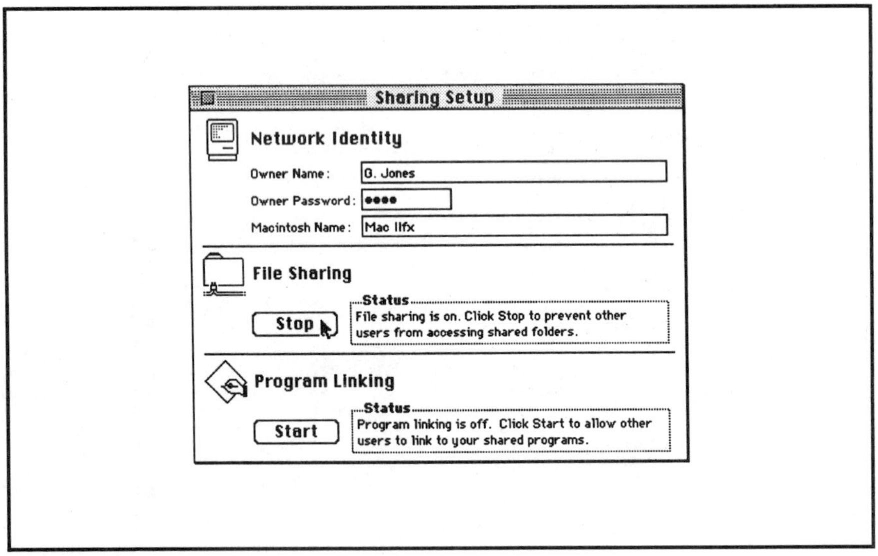

Figure 22.9: Ending file sharing

ESTABLISHING USER ACCESS

You control user access to your computer through the Users & Groups control panel. Follow this procedure to identify users and establish their access privileges:

1. Pull down the Apple menu, select Control Panels, and then, from the Control Panels window, double-click the Users & Groups icon. This action displays the Users & Groups Setup control panel. Initially, this control panel contains two icons, each resembling a human face in profile. One of these icons is labeled Guest, and the other bears your own name (picked up from your entries in the Sharing Setup control panel). The Guest icon represents any guest user of your computer who has not been identified by name and granted specific privileges. You can allow unnamed guests on the network complete access to your computer and files (the default setting), as well as permit linking privileges to your programs (by clicking a box in the Guest dialog box). By default, as the owner, you have complete access to all of the features of your computer. You can add icons with the names of individual users, as well as icons for groups of users, and you can assign privileges to each. Group icons display two human faces in profile. Figure 22.10 shows a typical Users & Groups control panel containing both user and group icons.

2. To add a new user, with the Users & Groups control panel open, pull down the File menu and select the New User command. (Shortcut: Press ⌘-N.) This command (and the New Group command, which works the same way) appears on the File menu only when the New User control panel is open. Figure 22.11 shows these commands.

3. When you select the New User command, a New User icon is added to the control panel. With the added icon still active, type the name or title of the new user and press Return. The icon displays the new name.

4. To add a new group, pull down the File menu and select the New Group command. An icon appears bearing the name New Group.

5. Type a name for the new group and press Return. The icon displays the new name.

6. To make an individual part of a group, drag that user's icon into the appropriate group icon. Figure 22.12 shows a group icon named

Marketing, which has been opened to display icons for the two members of the group. The icons for these members resemble portraits hanging on a wall. Even when individuals become part of a group, the control panel still also displays the original individual user icons for the group members. You can make an individual a member of as many groups as you like.

7. To designate privileges for a user, double-click the user's icon. You'll bring up a dialog box like the one in Figure 22.13. Here you can enter an individual password for the user and choose whether or not to let the user change the password. You can also specify whether or not the user can connect to shared folders and link to programs on your Macintosh. Select the alternatives you want by clicking the clearly labeled boxes to select or deselect them. This dialog box also displays a list of the groups to which the user belongs, although you can change these group memberships only by dragging icons within the User Setup control panel, as previously explained.

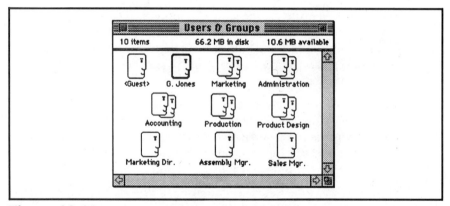

Figure 22.10: A Users & Groups control panel

SHARING FILES AND FOLDERS

Although System 7 menus refer to *file* sharing, the operating system actually provides mainly for *folder* sharing. A network user automatically receives either access to all files within a folder for which access has been granted or access to no files. Of course, if you want to restrict access to a

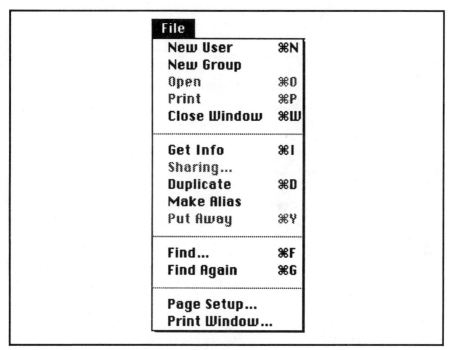

Figure 22.11: The File menu for the Users & Groups control panel

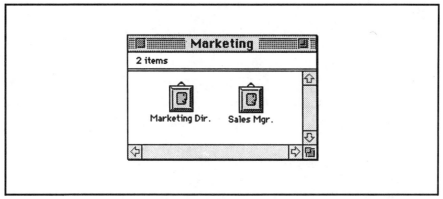

Figure 22.12: Members of a user group

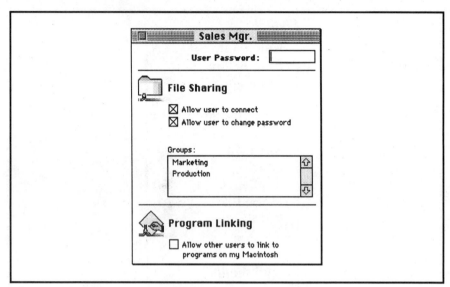

Figure 22.13: A user dialog box

particular Excel file, you can protect it with a password, as explained in Chapter 4; this feature of Excel itself does not require System 7 to function.

Other users of your AppleTalk network cannot open any folder on your computer unless you designate the folder as shared. Here's how to select a folder for sharing:

1. Suspend any application currently active by hiding it through the Applications menu (the icon at the far right of your menu bar). The System 7 Finder menu should then appear.

2. Open folders, scrolling as necessary, until you see the icon for the folder you want to share.

3. Highlight the icon for the folder to select it. (However, do *not* double-click to open the folder.)

4. Pull down the Finder File menu and select the Sharing... command (shown in Figure 22.14). This action displays a Sharing dialog box (see Figure 22.15).

5. Near the top of the dialog box, you will see a box labeled Share This Item and Its Contents. Click the box to place an X in it and activate sharing.

6. Below this box, you will see an area labeled Owner. Place the mouse pointer on the down-pointing arrow at the right of the owner area and depress the button to pop up a list of network users and groups. Select the user you want to designate as owner of this folder. (If you don't want to place any restrictions on the folder, you can select the Any User option, meaning that you're granting owner status to any user of the folder.)

7. By default, the three boxes to the right of the down-pointing arrow are selected, granting privileges to the owner. Deselect the appropriate box if you want to prevent the owner of the folder from seeing folders or files within this folder or from making changes.

8. Below the Owner area is the User/Group area. Here you can pop up the same list of users and groups from which to select a user or group for special access to the folder. Using the boxes to the right of the down-pointing arrow, you can select the privileges to be granted to this user or group.

9. Below the User/Group area is another area, labeled Everyone. Here you establish privileges for all other network users. Figure 22.15 shows an example of assignment of user privileges. In the figure, the marketing director can view any folders and files in the Monthly Expenses folder, but cannot change their contents. The owner of the Monthly Expenses folder is the accounting department, which has denied all access to other users of the network.

TIP

You can let everyone use a folder as a confidential in-box by checking the Make Changes box so users can deposit files or folders in the designated folder without being allowed to see the files or folders enclosed.

---

10. Below the Everyone area is a box you can select to apply the same privileges to all folders within the current folder. You can select a second box to keep users from moving, renaming, or deleting the folder. If you select the first box, you will see the alert box shown in Figure 22.16, asking if you're certain you want to grant the same privileges to all subsidiary folders. Click OK if that is your intention or Cancel to return to the dialog box.

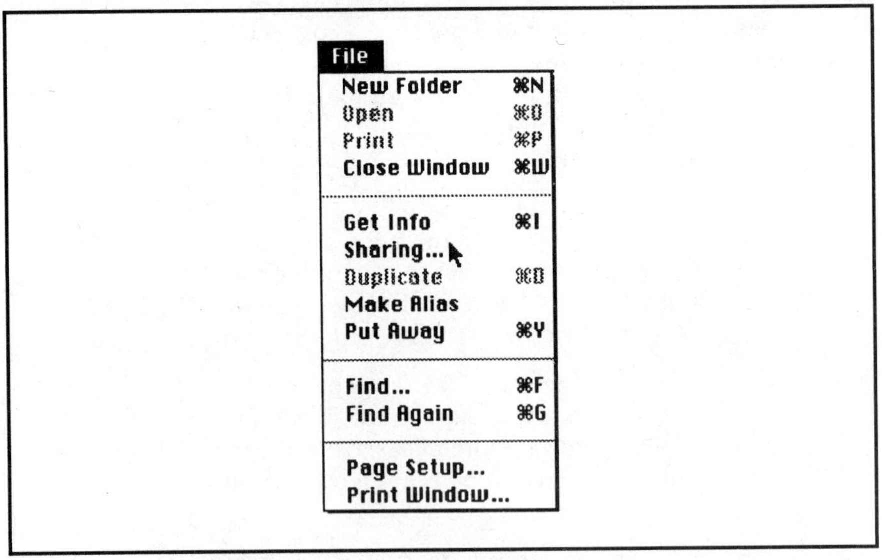

Figure 22.14: The Finder File menu showing the Sharing... command

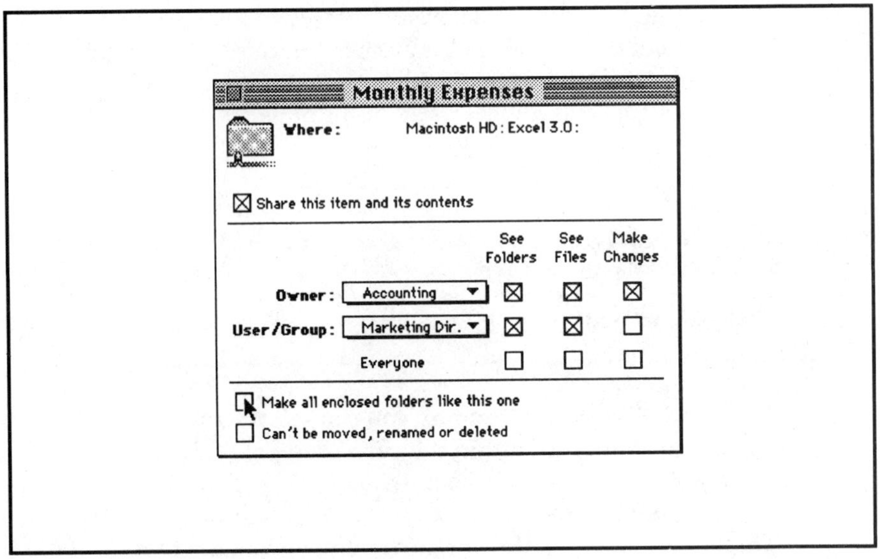

Figure 22.15: The Sharing dialog box

11. When you've completed your selections for the current folder in the Sharing dialog box, click the close box to enter the changes and close the dialog box.

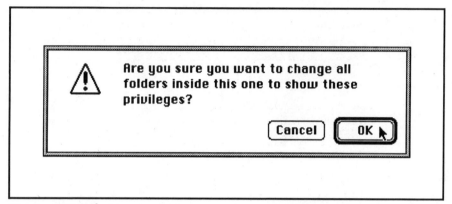

Figure 22.16: Alert box relating to sharing folders

Once a folder has been selected for sharing, the appearance of its icon changes to permit easy recognition of shared folders. Figure 22.17 shows both a standard, nonshared folder (on the left) and a shared folder (on the right). The shared folder icon includes a representation of network cables.

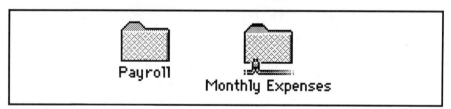

Figure 22.17: Standard, nonshared folder icon (left) and shared folder icon

You can select the control panel named File Sharing Monitor (see Figure 22.18) to find out which folders are currently being accessed by various network users. A scale at the bottom of the panel indicates whether file-sharing activity is relatively light or heavy.

CHAPTER TWENTY-TWO

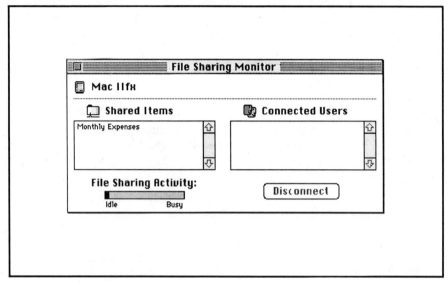

Figure 22.18: The File Sharing Monitor

SUMMARY

This chapter discussed how to use Excel on a network. including how to set up publishers and subscribers, connect to an AppleTalk network, and share files.

Most of the features mentioned in this chapter require a network operating under System 7. However, this specification will probably not be a problem for you. The networking capabilities of System 7 are so superior to those available under previous versions of the operating system that most network supervisors have installed System 7.

Chapter

23

Using the
Solver

$\mathbf{Y}$ou can solve optimization problems in Excel through a utility called the Solver, accessed from the Formula menu. The Solver adjusts values in specified worksheet cells to answer questions such as "Which combination of investments will bring the greatest return?" and "What is the ideal feed mix for providing cattle with all of their nutritional requirements at a minimum cost?"

The mathematical techniques used in optimization are often referred to as *linear programming*. Linear programming is an iterative procedure: The procedure recalculates the problem over and over, each time (hopefully) getting closer to the optimum combination of numbers. Linear programming works with *linear formulas*: formulas that express straight-line relationships. Most formulas in worksheets fall into this category. The Solver can also solve problems involving *nonlinear formulas*. A nonlinear formula contains two or more adjustable cells being multiplied or divided by each other.

You need three elements to make linear programming (or the Solver) work: (1) a value to be optimized, (2) other values that can be adjusted to achieve the goal, and (3) constraints. Constraints are what make the problem exist. For example, you'd never have to worry about the most efficient shipping route from one city to another if there were no constraints such as time and money. In the Solver, you must identify the applicable worksheet cells for each of the three elements.

You must link the elements through formulas. Wherever connecting formulas are missing, no relationship can exist between the cells.

PREPARING A
WORKSHEET FOR THE SOLVER

By making a few quick adjustments, you can use the Performance Report worksheet to sample the capabilities of the Solver. If you followed the suggestion in Chapter 22, you've already made a copy of the Performance Report worksheet by saving it as the Optimize Budget worksheet. If you haven't already created an Optimize Budget worksheet, do so now.

The next step is to modify the worksheet so you can use it for an optimization problem. Your goal will be to make the worksheet look like Figure 23.1.

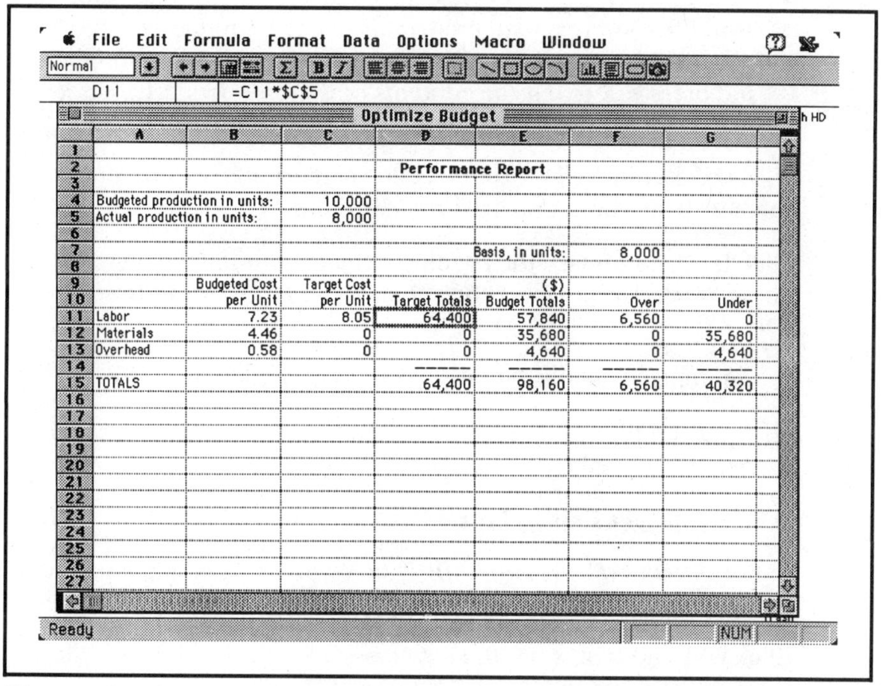

Figure 23.1: The completed Optimize Budget worksheet

You'll solve a problem based on the assumption that the company featured in the spreadsheet has agreed to a new labor contract incorporating raises for production-line employees. Because of higher salaries, the labor cost per unit has increased from $7.23 to $8.05. You're using the Solver to determine by how much the budgets for materials and overhead must be reduced to continue manufacturing the products within the previously established total budget of $98,160 for 8,000 units.

1. First you need a new column within the data area of the worksheet. Select any cell in column C, pull down the Edit menu, and choose the Insert... command. (Shortcut: Press ⌘-I.) The Insert dialog box appears.

2. In the dialog box, click the Entire Column button to add a column to the left of column C. Then click OK.

3. Now the numbers that were in cells C4 and C5 are too far from the labels to their left that explain them, since these numbers (10,000 and 8,000) now appear in cells D4 and D5. Drag to select D4 and D5 and press ⌘-X to cut the contents of the cells from the worksheet and store those values on the clipboard.

4. Click the current cell C4 to select it. Then press ⌘-V to paste the numbers from the clipboard into cells C4 and C5.

5. Click D10 and replace the heading Actual by typing the words **Target Totals**. Press Tab to enter the text and move right to cell E10.

6. In E10, replace the heading Budget by typing **Budget Totals**.

7. Click C9 and type **Target Cost**. Press Return to enter the text and move down to cell C10.

8. In C10, type **per Unit** and press Return.

9. Drag to select both C9 and C10. Then click the right-alignment icon on the Toolbar to align the text at the right side of the cells.

10. Click C11 and type **8.05** (the new labor cost per unit). Press Tab to enter the number and move right to cell D11.

11. In D11, enter the formula **=C11*C5**. This formula will multiply the 8.05 figure in C11 by the actual production in units: 8,000, as shown in cell C5. You added dollar signs to make the reference to C5 an absolute reference. Now, when you copy the formula, the copied formulas will also refer to C5, not to some cell lower in the worksheet.

12. Drag to select the range D11:D13. Then press ⌘-D to copy the formula in D11 into D12 and D13 as well. You've completed the necessary modifications to the worksheet so you can use it with the Solver. Your screen should resemble Figure 23.1.

You could also change the Performance Report title stored in E2 to something more appropriate for the task at hand. However, this change is not necessary for learning how to use the Solver.

SETTING UP AND
SOLVING THE PROBLEM

Now activate the Solver and tell it which cell to optimize, which cells can be changed, and what constraints to apply.

1. Pull down the Formula menu and select the Solver... command, shown in Figure 23.2. The Solver Parameters dialog box appears (see Figure 23.3).

2. Drag the dialog box by its title bar to the bottom of the screen so you can see the contents of the worksheet as well. You'll start filling out the dialog box with your screen in this configuration.

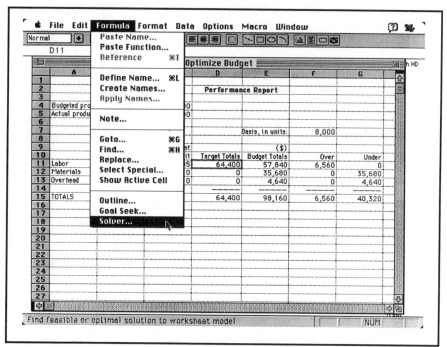

Figure 23.2: Issuing the Solver... command

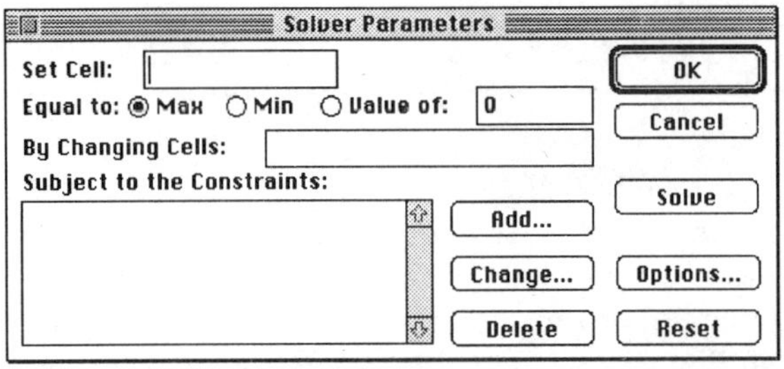

Figure 23.3: The Solver Parameters dialog box

TOURING THE
SOLVER PARAMETERS DIALOG BOX

The layout of the Solver Parameters dialog box makes providing the information needed by the Solver easy. At the top of the dialog box, you can see the Set Cell box. Here, by clicking a cell on the worksheet (or entering a cell address manually), you specify the cell to be optimized. Note that this dialog box provides option buttons you can click to instruct the Solver to make the cell contents equal to the maximum or minimum values that can be achieved. You can click the third button, labeled Value Of, and type a number in the data entry box to the right of the button label, to tell the Solver to match the typed value exactly.

The next line contains the By Changing Cells box. After clicking the data entry box to activate it, you drag a range on the worksheet or type individual cell address to inform the Solver which cells it can adjust to find the solution. Remember that no optimization problem can be solved without the adjustment of cell values.

The bottom area is where you define constraints. You add a constraint by clicking the Add... button and making entries in a subsidiary dialog box; the added constraint then appears in the Subject to the Constraints list box. You click the Change... button to modify an existing constraint highlighted in the list box. You click the Delete button to remove a highlighted constraint.

The right side of the dialog box displays the usual OK and Cancel buttons. Below these, you click the Solve button to start the Solver working on a problem. Click the Options... button to adjust the program's default methods of solving problems. (You'll use this button shortly.) Click the Reset button to return the dialog box contents to specifications previously saved with the worksheet. (When you save the worksheet, Excel saves the current settings in the Solver Parameters dialog box for future use.)

ESTABLISHING THE CELL TO OPTIMIZE

Begin filling out the Solver Parameters dialog box using the following steps:

1. Click cell F15 on the worksheet to specify that cell as the one to be optimized. This is the cell where the total appears for items that are over budget.

2. Click the Value Of button (to indicate that the goal is an exact match for a figure you'll enter, not an unspecified maximum or minimum value).

3. In the data entry box to the right of the Value Of button, type **6560**. This is the total labor cost for producing 8,000 units under the new contract at $8.05 per unit. (An existing formula on the worksheet has already done the necessary multiplication and entered the number 6560 in cell F11.) If cell F15 must contain the exact value 6560, then the increased labor cost will be the only over-budget item permitted. Therefore, for the problem to be solved successfully, the other items must be *under* budget by some amount to be determined by the Solver. This is the result you want. Press Tab to complete the entry and activate the data entry box below.

4. With the By Changing Cells box selected, drag to select the range C12:C13 on the worksheet. These cells will contain the per-unit prices the Solver will compute for materials and overhead costs. The Solver will continue recalculating the worksheet, trying different combinations of values in these cells until it either finds the optimum combination or decides it cannot solve the problem. Your screen should now resemble Figure 23.4.

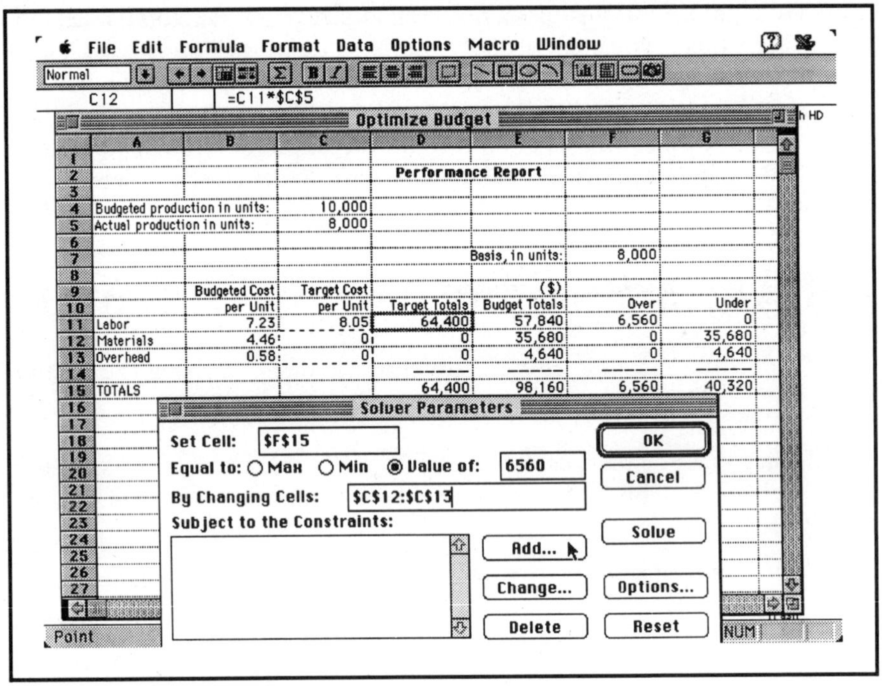

Figure 23.4: Specifying cells that can be changed

ADDING THE CONSTRAINTS

You add constraints through entries you make in the Add Constraint dialog box, which—like the Solver Parameters dialog box—you may want to drag by its title bar to a new position if it covers a worksheet area you want to see.

1. Click the Add... button to add the first constraint to the problem. The Add Constraint dialog box appears.

2. Click C12, the cell that will contain the target cost for materials. The cell address appears in the Cell Reference data entry box, configured with dollar signs as an absolute reference.

3. The next item to the right of the Cell Reference box defines the relationship of the designated cell to the restraint you will specify. By default, this box displays the characters < = , meaning that the

cell reference must be less than or equal to the specified constraint. The other two relationship options are an equal sign alone (=) and the characters $>=$, the greater-than symbol. You select a different option by positioning the pointer on the down arrow and pressing your mouse button to drop down the menu of these relationships. Simply highlight the alternative you want displayed instead of the default selection. In this case, make no change in the relationship item. Press Tab to activate the Constraint data entry box.

4. Type **4.46**. After this entry is completed, the contents of the dialog box will indicate that any value in cell C12 must be less than or equal to $4.46. In other words, you won't accept a higher value than the original budgeted cost of $4.46 per unit for materials—a logical decision if you must reduce costs to balance the budget! Your screen should now resemble Figure 23.5.

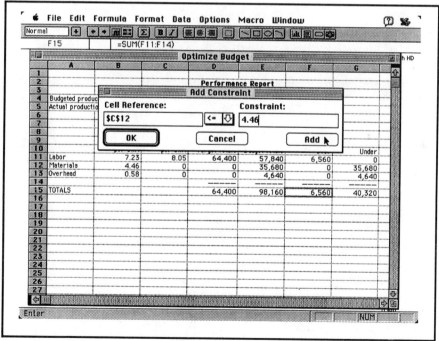

Figure 23.5: Adding a constraint

5. Now you can click any one of three buttons to complete the entry. Of course, if you click the Cancel button, you'll wipe out everything you've entered and return to the previous dialog box. If you click the OK button, you'll enter the specifications for the constraint and return to the previous dialog box. In this instance, select the third button, labeled Add. When you click Add, you'll enter the specifications for the constraint and return to the same Add Constraint dialog box, so you can add more constraints.

6. Look at Figure 23.6, which shows the completed Solver Parameters dialog box with all of the necessary constraints in place. Following the procedures you just used, enter the additional constraints. Click OK instead of Add to close the Add Constraint dialog box after you complete the final constraint.

Note that one effect of these constraints is to restrict the Solver from entering and using values *higher* than the original per-item budgeted figures for

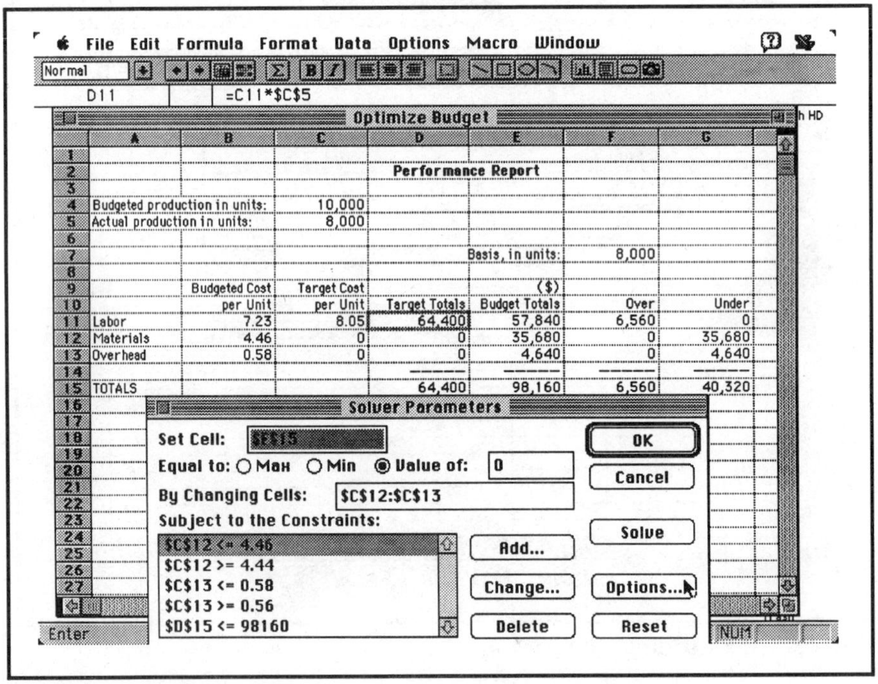

Figure 23.6: The completed Solver Parameters dialog box

materials and overhead. On the other hand, you have prevented the Solver from using values more than two cents *lower* than the original amounts, due to the constraints you entered with the greater-than-or-equal-to relationships. You entered these restrictions to find out if *minimal* budget cuts for materials and overhead will work in restoring the original budget bottom line, despite the increase in labor costs. The fifth constraint prevents the Solver from entering an amount greater than $98,160 in cell D15; in other words, the total new budget cannot exceed the original budget total displayed in cell E15.

CHANGING OPTIONS

Before clicking the Solve button to have the Solver work on any problem, you may want to change some of the program's options. Try this now.

1. From the Solver Parameters dialog box, click the Options... button. The Solver Options dialog box appears. Here you can set the maximum length of time that the Solver will try for a solution (default: 100 seconds), the maximum number of iterations (default: 100), and the precision you want for the answer (default: an accuracy of .000001).

2. Click the Precision box and type a new value: **.01**. (Since the numbers in this worksheet are in dollars and cents, a precision of two decimal places is appropriate. There is no reason to increase the time allowed or maximum number of iterations unless you find that the problem can't be solved with the default settings.)

3. Click to select the box labeled Show Iteration Results. When this box is selected, the Solver shows you the figures it enters as it completes each iteration. If a worksheet is very large, this display may slow down the iteration process too much to be practical. In a smaller worksheet, such as this one, you'll find it interesting to watch the Solver at work, since the program will require only a few seconds to complete all of the iterations. The dialog box should now resemble Figure 23.7.

If you're using a large worksheet and you're sure that the formulas are all linear, you can speed up the solving of the problem by clicking the box labeled Assume Linear Model. Then the Solver will not waste time constantly checking formulas for linearity.

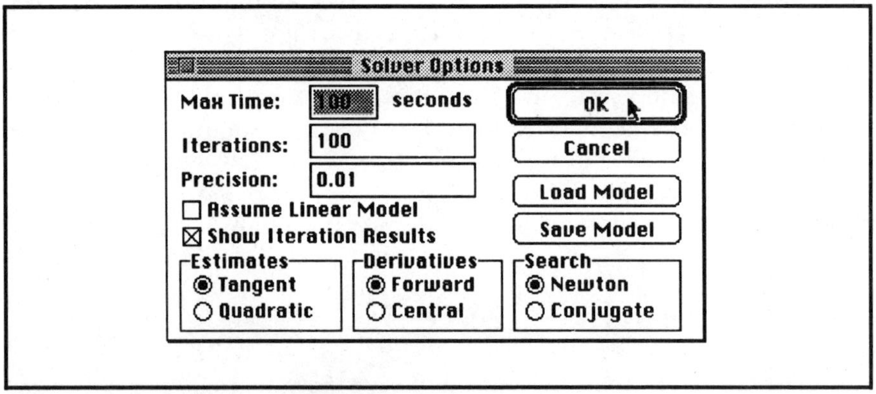

Figure 23.7: The Solver Options dialog box

USING ADVANCED OPTIONS

The lower portion of the Solver Options dialog box contains two rows of three option buttons each that you can click to control advanced options. By default, the buttons in the first row are selected; these are the correct settings for most problems. Unless you are experienced at mathematical programming, you should probably use these default settings.

In the Estimates area, you can choose the approach to be used in obtaining initial estimates of the basic variables. The default selection, Tangent, uses linear extrapolation from a tangent vector. The alternative selection, Quadratic, uses quadratic extrapolation, which may produce better results for some nonlinear problems.

In the Derivatives area, you can select forward (the default choice) or central differencing for estimates of partial derivatives. Choosing central differencing causes more worksheet recalculation but could produce better results for difficult problems.

In the Search area, you can select between a quasi-Newton method for computing the search direction (the default choice) and a conjugate gradient method of accomplishing the same goal. The latter method is slower but could help if progress is slow between successive trial points in the iterations.

SOLVING THE PROBLEM

It's time to find out if the Solver can solve the problem with the parameters you've provided.

Incidentally, although the Solver works by recalculating a problem again and again, substituting different values, programs of this sort do not always substitute the same values twice in succession. In other words, particularly in the case of a complicated worksheet, you could have the Solver try the same problem from scratch several times and each time end up with a slightly different answer, although each answer might satisfy the criteria you established. Therefore, it's possible that your worksheet might show final values that differ from those shown in samples.

1. Click OK to close the Solver Options dialog box and return to the Solver Parameters dialog box.

2. Click the Solve button to start the iterative process. After a few seconds, you should see the alert message displayed in Figure 23.8, stating that the Solver couldn't find an answer. In this box, you can click OK to save the current unsuccessful solution or click Cancel to return the worksheet to its original values. You'll click Cancel to start over, but first examine the values the Solver produced.

Apparently you made the constraints too restrictive. Note that the Solver inserted the lowest values you permitted into both C12 and C13. These values reduced the materials and overhead items in the budget by a total of only $320, as shown in cell G15. The total cost is now projected in D15 as $104,400 rather than the goal of $98,160.

The next step, therefore, is to change the constraints. The company will have to attempt to reduce materials and overhead expenses even more.

1. If you haven't already done so, click Cancel to close the alert box without saving the worksheet changes the Solver made in its unsuccessful attempt to solve the problem. This action also closes the Solver itself.

2. Pull down the Formula menu and select the Solver... command again, to reactivate the program. The Solver Parameters dialog box reappears.

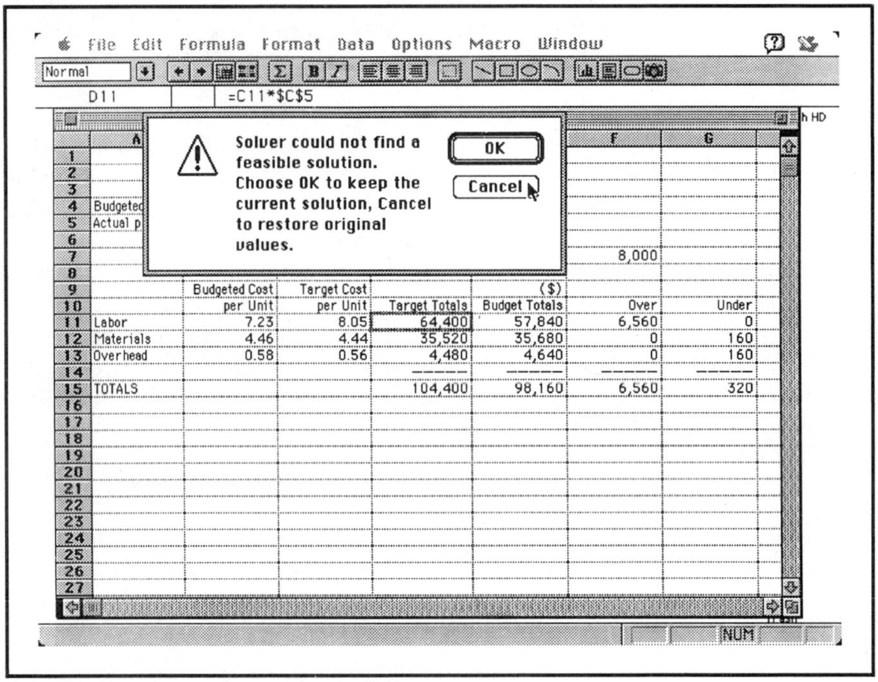

Figure 23.8: The Solver warns that it can't find a solution

3. In the Subject to the Constraints list box, highlight the second constraint, C12 > = 4.44, and click the Change... button. The Change Constraint dialog box appears. It looks exactly like the Add Constraint dialog box, except that it does not have an Add button.

4. Click the Constraint data entry box at the end of the number 4.44 to select that position as a data-entry point. Backspace to erase the number and type **3.5**. This action relaxes the constraint so that the Solver can place any value in cell C12 that is greater than $3.50 but less than the maximum of $4.46, which you established through another constraint.

5. Click OK to close the Change Constraint box and return to the Solver Parameters dialog box.

6. Highlight the fourth constraint in the Subject to the Constraints list box: C13 > = 0.56. Click the Change... button.

7. In the Change Constraint dialog box, click the end of the number 0.56 in the Constraint data entry box and backspace to erase only the 6. Now the Solver can use any value in cell C13 that is between 50 cents and the maximum of 58 cents.

8. Click OK to close the Change Constraint box and return to the Solver Parameters dialog box. Your screen should now resemble Figure 23.9.

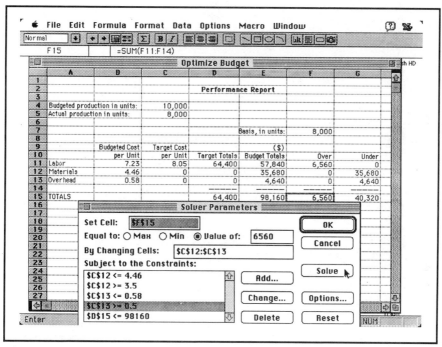

Figure 23.9: The changed Solver parameters

9. Click the Solve button to start the iterative process again. You will soon see a small dialog box displaying this message: *Solver found a solution. All constraints and optimality conditions are satisfied.* You can see the result in Figure 23.10.

As this figure shows, the Solver ended up using the minimum costs per unit you just entered for materials and overhead (see cells C12 and C13). If these cost-saving figures could be realized, under-budget items would total

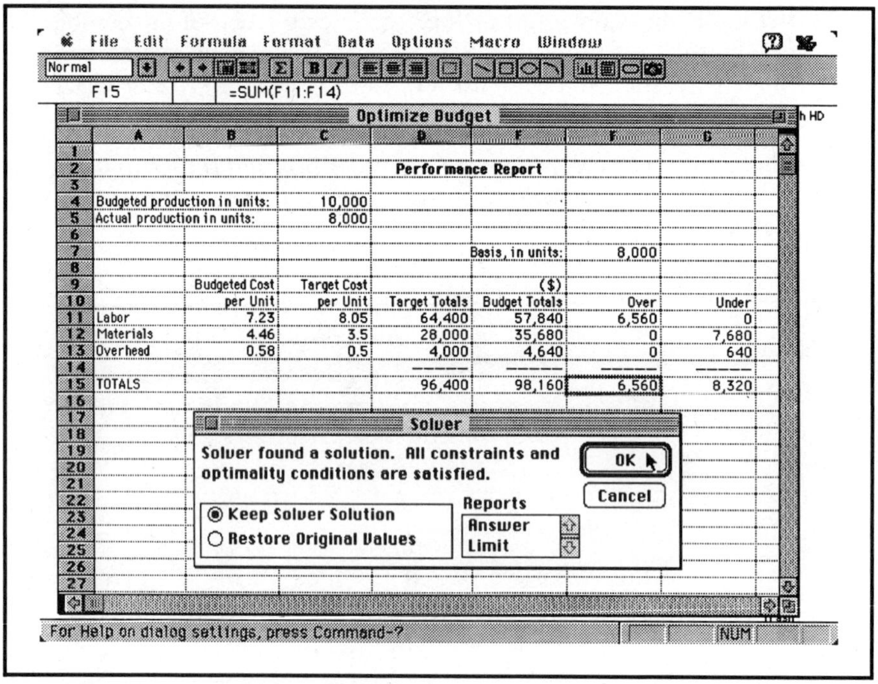

Figure 23.10: The Solver indicates it has found a solution

$8,320 (cell G15), more than offsetting the $6,560 over-budget item created by the increased labor costs (cell F15). In fact, rather than meeting the goal of a $98,160 total budget (cell E15), the new budget would be lower: $96,400 (cell D15). The saving would be $1,760, although this amount isn't specifically shown on the worksheet.

Note that this small Solver dialog box has a section headed Reports. The box also provides buttons you can click either to keep the Solver solution or discard it and restore the previously saved worksheet values.

To obtain a report, highlight either Answer or Limit. Then click OK to close the box. (If you click Cancel, no reports will be prepared, and the solution won't be saved.) If you highlight either Report option, the Solver will produce a report of its calculations. You can select both kinds of reports by holding down the Shift key and then clicking to highlight the words *Answer* and *Limit*. A selected report appears on your screen as another Excel worksheet with its own window. You can print the report by switching to that window and issuing the normal Print command.

The Answer report provides information about how well the constraints were met. The report calculates the *slack* in each constraint (slack is the difference between the value in the cell and the constraint). The Limit report shows the values obtained when each adjustable cell was at its upper and lower limits.

This completes the Solver example. If you save the Optimize Budget worksheet before closing it, the parameters you used will be saved with the worksheet and will be displayed again if you reopen the Solver while this worksheet is active.

SUMMARY

The example you completed in this chapter illustrates how the Solver works when you assign a specific value to the Set Cell box. Remember that you can also solve problems that search for maximum or minimum values, such as finding the largest audience that can be reached by buying commercials at a certain price from local TV stations or determining the smallest amount of overtime that will be required if employee work schedules are adjusted for peak efficiency.

However, the Solver won't function correctly if you use it with a worksheet that contains formula errors or cells specified for use that are not connected to formulas. Be sure to check cell relationships carefully before calling up the Solver.

Chapter 25 will introduce you to another useful decision tool: the goal-seeking feature.

Chapter

24

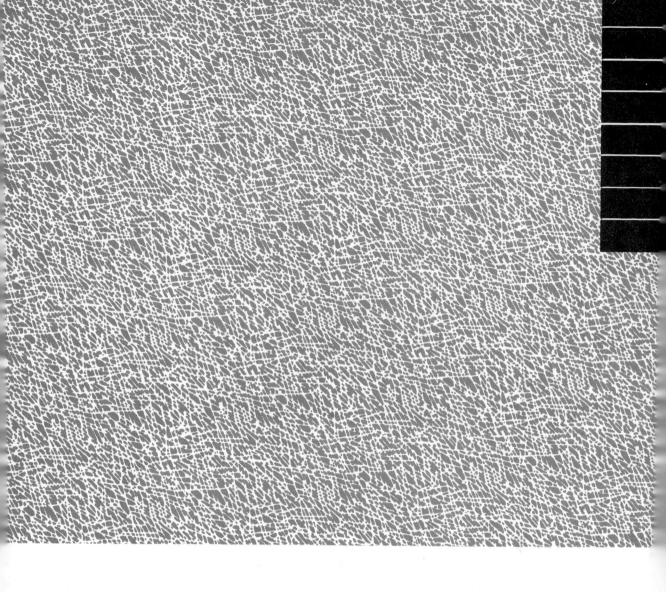

Using Color

You can work with color in Excel even if you have neither a color printer nor a color monitor. You can use menu formatting options to add background color to individual cells or ranges. You can configure numbers or headings for display in color. You can color gridlines and graphic objects and, of course, change the colors of items in a chart. Although without a color monitor you will see only the name of a color on menus, rather than the actual color, and no colors at all on your screen, you can save a worksheet or chart containing color specifications as a file to be printed either by another Macintosh connected to a color printer or by a professional printshop.

In addition, if you do have a color monitor, you can mix colors to create new colors, experimenting to your heart's content and seeing the results on the screen. Although screen colors on a Macintosh monitor are only an approximation of the actual colors that will be printed, with practice you can achieve very satisfactory results.

Of course, if you have a color printer, you can quickly run tests to determine exactly the settings required on screen to obtain the effect you want on paper.

This chapter discusses some of these options.

USING COLOR TO EMPHASIZE CELLS

You can easily use color to emphasize key numbers or areas of a worksheet.

Let's say you'd like to call attention to the highest temperature reading displayed in the High Temperatures worksheet. Try this:

1. Open the High Temperatures worksheet.

2. Select D7, the cell showing the highest temperature recorded for Honolulu: 80 degrees, on Monday.

3. Pull down the Format menu and select the Font... command. The Format Font dialog box appears.

4. Place the pointer on the down arrow in the Color area and depress the mouse button. A pull-down menu of available colors appears.

5. Select the color red (as shown in Figure 24.1) and click OK to close the dialog box.

The number 80 now appears in red.

In Figure 24.1, we used the Monitor control panel to configure the monitor to display only grays, thereby causing Excel to show the names of colors rather than bars containing the colors. We made this change so the figure would be more understandable for readers, since the illustrations in this book are not reproduced in color. We also dragged the window containing the High Temperatures worksheet toward the bottom of the screen so the selected cell would not be hidden by the dialog box.

Another excellent use for color is in worksheets dealing with dollar amounts. You can make negative numbers appear automatically in red.

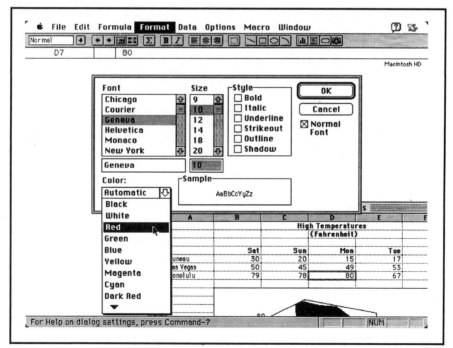

Figure 24.1: Adding color to a worksheet number

Here's how:

1. Open the worksheet containing negative dollar amounts.

2. Drag to highlight the area displaying dollar amounts.

3. Pull down the Format menu and select the Number... command.

4. Select one of the two dollar formats that include the word *Red* (see Figure 24.2).

5. Click OK to close the dialog box. Thereafter, negative dollar amounts in the formatted area will be displayed in red.

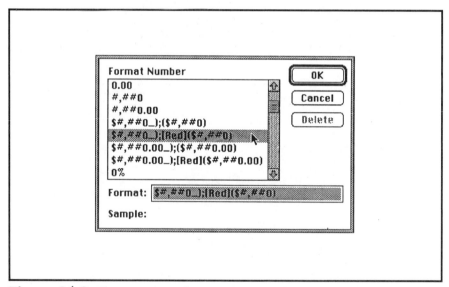

Figure 24.2: Formatting to show negative dollar amounts in red

You can achieve another eye-catching effect by shading the background of a cell or range in color. Follow this procedure:

1. Select the cell or range to which you want to apply a background.

2. Pull down the Format menu and select the Patterns... command. The Cell Shading dialog box appears, with drop down submenus titled Pattern, Foreground, and Background.

3. Select the Pattern submenu and pick a pattern for the colored background.

4. Select the Background submenu and choose the color.

5. Click OK to close the dialog box.

Sometimes you may want a color border around a key area or cell. The technique is similar to adding a background.

1. Select the cell or area for the border.

2. Pull down the Format menu and select the Border... command. The Border dialog box appears.

3. In the Border section, you can choose to outline the entire selected area or cell or to place a border line only at the left, right, top, or bottom of the area or cell. Click the appropriate selection.

4. In the Style section of the dialog box, choose the type of line you want. You can select light or heavy lines or lines made with dashes.

5. In the Color section, pick the color you want from the drop-down submenu.

6. Click OK to close the dialog box.

MIXING YOUR OWN COLORS

You can customize any of the colors on your current color palette, provided you have a color monitor so you can see the results of your changes. Use these steps:

1. Pull down the Options menu and select the color palette command (you must be using Full Menus to see this command). If you have a color monitor, the command will display representations of the colors in the current palette (see Figure 24.3). A color palette contains 16 colors.

2. Click the color on the palette you want to change.

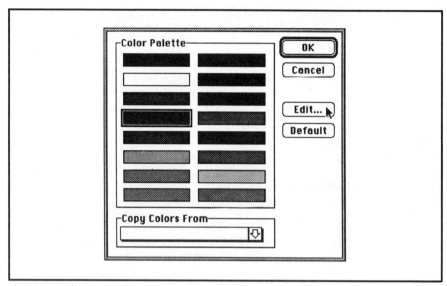

Figure 24.3: The Color Palette dialog box

3. Click the Edit... button to display the color wheel shown in Figure 24.4.

4. Use the up and down arrows to change the numbers in any of the color specification boxes shown at the left. In the upper left corner of the dialog box, the top half of the displayed square shows your color changes as you make them, while the bottom half of this square shows the original color before you started making changes.

5. As an alternative, you can also make changes in the color wheel itself. The small dot on the wheel indicates the point on the wheel represented by the current selection. Place the pointer on the wheel; it will assume the shape of a circle with a heavy outline. Click a new location on the circle to change the color or drag the pointer around the circle to see continuous changes. Drag the vertical bar located at the right of the wheel to control brightness.

6. Click OK to save your changes to the color or click Cancel to revert to previously saved changes for the color and display the color palette dialog box again.

7. In the Color Palette dialog box, click OK to save changes, Cancel to discard the changes, or Default to return to the default specifications.

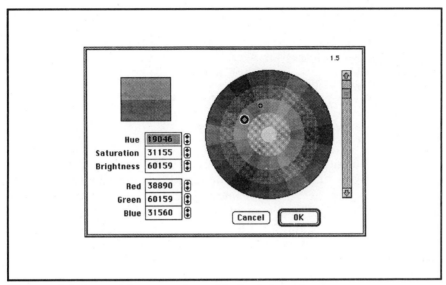

Figure 24.4: Modifying a color with the color wheel

The Red, Green, and Blue boxes control the percentages of these primary colors that Excel adds to the selected color. *Hue* refers to the color itself, the main characteristic of the color that makes it different from other colors. *Saturation* refers to the amount of gray present in a color; adding more gray reduces the saturation of the color. *Brightness* is the intensity of light in the color.

SELECTING AN
ALTERNATE COLOR PALETTE

Microsoft provides several alternate color palette files with Excel. These palettes are stored in the Macro Library folder under names descriptive of their contents: Autumn, BlueRed, Blues, Dusk, Pastel, Rainbow, Reds, Summer, Sunset, Winter, and YellGreen. In addition, this folder contains three other color palette files: Default, User1, and User2. Default contains the default palette that is shipped with Excel. Initially, User1 and User2 contain the same default palette; they are provided to allow customization by multiple users of a single Macintosh.

To switch to a different color palette, use this procedure:

1. Pull down the Excel File menu and select the Open... command. (Shortcut: Press ⌘-O.)

2. In the Macro Library folder, scroll to locate the alternate color palette you want and double-click the name to open it. The file opens but remains hidden from view.

3. Pull down the Window menu and select the Unhide... command.

4. From the list of hidden files shown in the Unhide dialog box, double-click the palette name to "unhide" it. (Probably the list will contain only the name of the color palette you just opened.) The new palette appears in a small window, as shown in Figure 24.5, and replaces the current color palette. However, as also shown in Figure 24.5, when you select a palette other than the Excel default color palette on a monochrome or gray-scale monitor, the program

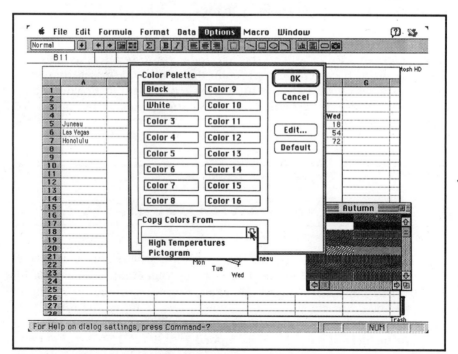

Figure 24.5: Copying the color palette from another file

shows the colors in the Color Palette dialog box as Black and White followed by colors numbered 3 through 16 (since Excel has no way to give a specific name to these nonstandard colors).

5. To switch to the color palette being used in some other open file (which may contain colors you've customized), place the pointer on the arrow in the Copy Colors From box of the Color Palette dialog box and depress the mouse button. You'll see a drop-down list of the open files (illustrated too in Figure 24.5). Highlight a file name to select it.

6. Click OK to close the Color Palette dialog box.

You can make a copy of any color palette file. With the currently saved palette as the active file, select the Save As... command on the Excel file menu and give the palette copy a new name.

SAVING A WORKSHEET OR CHART FOR COLOR PRINTING ELSEWHERE

If you've created a worksheet or chart using colors and don't have a color printer, or if you want to create a file that can be used by a professional publisher, you can save the file as a PostScript file by using an option in the Print dialog box (see Figure 24.6). A commercial printing service can then

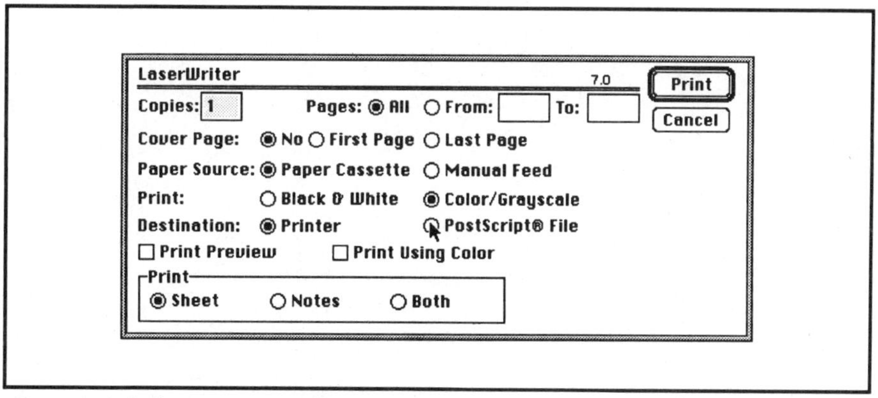

Figure 24.6: Saving your work to a PostScript file

use the data in this PostScript file to create a high-resolution version of your work, or you can have the file printed on another Macintosh that does have access to a color printer.

SUMMARY

The discreet use of color can increase the readability and impact of your printed Excel files. Remember that on-screen colors never duplicate printed colors exactly, and that you need a color monitor if you want to mix your own colors.

Chapter

25

Goal Seeking
and Data Tables

In previous chapters, you found that Excel provides many powerful features to help you analyze data and make decisions, including advanced templates such as Sales Tracking and macros such as Data Crosstabs. Now you'll learn about two additional tools you can add to your repertoire: goal seeking and data tables.

FINDING THE
VALUE THAT ACHIEVES A GOAL

The goal-seeking feature of Excel is simple to use and can be a real time-saver. All it does is adjust the value in a cell you designate so that the result of a formula will be the exact number you want. However, if you have a problem that requires changing multiple variables—perhaps with multiple constraints on the values that can be used—you must instead use the Solver, explained in Chapter 23.

The easiest way to understand the Goal Seek... command is to try it. For this purpose, you'll use the Optimize Budget worksheet from Chapter 23. Your goal will be to find what per-unit materials cost is necessary to allow the company to manufacture 8,000 units within the total budget of $98,160, assuming that labor and overhead costs cannot be changed.

In Chapter 23 you already established a fixed target labor cost of $8.05 (because of a new labor contract). Now you'll fix the target overhead cost at 58 cents per unit (which is the budgeted cost) and then use the Goal Seek... command to determine the value required for materials cost if the budget is to be met.

1. Open the Optimize Budget worksheet.

2. Change the zero in cell C13 to **.58** (the fixed target overhead cost).

3. Select cell D15, which contains the target total cost. (Your goal is to make the value in this cell the same as the value in E15, the budgeted total.)

4. Pull down the Formula menu and select the Goal Seek... command (shown in Figure 25.1).

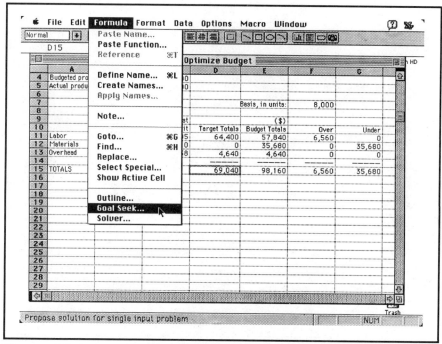

Figure 25.1: Selecting the Goal Seek... command

5. The Goal Seek dialog box appears. Click the To Value data entry box to select it and enter the value **98160**. (If you achieve this value in D15, the target total cost per unit will equal the budgeted total.)

6. Press Tab to move to the By Changing Cell data entry box and click cell C12 to enter it in this box. The cell address reference appears as an absolute reference (with dollar signs preceding both the column and row components of the address). Your screen should now resemble Figure 25.2.

7. Click OK to start the search for a solution. Excel adjusts cell C12 and soon displays the Goal Seek Status dialog box shown in Figure 25.3, announcing that a solution has been discovered. As you can see, the goal-seeking utility has discovered that a per-unit materials cost of $3.64 will produce the target total cost for 8,000 units, assuming that labor and overhead costs cannot be adjusted.

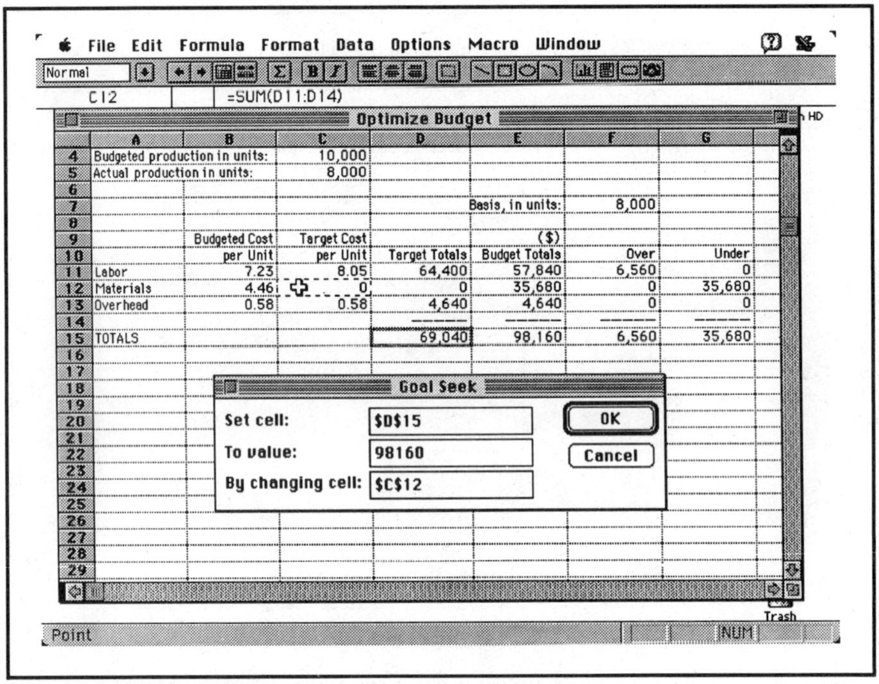

Figure 25.2: The completed Goal Seek dialog box

To see step by step how the Goal Seek... command solves a problem, you can click the Pause button at any time to halt the calculations and then click the Step button to resume goal seeking one step at a time. Excel will add a Continue button to the dialog box, which you can click at any time to resume full-speed calculation.

This concludes the discussion of the Goal Seek... command. Next you'll use the Optimize Budget worksheet again in creating a data table. However, to make the steps in the next section less confusing, select C12 again and restore this cell to its previous state by entering a zero in the cell.

MAKING A DATA TABLE

Using the Table... command (located on the Data menu), you can quickly produce a table showing what the result would be if any one of a series of values were entered into a specified cell on a worksheet.

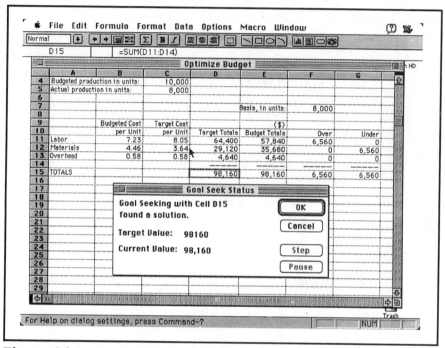

Figure 25.3: The Goal Seek... command finds a solution

However, once you've created such a table, you can no longer edit individual cells within the table. If you want to change the formatting of a number in a completed data table, you have no choice but to erase the entire table, make the change, and then start over. Therefore, for the table you're about to generate, you'll format cells before issuing the command to build the table.

This table will calculate the total manufacturing cost for 8,000 units in the Optimize Budget worksheet if the materials cost per unit is $3.00, $3.50, or $4.00, assuming that labor and overhead costs per unit are fixed at $8.05 and 58 cents, respectively. You will enter the materials cost-per-unit amounts in a row, to generate a series of possible results in the row below, though you could just as easily configure your table in columns rather than rows. Tables of this sort are referred to as *one-input* tables, because they change input values for only one cell in a formula. You can create a table that uses both rows and columns—termed a *two-input* table—using the same techniques.

The input cell that will change to produce the three possible results will be C12, the cell provided in the worksheet to contain the target materials cost per unit.

SETTING UP THE TABLE

First you'll set up identifying headings for the table. Then you'll enter the series of per-unit costs to be inserted one by one into the input cell.

1. With the Optimize Budget worksheet still active, select cell A17 and type **Materials Costs:**

2. Press Return to complete the entry and move to cell A18. Type **Total Costs:**

3. Press Return to complete the entry. Then drag to select both A17 and A18.

4. Click the Bold icon in the Toolbar to make the text in the selected cells appear in boldface.

5. Click cell C17 and type **3.0**. Press Tab to enter the number and activate cell D17.

6. In D17, type **3.5**. Press Tab to enter the number and activate cell E17.

7. In E17, type **4.0**. Press Tab again to complete the entry.

8. Drag to select the range C17:E17. Then click the Bold icon in the Toolbar to make the numbers appear in boldface.

9. With the range still selected, pull down the Format menu and select the Number... command.

10. Select the third choice (0.00) and click OK. The numbers are now formatted as dollar amounts, with two decimal places. You've completed the entry and formatting of the per-unit costs Excel will use in calculating the total manufacturing cost that would result from using each of the per-unit figures.

11. Next you must enter a formula that connects the table to the input cell in the worksheet. When you use a row configuration for the table, this connecting formula must appear in the column to the left of the table and in the row below the series of values to be entered

(the varying per-unit costs). (When you use a column configuration, you must enter the connecting formula in the row above the first input value and one cell to the right of the table.) Select cell B18 and enter this formula: **= D11 + D12 + D13**. Your screen should now resemble Figure 25.4.

12. Click the enter box in the formula bar to complete the formula. Cell B18 now displays the number 69040, the same total (although unformatted) that appears in D15.

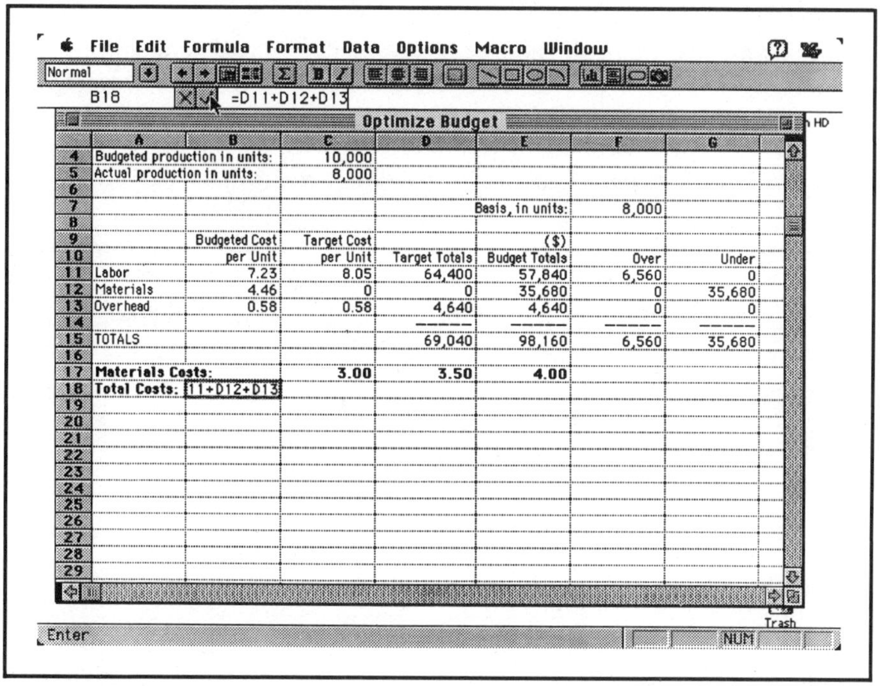

Figure 25.4: Entering a connecting formula for the input cell

The formula you entered for the table does not directly connect the input cell C12 to the table. The table formula adds the results of the worksheet formulas in D11, D12, and D13, thereby calculating the total manufacturing cost for 8,000 units using the per-unit costs in column C. One of these worksheet formulas—the one in D12—does refer to C12, and it is through this formula that the connection to the input cell is made.

As you can see from looking at Figure 25.4, the formula you entered in B18 is immediately to the right of the Total Costs heading, displayed between that heading and the table of values that will appear below the row of per-unit costs you entered. Although the formula must be in this position for the table to be created, it is certainly in the way from a readability standpoint; it will constitute an unwanted barrier between the heading and the table itself. Fortunately, you can hide the formula from view, though it will still be in place to perform its necessary function.

1. With B18 still selected, pull down the Format menu and select the Number... command again.

2. Instead of scrolling to choose one of Excel's standard number formatting options, simply type two double quotation marks: "" (see Figure 25.5). Then click OK to complete the formatting. The contents of B18 disappear (although when you select that cell, you'll still be able to see the formula it contains by glancing at the formula bar). This

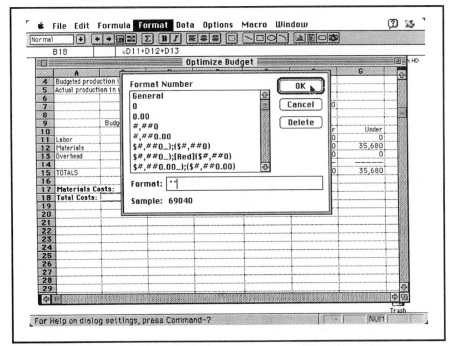

Figure 25.5: Formatting cell B18 to hide its contents

formatting entry actually tells Excel to use the format information provided between the quotation marks. Since there is no information between the quotation marks—not even a space—you're specifying no format at all—in other words, an invisible entry.

GENERATING THE TABLE

You're almost finished. Now you'll issue the command to generate the table.

1. Drag to select the range B17:E18. This range includes the hidden formula, the series of per-unit costs to be used in creating the alternate total-cost values, and the empty cells where the total-cost values will appear (C18 through E18).

2. Pull down the Data menu and select the Table... command. At this point, your screen should resemble Figure 25.6.

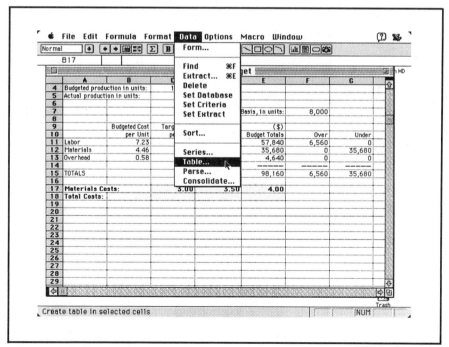

Figure 25.6: Issuing the Table... command

3. The Table dialog box appears. With the Row Input Cell data entry box selected, click cell C12 to enter it in that box. Your screen should now resemble Figure 25.7. (If you were making a two-input table, you would also enter a cell address for column input.)

4. Click OK. The dialog box closes, and Excel generates the table.

5. Finally, click D18 to observe the entry that appears in the formula bar (see Figure 25.8).

The table shows that, with a per-unit cost of $3.00 for materials, the total cost for manufacturing 8,000 units would be $93,040 (assuming that labor and overhead costs are fixed at their present levels). With a per-unit materials cost of $3.50, the total cost would be $97,040. With a per-unit materials cost of $4.00, the total cost would be $101,040.

Now look at the entry displayed in the formula bar when D18 is selected. The displayed formula was produced by Excel and confirms that D18 is now part of a table and cannot be edited separately.

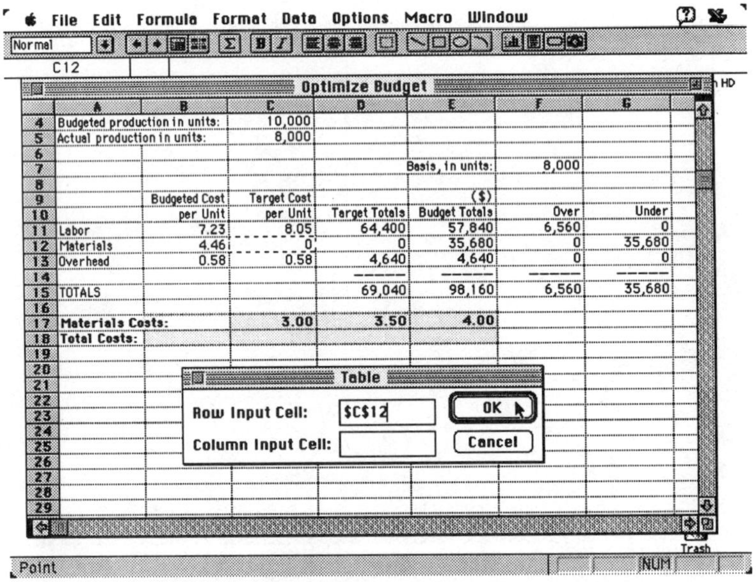

Figure 25.7: Specifying the input cell

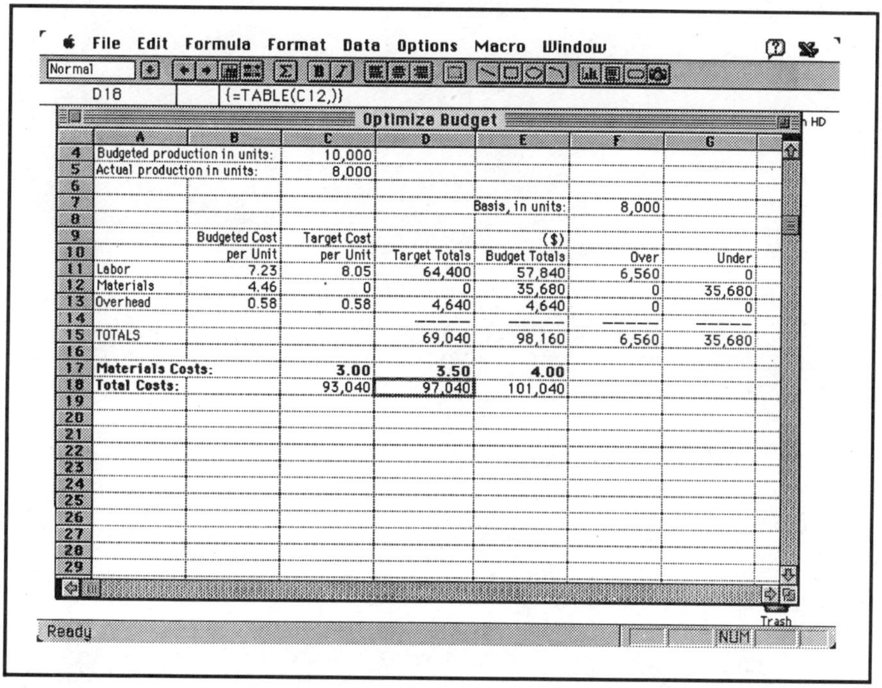

Figure 25.8: The completed table, showing the formula bar display

You can create very large tables of this sort. A common use is to calculate a series of automobile or mortgage payments.

If the series of input values you want will be in some regular progression (the values in this example qualify as regular, since each value is simply 50 cents higher than the preceding one), you can save time in constructing large tables by using the Series... command on the Data menu (explained in Chapter 6).

SUMMARY

Both the Goal Seek... and Table... commands rely on changing input values in cells *referred to by one or more formulas*. Remember: If this connection does not exist, neither command will work.

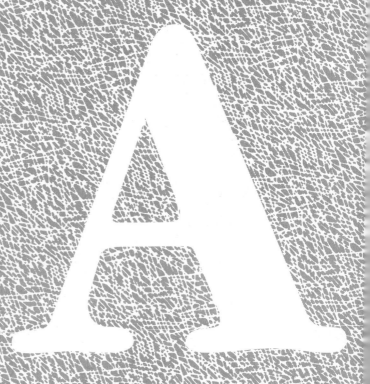

Appendix

Installing Excel

Installing Excel is a simple procedure, involving little more than inserting disks and following the directions on the screen. However, if you want to install all of the features of the program, you'll need a hard disk with at least 4 megabytes of free storage space, not counting the additional room you'll need for the files you'll create. Fortunately, if you're short on disk space, you can skip the installation of some items and reduce the space requirement for the Excel program to as little as 1.3 megabytes.

SELECTING
ITEMS FOR INSTALLATION

Here are the steps required to select items for installation:

1. Insert the Excel Setup disk into a floppy drive and double-click the icon for the disk to open it. You'll see a window containing the two file icons shown in Figure A.1. Double-click the icon on the left (labeled Microsoft Excel Setup) to begin installation.

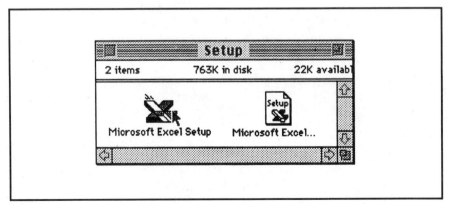

Figure A.1: Double-clicking the Setup icon to begin installation

2. Follow the directions on the screen to personalize your copy of Excel with your name and the name of your organization. Then click OK to continue. The Installation dialog box will appear (Figure A.2).

3. In this dialog box, select the Excel options you want to install. To help you make your decision, Microsoft lists the amount of space needed for each option, the total space required, and the space available on the hard disk.

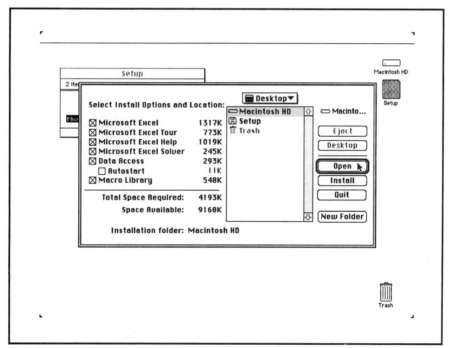

Figure A.2: The Installation dialog box

Actually, you can use Excel satisfactorily if you install only the first option: the program itself. However, this choice still results in the automatic installation of three additional items. You can remove these extra items later, if disk space is critical, by dragging their icons into the trash. The items are the Dialog Editor (explained in Chapter 20) and two sample files for use with tutorials in the manual. However, these items consume very little space; the

Dialog Editor occupies 38K of disk space, and the sample files occupy much less. If you have no intention of creating your own dialog boxes, you may want to remove the Dialog Editor. If no one else will be using your copy of Excel, you may want to delete the sample files, too, after you've finished with them.

Of course, if you will be sharing your Macintosh with others, you will have to consider their needs and wishes in selecting files for installation.

Here is a description of the additional optional files:

- **Microsoft Excel Tour**. This HyperCard file is a 773K tutorial. If you're the sole user of your Macintosh, you may want to delete this large file after you've viewed it.

- **Microsoft Excel Help**. The on-line help files occupy 1019K. However, you never know when you might want help on screen; using on-line help is often more convenient than searching through the manual or your copy of this book. If you have the space available, by all means retain this help capability.

- **Microsoft Excel Solver**. This feature was explained in Chapter 23. If you don't think you or anyone else using your Macintosh will use the Solver, delete it—through you'll save only 245K of disk space.

- **Data Access**. This 293K utility lets you access external databases. However, to use Data Access, your computer must be connected to a network, with the host system running Apple's CL/1 server program. You will also need authorization, in the form of an account and a personal password, from a network administrator. Through Data Access, you can issue commands in the structured query language (SQL), originally developed for use on IBM mainframe computers. As you can imagine, Data Access is of interest only to a small percentage of Excel users. Others would do well to delete the files and save the disk space.

- **Macro Library**. You became acquainted with the Macro Library in Chapter 16. The library requires 548K, but contains many items you may some day want to use. You should retain it if you can, considering the library second in importance only to the help files.

COMPLETING THE INSTALLATION

Once you've selected the options you want, you have only one more decision to make: You must choose the location where you want Excel installed—the folder in which you want it placed and, if you have multiple hard drives, the name of the drive. (A Drive button will appear in the dialog box, under the Eject button, only if your Macintosh system has more than one hard drive. You can click this Drive button repeatedly to cycle through your available hard drives until the screen displays the name of the drive you want.)

CREATING A NEW FOLDER

You can install a new version of Excel over an earlier version, in the same folder: Simply select the existing folder as the location for the installation. Otherwise, create a new folder to contain the software.

You create a new folder like this:

1. Click the New Folder button in the dialog box to create a new folder. A small New Folder dialog box will appear.

2. Type a name for the folder (such as **Excel** or **Excel 3.0**). Then click Create to complete the entry and return to the main installation dialog box.

FOLLOWING PROMPTS TO INSTALL THE FILES

Once you've determined where you want Excel, follow these steps to complete the installation:

1. Click the Open button, if necessary, to open the folder where you want Excel.

2. Click the Install button to start the installation from the Setup disk. The installation program informs you of its progress: The program

provides the name of the file currently being installed and also displays a horizontal bar that depicts graphically the percentage of the installation that has been completed.

3. When the program needs another floppy disk, it ejects the current disk. Follow the prompts on the screen to insert other disks as requested (see Figure A.3).

4. When the program has completed the installation, it displays a message to that effect (see Figure A.4). Click OK to close the message display.

To start using Excel, double-click the Excel folder to open it. Then double-click the Microsoft Excel icon to load the Excel program.

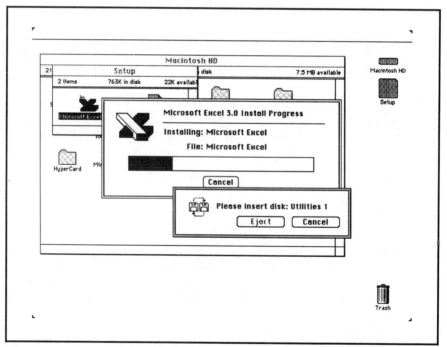

Figure A.3: The installation program requests another disk

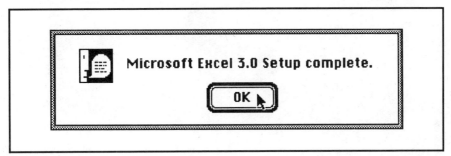

Figure A.4: The message indicating that Excel installation is completed

Appendix

B

Excel Functions

This appendix provides an alphabetical summary of Excel functions and what they do. If you're interested in using a particular function, you'll find the necessary arguments displayed when you select the function through the Paste Function... command on the Formula menu.

Some functions can be used on any worksheet or macro sheet. However, many Excel functions are designed for use on macro sheets only. Therefore, for your convenience this appendix identifies the intended use of each function in the third column of the following list. Functions that work with either worksheets or macro sheets are marked with a W; functions that work only with macro sheets are marked with an M.

Function	Use	W/M
A1.R1C1	Switches the display between A1 and R1C1 styles	M
ABS	Returns the absolute value of a number	W
ABSREF	Returns the absolute reference of offset cells	M
ACOS	Returns the arccosine of a number	W
ACOSH	Returns a number's inverse hyperbolic cosine	W
ACTIVATE	Activates a new window or a split-window pane	M
ACTIVATE.NEXT	Activates the next window	M
ACTIVATE.PREV	Activates the previous window	M
ACTIVE.CELL	Returns the active cell as an external reference	M
ADD.ARROW	Adds an arrow to the active chart	M
ADD.BAR	Adds a new menu bar	M
ADD.COMMAND	Adds a command to a menu	M
ADD.MENU	Adds a menu to a menu bar	M
ADD.OVERLAY	Adds an overlay to a two-dimensional chart	M

ADDRESS	Creates a cell address as text	W
ALERT	Displays an Alert dialog box	M
ALIGNMENT	Aligns the contents of selected cells	M
AND	Returns TRUE if all arguments are true	W
APP.ACTIVATE	Activates an application	M
APP.MAXIMIZE	Maximizes the Excel window	M
APP.MINIMIZE	Minimizes the Excel window	M
APP.MOVE	Moves the Excel window	M
APP.RESTORE	Restores a window to its previous size or location	M
APP.SIZE	Changes the size of an Excel window	M
APPLY.NAMES	Applies defined names to formulas	M
APPLY.STYLE	Applies a defined style to the current selection	M
AREAS	Returns the number of areas in a reference	W
ARGUMENT	Describes arguments used in a custom function	M
ARRANGE.ALL	Rearranges and sizes open windows to display them all	M
ASIN	Returns the arcsine of a number	W
ASINH	Returns a number's inverse hyperbolic sine	W
ASSIGN.TO.OBJECT	Assigns a macro to run when an object is clicked	M
ATAN	Returns the arctangent of a number	W
ATAN2	Returns the arctangent of X and Y coordinates	W
ATANH	Returns the inverse hyperbolic tangent of a number	W

ATTACH.TEXT	Attaches text to parts of a selected chart	M
AVERAGE	Returns the average (mean) of the arguments	W
AXES	Displays or hides axes on charts	M
BEEP	Sounds a tone to attract the user's attention	M
BORDER	Adds a border to a selected cell, range, or object	M
BREAK	Interrupts a loop	M
BRING.TO.FRONT	Displays the selected object in front of others	M
CALCULATE. DOCUMENT	Calculates the active document	M
CALCULATE.NOW	Calculates all open documents	M
CALCULATION	Controls how and when formulas are calculated	M
CALL	Calls a dynamic link library or code procedure	W
CALLER	Returns data about cells that call a custom function	M
CANCEL.COPY	Cancels the marquee after a Copy or Cut command	M
CANCEL.KEY	Disables macro interruption	M
CELL	Returns information about the upper-left cell in a reference	W
CELL.PROTECTION	Controls cell protection and display	M
CHANGE.LINK	Changes the supporting link to another document	M
CHAR	Returns the character for a code number	W
CHECK.COMMAND	Adds or removes a check mark from a command name	M

CHOOSE	Returns a value from a list of arguments	W
CLEAN	Removes all nonprintable characters from text	W
CLEAR	Clears data from a worksheet or macro sheet	M
CLOSE	Closes the active window	M
CLOSE.ALL	Closes all windows	M
CODE	Returns the numeric code of the first character in a string	W
COLOR.PALETTE	Copies a color palette between documents	M
COLUMN	Returns the column number of a given reference	W
COLUMN.WIDTH	Changes the width of specified columns	M
COLUMNS	Returns the number of columns in an array	W
COMBINATION	Changes a chart to the combination format	M
CONSOLIDATE	Consolidates data in multiple ranges or sheets	M
COPY	Defines the selection to be copied	M
COPY.CHART	Copies a chart in Excel version 1.5 or an earlier version	M
COPY.PICTURE	Copies a selection to the Clipboard as a graphic	M
COS	Returns the cosine of a given angle	W
COSH	Returns the hyperbolic cosine of number	W
COUNT	Counts the numbers in the list of arguments	W
COUNTA	Counts the number of nonblank values in arguments	W

CREATE.NAMES	Creates names from text labels in a worksheet	M
CREATE.OBJECT	Draws an object and returns a value identifying the object	M
CREATE.PUBLISHER	Publishes the selected range to an edition file	M
CUSTOM.REPEAT	Creates an Edit Repeat command for custom use	M
CUSTOM.UNDO	Creates an Edit Undo command for custom use	M
CUT	Defines the selection to be moved (pasted)	M
DATA.DELETE	Deletes data that matches specified criteria	M
DATA.FIND	Selects database records that match criteria	M
DATA.FIND.NEXT	Finds the next matching record in a database	M
DATA.FIND.PREV	Finds the previous matching database record	M
DATA.FORM	Displays the data form	M
DATA.SERIES	Enters an incrementally changing value series	M
DATE	Returns the serial number of a date	W
DATEVALUE	Returns the date serial number of an argument	W
DAVERAGE	Averages values that match criteria	W
DAY	Returns the day of the month from a serial number	W
DAYS360	Returns the number of days between two 360-day year dates	W

DCOUNT	Counts cells with numbers that match criteria	W
DCOUNTA	Counts nonblank cells that match criteria	W
DDB	Depreciates an asset for a specified period	W
DEFINE.NAME	Defines a name for an active worksheet or macro sheet	M
DEFINE.STYLE	Creates and changes cell styles	M
DELETE.ARROW	Deletes a selected arrow from a chart	M
DELETE.BAR	Deletes a custom menu bar	M
DELETE.COMMAND	Deletes a command from a custom or built-in menu	M
DELETE.FORMAT	Deletes a custom number format	M
DELETE.MENU	Deletes a menu from a menu bar	M
DELETE.NAME	Deletes a defined name	M
DELETE.OVERLAY	Deletes an overlay from a chart	M
DELETE.STYLE	Deletes a style from a document	M
DEMOTE	Demotes selected outline rows or columns	M
DEREF	Returns the value of cells in a reference	M
DGET	Extracts a value from a database	M
DIALOG.BOX	Displays the dialog box described in an argument	M
DIRECTORY	Makes the specified folder current	M
DISABLE.INPUT	Prevents all user input from the key-board or mouse	M
DISPLAY	Controls the display of attributes or Info commands	M
DMAX	Returns the largest number in database field	W

DMIN	Returns the smallest number in database field	W
DOCUMENT	Returns the names of open files alphabetically	M
DOLLAR	Converts a number to text in currency format	W
DPRODUCT	Multiplies values that match criteria	W
DSTDEV	Returns the standard deviation of a sample	W
DSTDEVP	Returns the standard deviation of a population	W
DSUM	Adds numbers that match criteria	W
DUPLICATE	Duplicates a selected object	M
DVAR	Returns the variance from a sample	W
DVARP	Returns the variance from a population	W
ECHO	Controls screen updating while a macro runs	M
EDIT.COLOR	Defines a color for a color palette	M
EDIT.DELETE	Removes selected cells from a worksheet	M
EDIT.REPEAT	Repeats actions or commands	M
EDIT.SERIES	Adds or modifies the chart SERIES formula	M
EDITION.OPTIONS	Sets publisher or subscriber options	M
ELSE	Marks functions to run if a logical test is FALSE	M
ELSE.IF	Marks functions to run if a logical test is TRUE	M
EMBED	Identifies the origin of an embedded object	W

ENABLE.COMMAND	Enables or disables a custom command or menu	M
END.IF	Ends functions associated with an IF function	M
ERROR	Specifies the action to take if an error occurs in a macro	M
EXACT	Compares two text strings; returns TRUE if the strings match	W
EXEC	Starts another program from within Excel	M
EXECUTE	Executes commands in a program other than Excel	M
EXP	Returns the constant e to a specified power	W
EXTRACT	Copies database records that meet criteria	M
FACT	Returns the factorial of a number	W
FALSE	Returns the logical value FALSE	W
FCLOSE	Closes a specified file	M
FILE.CLOSE	Closes the active document	M
FILE.DELETE	Deletes a file from a disk	M
FILES	Returns a horizontal text array of file names	M
FILL.DOWN	Copies top-row contents to the rest of a range	M
FILL.LEFT	Copies right-column contents to the rest of a range	M
FILL.RIGHT	Copies left-column contents to the rest of a range	M
FILL.UP	Copies bottom-row contents to the rest of a range	M

FILL.WORKGROUP	Copies a selection to other worksheets in a group	M
FIND	Finds a text string within another string	W
FIXED	Rounds a number and adds the decimal format	W
FONT	Sets the normal font style for Excel 1.5 macros	M
FOPEN	Opens a file with access permission specified	M
FOR	Starts a FOR-NEXT loop	M
FOR.CELL	Starts a FOR-NEXT loop, repeating instructions in each cell within a range	M
FORMAT.FONT	Applies a font to a selection	M
FORMAT.LEGEND	Determines the legend position and orientation	M
FORMAT.MAIN	Formats a chart according to arguments	M
FORMAT.MOVE	Moves an object to a specified position	M
FORMAT.NUMBER	Formats cell numbers, dates, and times	M
FORMAT.OVERLAY	Formats an overlay chart according to arguments	M
FORMAT.SIZE	Sizes a selected worksheet object	M
FORMAT.TEXT	Formats a worksheet text box or text item	M
FORMULA	Enters a formula in an active cell or reference	M
FORMULA.ARRAY	Enters a formula as an array in a specified range	M
FORMULA.CONVERT	Switches the formula style between A1 and R1C1	M
FORMULA.FILL	Enters a formula in a range or selection	M

FORMULA.FIND	Selects a cell that contains specified text	M
FORMULA.FIND. NEXT	Finds the next cell that matches text specified in the formula Find box	M
FORMULA.FIND. PREVIOUS	Finds the previous cell that matches text specified in the formula Find box	M
FORMULA.GOTO	Scrolls and selects a named area or reference	M
FORMULA.REPLACE	Finds and replaces worksheet characters	M
FPOS	Sets a specific position within a file	M
FREAD	Reads characters from the current file position	M
FREADLN	Reads file position characters to the end of a line	M
FREEZE.PANES	Freezes or unfreezes panes of windows	M
FSIZE	Returns the number of characters in a file	M
FULL	Changes the size of the active window to or from full	M
FV	Returns the future value of an investment	W
FWRITE	Writes text to a file from the current position	M
FWRITELN	Writes text followed by a return or line feed	M
GALLERY	Specifies one of a family of functions that selects a chart type	M
GET.BAR	Returns the number of the active menu bar or the name or position of a specified command on a menu	M
GET.CELL	Returns information about the selected cell	M

GET.CHART.ITEM	Returns the position of a point on a chart item	M
GET.DEF	Returns a defined name as text	M
GET.DOCUMENT	Returns information about a document	M
GET.FORMULA	Returns cell contents as shown in the formula bar	M
GET.LINK.INFO	Returns information about a specified link	M
GET.NAME	Returns the definition of a defined name	M
GET.NOTE	Returns the text of a note	M
GET.OBJECT	Returns information about a specified object	M
GET.WINDOW	Returns information about a window	M
GET.WORKSPACE	Returns information about the workspace	M
GOAL.SEEK	In a macro, functions like the Goal Seek... command	M
GOTO	Directs a running macro to another cell or range	M
GRIDLINES	Turns chart gridlines on or off	M
GROUP	Groups objects	M
GROWTH	Fits an exponential curve to argument data	W
HALT	Stops all macros from running	M
HELP	Displays the specified custom help topic	M
HIDE	Hides the active window	M
HIDE.OBJECT	Hides or displays the specified object	M
HLINE	Scrolls a window the specified number of columns	M

HLOOKUP	Returns a value starting from the top row of an array	W
HOUR	Returns the hour that corresponds to the serial number argument	W
HPAGE	Scrolls one window at a time	M
HSCROLL	Scrolls a window by a percentage or number of columns	M
IF	Returns TRUE or FALSE, according to logical test results	W
IF	A separate macro form of IF used with ELSE, ELSE.IF	M
INDEX	Returns the reference at a cell or array intersection	W
INDIRECT	Returns the reference specified in an argument	W
INFO	Returns information about the current environment	W
INITIATE	Opens a dynamic data exchange (DDE) channel to an application	M
INPUT	Displays a dialog box for user input	M
INSERT	Inserts blank cells or pastes Clipboard cells	M
INT	Rounds a number down to the nearest integer	W
IPMT	Returns the interest payment on an investment	W
IRR	Returns the cash flow internal rate of return	W
IS	Performs nine functions that test the value or reference type	W
JUSTIFY	Justifies text in a range	M

LAST.ERROR	Returns a reference to the cell where the last macro error occurred	M
LEFT	Returns the first character in a text string	M
LEGEND	Adds or removes the chart legend	M
LEN	Returns the number of characters in a text string	W
LINEST	Calculates least-squares linear regression	W
LINKS	Returns the names of worksheets linked externally	M
LIST.NAMES	Lists the names defined on a worksheet	M
LN	Returns the natural logarithm of a number	W
LOG	Returns the logarithm of a number to a specified base	W
LOG10	Returns the base-10 logarithm of number	W
LOGEST	Calculates an exponential curve to fit data	W
LOOKUP	Returns a specified value from an array	W
LOWER	Converts uppercase letters to lowercase letters	W
MAIN.CHART.TYPE	Specifies the main chart type in an Excel 1.5 macro	M
MATCH	Returns the position of an item that matches a value	W
MAX	Returns the largest number from arguments	W
MDETERM	Returns the matrix determinant of an array	W
MEDIAN	Returns the median of given numbers	W

MERGE.STYLES	Merges the styles of another file into the current file	M
MESSAGE	Displays or removes messages in the status bar	M
MID	Returns specified characters from a text string	W
MIN	Returns the smallest number from arguments	W
MINUTE	Returns the minute that corresponds to a serial number argument	W
MINVERSE	Returns the inverse matrix from an array matrix	W
MIRR	Returns the modified internal rate of return	W
MMUL	Returns the matrix product of two arrays	W
MOD	Returns the remainder (modulus) after division	W
MONTH	Returns the month that corresponds to a serial number argument	W
MOVE	Moves a window to a new position	M
N	Returns a value converted to a number	W
NA	Returns an error value (used for empty cells)	W
NAMES	Returns an alphabetical list of defined names	M
NEW	Creates a new Excel document or opens a template	M
NEW.WINDOW	Creates a new window for an active macro sheet	M
NEXT	Ends a loop and executes the next macro formula	M

NOT	Reverses the value of its argument	M
NOTE	Creates a note or replaces characters in a note	M
NOW	Returns the serial number of the current date and time	W
NPER	Returns the number of periods of an investment	W
NPV	Returns the net present value of an investment	W
OBJECT. PROTECTION	Changes the protection status of the selected object	M
OFFSET	Returns an offset reference according to arguments	W
ON	Specifies one of a family of functions that run a macro when an event occurs	M
ON.DATA	Starts a macro when data is sent via dynamic data exchange (DDE)	M
ON.KEY	Runs a macro when the specified key is pressed	M
ON.RECALL	Runs a macro when a document is recalculated	M
ON.TIME	Runs a macro at a specified time of day	M
ON.WINDOW	Starts a macro when a specified window is opened	M
OPEN	Opens an existing file or workspace	M
OPEN.LINKS	Opens a document linked to another document	M
OPEN.MAIL	Opens files sent by Microsoft Mail	M
OR	Returns TRUE if one or more arguments are TRUE	W
OUTLINE	Creates an outline; defines outline settings	M

OVERLAY	Formats the overlay for Excel 2.2 macros	M
OVERLAY.CHART. TYPE	Formats the overlay for Excel 1.5 macros	M
PAGE.SETUP	Controls the printed appearance of document	M
PARSE	Apportions column contents to adjacent columns	M
PASTE	Pastes a selection or object from the Clipboard	M
PASTE.LINK	Pastes copied data or objects and links them to their sources	M
PASTE.PICTURE	Pastes the Clipboard contents to an active cell	M
PASTE.PICTURE.LINK	Pastes a linked picture from the Clipboard	M
PASTE.SPECIAL	Pastes specified elements from the copy area	M
PATTERNS	Changes the appearance of a selection according to arguments	M
PLACEMENT	Sets the way selected objects attach to cells	M
PMT	Returns the periodic payment for an annuity	W
POKE	Sends data to another application through dynamic data exchange (DDE)	M
PPMT	Returns the payment on principal for a given period	W
PRECISION	Controls the way values are stored in cells	M
PREFERRED	Changes the format of the active chart to preferred	M

PRINT	Prints the active document	M
PRINT.PREVIEW	Previews pages or page breaks before printing	M
PRODUCT	Multiplies arguments and returns the product	W
PROMOTE	Promotes the current selection in an outline	M
PROPER	Capitalizes the first letter in text	W
PROTECT. DOCUMENT	Adds or removes protection for the current file	M
PV	Returns the present value of an investment	W
QUIT	Quits Excel and closes open, saved documents	M
RAND	Returns a random number greater than 0 and less than 1	W
RATE	Returns the interest rate per period for an annuity	W
REFTEXT	Makes a text reference absolute	M
REGISTER	Makes the specified code resource available	M
RELREF	Returns R1C1-style relative cell references	M
REMOVE.PAGE. BREAK	Removes manual page breaks	M
RENAME.COMMAND	Changes the name of a command or menu	M
REPLACE	Replaces the specified number of text characters	W
REPLACE.FONT	Replaces a font with a new font and style	M
REPT	Replaces text a given number of times	W

REQUEST	Requests an array of data from a linked application	M
RESTART	Specifies which macro regains control of a sequence	M
RESULT	Specifies the data type returned from a function or subroutine	M
RETURN	Ends the macro currently running	M
RIGHT	Returns the last character in a text string	W
ROUND	Rounds a number to the specified number of digits	W
ROW	Returns the row number of an argument	W
ROW.HEIGHT	Changes the height of specified rows	M
ROWS	Returns the number of rows in a reference or array	W
RUN	Runs a macro	M
SAVE	Saves the active document	M
SAVE.AS	Saves a version of the active document under a new name	M
SAVE.NEW.OBJECT	Saves a copy of the current object under a new name	M
SAVE.WORKSPACE	Saves a workspace file	M
SCALE	Changes the scale of a chart axis	M
SEARCH	Returns the location of specified text	W
SECOND	Returns the second (time) according to an argument	W
SELECT	Selects the active cell, object, or chart	M
SELECT.CHART	Selects a chart for Excel 1.5 macros	M
SELECT.END	Selects a cell at the specified edge of a range	M

SELECT.LAST.CELL	Selects the last cell that contains data	M
SELECT.PLOT.AREA	Selects the plot area in old-version Excel macros	M
SELECT.SPECIAL	Selects groups of cells	M
SELECTION	Returns an external reference from a selection (object, range, button, and so on)	M
SEND.KEYS	Sends keystrokes to the active application	M
SEND.MAIL	Sends the active document by Microsoft Mail	M
SEND.TO.BACK	Places selected objects behind other objects	M
SERIES	Represents a data series in the active chart	W
SET.CRITERIA	Defines the selected range under the name Criteria	M
SET.DATABASE	Defines the selected range under the name Database	M
SET.EXTRACT	Defines the selected range under the name Extract	M
SET.NAME	Defines a macro sheet name to refer to a value	M
SET.PAGE.BREAK	Sets manual page breaks for printing a worksheet	M
SET.PREFERRED	Sets the default chart format	M
SET.PRINT.AREA	Defines the area to be printed	M
SET.PRINT.TITLES	Defines text for printed titles	M
SET.UPDATE.STATUS	Sets the update status of a link	M
SET.VALUE	Changes the values, not the formulas, of cells	M

SHORT.MENUS	Switches between short and full menu display	M
SHOW.ACTIVE.CELL	Scrolls the window so the active cell becomes visible	M
SHOW.BAR	Displays a specified menu bar	M
SHOW.CLIPBOARD	Displays Clipboard contents in a new window	M
SHOW.DETAIL	Expands or collapses outline detail	M
SHOW.INFO	Controls the Info window display	M
SHOW.LEVELS	Displays the specified outline rows or columns	M
SIN	Returns the sine of a given angle	W
SINH	Returns the hyperbolic sine of a number	W
SIZE	Changes the size of a window	M
SLN	Returns straight-line depreciation for an asset	W
SORT	Sorts selected rows or columns	M
SPLIT	Splits the active window into panes	M
SQRT	Returns a positive square root	W
STANDARD.FONT	Sets the standard font for old-version macros	M
STDEV	Returns the standard deviation of a sample population	W
STDEVP	Returns the standard deviation of an entire population	W
STEP	Makes a macro proceed one cell at a time	M
STYLE	Changes font styles for old-version macros	M

SUBSCRIBE.TO	Inserts an edition into the active document	M
SUBSTITUTE	Replaces specific text in a text string	W
SUM	Returns the sum of all numbers in arguments	W
SUMPRODUCT	Multiplies array components; returns the sum	W
SYD	Returns sum-of-years' digits depreciation	W
T	Returns text referred to by an argument	W
TABLE	Creates table form input values and formulas	M
TAN	Returns the tangent of the given angle	W
TANH	Returns the hyperbolic tangent of a number	W
TERMINATE	Terminates the dynamic data exchange (DDE) channel opened with INITIATE	M
TEXT	Converts a value to text in number format	W
TEXT.BOX	Replaces text box characters as specified	M
TEXTREF	Converts text to an absolute reference	M
TIME	Returns the serial number of a particular time	W
TIMEVALUE	Converts time represented as text to a serial number	W
TODAY	Returns the serial number of the current date	W
TRANSPOSE	Transposes the rows and colums of an argument array	W
TREND	Reforms linear regression; fits a straight line to arrays	W

TRIM	Removes text spaces, except spaces between words	W
TRUE	Returns the logical value TRUE	W
TRUNC	Truncates a number to an integer	W
TYPE	Returns the type of a value in a cell	W
UNDO	Reverses some actions and commands	M
UNGROUP	Separates grouped objects	M
UNHIDE	Displays hidden windows	M
UNLOCKED	Moves to the next or previous unlocked cell	M
UNREGISTER	Frees memory after code resources are used	M
UPDATE.LINK	Updates a link to another document	M
UPPER	Converts text to uppercase	W
VALUE	Converts text to a number	W
VAR	Returns the population variance from a sample	W
VARP	Returns the population variance from the whole	W
VDB	Returns the depreciation of an asset for a period	W
VIEW.3D	Adjusts the view of an active 3-D chart	M
VLINE	Scrolls the active window vertically by rows	M
VLOOKUP	Returns a value starting from the left-most column of an array	W
VOLATILE	Specifies that a custom function is volatile	M
VPAGE	Scrolls the active window vertically one screenful	M

VSCROLL	Scrolls the active document by a percentage or row	M
WAIT	Pauses a macro until the specified time	M
WEEKDAY	Returns the day of the week from a serial number	W
WHILE	Specifies an action in WHILE-NEXT loops	M
WINDOWS	Returns names of all (even hidden) open windows	M
WORKGROUP	Creates a workgroup	M
WORKSPACE	Changes workspace settings	M
YEAR	Returns the year from a serial number	W

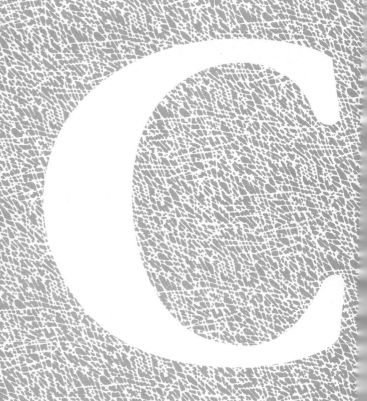

Appendix C

Excel for Users
of Lotus 1-2-3

If you've been using the Lotus 1-2-3 spreadsheet program (or a Lotus-compatible application), you won't have to throw away your old 1-2-3 files or recreate them when you start using Excel. Excel can import most 1-2-3 files automatically and convert them to the Excel format. In fact, Excel can import Lotus Symphony files too.

In addition, you can export Excel files to 1-2-3, saving them in your choice of 1-2-3 worksheet formats.

This appendix discusses both the importing and exporting of files. It also tells you how to adjust to the differences between Excel and 1-2-3.

IMPORTING LOTUS 1-2-3 FILES

Before you can load a 1-2-3 worksheet into Excel, the file must be available to your Macintosh. You can accomplish this goal in several ways. For example, if your Macintosh is connected to a network, you may be able to access files from MS-DOS computers.

Since file-access methods can vary greatly, depending on the equipment and software involved, we'll discuss only one method here, which is available to all Macintosh users: importing through the Apple File Exchange utility.

These are the steps to follow:

1. On an MS-DOS computer, save the 1-2-3 file in its normal WKS, WK1, or WK3 format.

2. Copy the file onto a 3-1/2 inch floppy disk that has been formatted under the MS-DOS operating system.

3. Take the floppy disk to your Macintosh (but do not insert it yet).

4. Load the Apple File Exchange utility, provided with your Macintosh operating system, by double-clicking the Apple File Exchange icon. A dialog box will appear, with a list box at the left showing the contents of the current folder.

5. If the current folder is not where you want to store the 1-2-3 file to be imported, place the pointer on the name of the folder at the top of the list box, hold down the mouse button, and drag downward to reveal

other storage options. Select the folder in which you want to store the imported file.

6. Insert the MS-DOS disk into the floppy drive of your Macintosh. You should immediately see a list of MS-DOS files on the floppy disk. The list will be displayed in the list box at the right of the Apple File Exchange dialog box.

7. Highlight the name of the file you want to import and click the Translate button, as shown in Figure C.1. The utility will quickly translate the file to a Macintosh format, displaying a horizontal bar that moves to the right as the translation is completed.

8. Close Apple File Exchange. You can now load the translated 1-2-3 file through the Open command on the Excel File menu. If the file contains graphs, you will be asked, *Create Lotus 1-2-3 graphs?* If you answer yes, Excel will re-create the 1-2-3 graphs as separate Excel chart files. If you answer no, the 1-2-3 graphs will not be duplicated.

9. Save the imported worksheet in the normal Excel format to preserve it as an Excel file. If the original file contained graphs you

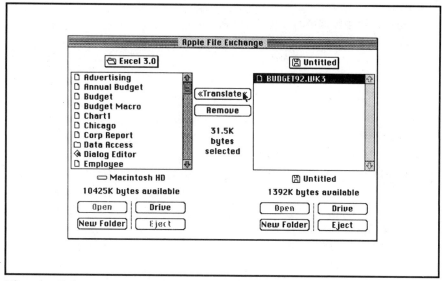

Figure C.1: Importing a Lotus 1-2-3 worksheet

decided not to re-create as Excel charts, you may want to retain the Macintosh file made by Apple File Exchange; you can then import the file into Excel again later and re-create the charts at that time, if you desire.

Since the Excel menu and command structure differ from those of 1-2-3, you cannot use 1-2-3 macros in Excel. However, you can import most other 1-2-3 features correctly, including database and other range names.

EXPORTING WORKSHEET FILES TO LOTUS 1-2-3

You can save an Excel file in any of three Lotus 1-2-3 file formats: WKS (for older versions of 1-2-3), WK1 (for Release 2.X), or WK3 (for Release 3.X). This capability means that you can import a Lotus 1-2-3 file into Excel, work with it, and save it again as a 1-2-3 file; in other words, you can use 1-2-3 files on your Macintosh without having either an MS-DOS computer or the Lotus 1-2-3 program. Conversely, someone using Lotus 1-2-3 on an MS-DOS computer can work with Macintosh Excel files without having a Macintosh.

Here is the procedure for saving Excel files as 1-2-3 files:

1. Pull down the Excel File menu and select the Save As... command.

2. In the Save As dialog box, click the Options button. The Save Options dialog box will appear.

3. Place the pointer on the down arrow beside the File Format section of the dialog box and depress the mouse button to see the list of file format options (shown in Figure C.2).

4. Highlight the Lotus 1-2-3 format you want and click OK to close the Save Options dialog box and return to the Save As dialog box.

5. Type the name you want for the 1-2-3 version of the worksheet. (Remember that MS-DOS rules limit you to an eight-character name starting with a letter and followed, optionally, by a period and three more characters. In this case, you should type a three-character extension of WKS, WK1, or WK3, depending on the format you've chosen, so Lotus 1-2-3 will recognize the name as a 1-2-3 worksheet.)

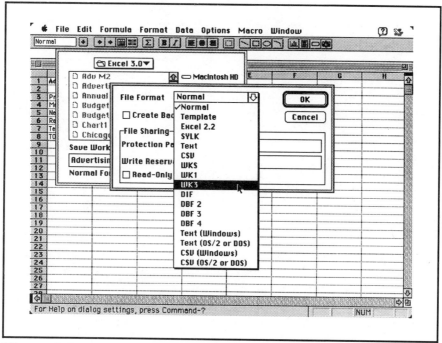

Figure C.2: Saving an Excel worksheet as a 1-2-3 file

6. Click the Save button to save the 1-2-3 version of the file.

7. Use the Apple File Exchange utility again to export the 1-2-3 file to an MS-DOS floppy disk.

Excel imports three-dimensional worksheets from 1-2-3 as a set of linked two-dimensional worksheets. When exporting 3-D worksheets to Lotus 1-2-3, Excel must export them as separate, linked worksheets. To approximate the creation of a 3-D worksheet for 1-2-3, therefore, you must export a set of linked Excel 2-D worksheets.

Excel can *open* 1-2-3 files that contain either 2-D or 3-D graphs in the WK3 format, but can *save* only 2-D charts to WK3 files.

Lotus 1-2-3 does not support Excel's array capabilities. When you export an Excel worksheet that contains formulas involving arrays, the values in the arrays are used instead of the arrays themselves.

HOW EXCEL
DIFFERS FROM LOTUS 1-2-3

In Excel you have many handy tools displayed all the time to help you build files and work with them efficiently. For example, creating a formula in the active cell to add a column of numbers requires only one mouse click. If you're new to Excel, be sure to read Chapter 2, where the Toolbar is explained carefully.

Often, selecting one Excel command displays a dialog box, where you can make a variety of choices related to that command.

To access a menu in Lotus 1-2-3, on the other hand, you press the slash key followed by a letter, and you frequently must use multiple menus to make a series of choices regarding a subject.

When you work in Excel, you select a range and then a command you wish to apply to the range. This procedure lets you perform several operations on a range without reselecting it.

When you use 1-2-3, you first select the command and then the range. If you want to issue a second command relating to the same range, you must select the new command and then select the range again.

In Lotus 1-2-3 you become accustomed to issuing familiar commands quickly by merely typing a series of keystrokes. Although you can issue many Excel commands from the keyboard too, you will often find that the use of the mouse is a time-saver and is sometimes essential. The Excel keyboard commands are different from those in 1-2-3. Fortunately, Excel's on-line Help screens include special features to assist you in making the transition. We'll discuss these Help screens shortly.

SWITCHING TO EXCEL COMMANDS

You receive some minor help in switching to Excel commands through a default Excel setting. The slash key is defined as an alternate key for displaying a menu. For example, to load a file in 1-2-3, you press /FR (the slash key followed by the letters F for File and R for Retrieve). To perform the same action in Excel, you can press the slash key and F to bring up Excel's File menu; however, then you must press the O key (for Open). The O in Open is underlined on the File menu, to indicate that you can press the key to issue the command. The other keyboard method of selecting a file to load in Excel is to hold down the Macintosh ⌘ key while pressing O (which bypasses the display of the File menu entirely and takes you immediately to a list of files available for loading).

You can control both the display of command letter underlining and the use of the slash key through menu options. Here's how:

1. Use the mouse to pull down the Options menu (or press / and then O) and select the Workspace... command. You'll see the Workspace dialog box shown in Figure C.3. The Alternate Menu Key text box will already be highlighted, showing the slash key (/).

2. If you want to call up menus by pressing some key other than the slash, type another character—though if you're accustomed to using 1-2-3's slash key, you will probably prefer to continue to use the slash key. If someone else has been using your copy of Excel and has changed the default alternate key to something else, you may want to type a slash to switch back (with the other party's approval, of course).

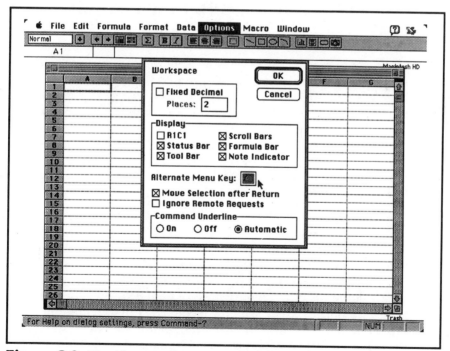

Figure C.3: The Alternate Menu Key text box in the Workspace dialog box

3. By default, the Command Underline button labeled Automatic is
    selected at the bottom of the dialog box, meaning that the letter you
    can press in a command name to issue that command is underlined
    when appropriate. If the On button is selected, the appropriate
    letter is *always* underlined in menus commands. If the Off button is
    selected, *no* letters are underlined in menu commands. Again, if
    someone has changed this feature from the default setting, as a
    1-2-3 user you may want to place your mouse pointer on the Auto-
    matic option and click your mouse button to restore the default
    setting so you can select commands from the keyboard using con-
    ventions similar to those used in 1-2-3.

4. When you finish with this dialog box, place the pointer on the OK
    button and click your mouse button to close the box and return to
    the worksheet. (If the default settings are still in effect when you
    display the dialog box, you can click the Cancel button instead to
    close the box without making changes.)

FINDING THE EXCEL EQUIVALENT
OF A LOTUS 1-2-3 COMMAND

If you want to look up the Excel equivalent for a common 1-2-3 command, Microsoft has provided an easy way to find it. Try this:

1. Place the pointer on the balloon-shaped icon containing a question
    mark; the icon is located near the right edge of the menu bar at the
    top of your Excel screen and represents the Help menu. Then hold
    down your mouse button and drag this small menu down to open
    it. Move the pointer to highlight and select the Microsoft Excel
    Help... command.

2. If you have a small-screen Macintosh system (a 12-inch monitor
    such as often is sold with a Macintosh IIsi or the 9-inch monitor
    built in to the Macintosh Classic), you probably won't see the bal-
    loon Help icon when a worksheet is displayed on the screen.
    Because of the number of Excel menus that are shown, the screen
    simply doesn't have room for that separate Help menu. You'll find a
    Help... command on the Window menu. You can select the com-
    mand through keystrokes by typing a slash followed by W and then
    P (the H is already used for the Hide... command on the same

menu). You will also find Help on the Window menu if your system software is a version earlier than System 7.

3. Once you have issued the Help command, you'll see the Microsoft Excel Help Index screen shown in Figure C.4. Click the Lotus 1-2-3 button in the lower right corner of the Help window to obtain help on how to convert many 1-2-3 commands to their Excel equivalents.

4. Once you've clicked the Lotus 1-2-3 button, the small dialog box shown in Figure C.5 appears. To test this feature, type **/FR** (the keystroke sequence for the 1-2-3 File Retrieve command).

5. When you've finished typing, click the OK button. You'll see the Help screen shown in Figure C.6, which explains exactly how to retrieve a file in Excel.

6. After you've read the Help screen, click the Topics button to return to the Help Index screen. You'll work with the index in the next section.

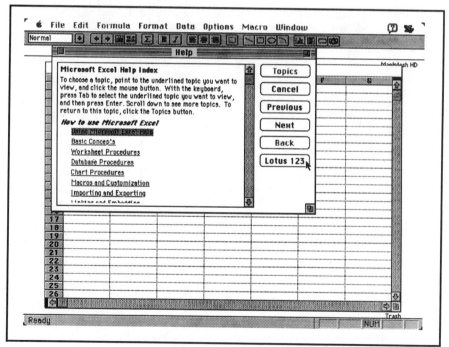

Figure C.4: The Lotus 1-2-3 button in the Help window

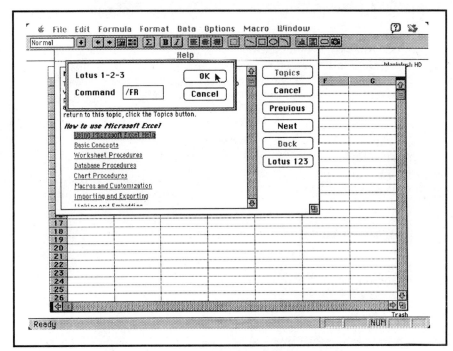

Figure C.5: Getting help with a 1-2-3 command in Excel

OTHER HELP IN CONVERTING TO EXCEL

You can find a long list of Excel equivalents for regularly used Lotus 1-2-3 commands within the layers of the Excel Help screens, as well as assistance with menus, file formats, and functions.

Take a look at this area now.

1. With the Excel Help Index screen still displayed, scroll the list of subjects until you see Switching from Lotus 1-2-3, shown in Figure C.7. Click this subject to select it.

2. You'll now see a smaller list of subjects, all related to Lotus 1-2-3 and displayed in Figure C.8. Click any one of these items to learn more about converting to Excel. Some of these choices bring up additional lists of items you can select to obtain information about aspects of a particular category.

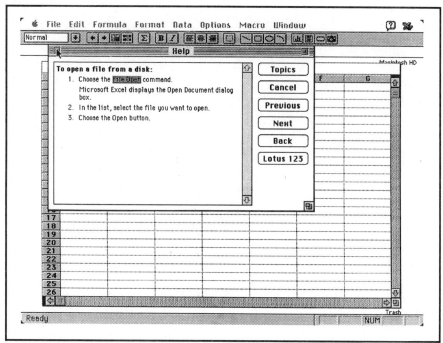

Figure C.6: Displaying the Excel equivalent for the 1-2-3 command

3. When you've finished exploring the Help menus, click the close box to close the Help window.

DIFFERENCES BETWEEN
EXCEL AND LOTUS 1-2-3 FORMULAS

Here is a list of some of the differences between Excel and Lotus 1-2-3 formulas.

- Lotus 1-2-3 provides several ways to start a formula. Excel provides only two: You must enter either an equal sign (=) or a plus sign (+).

- In Lotus 1-2-3, you must precede function names with the "at" symbol (@). In Excel, you can use the @ symbol if you want, but no symbol is required.

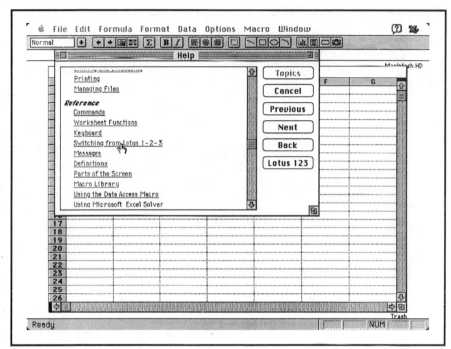

Figure C.7: Finding 1-2-3 help in the index

- Lotus 1-2-3 uses two periods (..) in designating a range to separate the two cell addresses that define the beginning and end of the range. Excel uses a colon (:) instead of the periods.

- Lotus 1-2-3 evaluates the exponentiation operator (^) before the negation operator (–); the reverse is true in Excel. Be aware that not attending to this difference can alter the result of formulas.

- Lotus 1-2-3 does not use the percentage operator (%). Therefore, 6% in Excel becomes 0.06 in 1-2-3.

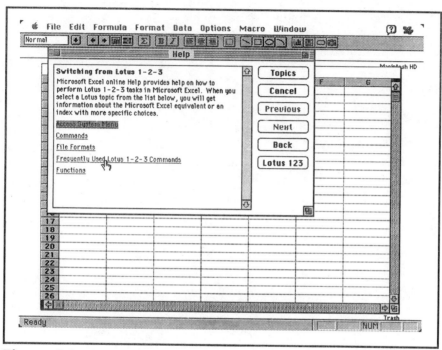

Figure C.8: The second level of three-level 1-2-3 Help screens

Index

X

Y

Selections from The SYBEX Library

APPLE/MACINTOSH

ABC's of Excel on the Macintosh (Second Edition)
Douglas Hergert
334pp. Ref. 634-0

Newly updated to include version 2.2, this tutorial offers a quick way for beginners to get started doing useful work with Excel. Readers build practical examples for accounting, management, and home/ office applications, as they learn to create worksheets, charts, databases, macros, and more.

Desktop Publishing with Microsoft Word on the Macintosh (Second Edition)
Tim Erickson
William Finzer
525pp. Ref. 601-4

The authors have woven a murder mystery through the text, using the sample publications as clues. Explanations of page layout, headings, fonts and styles, columnar text, and graphics are interwoven within the mystery theme of this exciting teaching method. For Version 4.0.

Encyclopedia Macintosh
Craig Danuloff
Deke McClelland
650pp. Ref. 628-6

Just what every Mac user needs—a complete reference to Macintosh concepts and tips on system software, hardware, applications, and troubleshooting. Instead of chapters, each section is presented in A-Z format with user-friendly icons leading the way.

Mastering Adobe Illustrator
David A. Holzgang
330pp. Ref. 463-1

This text provides a complete introduction to Adobe Illustrator, bringing new sophistication to artists using computer-aided graphics and page design technology. Includes a look at PostScript, the page composition language used by Illustrator.

Mastering AppleWorks (Second Edition)
Elna Tymes
479pp. Ref. 398-8

New chapters on business applications, data sharing DIF and Applesoft BASIC make this practical, in-depth tutorial even better. Full details on AppleWorks desktop, word processing, spreadsheet and database functions.

Mastering Microsoft Word on the Macintosh
Michael J. Young
447pp. Ref. 541-7

This comprehensive, step-by-step guide shows the reader through WORD's extensive capabilities, from basic editing to custom formats and desktop publishing. Keyboard and mouse instructions and practice exercises are included. For Release 4.0.

Mastering Powerpoint
Karen L. McGraw, Ph.D.
425pp. Ref. 646-4

The complete guide to creating high-quality graphic presentations using PowerPoint 2.01 on the Macintosh— offering detailed, step-by-step coverage of everything from starting up the software to fine-tuning your slide shows for maximum effect.

Mastering Ready, Set, Go!
David A. Kater
482pp. Ref. 536-0
This hands-on introduction to the popular desktop publishing package for the Macintosh allows readers to produce professional-looking reports, brochures, and flyers. Written for Version 4, this title has been endorsed by Letraset, the Ready, Set, Go! software publisher.

Understanding Hard Disk Management on the Macintosh
J. Russell Roberts
334pp. Ref. 579-4
This is the most comprehensive and accessible guide to hard disk usage for all Macintosh users. Complete coverage includes SCSI and serial drives and ports, formatting, file fragmentation, backups, networks, and a helpful diagnostic appendix.

Understanding HyperCard (Second Edition)
Greg Harvey
654pp. Ref. 607-3
For Mac users who want clear-cut steps to quick mastery of HyperCard, this thorough tutorial introduces HyperCard from the Browsing/Typing and Authoring/Painting levels all the way to Scripting with HyperTalk, the HyperCard programming language. No prior programming experience needed. For Version 1.2.

Using the Macintosh Toolbox with C (Second Edition)
Fred A. Huxham
David Burnard
Jim Takatsuka
525pp. Ref. 572-7
Learn to program with the latest versions of Macintosh Toolbox using this clear and succinct introduction. This popular title has been revised and expanded to include dozens of new programming examples for windows, menus, controls, alert boxes, and disk I/O. Includes hierarchical file system, Lightspeed C, Resource files, and R Maker.

SPREADSHEETS AND INTEGRATED SOFTWARE

1-2-3 for Scientists and Engineers
William J. Orvis
341pp. Ref. 407-0
Fast, elegant solutions to common problems in science and engineering, using Lotus 1-2-3. Tables and plotting, curve fitting, statistics, derivatives, integrals and differentials, solving systems of equations, and more.

The ABC's of 1-2-3 (Second Edition)
Chris Gilbert
Laurie Williams
245pp. Ref. 355-4
Online Today recommends it as "an easy and comfortable way to get started with the program." An essential tutorial for novices, it will remain on your desk as a valuable source of ongoing reference and support. For Release 2.

The ABC's of 1-2-3 Release 2.2
Chris Gilbert
Laurie Williams
340pp. Ref. 623-5
New Lotus 1-2-3 users delight in this book's step-by-step approach to building trouble-free spreadsheets, displaying graphs, and efficiently building databases. The authors cover the ins and outs of the latest version including easier calculations, file linking, and better graphic presentation.

The ABC's of 1-2-3 Release 3
Judd Robbins
290pp. Ref. 519-0
The ideal book for beginners who are new to Lotus or new to Release 3. This step-by-step approach to the 1-2-3 spreadsheet software gets the reader up and running with spreadsheet, database, graphics, and macro functions.

The ABC's of Excel on the IBM PC
Douglas Hergert
326pp. Ref. 567-0

This book is a brisk and friendly introduction to the most important features of Microsoft Excel for PC's. This beginner's book discusses worksheets, charts, database operations, and macros, all with hands-on examples. Written for all versions through Version 2.

The ABC's of Quattro
Alan Simpson
Douglas J. Wolf
286pp. Ref. 560-3

Especially for users new to spreadsheets, this is an introduction to the basic concepts and a guide to instant productivity through editing and using spreadsheet formulas and functions. Includes how to print out graphs and data for presentation. For Quattro 1.1.

The Complete Lotus 1-2-3 Release 2.2 Handbook
Greg Harvey
750pp. Ref. 625-1

This comprehensive handbook discusses every 1-2-3 operating with clear instructions and practical tips. This volume especially emphasizes the new improved graphics, high-speed recalculation techniques, and spreadsheet linking available with Release 2.2.

The Complete Lotus 1-2-3 Release 3 Handbook
Greg Harvey
700pp. Ref. 600-6

Everything you ever wanted to know about 1-2-3 is in this definitive handbook. As a Release 3 guide, it features the design and use of 3D worksheets, and improved graphics, along with using Lotus under DOS or OS/2. Problems, exercises, and helpful insights are included.

Lotus 1-2-3 2.2 On-Line Advisor Version 1.1
SYBAR, Software Division of SYBEX, Inc.

Ref. 935-8

Need Help fast? With a touch of a key, the Advisor pops up right on top of your Lotus 1-2-3 program to answer your spreadsheet questions. With over 4000 index citations and 1600 pre-linked cross-references, help has never been so easy to find. Just start typing your topic and the Lotus 1-2-3 Advisor does all the look-up for you. Covers versions 2.01 and 2.2. Software package comes with 3½" and 5¼" disks. **System Requirements:** IBM compatible with DOS 2.0 or higher, runs with Windows 3.0, uses 90K of RAM.

Lotus 1-2-3 Desktop Companion SYBEX Ready Reference Series
Greg Harvey
976pp. Ref. 501-8

A full-time consultant, right on your desk. Hundreds of self-contained entries cover every 1-2-3 feature, organized by topic, indexed and cross-referenced, and supplemented by tips, macros and working examples. For Release 2.

Lotus 1-2-3 Instant Reference Release 2.2 SYBEX Prompter Series
Greg Harvey
Kay Yarborough Nelson
254pp. Ref. 635-9, 4 ¾" × 8"

The reader gets quick and easy access to any operation in 1-2-3 Version 2.2 in this handy pocket-sized encyclopedia. Organized by menu function, each command and function has a summary description, the exact key sequence, and a discussion of the options.

Lotus 1-2-3 Tips and Tricks (2nd edition)
Gene Weisskopf
425pp. Ref. 668-5

This outstanding collection of tips, short-cuts and cautions for longtime Lotus users is in an expanded new edition covering Release 2.2. Topics include macros, range names, spreadsheet design, hardware and operating system tips, data analysis, printing, data interchange, applications development, and more.

SYBEX ®

FREE CATALOG!

Mail us this form today, and we'll send you a full-color catalog of Sybex books.

Name _____

Street _____

City/State/Zip _____

Phone _____

Please supply the name of the Sybex book purchased.

_____

How would you rate it?

_____ Excellent _____ Very Good _____ Average _____ Poor

Why did you select this particular book?

_____ Recommended to me by a friend

_____ Recommended to me by store personnel

_____ Saw an advertisement in _____

_____ Author's reputation

_____ Saw in Sybex catalog

_____ Required textbook

_____ Sybex reputation

_____ Read book review in _____

_____ In-store display

_____ Other _____

Where did you buy it?

_____ Bookstore

_____ Computer Store or Software Store

_____ Catalog (name: _____)

_____ Direct from Sybex

_____ Other: _____

Did you buy this book with your personal funds?

_____ Yes _____ No

About how many computer books do you buy each year?

_____ 1-3 _____ 3-5 _____ 5-7 _____ 7-9 _____ 10+

About how many Sybex books do you own?

_____ 1-3 _____ 3-5 _____ 5-7 _____ 7-9 _____ 10+

Please indicate your level of experience with the software covered in this book:

_____ Beginner _____ Intermediate _____ Advanced

Which types of software packages do you use regularly?

_____ Accounting	_____ Databases	_____ Networks
_____ Amiga	_____ Desktop Publishing	_____ Operating Systems
_____ Apple/Mac	_____ File Utilities	_____ Spreadsheets
_____ CAD	_____ Money Management	_____ Word Processing
_____ Communications	_____ Languages	_____ Other _____
		(please specify)

Which of the following best describes your job title?

_____ Administrative/Secretarial	_____ President/CEO
_____ Director	_____ Manager/Supervisor
_____ Engineer/Technician	_____ Other _____
	(please specify)

Comments on the weaknesses/strengths of this book: _____

_____

_____

_____

_____

PLEASE FOLD, SEAL, AND MAIL TO SYBEX

– –

SYBEX, INC.
Department M
2021 CHALLENGER DR.
ALAMEDA, CALIFORNIA USA
94501

SYBEX ®

SEAL

Chart Full Menus
(System 7)

File

New...	⌘N
Open...	⌘O
Close	⌘W
Links...	
Save	⌘S
Save As...	
Save Workspace...	
Delete...	
Print Preview	
Page Setup...	
Print...	⌘P
1 Pictogram	
2 Return on Investments	
3 Quality Control Database	
4 Rapid Transit Proposal	
Quit	⌘Q

Edit

Can't Undo	⌘Z
Repeat Close	⌘Y
Cut	⌘X
Copy	⌘C
Paste	⌘V
Clear...	⌘B
Paste Special...	
Create Publisher...	

Gallery

Area...
Bar...
✓ Column...
Line...
Pie...
XY (Scatter)...
Combination...
3-D Area...
3-D Column...
3-D Line...
3-D Pie...
Preferred
Set Preferred

Format

Patterns...
Font...
Text...
Scale...
Legend...
Main Chart...
Overlay...
3-D View...
Move
Size

Macro

Run...
Record...
Start Recorder

Chart

Attach Text...	
Add Arrow	
Add Legend	
Axes...	
Gridlines...	
Add Overlay	
Edit Series...	
Select Chart	⌘A
Select Plot Area	
Protect Document...	
Color Palette...	
Calculate Now	⌘=
Short Menus	

Window

Show Clipboard
Arrange All
Hide
Unhide...
✓ 1 Chart1

Chart Full Menus
(System 7)